THE ILLUSTRATED HISTORY OF
THE POPES

THE ILLUSTRATED HISTORY OF
THE POPES

AN AUTHORITATIVE GUIDE TO THE LIVES AND WORKS OF
THE POPES OF THE CATHOLIC CHURCH, WITH 450 IMAGES

CHARLES PHILLIPS

LORENZ BOOKS

CONTENTS

INTRODUCTION
AN INSTITUTION AS OLD AS THE CHURCH

The thousands of pilgrims huddled beneath umbrellas in St Peter's Square in Rome on 13 March 2013 knew they would be witnessing history when the new pope was announced: the election of every new pope is an historic occasion. But when French Cardinal Jean-Louis Tauran pronounced the famous words *Habemus papam* ('We have a pope!') and then revealed the identity of the new leader of the Roman Catholic Church, the event was doubly exceptional, for the election of Argentinian Cardinal Jorge Maria Bergoglio, former Archbishop of Buenos Aires, as Pope Francis was the first of its kind in no fewer than three ways.

Francis is the first Latin American pope, the first Jesuit pope and the first pope from the southern hemisphere. In other ways he is, if not unique, then certainly a rare specimen. He is the first non-European pope for more than

1,000 years – since Pope Gregory III (731–41), a Syrian by birth – and the first to take a new papal name (one that has never been used before) since Pope Lando (913–14). Moreover, following as he does the abdication of Pope Benedict XVI (2005–13), he is the first leader of the Church to succeed a pope who had resigned since Celestine V (5 July–13 December 1294) was replaced by Boniface VIII (1294–1303) in 1294.

SURPRISE APPOINTMENT

The election of Cardinal Bergoglio to the leadership of the Church was unexpected. He had been considered a possible candidate to become pope at the 2005 conclave that elevated Benedict XVI but reputedly made a plea to other cardinals not to elect him. In 2013 several other candidates – notably Cardinal Angelo Scola, Archbishop of Milan, Cardinal Odilo Scherer, Archbishop of Sao Paolo and Cardinal Peter Turkson, Archbishop Emeritus of Cape Coast – were considered more likely than Bergoglio to be elected as Benedict's replacement.

There is a celebrated saying among those who follow papal elections: 'He who enters the conclave a pope leaves a cardinal' – meaning that those who are considered favourites for the papacy very, very rarely actually become pope. Well-known examples include 1958, when the election of Cardinal Angelo Roncalli as Pope John XXIII (1958–63) was a great surprise and Cardinal Giuseppe Siri, Archbishop of Genoa, was a strong favourite.

Pope Francis began his pontificate in light-hearted vein. His first words were: 'Brothers and sisters, good evening. You all know that the duty of the conclave was to give a bishop to Rome. It seems that my brother cardinals have gone almost to the ends of the earth to get him … But we're here.' He subsequently

Above: A mosaic in the Hagia Sophia in Istanbul honours Emperor Constantine, founder of the city as Constantinople in 330.

declared he was taking this name in honour of St Francis of Assisi (1182–1226), founder of the Franciscans, and because he was especially concerned for the poor; before becoming pope he had praised St Francis: 'He brought to Christianity an idea of poverty against the luxury, pride, vanity of the civil and ecclesiastical powers of the time… He changed history.' As pope he declared 'How I would like a Church which is poor, and for the poor.'

TWO THOUSAND YEARS OF POPES

The pope's authority to lead the Church depends on his status as a successor of St Peter. Francis is the 266th pope in direct line from St Peter. He stands at the end of almost two millennia of history of the Church in Rome, since the time of Peter.

Witness to the events of Jesus's life and the leader of his disciples, Peter was established by him in Rome as leader of

---

THE PAPACY IN FIGURES

Of the 266 popes, a round 100 (well over one-third of the total) have been Italian-born – although in the modern era we have not had an Italian pope since John Paul I in 1978. There have been 14 French popes (the last being Gregory XI, 1370–78), 11 Greek (the last, Zacharias in 741–52), seven German (the last, Benedict XVI in 2005–13), six Syrian (the last, Gregory III in 731–41), three Sicilian (the last, Stephen III in 768–72), two Portuguese (the last, John XXI in 1276–7), two Spanish (the last, the notorious Alexander VI in 1492–1503) and two African (the last, Miltiades in 311–14). Three nationalities can claim only one pope: English (Hadrian IV, 1154–9), Dutch (Hadrian VI, 1522–3) and Polish (John Paul II, 1978–2005).

Above: In the 11th century Pope Gregory VII clashed with Holy Roman Emperor Henry IV in the celebrated 'Investiture Controversy' over the right to invest or appoint abbots and bishops.

the Christians there. After he died a martyr in Rome in *c.*64 AD, Christians faced persecution for more 200 years until the Roman Empire recognized their faith with the Edict of Milan of 313. Peter's successors in Rome attempted to establish their pre-eminence over other bishops and centres of the faith – notably Constantinople (modern Istanbul), the city founded by Emperor Constantine in 330 as a new, eastern capital for the Roman Empire.

Following the collapse of the Roman Empire in the West in 410, Rome struggled to escape the heavy hand of Constantinople until in the 8th century popes aligned themselves with the new European power of Charlemagne and the Franks and in 1054 the Western and Eastern Churches of Rome and Constantinople – in a dramatic exchange of excommunications – brought about a split that has endured to the 21st century.

PRINCELY POPES

Over the early centuries the papacy acquired territory in central Italy known as the Patrimony of St Peter. This was significantly expanded with grants of land made by the Frankish kings to create the papal states. As ruler of the papal states, the pope was effectively a temporal prince. He was drawn into worldly disputes, and faced the challenge of a series of rival powers, including the Holy Roman Emperor, the Normans in Sicily and the kings of France.

For 500 years from 1096 onwards, pontiffs beginning with Urban II (1088–99) used crusades or holy wars to fight Muslims and heretic Christians – and also to further the papacy's territorial

Below: 'Thou art Peter, and upon this rock I will build my church.' Italian Baroque painter Bernardo Strozzi painted this vision of Christ granting authority to Peter.

universities, while others such as Julius II (1503–13) were great patrons of the arts, responsible for funding such masterpieces as Michelangelo's Sistine Chapel ceiling and the frescoes by Raphael in the Vatican. The financial extravagance this involved – and the licentiousness that accompanied it – fuelled increasingly urgent calls for reform of the Church and led to the Protestant Reformation, launched by German pastor Martin Luther in 1517.

REFORMING PAPACY

Under Pope Paul III the papacy and the Church fought back against Protestantism, launching the Counter-Reformation with the calling of the Council of Trent (1545–63), the establishment of the teaching order of the Society of Jesus (Jesuits) in 1540 and in 1542 the creation of the Holy Office of the Inquisition to stamp out heresy. In addition popes such as Urban VIII

Below: John XXII was the longest-reigning of the Avignon popes, ruling for 18 years from 1316–34. Under him, the papacy had a close relationship with the French crown.

and political interests. These wars were fought under crusade indulgences, which promised those who took part freedom from all temporal punishment for their sins. Nine crusades from 1096–1272 were directed largely towards the holy places of Palestine and Syria, and alongside years of bitter military conflict in which great suffering was caused on both sides, opened up communications between Christian Europe and the Muslim Middle East – which greatly enriched European culture.

AVIGNON POPES

Under French influence, Pope Clement V moved the seat of the papacy to Avignon in southern France for 68 years, 1309–77, and these years of the 'Avignon Exile' were followed by the Great Papal Schism of 1378–1417, in which rival popes in Rome and Avignon set themselves up against one another and the reputation of the papacy was badly damaged. In the Italian Renaissance, however, many learned popes developed canon law and founded enduring

(1623–44) and Innocent X (1644–55) were great patrons influencing the rebuilding of the churches, streets and squares of Rome in the intensely appealing baroque style that sought to capture the drama of religious encounter.

MARGINALIZED

Thereafter, however, a succession of pontiffs were unable to stem the rising tide of materialism in the 'Age of Reason' while politically the papacy became increasingly marginalized on the European map. After the establishment of the Kingdom of Italy in 1861 and the choice of Rome as its capital in 1870, the popes were temporal rulers no more – save for in the enclave of Vatican City. This situation was formalized under the Lateran Treaty of 1929.

VOICE FOR PEACE

Popes increasingly concentrated on their roles as spiritual leaders and teachers. Through the terrible violence and ideological conflict of the 20th century, pope after pope called for peace and reconciliation.

The leaders of the Church tried to lead humanity away from violence towards negotiation. Benedict XV (1914–22) denounced the First World War as 'horrible butchery' and 'the suicide of Europe' and circulated – without

success – a detailed peace plan in 1917. At the height of the Cold War between East and West, John XXIII (1958–63) issued a celebrated encyclical on 11 April 1963, *Pacem in Terris* ('Peace on Earth'), which called on people to solve disputes by negotiation rather than through recourse to arms and began 'Peace on Earth – which man throughout the ages has so longed for and sought after – can never be established, never guaranteed, except by the diligent observance of the divinely established order.'

John Paul II (1978–2005) declared that 'War… is always a defeat for humanity,' and in 1995 said in an address to the General Assembly of the United Nations that a moral law common to all could help the world progress from 'a century

Above: Fra Angelico's painting of the Crucifixion, with Saints Cosmas, Damian, Francis and Bernard, has a border of prominent Dominicans including Pope Innocent V and Pope Benedict XI.

of violent coercion' to 'a century of persuasion'. He supported and encouraged people working for justice and freedom – notably against communism in his native Poland – but always stressed that those seeking change should do so peacefully; he was a major influence on keeping the Polish *Solidarity* trade union movement non-violent even during an era of martial law and repression.

Then in the economic upheaval of the early 21st century, popes taught that people need to turn away from sterile, secular thinking and the obsession with money. John Paul II criticized materialism and the effects of untamed capitalism in the West; he also identified a 'culture of death' in which people accepted abortion, euthanasia and capital punishment. In his encyclical *Caritas in veritate* ('Charity in Truth'), Benedict XVI (2005–13) taught that the prevailing economic system showed 'the pernicious effects of sin' and declared that people should seek to

Left: Pope Clement V moved the seat of the papacy from Rome to Avignon, southern France, in 1309 – and it remained there for the 67 years of the 'Avignon Exile'. Clement VI (1342–52) lived in the style of a prince at the Palais des Papes.

Above: The faithful flock to Easter Sunday Mass at St Peter's Square in the Vatican. Pope Francis led his first Easter Sunday Mass on 31 March 2013.

use ethics in business. He called on people to leave 'the dead-end streets of consumerism' in order to find happiness.

LIBER PONTIFICALIS

Names and information for many early popes are taken from the Liber Pontificalis, a collection of papal biographies that was gradually compiled over centuries. Its first edition ended with Hadrian II (867–72), then further publications extended the information as far as Eugenius IV (1431–47) and later Pius II (1458–64). Until the 18th century many authors took its contents at face value and quoted from it uncritically, but modern scholars treat it more cautiously.

PAPAL TITLES

The title 'pope' derives from the Latin *papa* and Greek *pappas* meaning 'father'. By tradition the pope's position is akin to that of the father in a traditional patriarchal family. One of the pope's forms of

address is 'Holy Father'. The title was reserved in the Western church for the bishop of Rome only from around the 9th century; before that it was used for any bishop and even sometimes given to priests as a mark of respect. At the time of the Protestant Reformation, the word became charged for Protestants who refused to use pope and preferred to call the pontiff the 'bishop of Rome' – when they were not calling him the antichrist.

The title or name pontiff is also applied to the pope. This word originally referred to a high priest in Ancient Rome and was applied later to Christian bishops and the bishop of Rome – the pope.

The long history of the papacy is written in the list of the pope's official titles: Bishop of Rome, Vicar of Jesus Christ, Successor of the Prince of the Apostles, Supreme Pontiff of the Universal Church, Primate of Italy, Archbishop and Metropolitan of the Roman Province, Sovereign of the Vatican City State, Servant of the servants of God.

'Bishop of Rome' and 'Successor of the Prince of the Apostles' refer to his direct descent as leader of the Christians in Rome from St Peter. In the course of

Jesus's ministry, Peter became identified as leader of the 12 disciples. The word apostle derives from a Greek word for a person who is sent on a mission – as the disciples were sent by Jesus to teach the Gospel to people of all nations; as leader of the disciples, Peter was celebrated as 'Prince of the Apostles'. 'Vicar of Christ' means Christ's representative on Earth. The Second Vatican Council taught that all bishops are 'vicars and ambassadors of Christ'. 'Servant of the servants of God' was first widely used by Pope Gregory I the Great (590–604).

PAPACY AND SCANDALS

From the mid-1980s onwards, the Roman Catholic Church and wider society were shocked by a series of allegations of sexual abuse of young people by diocesan priests and members of the religious orders. There were major scandals in the United States, Ireland and Australia; in some cases, members of the church hierarchy were accused of trying to silence the accusations and even of moving abusers on from one scandal into a position where the person might commit a similar offence.

In 2001 John Paul II, at the urging of his friend Cardinal Ratzinger (the future Pope Benedict XVI), transferred the main responsibility for handling cases of sexual abuse by priests from dioceses to the Congregation for the Doctrine of the Faith. As its prefect, before becoming pope, Cardinal Ratzinger had made a number of changes to improve the Church's handling of the problem.

As pope, during a visit to the United States in 2008 he met victims of priestly sexual abuse and spoke out condemning perpetrators. In a pastoral letter to Irish Catholics of March 2010 he addressed victims of sexual abuse by priests: 'You have suffered grievously and I am truly sorry … Your trust has been betrayed and your dignity has been violated … I openly express the shame and remorse that we all feel.'

SAINTLY POPES

After Pope John Paul II's death, around four million people attended his Mass of Requiem, which was conducted on 8 April 2005 by Cardinal Joseph Ratzinger (soon to be Pope Benedict XVI). At the Mass several cried out 'Santo Subito!'

Below: Pope John Paul II made nine visits to his native Poland during his pontificate, the first in 1979 and the last in 2003. He greets the crowd from his popemobile.

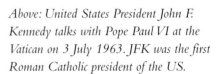

('Make him a saint at once!') No fewer than 78 popes have posthumously been declared saints. This process is known as canonization because a person raised to sainthood is added to the canon of saints.

The current process by which a person is identified as a saint in the Roman Catholic Church was established in 1983. The first stage is when a bishop authorizes opening an investigation into the virtues of the person in question (called a 'Servant of God'), usually not sooner than five years after his or her death; the pope can do this in his capacity as bishop of Rome and has the power to waive the five-year rule as John Paul II did in the case of Mother Teresa of Calcutta in 1997 and Benedict XVI

Above: United States President John F. Kennedy talks with Pope Paul VI at the Vatican on 3 July 1963. JFK was the first Roman Catholic president of the US.

did for John Paul II; the case is presented to the Congregation for the Causes of Saints. At the second stage the congregation may recommend to the pope that the Servant of God be declared 'Venerable'. The third stage is for the church to declare the person 'Blessed'. In the case of a martyr (someone who died for his or her faith), the pope simply declares the person a martyr. In the case of confessors (people who confessed or bore witness to their faith in the way they lived), it is necessary to show that God performed a miracle in response to the blessed person's prayers – usually a miraculous cure.

The final stage comes when at least two miracles can be shown to have occurred through the blessed person's prayers after his or her death: then he or she is declared a saint.

Recent popes on the path to sainthood include Pius XII, John XXIII and John Paul II. John Paul II declared Pius a 'Servant of God' in 1990 and John XXIII 'Blessed' in 2000; Benedict XVI declared Pius 'Venerable' in 2009. Benedict then declared John Paul II 'Venerable' in 2009 and beatified him in 2011. On 27 April 2014 Pope Francis canonized John XXIII and John Paul II.

TIMELINE

64–1054 *(Bracketed italic entries are antipopes, i.e. not popes in the real succession.)*

Above: Dome of the Rock, Jerusalem.

Above: St Peter's statue in Vatican.

Above: The first popes, Ravenna.

64-275

c.64 St Peter dies a martyr in Rome.
c.66–c.78 Pope St Linus.
c.79–c.91 Pope St Anacletus.
c.91–c.101 Pope St Clement I –
ordained by St Peter?
c.101–c.109 Pope St Evaristus.
c.109–c.116 Pope St Alexander.
c.116–c.125 Pope St Sixtus I.
c.125–c.136 Pope St Telesphorus.
c.138–c.142 Pope St Hyginus.
c.142–c.155 Pope St Pius I.
c.155–c.166 Pope St Anicetus.
c.166–c.174 Pope St Soter.
c.175–c.189 Pope St Eleutherius.
c.189–c.199 Pope St Victor I – first
African-born pope.
c.199–c.217 Pope St Zephyrinus.
211 Church Father Origen visits Rome.
c.217–c.222 Pope St Callistus I.
(217–35) Antipope St Hippolytus.
c.222–30 Pope St Urban I.
230–5 Pope St Pontian – first pope
to resign papacy.
235–6 Pope St Anterus.
236–50 Pope St Fabian.
250–1 Election of new pope delayed
due to imperial persecution of Church.
251–3 Pope St Cornelius.
(251–8) Antipope Novatian
253–4 Pope St Lucius I.
254–7 Pope St Stephen I – emphasizes
pre-eminence of Rome.
257–8 Pope St Sixtus II – early martyr.
260–8 Pope St Dionysius.
269–74 Pope St Felix I.

275–418

275–83 Pope St Eutychian.
283–96 Pope St Gaius.
296–304 Pope St Marcellinus.
301 Armenia is the first Christian state.
304–8 Severe persecution of Christians
causes break in line of popes.
c.308–9 Pope St Marcellus I.
310, 18 Apr–21 Oct, Pope St Eusebius.
311–14 Pope St Miltiades.
312 Battle of Milvian Bridge –
Roman Emperor Constantine I
defeats rival Maxentius.
313 Edict of Milan, Christians free to
practise faith in the Roman Empire.
330 Foundation of Constantinople.
314–335 Pope St Sylvester I.
325 Council of Nicaea – first ecumenical council; agrees Nicene Creed.
336, 18 Jan–7 Oct, Pope St Mark.
337–52 Pope St Julius I.
352–66 Pope Liberius – first pope not
to be canonized.
(355–65) Antipope Felix II.
366–84 Pope St Damasus I.
381 First Council of Constantinople –
confirms Nicene Creed.
(366–85) Antipope Ursinus.
384–99 Pope St Siricius.
399–401 Pope St Anastasius I.
397–401 St Augustine (Bishop of
Hippo c.395) writes his Confessions.
401–17 Pope St Innocent I.
410 Rome sacked by Visigoths.
417–18 Pope St Zosimus.
(418–23) Antipope Eulalius.

418–608

418–22 Pope St Boniface I.
422–32 Pope St Celestine I.
431 Council of Ephesus.
432–40 Pope St Sixtus III.
440–61 Pope St Leo I the Great.
451 Council of Chalcedon.
461–8 Pope St Hilarius.
468–83 Pope St Simplicius.
476 Last Roman emperor in West,
Romulus Augustulus, deposed.
483–92 Pope St Felix III.
492–6 Pope St Gelasius I.
496–8 Pope Anastasius II.
498–514 Pope St Symmachus.
*(498–9) Antipope Laurence; returned to
power 501–506.*
514–23 Pope St Hormisdas.
523–6 Pope St John I.
526–30 Pope St Felix IV.
(530) Antipope Dioscorus.
530–2 Pope Boniface II – first pope of
Germanic descent.
533–5 Pope John II – first pope to
change his name.
535–36 Pope St Agapitus I.
536–7 Pope St Silverius.
537–55 Pope Vigilius.
553 Second Council of Constantinople.
556–61 Pope Pelagius I.
561–74 Pope John III.
575–9 Pope Benedict I.
579–90 Pope Pelagius II.
590–604 Pope St Gregory I the Great.
604–6 Pope St Sabinian.
607, 19 Feb–12 Nov, Pope Boniface III.

Above: Monastery, County Limerick.

Above: The Temple Church, London.

Above: Notre Dame, Paris.

608–768

608–15 Pope St Boniface IV.
615–18 Pope St Adeodatus I.
619–25 Pope Boniface V.
625–38 Pope Honorius I.
632 Death of Prophet Muhammad –
birth of Islam.
640, 28 May–2 Aug, Pope Severinus.
640–2 Pope John IV.
642–9 Pope Theodore I.
649–53 Pope St Martin I.
654–7 Pope St Eugenius I.
657–72 Pope St Vitalian.
663/664 Synod of Whitby.
672–6 Pope Adeodatus II.
676–8 Pope Donus.
678–81 Pope St Agatho, said to have
been over 100 years old on election.
680–81 Third Council of Constantinople.
682–3 Pope St Leo II.
684–5 Pope St Benedict II.
685–6 Pope John V.
686–7 Pope Conon.
(687) Antipope Theodore.
(687) Antipope Paschal.
687–701 Pope St Sergius I.
701–5 Pope John VI.
705–7 Pope John VII.
708, 15 Jan–4 Feb, Pope Sisinnius.
708–15 Pope Constantine I.
715–31 Pope St Gregory II.
731–41 Pope St Gregory III.
741–52 Pope St Zacharias.
752, 26 Mar–26 Apr, Stephen II –
dies before consecration.
752–7 Stephen II – so named since his
immediate predecessor is discounted.
757–67 Pope St Paul I.
(767–68) Antipope Constantine II.
(768) Antipope Philip.

768–914

768–72 Pope Stephen III.
772–95 Pope Hadrian I.
787 Second Council of Nicaea.
795–816 Pope St Leo III – crowns
Charlemagne 'Emperor of the Romans'.
816–17 Pope Stephen IV.
817–24 Pope St Paschal I.
824–7 Pope Eugenius II.
827, Aug–Sep, Pope Valentine.
827–44 Pope Gregory IV.
(844) Antipope John.
844–7 Sergius II.
846 Muslim Saracens attack Rome.
847–55 Pope St Leo IV.
855–8 Pope Benedict III.
(855) Antipope Anastasius Bibliothecarius.
858–67 Pope St Nicholas I the Great.
867–72 Pope Hadrian II.
869–70 Fourth Council of
Constantinople.
872–88 Pope John VIII – first pope to
be assassinated.
882–4 Pope Marinus I.
884–5 Pope Hadrian III.
885–91 Pope Stephen V.
891–6 Pope Formosus.
896, May–Aug, Pope Boniface VI.
896–7 Pope Stephen VI.
897, Aug–Nov, Pope Romanus.
897, Nov–Dec, Pope Theodore II.
898–900 Pope John IX.
900–3 Pope Benedict IV.
903, Aug–Sep, Pope Leo V.
855–7 According to legend, reign of
female Pope Joan.
(903–4) Antipope Christopher.
904–11 Pope Sergius III.
911–13 Pope Anastasius III.
913–14 Pope Lando.

914–1054

914–28 Pope John X.
928, May–Dec, Pope Leo VI.
928–31 Pope Stephen VII.
931–5/6 Pope John XI.
936–9 Pope Leo VII.
939–42 Pope Stephen VIII.
942–6 Pope Marinus II.
946–55 Pope Agapitus II.
955–64 Pope John XII.
963–5 Pope Leo VIII – sometimes
listed as an antipope.
964, 22 May–23 Jun, Pope Benedict V.
965–72 Pope John XIII.
973–4 Pope Benedict VI.
*(974) Antipope Boniface VII – returns to
power 984–985.*
974–83 Pope Benedict VII.
983–4 Pope John XIV.
985–96 Pope John XV.
996–9 Pope Gregory V.
(997–1001) Antipope John XVI.
999–1003 Pope Sylvester II – first
French pope.
1003, 16 May–6 Nov, Pope John XVII.
1003–9 Pope John XVIII – abdicated.
1009–12 Pope Sergius IV.
(1012) Antipope Gregory VI.
1012–24 Pope Benedict VIII.
1024–32 Pope John XIX – first pope
to grant an indulgence.
1032–44; 1045; 1047–8 Pope
Benedict IX.
1045, 20 Jan–10 Mar, Pope Sylvester III.
1045–6 Pope Gregory VI.
1046–7 Pope Clement II.
1048, 17 Jul–9 Aug, Pope Damasus II.
1049–54 Pope St Leo IX.
1054 Great Schism – Western and
Eastern churches split.

TIMELINE
1054–1534

Above: The Duomo, Florence.

Above: The Crusaders before Antioch.

Above: The Vatican in Rome, Italy.

1054–1138
1054 The Eastern Orthodox Church formally parts company with Rome.
1055–7 Pope Victor II.
1057–8 Pope Stephen IX.
(1058–9) Antipope Benedict X.
1058–61 Pope Nicholas II – made important alliance with Norman leader Robert Guiscard.
1061–73 Pope Alexander II.
(1061–4) Antipope Honorius II.
1073–85 Pope St Gregory VII – clashed with Holy Roman Emperor Henry IV in 'Investiture Dispute'.
(1080 and 1084–1100) Antipope Clement III.
1086–7 Pope Blessed Victor III.
1088–99 Pope Blessed Urban II – launched First Crusade.
1096–9 First Crusade.
1099–1118 Pope Paschal II.
(1100–1) Antipope Theoderic.
(1101/2) Antipope Aleric.
(1105–11) Antipope Sylvester IV.
1118–19 Pope Gelasius II.
(1118–21) Antipope Gregory VIII.
1119–24 Pope Callistus II.
1122 Concordat of Worms ends Investiture Dispute.
1123 First Lateran Council.
1124–30 Pope Honorius II.
1129 Honorius grants papal approval to Knights Templar.
(1124) Antipope Celestine II.
1130–43 Pope Innocent II.
(1130–38) Antipope Anacletus II.

1138–1217
(1138) Antipope Victor IV.
1139 Second Lateran Council.
1143–4 Pope Celestine II.
1144–5 Pope Lucius II.
1145–53 Pope Blessed Eugenius III.
1147–9 Second Crusade.
1153–4 Pope Anastasius IV.
1154–9 Pope Hadrian IV – only English pope.
1159–81 Pope Alexander III.
(1159–64) Antipope Victor IV.
(1164–8) Antipope Paschal III.
(1168–78) Antipope Callistus III.
1179 Third Lateran Council.
(1179–80) Antipope Innocent III.
1181–5 Pope Lucius III.
1185–7 Pope Urban III.
1187 Pope Gregory VIII.
1187 Saladin recaptures Jerusalem for the Muslims.
1187–91 Pope Clement III.
1187–92 Third Crusade.
1191–8 Pope Celestine III – confirms Teutonic Knights.
1198–1216 Pope Innocent III – church reformer who calls Fourth and Fifth Crusades.
1202–4 Fourth Crusade.
1208 Innocent III calls crusade against Albigensians in southern France.
1209 St Francis of Assisi begins his ministry.
1215 Fourth Lateran Council.
1216–27 Pope Honorius III – approves Dominicans and Franciscans.

1217–1285
1217–21 Fifth Crusade.
1218 Crusade against Muslims in Spain.
1227–41 Pope Gregory IX canonizes Francis of Assisi and Dominic Guzman.
1231 Gregory IX founds Dominican inquisition.
1228–9 Sixth Crusade.
1241, 25 Oct–10 Nov, Pope Celestine IV.
1241–3 Cardinals take a year and a half to elect a new pope.
1243–54 Pope Innocent IV.
1245 First Council of Lyon.
1248–54 Seventh Crusade.
1254–61 Pope Alexander IV.
1261–4 Pope Urban IV.
1265–8 Pope Clement IV.
1266–74 St Thomas Aquinas writes the *Summa Theologica*.
1268–71 On Clement's death cardinals take three years to elect successor.
1270 Eighth Crusade.
1271–6 Pope Blessed Gregory X.
1271–2 Ninth Crusade.
1274 Thomas Aquinas dies.
1275 Second Council of Lyon.
1276, 21 Jan–22 Jun, Pope Blessed Innocent V.
1276, 11 Jul–18 Aug, Pope Hadrian V.
1276–7 Pope John XXI (due to an error in numbering, there has never been a Pope John XX).
1277–80 Pope Nicholas III.
1281–5 Pope Martin IV.

Above: Correggio's Madonna and Child.

Above: Michelangelo's Moses.

Above: San Jose de Laguna, New Mexico.

1285-1394

1285–7 Pope Honorius IV.
1288–92 Pope Nicholas IV.
1291 Last Christian holding in the Holy Land, at Acre, lost to army of Egyptian Mamluk Sultanate.
1294 Pope St Celestine V.
1294–1303 Pope Boniface VIII – founds University of Rome in 1303.
1297 Boniface canonizes King Louis IX of France.
1302 Boniface VIII issues *Unam Sanctam* bull – salvation depends on being subject to the pope.
1303–4 Pope Benedict XI.
1305–14 Pope Clement V.
1309–77 Avignon exile – papacy is based in city of Avignon, southern France, not Rome.
1311–12 Council of Vienne.
1312 Knights Templar dissolved.
1316–34 Pope John XXII.
(1328–30) Antipope Nicholas V.
1334–42 Pope Benedict XII.
1337–1453 Hundred Years' War between England and France.
1342–52 Pope Clement VI – purchases Avignon and surrounding area for papacy.
1352–62 Pope Innocent VI.
1362–70 Pope Blessed Urban V.
1367 Urban V attempts to return papacy to Rome but is forced by unrest to retreat to Avignon.
1370–78 Pope Gregory XI.
1377 Gregory returns papacy to Rome, ending Avignon exile.
1378–89 Pope Urban VI.
(1378–94) Antipope Clement VII.
1389–1404 Pope Boniface IX.

1394-1492

(1394–1417) Antipope Benedict XIII.
1404–6 Pope Innocent VII.
1406–15 Pope Gregory XII.
1408 Council of Pisa fails to resolve the Western Schism.
(1409–10) Antipope Alexander V.
(1410–15) Antipope John XXIII.
1417–31 Pope Martin V.
1414–18 Council of Constance.
1415 Czech reformer Jan Hus is condemned and burned as a heretic.
1431 Joan of Arc is found guilty of heresy and burned at the stake.
1431–47 Pope Eugenius IV.
1431–42 Council of Basel; moved to Ferrara and then Florence.
1447–55 Pope Nicholas V – founds Vatican Library.
1453 Constantinople sacked by Ottoman Turks.
1455–58 Pope Callistus III – first Borgia pope.
1456, Jul, In the Battle of Belgrade governor of Hungary John Hunyadi defeats the Ottomans. Pope Callistus III makes the Feast of the Transfiguration of Jesus a universal feast to celebrate victory,
1458–64 Pope Pius II.
1464–71 Pope Paul II.
1464 First printed books in the papal states.
1479 Bartolomeo Platina's *Lives of the Popes* is published.
1471–84 Pope Sixtus IV.
1473–79 Ponte Sisto built in Rome.
1478 Spanish Inquisition is established.
1483 Sistine Chapel opens.
1484–92 Pope Innocent VIII.

1492-1534

1492 End of Reconquista – Ferdinand and Isabella expel Muslims from Granada, ending 700 years of Islamic presence in Spanish peninsula.
1492 Christopher Colombus sets sail to Americas and starts opening up an empire for Spain there.
1492–94 Borgia Apartments laid out in Vatican.
1492–1503 Pope Alexander VI.
1503, 22 Sep–18 Oct, Pope Pius III.
1503–13 Pope Julius II.
1506 Julius II lays foundation stone for new St Peter's Basilica.
1508–12 Michelangelo paints Sistine Chapel ceiling.
1512–17 Fifth Lateran Council.
1506 Foundation of the Swiss Papal Guard, one of the oldest military units in the world.
1513–21 Pope Leo X.
1517 Martin Luther pins his '95 Theses' on the door of Wittenburg Cathedral – the beginning of the Protestant Reformation.
1521 Pope Leo X excommunicates Luther.
1522–3 Pope Hadrian VI.
1523–34 Pope Clement VII.
1527 Rome sacked by troops of Charles V. Pope Clement VII is taken prisoner during the Sack of Rome.
1529 The Ottoman Siege of Vienna is successfully repulsed.
1534 Henry VIII announces that he and his successors will henceforth be heads of the Church of England.
1534 St Ignatius Loyola founds the Society of Jesus, the Jesuits.

TIMELINE
1534–2016

Above: St Louis Cathedral, New Orleans.

Above: Statue of Mary, Santiago, Chile.

Above: Crowd in front of St Peter's Rome.

1534–1584

1534–49 Pope Paul III.

1536–41 Michelangelo paints *The Last Judgement* in the Sistine Chapel.

1540 Papal bull *Regimini militantis ecclesiae* gives official recognition to Jesuits.

1542 Paul III establishes the Holy Office of the Inquisition.

1545–63 Council of Trent.

1547 Paul III appoints Michelangelo principal architect on St Peter's Basilica.

1550–5 Pope Julius III.

1553 Catholicism restored in England.

1555, 9 Apr–1 May, Pope Marcellus II – died after 22 days.

1555–9 Pope Paul IV.

1557–8 Paul IV creates Index of Prohibited Books.

1559–65 Pope Pius IV.

1561–5 Porta Pia in Rome is built – to designs by Michelangelo.

1564 Michelangelo dies.

1566–72 Pope St Pius V – his reign is dated from 1566 because Pius IV died in Dec 1565.

1570 Pius V excommunicates Elizabeth I of England.

1571 Battle of Lepanto – victory for Catholic League against Turks.

1572–85 Pope Gregory XIII.

1572 Massacre of St Bartholomew's Day – slaughter of French Huguenots.

1580 Gregory XIII backs reform of Carmelites by Teresa of Avila.

1582 Gregorian calendar introduced to replace Julian calendar.

1584–1669

1584 The Gesù – mother church of the Jesuits – is consecrated.

1585–90 Pope Sixtus V.

1590 Dome of St Peter's completed.

1588 Spanish Armada – Sixtus V renews Elizabeth's excommunication.

1590, 15–27 Sep, Pope Urban VII – Fell ill at once and died 11 days later.

1590–1 Pope Gregory XIV.

1591, 29 Oct–30 Dec, Pope Innocent IX – 82 years old on election.

1592–1605 Pope Clement VIII.

1593 King Henry IV of France is reconciled to the Church.

1605, 1–27 Apr, Pope Leo XI.

1605–21 Pope Paul V.

1605 Paul V establishes Bank of the Holy Spirit.

1618–48 Thirty Years' War in Germany.

1621–3 Pope Gregory XV.

1622 Gregory XV canonizes Ignatius of Loyola, Francis Xavier, Philip Neri and Teresa of Avila.

1623–44 Pope Urban VIII.

1623–4 Gian Lorenzo Bernini designs the baldachin in St Peter's Basilica.

1633 Galileo is condemned by the Inquisition and forced to recant.

1644–55 Pope Innocent X.

1650 Diego Velazquez paints portrait of Innocent X.

1655–67 Pope Alexander VII.

1656–67 Gian Lorenzo Bernini design St Peter's Square.

1667–9 Pope Clement IX.

1669–1809

1669 Candia, last Christian stronghold on Crete, falls to the Ottoman Turks.

1670–6 Pope Clement X.

1673 John Sobieski defeats Turks.

1676–89 Pope Innocent XI.

1688 Catholic King James II driven from English throne and replaced by Protestant William and Mary.

1689–91 Pope Alexander VIII.

1691–1700 Pope Innocent XII.

1700–21 Pope Clement XI.

1721–4 Pope Innocent XIII.

1726 John of the Cross is canonized.

1724–30 Pope Benedict XIII.

1725 Benedict XIII opens Spanish Steps in Rome.

1730–40 Pope Clement XII.

1740–58 Pope Benedict XIV.

1758–69 Pope Clement XIII.

1751–2 French encyclopedia of Diderot and d'Alembert is published; Clement XIII has the book placed on the Index.

1762 Trevi Fountain in Rome, designed by Nicola Salvi, is completed.

1769–74 Pope Clement XIV.

1773, 16 Aug, Papal bull *Dominos ac Redemptor noster* dissolves Jesuits.

1775–99 Pope Pius VI.

1789 French Revolution.

1797 French army occupies papal states, proclaims Roman Republic and announces deposition of pope as head of state; Pius flees to Florence.

1800–23 Pope Pius VII.

Above: St Patrick's Cathedral, Manhattan.

Above: Sagrada Familia, Barcelona, Spain.

Above: John Paul II, the first Polish pope.

1809–1937

1809 Napoleon annexes papal states. Pius excommunicates Napoleon, who has the pope arrested and imprisoned.
1814 After Napoleon is defeated, the Congress of Vienna returns the papal states to the papacy.
1814 Jesuits are restored.
1823–9 Pope Leo XII.
1829–30 Pope Pius VIII.
1829 Catholic Emancipation Act in Britain.
1830 In the July Revolution Louis Philippe comes to the French throne.
1831–46 Pope Gregory XVI.
1846–78 Pope Pius IX.
1849 Creation of Roman Republic abolishes pope's secular powers.
1860 Establishment of Italy, with Rome as its capital – the papal states annexed.
1864, Dec, Pius issues Syllabus of Errors.
1869–70 First Vatican Council.
1878–1903 Pope Leo XIII.
1903–14 Pope Pius X.
1914–22 Pope Benedict XV.
1914–18 First World War.
1917 Russian Revolution.
1920 Benedict XV canonizes Joan of Arc.
1922–39 Pope Pius XI.
1929 Lateran Treaty establishes the pope as sovereign ruler of an independent neutral state in Vatican City.
1931 Pius XI becomes the first pope to make a radio broadcast.
1933 Papacy signs concordat with Hitler's German Reich.
1936–9 Spanish Civil War.

1937–1989

1937 Pius XI's encyclicals denounce Nazism and communism.
1939–58 Pope Pius XII.
1939–45 Second World War.
1949 Pius condemns Soviet Union and threatens excommunication for Catholics joining Communist Party.
1950 Pius invokes papal infallibility in defining dogma of the Assumption of Blessed Virgin Mary.
1958–63 Pope John XXIII.
1962–5 Second Vatican Council.
1962 Cuban Missile Crisis.
1963–78 Pope Paul VI.
1964 Paul VI is first modern pope to visit Holy Land.
1965 Pope Paul VI and Ecumenical Patriarch Athenagoras I issue a joint statement withdrawing the excommunications exchanged in 1054.
1965 Paul VI travels to USA, meets President Johnson, visits the United Nations and celebrates Mass in the Yankee Stadium.
1968 Pope Paul VI declares that bones under altar of St Peter's Basilica have been identified as Peter's.
1968 Paul VI's encyclical *Humanae vitae* condemns artificial birth control.
1969 Paul VI introduces revised form of Mass.
1978, 26 Aug–28 Sep, Pope John Paul I.
1978–2005 Pope John Paul II.
1980–1 Rise of Solidarity trade union and imposition of martial law in Poland.
1981, 13 May, John Paul II survives an assassination attempt in St Peter's Square.

1989–2017

1989–90 Solidarity forms coalition government and prominent Solidarity member Lech Walesa is elected President of Poland.
1993 The Holy See establishes diplomatic relations with the state of Israel.
2001, 11 Sep, Terrorist attacks launched by Islamic terrorists al-Qaeda hit New York City. John Paul II says: 'This was an attack, not just on the United States, but on all of humanity.'
2003 United States-led invasion of Iraq.
2005–13 Pope Benedict XVI.
2013, 11 Feb, Benedict announces his abdication.
2013 Francis is the first Latin American, Jesuit and non-European pope for more than 1,000 years.
2013, 23 Mar, Pope Francis meets and prays with pope emeritus Benedict – the first time such a meeting has been possible since 1294.
2014, 27 Apr, Francis canonizes Pope John XXIII and Pope John Paul II.
2014, 24–26 May, Francis visits Israel, Jordan and Palestine.
2015, 24 Sep, On visit to Cuba and the United States, Francis is the first pope to address the US Congress.
2016, 4 Sep, Francis canonizes Teresa of Calcutta.
2017, 1 Jan, In the 50th annual papal peace message, Francis says: 'May charity and non-violence govern how we treat each other as individuals, within society and in international life.'
2017, 13 May, Francis visits Portugal to celebrate 100th anniversary of Our Lady of Fatima.

PART ONE

THE FIRST POPES

The roll call of leaders of the Church begins with the first bishop to the Christians of Rome, founder of the papacy – Saint Peter, eyewitness to the deeds of Jesus of Nazareth. Peter died a martyr for his faith, as did many of his successors through more than 200 years of on-off persecution that followed until the 313 Edict of Milan that recognized Christianity in the Roman Empire. Across almost 1,000 years of history from Peter to Leo IX in 1054, almost 150 popes led the Church. Aside from Peter, the greatest must include Leo I who in 452 persuaded Attilla the Hun not to sack Rome and Leo III who crowned Charlemagne emperor in the West, and consolidated the relationship with the Franks that set Rome free from the heavy hand of Constantinople.

Left: Several early popes were celebrated as saints. This detail of a 6th-century mosaic in the Basilica of Sant'Apollinare Nuovo in Ravenna, Italy, shows Clement (died c.101) and Sixtus (died c.125) at the far left – both were sainted popes and said to have died as martyrs for their faith. Next to Sixtus is Saint Lawrence of Rome (d.258), another martyr but not a pope.

LAVACRVM
RENASCEN
TIS VITAE
C·VAL
CONSTANTINI

CLEMENS·VII
PONT·MAX
ALEONE·X
COEPTVM
CONSVMMAVIT
MDXXIIII

CHAPTER ONE
'UPON THIS ROCK...'
PETER TO SYLVESTER I, c.30/40–335

The origin of the papacy lies in a momentous encounter between Jesus Christ and the Apostle Peter, when Jesus gave Peter authority over the community of his followers. According to the Gospel of St Matthew 16:13–20, Jesus was with his disciples in Caesarea Philippi when he asked them, 'Whom do men say that I am?' and Peter made the ringing statement 'Thou art the Christ, the Son of the living God'. Then Jesus declared, 'Thou art Peter, and upon this rock I will build my Church; and the gates of hell shall not prevail against it. And I will give unto thee the keys of the kingdom of heaven: and whatsoever thou shalt bind on earth shall be bound in heaven: and whatsoever thou shalt loose on earth shall be loosed in heaven.' Peter was pre-eminent among the disciples while Jesus was alive, and after the crucifixion and resurrection, became leader of the fledgling Church. Each pope draws his authority as leader of the Church from his position as a descendant of Peter.

By tradition Peter left Jerusalem in c.44 and travelled to Antioch and then to Rome, where he established himself as bishop, leader of the community of Christians. He was crucified, probably in 64, in the persecution of Christians led by Roman Emperor Nero. Over the next three centuries, his successors as bishop of Rome tried to safeguard the Church's future in the face of often brutal official persecution; they worked to establish their authority as leaders of the Christian world and the pre-eminence of Rome as a centre of the faith.

In the early 4th century under Emperor Constantine the Great, the persecution was ended and the Roman Empire itself began to become Christian. Constantine founded a new imperial capital, Constantinople. This had the effect of diminishing the status of Rome, but gave added importance to the papacy's assumed role as a unifying force, a figurehead for the Christian world.

Left: Pope Sylvester I baptizes Constantine. According to legend Constantine – who established his imperial capital in Constantinople (modern Istanbul, Turkey) gave the pope authority to govern Rome and the Western empire. This fresco (1508/9–20) by Raphael is in the Vatican Palace.

ST PETER
THE FIRST POPE

The man Jesus singled out among his disciples and identified as the rock on which to build the community of Christians was originally a fisherman at Bethsaida on the northern shore of the Sea of Galilee (a large freshwater lake now in northeast Israel). He was roughly the same age as Jesus, having been born in *c.*4BC. The son of Jonas, he was originally known as Simeon (the Hebrew form; Simon in Greek) and worked alongside his brother Andrew with James and John, sons of Zebedee.

By the time Simeón encountered Jesus he had married, and was living in his mother-in-law's house further west along the shore of the Sea of Galilee, at Capernaum. With his brother Andrew he responded to Jesus's call, 'Follow me, and I will make you fishers of men,' and thereafter travelled with Jesus, gradually becoming the foremost disciple.

Below: A mosaic from St Peter's in Rome depicts Christ passing to Peter the key that represents papal authority over the church.

FACT BOX

Original name Simeon/Simon
Born *c.*4BC, Bethsaida, Sea of Galilee
Origin Jewish
Died *c.*AD64
Key fact Named by Christ as the rock on which the Church would be built

---

ENTRUSTED WITH CARE OF CHRISTIANS

When Simeon replied to Jesus's question, 'Whom do men say that I am?' with the words 'Thou art the Christ, the Son of the living God', Jesus named him the rock on which the Church would be founded (Matthew 16:13–20). He was then called Peter, from the Latin *Petrus* ('rock'). After the resurrection Jesus entrusted Peter with the care of his followers (John 21:15–17). Three times Jesus asked Peter if he loved him; and each time Peter replied, 'Lord, thou knowest that I love thee.' Jesus said, 'Feed my lambs … feed my sheep'.

Above: Leader of the early Christians, Peter is remembered as the first pope. Accounts of his life show that he had natural authority and, above all, a profound love for Jesus.

LEADER AND PREACHER

Peter was leader of the Christian community. He had the principal role in the election of Matthias to replace Judas Iscariot, who had betrayed Jesus and then hanged himself (Acts 1:15–26). He was the first to preach in explanation of the events of Pentecost when the Holy Spirit descended upon the faithful, making them speak in tongues (Acts 2: 14–40). He stood up and spoke as advocate for the Apostles before the religious authorities in Jerusalem (Acts 4:5–22).

In the early days of the Church, Peter travelled far and wide, preaching, guiding the first Christians and performing miracles – healing the sick and even raising the dead.

UNSHAKEABLE FAITH

We know that Peter was not learned – Acts 4:13 makes it clear that he was not trained in the Mosaic Law. He probably did not know Greek. However he always put his faith in the risen Christ.

Above: Peter was crucified upside down since he wanted to avoid comparisons with his Lord's Passion. A cherubic angel waits to deliver the saint's heavenly reward.

In *c*.44 he was arrested by Herod Agrippa I, but an angel visited him in jail, making the chains fall from his hands and leading Peter past sleeping guards to freedom (Acts 12:1–8). Thereafter he departed from Jerusalem, probably leaving leadership of the Church there in the hands of James 'the brother of the Lord'. He seems to have gone to Antioch (near modern Antakya, Turkey), which traditionally claims Peter as its first bishop.

CRUCIFIED IN ROME

After that he may have settled in Rome. There is no firm historical evidence that Peter was in Rome but many accounts by early Christian writers place him there. According to the historian Eusebius (*c*.260–*c*.340) Peter was martyred in Rome in the time of Emperor Nero (54–69) – probably in Nero's persecution of the Christians in 64.

Tradition has it that Peter went voluntarily to his death after an encounter with the Risen Christ. Peter was leaving Rome on the Via Appia to escape Nero's persecution when he met Jesus. He declared *Domine, quo vadis?* ('Where are you going, Lord?'); Jesus replied, 'To Rome, where I will be crucified once more.' At once Peter turned around and went to his death. According to the Alexandrian theologian Origen (*c*.185–*c*.254), Peter asked to be crucified upside down to avoid comparison with the death of his Lord.

The crucifixion took place beside an Ancient Egyptian obelisk that then stood near the Circle of Nero and today can be seen in St Peter's Square. By tradition Peter was buried by a Christian convert named Marcellus and a tomb was raised over his grave by Pope Anacletus (*c*.79–*c*.91). The first St Peter's Basilica was built on the site under Emperor Constantine in 319 onwards.

Below: The baroque bronze canopy (baldachin) over the high altar in St Peter's Basilica, Rome, is meant to mark Peter's tomb beneath. The baldachin was designed by Bernini and built in 1623–34.

ST PETER'S TOMB?

During alterations made to the burial crypt beneath St Peter's Basilica as part of the burial of Pope Pius XI in 1939, the remains of a man who died in the 1st century AD were found. They were in a tomb within a wall that was seemingly covered with marks made by pilgrims visiting the grave of St Peter. The bones – those of a powerfully built man who died in his 60s and wrapped in a splendid purple cloth engraved in gold – were declared by Pope Paul VI to be those of St Peter, on 26 June 1968.

LINUS TO PIUS I, 66–155
THE FIRST NINE POPES AFTER PETER

Pope Linus, first in a long line of successors to St Peter as head of the Church, was reputedly appointed by saints Peter and Paul acting together. The Church Father Irenaeus (130–202) identified this pope with the Linus mentioned by St Paul in 2 Timothy 4:21. The *Liber Pontificalis* ('Book of the Popes') dates Linus to 56–67, but St Jerome (*c*.347–420) places him at 67–78, and if he is right Linus would have been pope when the Second Temple was destroyed in Jerusalem by the Roman army of Emperor Titus and 20,000 Jewish slaves were transported to Rome and put to work building the Colosseum.

Linus was succeeded by Pope Anacletus (*c*.79–*c*.91). Tradition has it that he was a Roman, but took a Greek name (meaning 'called back', or when spelled Anencletus, 'beyond reproach'). He ordained priests to work in Rome, and like Linus is said to have died a martyr for his faith.

Below: St Sixtus (pope c.116–c.125) ruled that only ministers were permitted to touch the vessels used in the Mass. He was reputedly buried near St Peter's grave on Vatican Hill. His feast day is 6 April.

Above: Linus was pope at the time of the destruction of the Second Temple in Jerusalem by Emperor Titus in 70. This view (1625–26) is by Nicolas Poussin.

PAPAL EPISTLE

The fourth pope, Clement I (*c*.91–*c*.101) – who is said to have been ordained by St Peter himself – wrote an epistle *c*.96 to the Christians at Corinth that is one of the oldest surviving early Christian documents beside the New Testament. In the letter he attempted to reinforce the authority of presbyters (local church leaders) who had been deposed in Corinth, arguing that they should be honoured because they had been appointed by the Apostles.

The Basilica of San Clemente in Rome reputedly stands on the site of Clement's house. Some accounts identify him as the Clement mentioned by St Paul in Philippians 4:3 as a 'fellow-labourer' in Christ's service and others as a cousin of Emperor Domitian, Titus Flavius Clemens.

MARTYRED AT SEA

According to legend Clement was martyred after being exiled to the Crimean peninsula by Emperor Trajan. Sent to work in a quarry where the other labourers were desperate for water, he knelt in prayer and was granted a vision of a lamb on a nearby hillside. When he went to the spot, he struck with his quarryman's axe and brought forth a stream of the purest water.

Witnessing this miracle, many were converted to be followers of Christ, but Clement was martyred by being tied to an anchor and thrown from a boat into the Black Sea. In images he is often shown with an anchor.

THE POPE FROM BETHLEHEM

The next three popes were Evaristus (*c*.101–*c*.109), Alexander I (*c*.109–*c*.116) and Sixtus I (*c*.116–*c*.125). The *Liber Pontificalis* identifies Evaristus as being an Hellenic Jew, born in Bethlehem, and says he appointed seven deacons to the Church in Rome and assigned churches as titles to individual priests.

According to tradition, Alexander – who seems to have been born in Rome

– introduced the narration of the events of the Last Supper into celebration of the Mass. Sixtus I (spelled Xystus in the oldest documents) reputedly introduced the custom of the priest saying the Sanctus ('Holy, Holy, Holy') with the people during the Mass. Sixtus is recorded as being Roman by birth, the son of a man named Pastor.

THE PHILOSOPHER POPE

Pope Telesphorus (c.125–c.136) was from a Greek family and was said to have been a monk before being elected pope – according to tradition on Mount Carmel, Israel, so that the religious order of the Carmelites view him as their patron saint. An unexplained gap of two years in the papal lists interrupts the succession from Telesphorus to Pope Hyginus (c.138–c.142), a Greek, born in Athens, who was a philosopher before becoming pope. Gnostic theologians

Below: A 6th-century fresco in the Basilica of San Clemente, Rome, shows Clement I (pope c.91–c.101) celebrating Mass. The basilica is said to be on the site of his house.

Above: The Gnostic Valentinus claimed to have received esoteric spiritual knowledge from his teacher Theudas, who received it from St Paul. It was said to be derived from Paul's encounter with the risen Christ.

Valentinus and Cerdo visited Rome during Hyginus's pontificate, a time of ferment and theological debate.

Pope Pius I (c.142–c.155) was according to Church tradition from Aquileia, northern Italy, and the brother of a poet named Hermas who wrote 'The Shepherd', a series of visions and parables.

He excommunicated another Gnostic, Marcion, who subsequently founded the heretical sect of the Marcionites, teaching a form of dualism (belief in two gods) under which Christ was not the Son of the God of the Jews and the Old Testament but the offspring of a different, good God.

ANICETUS TO URBAN I, 155–230
THE PAPACY GROWS IN CONFIDENCE

Pope Anicetus (*c.*155–*c.*166) was a Syrian by birth, from Emesa (modern Homs). The fact that he was visited by the early Christian historian Hegesippus (110–180) suggests that the pope and the Church in Rome were beginning to hold a prime position in the Christian world.

Italian-born Pope Soter (*c.*166–*c.*174) was noted for his charity to Christians in need throughout the empire. Pope Eleutherius (*c.*175–*c.*189), a Greek born in Nicopolis, continued the struggle against Gnostics and followers of Marcionism begun under his predeces-

Below: Christians were traditionally said to have been martyred in the Colosseum, though modern historians doubt this – thinking the faithful were put to death at the Circus Maximus. In 1749 Pope Benedict XIV consecrated the Colosseum because of its link to early martyrs.

sors and took a stand against non-conformity in explicitly condemning Montanism, a charismatic Christian movement that had originated in Asia Minor (Anatolia). The followers of Montanism emphasized simplicity in the Church and reliance on the power of the Holy Spirit, and their meetings featured prophecies and also speaking in tongues.

EASTER ON A SUNDAY
The first African-born pope, Victor I (*c.*189–*c.*199), seems to have been a strong-willed man who set out to establish the authority of the papacy. He decided that Easter should always be celebrated on a Sunday and called synods in the major church centres in both Western and Eastern parts of the Christian world to consider the issue. By this date a tradition had been established whereby the

Above: Victor I (c.189–c.199) was the first African pope. This portrait is based on a medallion in the Basilica of Saint Paul Outside the Walls, Rome.

Roman Church celebrated Easter on a Sunday since this was the day of the week on which Christ rose from

Above: Callistus I (pope c.217–c.222) is buried in the basilica of Santa Maria in Trastevere in Rome. He built the first sanctuary on the site of the church.

the dead, but Christians in the East celebrated it on any day of the week according to the date of the Jewish festival of Passover – since the events of Christ's Passion took place at Passover.

The Western synods agreed with Victor's decision to fix Easter on a Sunday, but the ones in Asia Minor (Anatolia) did not; his response was to excommunicate those who challenged him. He also excommunicated Theodotus of Byzantium, who had argued that Jesus – although born of the Virgin Mary by the action of the Holy Spirit – was not divine until after his Resurrection.

PERSECUTION – AND HERESY

His successor, another Italian named Zephyrinus (c.199–c.217), ruled in difficult times.

Christians faced increasingly severe persecution under the Roman Emperor Septimius Severus, and Zephyrinus had to face down heretics including followers of the excommunicated Theodotus of Byzantium as well as the Montanists, Marcionists and Gnostics who had troubled his predecessors.

Right: Persecution at the hands of Marcus Aurelius struck fear into the hearts of the early Christians. This ancient bronze statue of the emperor stands on the Capitoline Hill in Rome.

In a dialogue written by a leading Christian named Caius to refute the teachings of the Montanist Proclus, we find the first reference to the graves of St Peter and St Paul in Rome. In exerting papal authority against the heretics, Zephyrinus made enemies. Hippolytus the Martyr dismissed this pope as 'ignorant' and 'a receiver of bribes and lover of money'.

TWICE CHEATED DEATH

Pope Callistus I (c.217–c.222), another Italian, came to power by taking advantage of the weakness of Zephyrinus towards the end of a wild and colourful life in which he bankrupted several Christians and twice narrowly escaped death.

As a young man he was a slave owned by a Christian named Carpophorus. Trusted by his master with substantial amounts of money, he launched a banking operation in which other Christians, including widows, invested. When Callistus lost all the money, he fled but was caught by his master just as he was about to embark on a cargo ship. The fugitive leapt into the sea but was hauled out and set to work at the hand-mill –

ANTIPOPES

Hippolytus of Rome was the first of the antipopes, the name given to the many individuals over the centuries who claimed the rights and authority of the papacy without proper authority. The term was first used in the late 12th century. Some antipopes arose because of disputes over doctrine, others when one candidate was preferred by the secular authorities but church leaders refused to give way, others as a result of papal exile. The last antipope was Felix V (1439–49).

a punishment used for slaves. Christians called for his release, and after further adventures he was sent to Antium with a pension by Pope Victor. Under Zephyrinus he was recalled to Rome and managed to ingratiate himself with the church hierarchy.

This account of his life is from the early 3rd-century *Philosophumena* (or 'Refutation of All Heresies'), probably written by Hippolytus of Rome. Callistus died a martyr, perhaps killed during an uprising in Rome; according to tradition his body was thrown down a well on the site of the Church of San Callisto in Rome that bears his name.

POWER OF PRAYER

The election of Callistus's successor, Urban I (c.222–230) was challenged and Hippolytus of Rome, author of the *Philosophumena* and a noted scholar, set himself up as a rival pope. Urban defied Hippolytus and maintained his hold on the papacy. The number of Christians in Rome increased under his rule. Legend has it that he converted many people through his sermons, and baptized the husband and brother-in-law of Saint Cecilia. It is also said that he succeeded in knocking a pagan idol over through the power of prayer alone and for this was seized and beheaded.

PONTIAN TO STEPHEN I, 230–57
STEPHEN ASSERTS PRIMACY OF POPE OVER OTHER BISHOPS

Roman-born Pontian (230–5) was the first pope to resign the papacy. The Roman Emperor Maximinus Thrax reinstituted persecution of Christians and banished Pontian and the antipope Hippolytus into exile in the Sardinian mines. Pontian resigned to allow a new pope to be elected in Rome. He had to live in terrible conditions in Sardinia and died as a result. Before his exile he had presided over a synod in Rome that condemned the Alexandrian theologian Origen.

The reign of Pontian's successor Anterus, a Greek, lasted just under six weeks from 21 November 235 to 3 January 236. He probably died of natural causes although some sources claim he was martyred during the persecutions of Maximinus.

THE TOUCH OF THE DOVE

Pope Fabian (236–50) was singled out for election as pope by a most unusual method – the intervention of a dove, symbol of the Holy Spirit. According to the 4th-century church historian Eusebius, Fabian was both a layman and a stranger to the Christians in Rome, but when they saw the dove land on his head while they were meeting to choose a new pontiff they acclaimed him as a bishop and elected him pope. From these unorthodox beginnings, he went on to become a quietly efficient leader, an important figure in the history of the early papacy who reorganized the Church in Rome and sent seven bishops to preach the Gospel in France.

Fabian also appointed officials to record the deeds of the Christian martyrs and corresponded with the theologian Origen. He was martyred on 20 January 250 during the persecution of Christians under Emperor Decius and after his death the Church was governed by a committee in the teeth of fierce official persecution for 14 months.

THE SECOND ANTIPOPE

Pope Cornelius finally succeeded in March 251 during a lull in the persecutions, but he was then faced by a second antipope, Novatian.

Novatian was the first Roman theologian to use the Latin language. He was consecrated by three bishops in 251. The principal disagreement between the

Left: Pope Fabian (pope 236–50) brought back the bodies of Pontian and the first antipope, Hippolytus, from their place of death in Sardinia for burial in Rome.

two leaders was over whether Christians who had lapsed in the face of persecution could be readmitted to the Church: Novatian said that they could not unless they were rebaptized, but the official position of the Church was that they could, without the need for a second baptism.

Cornelius prevailed and Novatian was excommunicated. From figures quoted in Cornelius's letters, we know that there were around 50,000 Christians in Rome by this time; the letters also make the first reference to the office of exorcist. Cornelius was exiled by Decius's successor Trebonianus Gallus to Centumcellae (modern Civitavecchia, Italy), where he died as a result of the hardships he endured.

ORIGEN

Origen (c.185–c.254) was a theologian and preacher, author of many biblical commentaries including the *Hexapla*, a comparative edition of the six extant versions of the Old Testament. He was

celebrated for his chastity, and according to the 4th-century church historian Eusebius castrated himself. He was head of a catechetical school first in Alexandria, Egypt (his probable birthplace) and – after he was exiled by Bishop Demetrius of Alexandria – in Caesarea, Palestine. In the persecution of Christians under Emperor Decius he was imprisoned and tortured but survived to die in Tyre, Phoenicia (modern Sur in Lebanon). Among the controversial ideas associated with him are that souls exist before bodies, that humans might endure a second Fall from Grace and that the devil was not beyond salvation.

Left: Origen was never sainted because his teaching was so controversial. Some historians hold he believed in reincarnation.

PATRON SAINT OF COPENHAGEN

Lucius I (253–4) seems to have been a prudent man who, although initially exiled under Emperor Trebonianus Gallus, won permission to return to Rome under Emperor Valerian. He is the patron saint of the Danish capital Copenhagen: according to tradition, his skull (within a reliquary) was taken to the area in *c.*1100 to banish local demons.

FROM THE CHAIR OF PETER

Stephen I (254–7) was a forthright exponent of the primacy of Rome. He opposed African and other churches that rebaptized heretic and lapsed Christians and threatened Cyprian, Bishop of Carthage, and other African bishops with excommunication; Cyprian wrote a spirited defence, asserting the right of each bishop to govern his own see, and sent envoys and threatened schism between Africa and Rome, but Stephen declared the primacy of the pope over other bishops, on the grounds that he followed in direct succession from Peter, the rock on

Below: Fabian was a surprise candidate for the papacy, elected after a dove alighted on his head, as depicted in this 15th-century image of the Spanish school.

Above: In the biblical account the Spirit of God descended to Jesus in the form of a dove after John the Baptist had baptized him in the River Jordan.

whom the Church's foundations were laid. He is associated with the phrase *cathedra Petri* ('The Chair of Peter') that symbolized the pre-eminence of the pope in Rome.

The Church does not celebrate Stephen as a martyr, although for many centuries he was remembered as such, following the tradition recorded in the 13th-century book the *Legenda aurea* ('Golden Legend') that he was sitting on the papal throne celebrating Mass on 2 August 257 when the Emperor Valerian's men burst in and beheaded him there and then.

THE POPE AND THE BISHOPS OF THE ROMAN CATHOLIC CHURCH

The pope and college of bishops derive their authority to teach and govern the Church from their status as direct spiritual descendants of St Peter and Jesus's other disciples.

Jesus gave the name Peter (from Greek *petros*, the translation of Syriac *cephas* – 'rock') to his disciple Simon, son of John, and told him he was the rock on which the Church would be built. He said 'I will give unto thee the keys of the kingdom of heaven: and whatsoever thou shalt bind on earth shall be bound in heaven: and whatsoever thou shalt loose on earth shall be loosed in heaven.' The pope is regarded as the direct spiritual descendant of St Peter – Pope Francis is 266th in line from Peter – and has these keys as his emblem, signifying his authority as 'Vicar' or representative of Christ.

Simon Peter became the foremost of Jesus's disciples and first leader of the Christians in Rome, where according to tradition he was martyred and buried in the spot where the high altar stands in St Peter's Basilica.

THE CHRISTIAN NARRATIVE

The profoundly inspirational narrative of the Christian Gospels taught by the pope and the Roman Catholic Church tells that the Son of God – born Jesus, son of the Virgin Mary in Bethlehem, Judea, roughly 2,000 years ago – gathered 12 disciples and for around three years was an itinerant preacher who taught in vivid parables or teaching tales and performed breathtaking miracles such as resurrecting Lazarus from the dead and calming a wild storm. He was betrayed to the Roman authorities, crucified in Jerusalem on the orders of the Roman prefect, Pontius Pilate, suffered, died and was buried, then on the third day rose again to life – and afterwards ascended into Heaven; by his death he redeemed all humankind who come to believe in Him from punishment due as a result of the sins of the first man, Adam, and the first woman, Eve.

These events fulfilled prophecies in Jewish tradition that a prince or king, the Messiah, would come to inaugurate an

Above: Jesus Christ, the Son of God, gave himself up to die on the cross and redeem humankind from the consequences of sin.

era of peace and justice: the name 'Christ' (Greek *Christos*, 'Anointed One') is the translation of the Hebrew word (*Meshiah*) for the Messiah and was given to Jesus by his followers after his death to signify that they knew him to be the Messiah.

After Jesus ascended into Heaven, at the Jewish festival of Pentecost, the disciples led by Peter felt the inspiration of God's Holy Spirit come upon them to inspire their preaching as they set about spreading the new faith that Jesus the Christ had founded. Roman Catholics and members of most other Christian denominations believe that God exists and is experienced in a Trinity of three forms: God the Father, God the Son and God the Holy Spirit.

Disagreement over the precise nature or origin of the Holy Spirit was later a matter of controversy between Western

Left: This ancient mosaic is at Tabgha, Israel – sometimes identified as the site of the miracle of the Feeding of the Five Thousand.

Left: The Angel Gabriel broke the news to Mary that she was to become pregnant with the Son of God. Fra Angelico painted several versions of the 'Annunciation'.

and Eastern Christian churches for centuries: while Latin (Roman) Christians held that the Holy Spirit proceeds from the Father and the Son together, their Eastern counterparts held that the Holy Spirit proceeds from the Father alone. This was a significant factor in the Great Schism between the churches in 1054.

THE EARLY CHURCH

The first Christians carried the new faith to many places in the Roman Empire, including the capital Rome. According to church tradition, Peter became bishop or leader of the Christians in Rome and in 64 died a martyr there. The Christians faced violent persecution for more than two centuries until under the Edict of Milan in 313 the empire recognized the legitimacy of the Christian Church.

COLLEGE OF BISHOPS

After he rose from the dead, Jesus commanded the disciples to 'go and make disciples of all nations' (Matthew 28:19); in Christian tradition the disciples are known as the Twelve Apostles, from the Greek word meaning one who is sent on a mission. Roman Catholics understand that, just as the pope is the spiritual successor of St Peter, so the bishops of the Church are successors of the apostles.

In the words of the Dogmatic Constitution of the Church as agreed by the Second Vatican Council (1962–5), the church is governed 'by the successor of Peter and by the bishops in communion with him'. The same council's Decree on the Bishops Pastoral Office identified the bishops of the Roman Catholic Church as a college that succeeded the Apostles as a group to teach and govern the Church.

At the time some scholars were concerned that this conception of the bishops' role would revive the idea that a general council of the Church should have equal or greater power than the pope himself – the 'conciliar theory' that caused a good deal of conflict between pope and council in the 15th century. A preliminary explanatory note to the decree established that the college of bishops cannot challenge the pope since: 'There is no such thing as the college without its head ... and in the college the head preserves intact his function as Vicar of Christ and pastor of the universal Church.'

Below: Christ said to Peter: 'I will give unto thee the keys of the kingdom of heaven.' The pope is Peter's descendant as Christ's 'Vicar'.

SIXTUS II TO EUSEBIUS, 257–310
POPES ARE MARTYRED BUT THE CHURCH SURVIVES PERSECUTION

Stephen's successor Sixtus II (257–8) is one of the most celebrated martyrs of the early Church. When Emperor Valerian launched a new round of violent persecution, Sixtus was seized and beheaded with six deacons while conducting a service in the catacomb of Praetextatus on the Appian Way. Sixtus prophesied the death of his best-known deacon, Lawrence of Rome, who was killed three days after the pope.

During his reign, Sixtus repaired relations with the Eastern churches, reputedly under the influence of Bishop Dionysius of Alexandria. He may or may not have written the *Sentences of Sextus*, a collection of spiritual teachings that bears his name.

For two years the severity of Valerian's persecution made election of a new pope impossible but after the emperor's humiliating death while a caged prisoner

Above: Pope Marcellinus. His martyr's death led to the veneration of his tomb by early Christians. He was buried in the Catacomb of Priscilla on the Via Salaria.

of the Persian King Shapur I, Pope Dionysius (260–8) took up the reins and the new emperor, Gallienus, issued an edict of toleration towards Christians.

STATEMENT OF FAITH
Dionysius was an able administrator who reorganized the Church in Rome, sent funds to support Christians in Cappadocia (modern Turkey) and reinforced the authority of Rome and the papacy: in a dispute with Bishop Dionysius of Alexandria – known as 'the affair of the two Dionysii' – the Pope clarified an orthodox position in which Father, Son and Holy Spirit were clearly seen as aspects of the Trinity rather than separate deities and the Bishop accepted the Pope's authority. This laid some of the groundwork for the statement of faith in the Nicene Creed of 325.

We know very little about popes Felix I (269–74), Eutychian (275–83) and Gaius (283–96), beyond the fact that

Left: Emperor Diocletian introduced the Tetrachy: rule by four emperors. This porphyry sculpture – now in St Mark's Basilica, Venice – celebrates the concept.

Felix issued an important dogmatic letter establishing the unity of the person of Christ and Eutychian was the last pope to be buried in the catacombs of Rome.

THE APOSTATE POPE

When Emperor Diocletian renewed violent persecution of the Roman Empire's Christians in 303, Pope Marcellinus (296–304) caved in. In a shocking abnegation of his responsibility, the pope simply gave in to Diocletian's demands that he hand over the Scriptures. Marcellinus even offered sacrifices to the pagan gods of Rome. After this failure, Marcellinus repented and again professed his faith as a Christian – and died a martyr.

(This is the widely circulated account, although St Augustine of Hippo denied its truth.) His reign, whether or not stained by this apostasy, is also marked by a great positive: the declaration of the first Christian state, when in 301 King Tiridates III of Armenia made Christianity the official faith of his country.

EXILED FROM ROME

Several years of trouble followed Marcellinus's death – persecution eased after Diocletian abdicated in 305 and

Above: This 3rd-century fresco of The Last Supper *in the Catacombs of Callixtus was rediscovered beneath Rome by Giovanni Battista de Rossi in 1854: Pius IX (pope 1846–78) visited to inspect the Crypt of the Popes.*

was succeeded as emperor by Maxentius. A new pope, Marcellus I (c.308–9), was not elected for around four years. Once in office, he reorganized the administration of the Church in Rome and established a burial place on the Via Salaria. But he did not last long. The very severe penalties he imposed on Christians who had lapsed under Diocletian's persecution led to rioting and Maxentius exiled the pope in an attempt to keep the peace. Marcellus died in exile. His remains were later returned to Rome where they are kept beneath the altar in the Church of San Marcello.

CHURCH IN TURMOIL

Marcellus's successor Eusebius was also embroiled in violent disagreements over whether lapsed Christians needed to perform penance to be readmitted to the Church. His reign lasted just six months, from 18 April to 21 October 310. Such was the upheaval among Christians in Rome that he, too, was sent into exile by Emperor Maxentius. He died shortly afterwards, in Sicily.

CATACOMBS

In times of persecution early Christians took refuge in a network of underground cemeteries (catacombs) beneath Rome: to worship; to honour the remains of martyrs of the faith; and, when necessary, as a hiding place. The first underground cemeteries had been made by pagan Romans in pre-Christian times and these were greatly extended by the Christians. Excavation was relatively easy in the soft tuff (volcanic ash) that lies beneath much of Rome, and large complexes developed, sometimes with four layers of tunnels built on top of one another. San Callisto, the largest of the catacombs – covering 15 hectares (37 acres) and containing more than 20km (12½ miles) of tunnels – is named after and was probably built by Pope Callistus I, although he was not buried in the 'Crypt of the Popes' within the complex. The origin of the word catacomb is not known; it was initially applied to the cemetery beneath the Basilica of San Sebastiano on the Appian Way and afterwards applied to other underground burial sites. Frescoes on the walls of the catacombs – treasured examples of early Christian art – represent incidents from Jesus's life as well as well as Old Testament scenes.

MILTIADES AND SYLVESTER I, 311–335
IMPERIAL CHRISTIANITY AND THE DONATION OF CONSTANTINE

The reigns of popes Miltiades (311–14) and Sylvester I (314–35) saw the birth of the Christian Roman Empire. In 312, prior to the Battle of the Milvian Bridge, Emperor Constantine had a vision of the Christian cross written in light on the midday sky, together with the words 'In this sign you will triumph', and this profoundly transformative event set him on the road to victory over his rival for power, Maxentius, and conversion to the Christian faith. In 313 in the Edict of Milan, Constantine and his co-ruler Licinius declared that Christians should be free to profess their faith, removed all existing penalties for being Christian and returned Church property. Constantine also donated the Lateran Palace in Rome to Miltiades as a papal residence.

Pope Miltiades was probably North African. Towards the end of his reign he was in charge of a church synod at the Lateran Palace that condemned Donatus

Magnus, leader of the Donatist sect, for rebaptizing clergy who had lapsed from their faith but who wanted to return to the Church. Miltiades died on 10 January 314 before he could attend the Council of Arles, a gathering of bishops called by Emperor Constantine. The Council rejected an appeal by the Donatists against the Rome decision and excommunicated Donatus.

COUNCIL OF NICAEA
The meeting at Arles was the forerunner of the Council of Nicaea, called by Constantine in 325 with the backing of Miltiades's successor Pope Sylvester I, to meet in Nicaea (modern Iznik, Turkey). Sylvester did not attend the council in person but sent the legates Vitus and Vincentius to represent him.

The council's principal task was to find a solution to problems in the Eastern Church caused by disagreements

Above: Arius of Alexandria, who argued that Christ was a created being and so not the equal of God the Father, was condemned by both the emperor and the pope.

over Arianism, the teachings of the presbyter Arius of Alexandria (c.250–336) – in particular, the idea that God is unique and self-existent (He exists of and in Himself) and that Christ, as God's Son, is a created being, not self-existent and therefore not fully divine.

The council condemned Arianism and issued the Nicene Creed as a statement of orthodoxy. The creed specified that Christ was 'of one substance' with the Father, so could not be differentiated from God the Father as Arius had suggested. Sylvester approved the council's decision; Constantine exiled Arius from the Roman Empire. Church and secular authority stood side by side.

A NEW ROME
Another event of Pope Sylvester's reign that had major and enduring consequences was Constantine's foundation of the city of Constantinople (modern

Left: In moving the seat of imperial rule to the new capital of Constantinople the emperor, according to legend, recognized the papacy's right to Rome.

Istanbul, Turkey) as a new capital for the Roman Empire in 330. After defeating his rival Licinius at Chrysopolis (now a district of Istanbul) in 324, so establishing himself as sole ruler of the Roman Empire, East and West, he determined to establish an Eastern imperial capital on the site of the Greek trading colony of Byzantium. The new capital undermined the importance of Rome, and of the western regions of the Roman Empire.

THE POPE AND THE EMPEROR

According to legend, Pope Sylvester baptized Constantine and in doing so cured the emperor of leprosy. As a sign of his gratitude Constantine declared that the pope had primacy over all other bishops and gave him the 'Donation of Constantine'.

The legend also recounts how Constantine gave up his insignia and led Sylvester's horse by the bridle, humbly acting as his groom. The pope then gave Constantine his imperial crown, and the emperor determined to give up Rome to the pope's control and move his own residence to Constantinople. The legend,

probably created in the 6th century, establishes the supremacy of the pope even over the Roman emperor.

A PIECE OF JERUSALEM IN ROME

In Sylvester's reign the Basilica di Santa Croce in Gerusalemme was established in Rome, in around 325. One of the many legends surrounding this pope tells that the church was built to contain relics of Christ's passion brought from the Holy

Above: The story of Pope Sylvester and Emperor Constantine seeks to establish the supremacy of papal authority and its role in guiding imperial power.

Land by Emperor Constantine's Christian mother, St Helen. The floor of the basilica was covered in soil from Jerusalem, thus giving the building its name in Gerusalemme. The first St Peter's Basilica in Rome was also begun during Sylvester's reign.

'DONATION OF CONSTANTINE'

This document was supposedly a decree made by Emperor Constantine in 315 or 317 that gave Pope Sylvester and his successors imperial authority to govern Rome and the Western empire, possession of the imperial palace in Rome and primacy over the bishops of Antioch, Alexandria, Constantinople and Jerusalem and all the world's churches. It was proved by Italian humanist Lorenzo Valla to be a forgery in the 15th century. The forgery was made by a cleric at the Lateran in

the 750s/760s, perhaps with the backing of Pope Stephen II (752–7). This was a time when the papacy was embarking on a close relationship with the Frankish monarchy, which led to the creation of the Holy Roman Empire in the West, and so was seeking to challenge the authority of the Byzantine Empire. Surprisingly, given the document's importance for claims of papal authority, no pope before Leo IX (1049–54) cited the Donation in any official document.

CHAPTER TWO

FALL OF THE WESTERN EMPIRE

MARK TO PELAGIUS II, 336–590

In 410 Rome was sacked for three days by the Germanic tribe of the Visigoths while Pope Innocent I took refuge in Ravenna. St Jerome, former secretary to Pope Damasus I, was aghast. He wrote: 'The bright light of the whole world was put out ... the Roman Empire was beheaded ... The entire world perished in one city...' The status of Rome as principal city of the Western Roman Empire was in sharp decline, yet it remained the base of the papacy and arguably the centre of the Christian world. Throughout the years 336–590, the popes sought to maintain their authority over rival church leaders, and to elevate Rome above all other Christian cities.

Pope Damasus I claimed Rome as the city of saints Peter and Paul; in an epitaph on their joint shrine he declared that as the place of their martyrdom Rome had the right to claim them as citizens. Pope Leo I based his claim to a pope's absolute authority as leader of the Church on the fact that he and other popes were in direct descent from St Peter. The popes won secular backing: in 380 co-emperors Theodosius I and Gratian declared the empire's inhabitants must follow the form of Christianity 'handed down by the Apostle Peter to the Romans'; in 445 Emperor Valentinian III issued an edict giving Leo I and his successors authority over all the other bishops of the Christian Church.

The struggle to establish pre-eminence met constant challenges. The Council of Chalcedon in 451 accepted as the ultimate truth Pope Leo's declaration that Christ had two natures in the course of His incarnation, one human and one divine: the bishops stated that 'Peter had spoken through Leo'. But they also declared that as capital of the Eastern Roman Empire, Constantinople was 'the new Rome'.

Left: Protector of Rome: Pope Leo I rode north to confront Attila the Hun who had invaded northern Italy; Attila withdrew – and Rome was safe. This grand vision of the event (1514) is by Raphael in the Apostolic Palace.

MARK TO LIBERIUS, 336–66
CHURCH IN TURMOIL OVER ARIAN HERESY

The most enduring legacy of Pope Mark, who reigned for less than nine months in 336, was the Basilica San Marco, which he founded in Rome in honour of St Mark the Evangelist. The church has been rebuilt several times, beginning in 792 under Pope Hadrian I (772–95), and underwent a major reconstruction in the Renaissance under Pope Paul II (1464–71).

A Roman clergyman before becoming pope, Mark was consecrated on 18 January 336. During his rule he ordained that the Bishop of Ostia would have the honour of consecrating each new pope and invested the bishop with the *pallium*, an ecclesiastical robe that served as a symbol of spiritual authority. He died of natural causes on 7 October 336.

POPE'S PRIMACY

Pope Julius I (337–52) played a key role in resurgent controversy over Arianism in the Eastern Church, in the course of

Above: Pope Mark. He was buried in the Catacomb of Balbina, although in the 12th century his remains were moved to the Basilica San Marco, where they are kept in an urn beneath the altar.

Above: Antipope Felix II, who came to power when Liberius was banished by Emperor Constantius II, was in the end ousted by Liberius and died in Porto, near Rome.

> ### ARIUS
>
> The man who gave his name to the heresy of Arianism was a Christian presbyter from Alexandria, born in *c*.250. His principal teaching was that God the Father was timeless, without beginning and without equal and that because Jesus Christ his Son was created by the Father and so had a beginning, therefore Christ had a distinct and different nature and a lesser divinity. His main work was Thalia ('Plenty') and elements of his teaching were spread in popular songs accessible to those who were not learned. Arius dropped dead while walking in Constantinople – possibly having been poisoned by his enemies – in 336, but the controversies over Arianism were to continue for many years in both Western and Eastern churches.

which he made a significant statement asserting the primacy of the pope and of Rome over other bishops and regions. Arianism – the theological teachings of Arius of Alexandria, who held that Christ was created by God the Father and therefore a lesser divinity – had been condemned and Arius declared a heretic at the Council of Nicaea of 325. The orthodox position, fervently held by churchmen such as Athanasius, Archbishop of Alexandria, was that God exists in three equal persons – Father, Son and Holy Spirit – all of one substance and therefore of equal divinity.

The controversy continued: after followers of the pro-Arian Eusebius, Patriarch of Constantinople, had succeeded in ousting Athanasius from his position, Athanasius travelled to Rome, where he was backed at a synod called by Pope Julius in 342. Julius then wrote to the Eastern bishops in an attempt to

quell the dispute, declaring Athanasius reinstated and asserting that in such matters bishops should apply to Rome before making decisions so that the pope could define what was just.

COUNCIL OF SARDICA

Subsequently Julius called a church council at Sardica (modern Sofia, Bulgaria) in 343 but was unable to impose his will on the Eastern bishops, who at the rival council of Philippopolis (modern Plovdiv, Bulgaria) voted to depose the pope, along with Athanasius and other leading churchmen. However, the Council of Sardica remained in session, attended by around 300 Western bishops, and backed the pope's authority to intervene in ecclesiastical disputes.

Julius declared Athanasius restored to his bishopric and his decision was initially accepted by pro-Arian Roman emperor Constantius II. When Athanasius returned to Alexandria in 346, Julius wrote to the priests, deacons and people of Alexandria to congratulate them.

ROMAN CHURCH THRIVES

In Rome, Julius presided over a thriving and expanding Church, with greatly increasing numbers of the faithful, and established two churches, the first now Santa Maria in Trastevere and the second now Santi XII Apostoli. On his death on 12 April 352 he was buried in the Catacomb of Calepodius on the Aurelian Way, then later his remains were moved to Santa Maria in Trastevere.

The Arian issue came to the fore once more under Julius's successor Pope Liberius. The pro-Arian Emperor Constantius wanted to establish religious unity in the empire: he condemned Athanasius, and required all Western bishops to approve this decision. When Liberius refused to agree to the condemnation, he was exiled by Constantius while antipope Felix II took power in Rome.

Below: A veteran of the First Council of Nicaea, Patriarch Athanasius of Constantinople fought long and hard against the Arian heresy. This altar mosaic is from a Ukrainian monastery.

In exile, Liberius submitted to the emperor, agreeing to break off relations with Athanasius and accepting changes to the Nicene Creed to eliminate anti-Arian elements. Recalled to Rome, he was rapturously welcomed by the people, but ordered by Constantius to rule alongside Felix II.

FIRST POPE NOT TO BE CANONIZED

Liberius's failure to manage the controversy, and his weakness in the face of the emperor, brought the papacy's standing low. When Constantius called the Council of Ariminum (modern Rimini, Italy) in 359, Liberius and Felix II were not invited. The Western bishops at

Above: The beautiful Roman church of Santa Maria in Trastevere, founded by Callistus I, was enlarged and rebuilt by Julius I. Like Callistus, Julius is buried there.

Ariminum were mostly orthodox but were outmanoeuvred and ended up approving an Arian creed.

After the death of Constantius in 361, Liberius attempted to revive the papacy's flagging authority, repudiating the creed agreed at Ariminum and then patched up differences with the moderate among the Arian Eastern bishops. Nevertheless after his death on 24 September 366 he gained the unenviable distinction of being the first pope not to be declared a saint.

DAMASUS I, 366–84
POPE WHO PROMOTED PRIMACY OF CHRISTIAN ROME

Damasus I (366–84) was a ruthless operator who won the papacy by force. When he was elected pope in October 366, he immediately faced the challenge of a rival, Ursinus. The conflict was played out in the streets between marauding gangs, and Damasus prevailed because his supporters were more numerous and tougher – his street fighters, who included groups of the fearsome *fossores* (diggers of catacombs) slaughtered 137 of Ursinus's supporters amid scenes of carnage at the Basilica of Sicinius (now the Basilica di Santa Maria Maggiore).

Rioting was so severe that Emperor Valentinian intervened to restore public order. The emperor backed Damasus and exiled Ursinus first to Cologne and afterwards to Milan.

TICKLER OF WOMEN'S EARS
Yet Damasus was also a charming man, an urbane priest with a particular influence among the wealthy women and heiresses of Rome – to such an extent that he was dubbed *matronarum auriscalpius* ('tickler of women's ears').

By this period Christianity was increasingly acceptable among the well-to-do in Rome who exchanged gifts that featured Christian symbols alongside pagan iconography such as pictures of Venus. Once established in the papacy, Damasus lived in great style – dressing well, travelling by carriage and enjoying lavish banquets. He was never without

Above: An 11/12th-century French manuscript Bible shows Pope Damasus I engaging the youthful St Jerome as his secretary. Before his stint in Rome, Jerome studied in Constantinople.

Below: Albrecht Durer shows St Jerome in his study (1521). Jerome is often shown with a lion – a legend told how he healed a lion.

his enemies and faced accusations of adultery, but was cleared by a synod of 44 bishops.

CHRISTIAN ROME
Damasus may have been a worldly cleric, but he conducted an effective papacy that enhanced the prestige of the pope and the Roman Church. He set out to establish Rome as a great Christian rather than pagan city.

He was the first pope to refer to Rome as the Apostolic See – the one established by the Apostle Peter. He claimed that Christ's words to Peter in

---

FACT BOX
Original name Damasus
Born *c.*304
Origin Roman
Date elected pope 1 October 366
Died 11 December 384
Key fact First pope to refer to Rome as the Apostolic See – established by the Apostle Peter

Matthew 16:18 ('thou art Peter and it is upon this rock that I will build my church') established the primacy of Rome over other centres of the faith. He promoted the veneration of Rome's Christian martyrs, restoring the catacombs, gathering and reburying the bodies of the saints beneath verse epitaphs.

For the joint shrine of saints Peter and Paul he wrote a celebrated epitaph: while acknowledging that the Apostles came from the East, he claimed them as citizens of Rome because they died as martyrs in Rome. In 384 he prevailed over non-Christian senators who wanted to maintain a pagan altar of Victory in the Senate, and had the altar abolished.

ENEMY OF HERESY

Damasus fought hard to maintain orthodoxy, writing no fewer than 24 anathemas against various heresies. At Roman synods in 368 and 369 he condemned Apollinarianism (the teaching of Bishop Apollinaris the Younger of Laodicea, according to which, while Christ had a human body and soul, He did not have a normal human mind, but

the divine Logos in its place) and Macedonianism (the theories of Bishop Macedonius of Constantinople, according to which the Holy Spirit was created by Jesus and thus had a lesser divinity than the Father and the Son).

He also continued the battle against Arianism, excommunicating the Arian Bishop of Milan, Auxentius, in 369 and negotiating at length with Bishop Basil of Caesarea – but in the end to little effect. In 380 this work gained imperial sanction when Eastern Emperor Theodosius I and Western Emperor Gratian jointly decreed that the empire's inhabitants must follow the form of Christianity 'handed down by the Apostle Peter to the Romans' as defined by the bishops of Rome and Alexandria.

LATIN BIBLE AND LITURGY

Another Roman synod, in 382, proclaimed the primacy of Rome. One of the delegates at the conference, Jerome, remained in Rome and became the pope's secretary. Damasus asked Jerome to revise the Latin translations of the Bible in the light of the Greek Septuagint (Old Testament) and New Testament, so creating the celebrated

Above: Western Emperor Gratian. His joint decree with Theodosius backing the form of Christianity 'handed down by … Peter to the Romans' was an important landmark.

Vulgate version of the Bible. In Damasus's reign, Latin became established as the language of the liturgy.

Below: Eastern Emperor Theodosius I holds a victory laurel. This detail is from the pedestal to an Ancient Egyptian column that Theodosius erected in Constantinople.

SIRICIUS AND ANASTASIUS, 384–401
FIRST DECREES IMPOSING CLERICAL CELIBACY

The first Roman bishop to call himself 'pope' in the modern sense, Siricius (384–99) was an uncompromising disciplinarian. He is celebrated above all for his surviving letters that enforce church discipline, with threats of sanctions against any who failed to abide by his decisions – notably on the celibacy of priests, penance, ordination and baptism.

FIRST PAPAL DECRETAL

Almost his first act as pope in 385 was to pen a letter to Bishop Himerius of Tarragona in Spain requiring that all priests should be celibate – this was the first statement from any pope on this matter and the letter is the first surviving papal decretal (authoritative statement on discipline or canon law).

Siricius emphasized the supremacy of Rome, exhorting Himerius to pass on his ordinances to bishops of the surrounding provinces and praising him for having consulted Rome, which he likened to the head of the Christian body. Now the pope was the supreme authority, the final arbiter and definer of the law.

When Priscillian, ascetic Bishop of Avila in the Roman province of Gallaecia (parts of northwest Spain and northern Portugal) was charged with magic and executed by Emperor Magnus Maximus, Siricius and Bishop Ambrose of Milan complained to the imperial authorities and were able to limit the persecution of his followers.

Siricius sought to exercise papal authority in the Eastern as well as the Western Church. He declared that no bishop should be consecrated without papal approval and succeeded in finding a temporary solution in 393 to the Meletian Schism, a dispute over the bishopric of Antioch.

Above: Pope Anastasius I. He was succeeded by his son (Innocent I) – perhaps the only case of a pope being followed in the papacy by his offspring.

ON ST PAUL'S GRAVE

In Rome, Siricius dedicated the Basilica di San Paolo fuori le Mura in 390. The church had originally been founded on the site of the grave of St Paul by Emperor Constantine but was beautifully expanded as an elegant, five-aisled basilica by Emperor Theodosius. A column naming Siricius and commemorating the dedication still stands today in the vestibule to the side entrance of the transept.

Siricius died on 26 November 399 and was interred in the Catacomb of Priscilla on the Via Salaria. His forthright statements ruffled feathers and divided opinion on his character. French-born letter-writer and later bishop Paulinus of Nola declared Siricius to be reserved and haughty, but Emperor Valentinian III noted his piety. The former papal secretary Jerome, meanwhile, held that Siricius lacked judgement.

His successor Anastasius I (399–401) was warmly praised by Paulinus, Augustine of Hippo and Jerome, who were all his friends. Jerome celebrated Anastasius as saintly and blessed, 'of very rich poverty and Apostolic solicitude'.

ST AUGUSTINE

Augustine of Hippo (354–430), or Aurelius Augustinus, was one of the most important of the Church Fathers, who adapted classical ideas to Christian thinking. His essential works are his 13-book spiritual autobiography *Confessions* (397–398) and the 22-book *City of God* (413–26), which celebrates Divine Providence and justifies the Church. Born in Tagaste, Numidia (modern Souk Ahras, Algeria) in 354, the son of Patricius and Monica, a devout Christian. He converted to Christianity in 386 and was baptized alongside his son Adeodatus by Bishop Ambrose of Milan the following year. After being ordained a priest in 391 he was Bishop of Hippo (modern Anaba in Algeria) from 396 to his death in 430. He had an immense influence on Christian thought and Western philosophy and the concepts of original sin and the just war derive from his work.

Above: St Augustine meditates on the fundamentals of Christianity in his study. Jerome said Augustine 'established anew the ancient Faith'. This image was made by Sandro Botticelli in 1480.

Above: The pope in the legend of St Ursula (shown here) is sometimes said to be Siricius. Ursula made a pilgrimage to Rome with her newly converted husband.

ORIGEN DENOUNCED

Some of this praise may be due to the pope's willingness to deliver what these friends wanted – in particular, under pressure from Jerome and Theophilus, patriarch of Alexandria, he was willing to anathemize the works of 3rd-century Alexandrian theologian Origen (*c.*185–*c.*254), whose *First Principle* had recently been translated from Greek into Latin by the monk and theologian Rufinus of Aquileia (345–410). The work is the first endeavour to present Christianity as a complete theory of the universe.

Anastasius called a council in 400 that denounced Origen, and when Rufinus wrote to defend his own work and Origen, the pope upheld the verdict despite the fact that he seems not to have read the offending work. He also wrote several papal letters denouncing Origen.

DONATIST DISPUTE

Anastasius also moved against Donatism in North Africa. He wrote to African bishops at the Council of Carthage in 401, who were struggling with a shortage of clergy, urging them not to lift the ban on Donatists (followers of Donatus Magnus, who had been excommunicated at the Council of Arles in 314 for requiring the rebaptism of clergy who had lapsed under persecution but wanted to re-enter the Church). In the end the bishops resisted papal pressure and did lift the ban.

Anastasius died on 19 December 401 after just over two years as pope. He was buried in the Catacomb of Pontian on the Via Portuensis.

INNOCENT I, 401–17
WHEN ROME WAS SACKED BY THE VISIGOTHS

Innocent I – elected to the papacy on 21 December 401 – was reputedly the son of his predecessor Anastasius, making this the only instance of a son succeeding his father as pope. In addition to being the pontiff who endured the Sack of Rome by the invading Visigoths in 410, Innocent was embroiled in the campaign led by St Augustine of Hippo to anathemize the British/Irish monk Pelagius, who argued against Augustine's concept of original sin in favour of humans exercising free will. Innocent excommunicated Pelagius on 27 January 417.

RAMPAGING VISIGOTHS

King Alaric I of the Visigoths (a Germanic tribe) saw the vulnerability of the Western Roman Empire under its profoundly ineffective young emperor Honorius and invaded Italy in 401. He was defeated by the brilliant Roman

Right: Innocent I. He reputedly allowed pagan worship in Rome after the city was sacked, but it is said there were few takers. Christianity was secure in Rome.

general Flavius Stilicho in 402 but moved again after Stilicho was executed by Honorius on suspicion of treachery in 408.

Alaric besieged Rome and would have accepted a negotiated settlement that included a vast ransom except that Honorius, safely ensconced at Ravenna, refused to agree to it – even though a deposition of Romans, including Pope Innocent, went there to try to persuade him to make a deal.

Alaric then besieged Rome again in 409 and for a third time in summer 410, and when on 24 August 410 allies within the city opened the gates, the Visigoth army poured into the city, ransacking, burning and looting.

'WHO WOULD BELIEVE IT?'

This was the first time Rome had been captured by a foreign enemy for almost 800 years, but the damage was not as bad as it might have been since Alaric was a Christian and ordered his men not to damage Christian buildings or hurt any of the devout. St Jerome, in the preface to his *Commentary on the Book of Ezekiel*, bewailed the event as the end of an era: 'Who would believe that Rome, built up by the conquering of the entire world, had collapsed, that the mother of all countries had been made their tomb…?'

In the aftermath Alaric led the Visigoths southwards, intending to invade Africa, but he died from a sudden

Left: Visigoth leader Alaric I died after taking Rome. He had given up on plans to invade Sicily and North Africa and then passed away as his army returned northwards.

FACT BOX

Original name Damasus

Born Not known

Origin Italian

Date elected pope 21 December 401

Died 12 March 417

Key fact Promoted papal authority and excommunicated Pelagius

---

PELAGIUS AND THE PELAGIAN HERESY

A British or Irish theologian, Pelagius (c.354–418) took issue with Augustine of Hippo on original sin, predestination and the workings of divine grace, arguing that humans could achieve salvation by their own efforts in exercising free will. He taught in Rome where he emphasized the need for ascetic self-denial and was shocked by the self-indulgence and laxity of many Christians. The fall of Rome in 410 led him to settle with his close supporter, a lawyer named Celestius, in northern Africa and he came into direct conflict with Augustine. After he moved to Palestine in c.412, his work *De libero arbitrio* ('On Free Will', 416) was condemned by two church councils in Africa and the following year he was excommunicated, along with Celestius, by Pope Innocent I. The election of Pope Zosimus would bring respite, and Pelagius was cleared after writing his *Libellus fidei* ('Brief Statement of Faith') but he was again condemned as a heretic at the Council of Carthage in 418. He was expelled from Jerusalem but granted sanctuary by Patriarch Cyril of Alexandria, in Egypt, where he probably died.

fever; his army thereafter marched north to Gaul (modern France). Innocent was in Ravenna at the time of the sacking, but he was able to return to Rome in 412.

AUTHORITY OF ROME

The pope had done all that he could to avert the catastrophe. In any case, the principal responsibility for the Sack of Rome lies not with Innocent but with the Western emperor, Honorius, who was reputedly more interested in raising chickens at Ravenna than saving Rome from the barbarian hordes. Despite the terrible events with which his name is associated, Innocent I was a gifted, deter-

Above: Innocent was unable to help John Chrysostom, who was deposed as Patriarch of Constantinople after confronting Empress Aelia Eudoxia over her life of luxury, shown here in a painting by Jean-Paul Laurens.

mined and effective pope, full of energy and zeal, who maintained and strengthened the authority of the papacy and of the Roman Church.

In particular, Innocent sought to exercise the pope's authority as leader of both Eastern and Western churches. For example, he wrote to Archbishop Anysius of Thessalonica confirming papal approval for the archbishop's rights as a vicar of the pope in Illyria (part of the Balkan peninsula) that he said had been granted by previous popes including Damasus and Siricius. In other letters and judgements he demanded absolute papal supremacy, declaring that all ecclesiastical disputes should be submitted to the pope for judgement.

JOHN CHRYSOSTOM

In one celebrated matter Innocent attempted but failed to exert the pope's authority in the East: in 404 he called for a synod at Thessalonica to decide the case of the saintly John Chrysostom. John had been deposed as Patriarch of

Constantinople and exiled by the Patriarch Theophilus of Alexandria and the Eastern empress Aelia Eudoxia, who was estranged from her husband and Eastern emperor Arcadius. The bishops he sent to communicate this decision to Arcadius were imprisoned and badly treated and the synod was not held. John Chrysostom remained in exile until his death.

Below: The might and glory of Rome – evidenced by scenes of the looting of Jerusalem in AD70 on the triumphal Arch of Titus – was no more.

ZOSIMUS TO SIXTUS III, 417–40
POPES FIGHT PELAGIANISM – AND OTHER HERESIES

The four popes from Zosimus to Sixtus III committed themselves to maintaining and where possible extending the prestige and authority of the papacy. They were also staunch defenders of orthodoxy who maintained a firm line against heresy.

The first, Zosimus (417–18), was a hasty and somewhat tactless man whose attempts to assert the supremacy of the papacy led the Roman Church into conflict with both French and African bishops in a short and turbulent reign of less than two years. When he declared Bishop Patroclus of Arles to be papal vicar in Gaul this provoked strong opposition from the bishops of Marseille, Vienne and Narbonne, particularly because the decision was made on the grounds that Arles was historically the prime see in Gaul. Outraged at the chal-

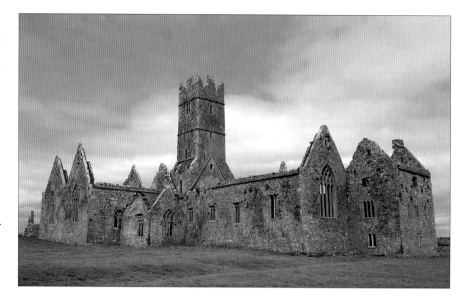

Below: The core structure of Santa Maria Maggiore remains as built by Sixtus III before 440. Its triumphal arch bears an inscription naming 'Sixtus, bishop to the people of God'.

lenge to his authority, Zosimus issued a threat of excommunication but he died before he could carry it through.

The dispute with the African bishops was over Pelagius, who had been condemned by African councils of the church and excommunicated by Innocent I: Zosimus was initially moved to accept Pelagius back into the church and he reprimanded the African bishops for being hasty in their condemnation, but he later changed his mind and confirmed Pelagius's excommunication in his *Epistola tractoria* ('Epistolary Sermon').

Zosimus was so unpopular that the announcement of his death on 27 December 418 caused celebrations in the streets of Rome.

STRUGGLE FOR POWER
His successor Boniface I (418–22) faced and overcame the challenge of an antipope, Eulalius. While the candidates were in dispute, Emperor Honorius ordered them to leave Rome and passed the decision on who should take precedence to a church synod scheduled to meet at Spoleto in June, but Eulalius defied the emperor's orders in returning to Rome and so lost the support of the secular authorities.

Above: Celestine contributed to the spread of Christianity in Ireland. Some historians hold that the bishop he sent in 431, Palladius, was confused with St Patrick in some traditions.

Emperor Honorius recognized Boniface as pope on 3 April 419. In a four-year reign, the new pope continued the work of his predecessors in

---

VIRGIN MARY

In Sixtus III's redevelopment the Liberian Basilica, the Roman church now known as Santa Maria Maggiore, was one of the earliest churches to feature images of the Virgin Mary and in this period, following the decree by the Council of Ephesus of 431 that she should be called *Theotokos* ('Bearer of God'), Mary was playing an increasingly important role in Christian worship. Devotion to the Virgin Mary goes back to the 2nd century, and was well established by the 3rd century in Egypt – the earliest surviving prayer to Mary, *Sub Tuum Praesidium* ('Beneath Thy Compassion'), dates to c.250 and uses the word *Theotokos*.

defending and exerting the rights of the papacy and in fighting against the beliefs of Pelagianism.

THEOTOKOS – BEARER OF GOD

Celestine I (422–32) was a vigorous defender of orthodoxy. He took a strong line against Nestorianism – the teachings of Nestorius, Patriarch of Constantinople in 428–31, who proposed that Christ has two natures, one human, one divine and argued that the Virgin Mary should be viewed as mother of the human Christ only and should not be celebrated as *Theotokos* ('Bearer of God').

Celestine called a church council in Rome that backed the use of the title *Theotokos* and called on Nestorius to renounce his errors. Then at the Council of Ephesus in 431 Nestorius was condemned as a heretic, deposed as Patriarch and banished.

ENVOYS TO IRELAND AND ENGLAND

Celestine also took an interest in nurturing the growth of Christianity in the British Isles. He sent Palladius, the first bishop to spread the Gospel in Ireland, and carried on the fight against Pelagianism by despatching bishops

Left: The two facial expressions in this exquisite 6th-century panel from the Monastery of St Catherine, Egypt, perhaps suggest twin natures, divine and human, in Christ – a doctrine propounded by Nestorius.

Germanus of Auxerre and Lupus of Troyes from Gaul to fight the heresy in England, where it was strong.

The Pelagians hoped for better when Sixtus III (432–40) was elected because this Roman priest was thought to be sympathetic to their theology. However, once installed as pope, he followed his predecessors in taking a hard line on orthodoxy and rejected an approach from the Pelagians to re-enter communion with the Church.

SANTA MARIA MAGGIORE

Sixtus set to work rebuilding Rome, which was still suffering from the effects of the Visigoths' three-day rampage through the city in 410. In particular, he rebuilt the Liberian Basilica, which had been constructed by Pope Liberius (352–66) and is now known as Santa Maria Maggiore. This church, which – as rebuilt by Sixtus III – featured exquisite mosaics of the Blessed Virgin Mary, has had a number of names associated with Mary, including Sancta Maria ad Praesepe ('Saint Mary of the Crib'), because it contains a relic of the crib in which Jesus lay as a baby, and Our Lady of the Snows because of the legendary account of its initial foundation according to which the church was built by a Roman named John, together with his wife, after they were instructed by Mary in a vision to build a church on the spot where she made snow fall at the height of summer.

Below: The Blessed Virgin was becoming increasingly important. This mosaic of her coronation was installed by Sixtus III as part of his rebuilding of Santa Maria Maggiore in Rome.

LEO I, 440–61
FIRST POPE TO WIN ACCOLADE 'THE GREAT'

The highly talented Pope Leo I (440–61) proved a courageous leader for the Church, assured in exercise of the authority he saw himself as having inherited directly from St Peter. He was a stern opponent of heresy and defiant of challenges to his position, as well as a fearless protector of Rome who twice confronted invading armies and in so

Below: Leo the Great showed courage and profound faith in confronting Attila the Hun.

doing greatly enhanced the prestige of the pope as a leading figure in the Western World.

LEO AND ATTILA

In 452 Leo met face to face with Attila the Hun whose army had invaded northern Italy, sacked Aquileia and was preparing to march on Rome. Leo travelled north to meet Attila at Lake Garda, where he persuaded him – one of the sternest enemies of the Roman Empire, both East and West – to retreat and spare Rome.

According to the 6th-century Roman historian Jordanes, Attila was fearful that he would meet the fate of the last man to invade Rome, Alaric of the Visigoths, who had died suddenly shortly after his men attacked the city in 410; in the 8th century Paul the Deacon recorded that Attila had a vision of a great warrior in priestly garb and armed with a naked sword while discussing with Leo – on the strength of which, he decided to abandon his invasion plans. Modern his-

Above: In Raphael's version of the encounter with Attila, Leo is supported by saints Peter and Paul in the sky above. Raphael painted Leo with the face of Leo X (pope 1513–21).

torians suggest that Attila's decision may have been influenced by an outbreak of plague in his army.

No doubt emboldened by this success, Leo again confronted a general three years later when Gaiseric, leader of the Germanic Vandals, had marched to the very gates of Rome. Although

---

FACT BOX

Original name Leo

Born Not Known

Origin Tuscan

Date elected pope 29 September 440

Died 10 November 461

Key fact Defined unity of divine and human natures in Jesus Christ

Left; 'Thou art Peter, and upon this rock I will build my church.' *Italian Baroque painter Bernardo Strozzi painted this vision of Christ granting authority to Peter.*

his human element had been absorbed into his nature as the Son of God. This undermined the extent to which Jesus could be said to be truly human. After Patriarch Flavian of Constantinople excommunicated Eutyches, Leo issued a forthright response in a celebrated letter to Flavian, emphasizing that Christ had two natures – both human and divine – unmixed and distinct, but not separate.

The Council of Chalcedon (see box) met in 451 and endorsed Leo's statement or *Tome*. The Council noted that they recognized in Leo's words 'the voice of Peter' – a notable endorsement of the pope's claim to be operating as Peter's representative and with his authority.

HONOURED FATHER

On his death Leo was buried in the porch of St Peter's but in 668 he was moved and given a monument within the basilica – and he was the first pope to receive this honour. Leo was declared a doctor of the Church by Pope Benedict XIV in 1754.

Leo could not prevent the army taking Rome, he persuaded Gaiseric to stop his men sacking the city.

AUTHORITY OVER BISHOPS

The 432 letters and 96 sermons that survive from Leo's hand assert that the pope has authority over all other Christian bishops and define the legal basis by which the authority of the pope is inherited. He established that Christ gave authority to St Peter alone, and that each new pope drew his authority not from his predecessor but from Peter. If a pope disgraced his position it should have no effect on the authority of the papacy, which derived from Peter and through him, from Christ himself. Bishops had authority over their flocks, but the pope had authority, derived from Peter, over the entire Church.

In 445 Leo won a formal statement of the papacy's ultimate authority over the Church from Emperor Valentinian III. Leo was in dispute with Bishop Hilary of Arles who had exceeded his powers in operating as papal vicar in Gaul (a position granted to the bishops of Arles, amidst much controversy by the ineffectual Pope Zosimus). Valentinian's edict of 8 July 445 stated that the pope had jurisdiction over all Western churches and even allowed for any bishops to be forcibly removed to Rome by secular governors if they refused to attend when summoned by the pope.

CHRIST'S SINGLE NATURE

The major controversy of Leo's reign was over the teachings of Eutyches, a Constantinople monk who held that Christ had only one, divine, nature since

---

THE NATURE OF CHRIST

The Fourth Ecumenical Council of the Church was called by Emperor Marcian with the backing of Pope Leo I. It met at Chalcedon (at the time a city in the Roman province of Bythnia, but now a suburb of Istanbul) in 451 and accepted Pope Leo's Tome as the basis of the 'Chalcedonian Definition' on the nature of Christ: He had two natures (divine and human), both complete, unmixed yet permanently united in hypostasis. The Council's decision led to schisms in the Church between those who supported Chalcedonian orthodoxy and the Monophysites who held Christ had only one (divine) nature.

HILARIUS TO SILVERIUS, 461–537
GELASIUS I DEVELOPS THEORY OF ROYAL AND EPISCOPAL POWER

Hilarius (461–68) built on the achievement of Leo the Great. He had served as a legate for Leo, and carried on where his predecessor had left off in consolidating the authority of the papacy, particularly in relation to churches in Gaul and Spain. In letters to the bishops in the East he underlined the primacy of Rome.

END OF THE WESTERN EMPIRE

In the reign of Pope Simplicius (468–83), the last Roman emperor in the West, Romulus Augustulus, was deposed in 476 by a German warrior, Odoacer, who became the effective ruler of Italy. The Western empire fell apart into principalities. In matters of religion, Simplicius struggled to contain conflict in the Eastern Church between those who accepted the orthodox definition of Christ's dual nature agreed at the Council of Chalcedon and the increasingly troublesome Monophysites (who held that Christ had one – divine – nature).

In 482 the Eastern (Byzantine) Emperor Zeno and Patriarch Acacius of Constantinople tried to make peace with the *Henotikon* ('Statement of Union'), which appeased the Monophysites; but among the first acts of Simplicius's successor Pope Felix III (483–92) was to excommunicate Acacius and so bring about a schism between Rome and Constantinople that was to last until 519.

CHURCH AND STATE

Gelasius I (492–6) was a great writer of treatises and letters, said to be the most prolific writer of any pope in the first 500 years of the papacy, celebrated for his vigorous prose style, although relatively few of his compositions have survived. In a letter to Acacius of 494 he developed the theory of two distinct governmental powers – one royal (held by emperor or king) and one episcopal, the 'sacred authority of bishops' (held by the pope) – that would influence Western political theory for centuries.

Anastasius II (496–8) tried without success to repair relations with the Eastern Church. The pontificate of Symmachus (498–514) never really recovered from the fact that it took him eight years to overcome the challenge of an antipope, Lawrence. His successor Hormisdas (514–23) succeeded in ending the schism with the Eastern Church in 519.

Left: Emperor Justinian I, shown here in a mosaic from Sant'Apollinare Nuovo, Ravenna, retook part of the Western empire and oversaw the rewriting of Roman law. He rebuilt the Hagia Sophia in Constantinople.

Above: Gelasius I wrote De duabus in Christo naturis *('On Christ's twofold nature'), which reiterated the orthodox position on the Monophysite controversy.*

Above: Silverius was the legitimate son of Pope Hormisdas, born before his father entered the priesthood. He was deposed in 537, a few months before his death.

Above: John I visited Constantinople at the behest of Theodoric of the Ostrogoths, but failed to convince Emperor Justin to end his persecution of Arian Christians.

FIRST POPE TO VISIT CONSTANTINOPLE

When Byzantine Emperor Justin I began to persecute Arian Christians, it provoked the ire of Theodoric the Great of the Ostrogoths, who had succeeded Odoacer as secular ruler in Italy and was himself an Arian Christian. Theodoric ordered John I (523–6) to Constantinople to seek a solution.

John received a splendid welcome but failed in his mission, much to Theodoric's disgust: on John's return to Italy, Theodoric had him imprisoned and, according to some traditions, executed him.

Felix IV (526–30) had a steady pontificate and built the Basilica of Santi Cosma e Damiano in the Forum of Vespasian, but caused chaos at the end of his reign by nominating archdeacon Boniface as his successor. Roman clergy elected Dioscorus of Alexandria in his place, and both candidates were consecrated in rival ceremonies – but the disagreement ended when Dioscorus died after around a month. Boniface ruled for two years, 530–2, the first pope of Germanic descent.

FIRST PAPAL NAME

A very messy election campaign followed, with corruption and bribery rife in Rome for more than two months, so that King Athalaric, successor to Theodoric the Great, passed a law to stop it happening again. In the end a Roman presbyter named Mercurius was elected John II (533–5) – he was the first pope to change his name, abandoning his birth name because of its associations with the Roman god Mercury and choosing a papal name that honoured Pope John I.

In the pontificate of Agapitus I (535–36), Byzantine Emperor Justinian I drew up plans to invade Italy and reincorporate it into the empire. King Theodahad of the Ostrogoths despatched Agapitus to Constantinople to broker a solution. Agapitus failed to change the emperor's mind but did succeed in ousting the Monophysite Patriarch of the city, Anthimus I, and consecrating Mennas as his successor. This angered Justinian's wife, Empress Theodora, who had Monophysite sympathies and wanted Anthimus restored.

When Agapitus died while still in Constantinople, Silverius (536–7) was elected in Rome and refused to restore Anthimus. Theodora then offered the papal throne to a Roman deacon named Vigilius if he would agree to back Anthimus, and ordered Byzantine general Belisarius to invade Rome and depose Silverius. Vigilius is considered the first pope of the Byzantine Papacy. Belisarius sent Silverius into exile, but when the matter was referred to Emperor Justinian he ordered Silverius back to Rome. Finally Vigilius used force to drive Silverius back into exile – on the island of Palmarola, near Naples – where he died.

ST VALENTINE'S DAY

In 496 Pope Gelasius I succeeded in suppressing the ancient pagan purification festival of Lupercalia and introduced the feast day of St Valentine on 14 February. The original St Valentine may have been a Roman priest who was martyred under Emperor Claudius II Gothicus (268–70) and buried on the Via Flamini. The saint's day became a lovers' festival in the 14th century. According to legend Valentine fell in love with the jailer's daughter while imprisoned and wrote her a letter signed 'your Valentine'.

ROME AND THE ACQUISITION OF THE PAPAL STATES

A succession of popes worked to make Rome the foremost Christian city and then built up the associated territories of the papal states that survived in various forms until the creation of the Kingdom of Italy in the 19th century.

The papacy established Rome's pre-eminence over other Christian cities in the course of several centuries. The city's status rested on the pope's spiritual descent from St Peter and his claim that as a result he took precedence over other bishops. Rome was rivalled by Jerusalem and Antioch, as well as Alexandria and from 330 by Constantinople, set up by Emperor Constantine as a new capital for the Roman Empire, but the popes contended that their city could outrank these others because of its association with saints Peter and Paul.

Below: Pope Stephen anoints Pepin III of the Franks, who in return – in the 'Donation of Pepin' (754) – granted the lands that formed the basis of the papal states.

Pope Damasus I (366–84) was the first to claim that Rome was the 'Apostolic See' – that is, the See established by the Apostle Peter – and stated that it outranked all other Christian cities because it was the place where saints Peter and Paul died as martyrs. Pope Siricius (384–99) declared that Rome was the head of the Christian body.

After Christianity became the state religion of the Roman Empire, Emperor Theodosius I announced in 380 that the empire's inhabitants must follow the form of the faith 'handed down by the Apostle Peter to the Romans'; subsequently in 445 Emperor Valentinian III gave Pope Leo I and his successors as pope authority over all other bishops.

Over centuries this struggle for pre-eminence continued and there were many more challenges to the status of the pope and of Rome; meanwhile, the city itself had many ups and downs: it was sacked several times, notably by the Visigoths in 410, the Muslims in 846 and

Above: Charlemagne the Great was deeply pious and mourned Pope Hadrian I as 'a father'. The 'Donation of Charlemagne' in 774 consolidated the papal territories.

the Holy Roman Emperor Charles V in 1527, but was enriched with architectural and artistic jewels in the Renaissance and beautified by the popes of the Counter-Reformation. Yet – save for the period of 1309–77, when the papacy removed to southern France in the 'Avignon Exile' – the city of St Peter's martyrdom remained and is still the base for the pope's rule of the Church.

PAPAL STATES

From as early as the 300s the papacy acquired territory close to Rome – known as the Patrimony of St Peter. Following the collapse of the Roman Empire the popes faced the threat of invasion by northern tribes – not least, from the sixth century onwards, by the Lombards.

The lands held by the papacy in this era were part of the Byzantine Empire, and in theory protected by Constantinople, but the Byzantines failed to defend papal lands against the Lombards: in the 8th century Pope Stephen II (752–7) appealed to the rising power of the Franks

STEPHANVS PP

PIPINVS REX

Above: Saint Augustine teaching rhetoric in Rome. Many leading figures of the early Church, including Jerome and Tertullian, came to and worked in the seat of the papacy.

for help and from Pepin III, Charlemagne, Louis the Pious and Lothar I the papacy received the basis of what became the papal states – the duchy of Rome, territories around Ravenna and the area known as the Pentapolis.

CONSOLIDATION

In the Middle Ages the papacy maintained control of the papal states and even expanded them with the addition of Spoleto, Benevento and Avignon in southern France; but during the period of the Avignon Exile and the Papal Schism the popes' authority was weak and there were many challenges – including the brief declaration of a republic in Rome in 1347.

Fifteenth-century popes reimposed their authority over the central Italian peninsula and the papal states were further expanded by the warlike Julius II (1503–13), but then as the standing of the papacy declined the popes were increasingly unable to maintain this territory until by the 18th century,

international powers felt free – for example in the treaties that ended the War of the Spanish Succession (1701–14) – to dispose of former papal territories as they saw fit.

ANNEXED BY FRANCE

The French Revolution of 1789 and the rise of post-revolutionary France under Napoleon Bonaparte had a major impact. First Avignon was annexed in 1791, then Pius VI (1775) could do nothing as France seized the papal states and declared a Roman Republic. Pius VII (1800–23) made peace with France: Rome along with several of the papal states were restored to the papacy, but

the new peace fell apart and Rome was occupied and the papal states annexed once more in 1808.

When Napoleon was defeated, the Congress of Vienna (1814–15) restored Rome and the papal states to the pope. (Napoleon's brief return did not change this.) There were revolts against papal rule in the states in 1830–1 and 1849 when Pius IX (1846–78) could not prevent the brief establishment of another Roman Republic.

RISORGIMENTO

In the end *Risorgimento*, the 19th-century movement for a unified Italy, proved unstoppable. In 1861 the former papal states – apart from Rome and its surrounding area – were made part of the new Kingdom of Italy; in 1870 Italian troops took Rome and it was made the capital of the new kingdom.

Pius IX refused to recognize this new situation: he and his successors declared themselves 'prisoners in the Vatican'. However, in 1929 Pope Pius XI (1922–39) oversaw the Lateran Treaty under which the papacy renounced its claim to the papal territories (in return for compensation equivalent to £21 million) and the independent ecclesiastical state of Vatican City was set up.

Below: Saints Peter (right, holding key) and Paul. Damasus I said the fact that they were martyred in Rome gave the city its pre-eminent status.

VIGILIUS TO PELAGIUS II, 537–90
POPES DEPENDENT ON BYZANTINE EMPERORS

The reign of Vigilius (537–55) is one of the low points in the history of the papacy. He did not recover from the sordid machinations through which he became pope, when he schemed with the Byzantine Empress Theodora to oust the elected pontiff, Silverius, and took power with the military backing of the Byzantine general, Belisarius.

Thereafter he struggled to assert his independence and proved himself a weak and vacillating leader who seriously damaged the standing of the papacy. He quickly became embroiled in 'The Three Chapters controversy' – a clash between the orthodox position that Jesus Christ had a dual human/divine nature and the Monophysite teaching (declared heretical at the 451 Council of Chalcedon) that Christ's nature was divine.

SECOND COUNCIL OF CONSTANTINOPLE

Emperor Justinian issued a pro-Monophysite decree in 544, repudiating the works (the 'three chapters') of three writers who supported the orthodox position, and demanded Vigilius ratify it.

When Vigilius initially refused, Justinian had him arrested and dragged to Constantinople.

There he vacillated until in 548 Vigilius issued a *Judicatum* ('Verdict') in which he backed the emperor's condemnation, but with some reservations. This caused uproar in the Western Church and Justinian called a general church council to settle the matter, while also repeating his own repudiation of the three chapters.

Then Vigilius snapped. He broke off relations with Justinian and took refuge in a sanctuary, before fleeing to Chalcedon. The Second Council of Constantinople met without him and backed the condemnation of the three chapters. Vigilius first issued a *Constitutum* ('Resolution') on 24 May 553 in which he refused to back the council, then the following February revoked this and issued a new statement backing the council's statement.

Above: The Visigoth king Reccared I who converted from Arian to Roman Christianity in the reign of Pope Pelagius II.

Now Vigilius lost the backing of his loyal nuncio and eventual successor, Pelagius I, whom he excommunicated and who was shortly afterwards imprisoned by Justinian. Finally, ill and dispirited, Vigilius was allowed by

Below: Pelagius II (far left) offers his rebuilt Church of San Lorenzo fuori le Mura to Christ and saints Lawrence, Peter and Paul.

Above: A gold triens (type of coin) minted for King Reccared I of the Visigoths.

Justinian to head back to Rome, but he died en route on 7 June 555 from an attack of gallstones.

On Vigilius's death, Pelagius was released from prison, and with the backing of Emperor Justinian elected pope. He was consecrated Pope Pelagius I in Rome on 16 April 556. A committed opponent of the imperial condemnation of the Three Chapters who even wrote a book in defence of the three denounced authors, he reversed his position once pope and backed the verdict of the Council of Constantinople. This caused a schism within the Western Church with the bishops of Milan and Istria. But Pelagius had considerable success in patching up Rome, which had been ravaged by the Ostrogoths, and in reforming clerical behaviour.

LOMBARD THREAT

John III (561–74) faced invasion by the Lombards and took flight to Naples, where in 571 he asked the former Byzantine general, Narses, to mount a defence of Rome. But the Romans who knew and hated Narses from of old, rose up and John was forced to seek refuge

Right: Justinian I brooked no opposition in the Three Chapters controversy. This mosaic of the forceful emperor is from San Vitale Cathedral in Ravenna and shows him carrying Eucharistic bread or a symbolic basket for receiving tribute.

in the catacombs, from where he conducted his administration until Narses died in 573.

Benedict I (575–9) faced calamity after calamity – plague, famine, the flooding of the Tiber and further southward invasions by the Lombards who laid siege to Rome in 579. He died with Rome in the grip of a severe famine and was succeeded by Pelagius II (579–90), who turned to Constantinople for support against the Lombards. But little help was forthcoming, since the emperor had pressing problems in fighting off attacks by the Persian Sassanian empire.

ENTER THE FRANKS

So Pelagius fixed on a new source of help, a people who would loom large in the history of Western Europe and the papacy: the Franks. He wrote to the Frankish bishop of Auxerre, declaring it the Franks' duty as Christians to defend Rome against the Arian Lombards. The Franks invaded Italy but were then bribed to hold off by the Lombards and Pelagius was forced to appeal to Constantinople again.

The matter was not resolved until 585 when Exarch Smaragdus of Ravenna, the Byzantine representative in Italy, agreed a peace settlement with the Lombards.

THE LOMBARDS

Originally a tribe from northwestern Germany, the Lombards began to migrate southwards in the 4th century, initially settling in an area that roughly matches that of modern Austria. In 567–8 they invaded Italy, and by the end of 569 had captured all the major cities northwards of the River Po, save Pavia – which survived only until 572. They made several incursions further southwards, and besieged Rome, but eventually established a Lombard Kingdom in Italy further north, with the capital at Pavia. They were defeated by the Frankish king Charlemagne in 774.

VISIGOTHS CONVERT

In around 589 the Visigoths in Spain under King Reccared I were converted from Arian Christianity to the faith of the Roman Church. Then Pelagius came into conflict with the Patriarch of Constantinople who claimed the title 'Ecumenical Patriarch', which the pope saw as undermining papal authority. The issue was still undecided when Pelagius died, in February 590 from the plague that had swept Rome after a terrible flooding in the autumn of 589.

CHAPTER THREE

ENTER THE FRANKS

GREGORY THE GREAT TO HADRIAN I, 590–795

On Easter Saturday 774 Charlemagne, King of the Franks, was greeted on the steps of St Peter's in Rome by Pope Hadrian I. In the celebrated 'Donation of Charlemagne', the Frankish king confirmed the gift of territories made by his father Pepin III to Hadrian's forerunner Stephen II, and greatly expanded the lands to be passed into papal governance. For much of the 8th century the popes had struggled to extricate the Church from the control of overbearing Eastern Roman (Byzantine) Emperors in Constantinople, while seeking to defend Rome and its earliest associated lands from attack by the Lombards who had invaded northern Italy in the 560s. This momentous encounter between Charlemagne and Hadrian freed the papacy from Constantinople, created the basis of the papal states and established the pope as a worldly prince. Charlemagne went to capture Pavia, crush the Lombards, then overcome the Saxons and Avars to create a great Western empire in opposition to the Eastern Roman Empire of Constantinople.

The consequences for the pope and the Church were significant. While the papacy was increasingly able to operate free of interference from Constantinople, it now had a new secular ruler to deal with. Charlemagne declared his intention to impose unity on the churches in his territories, and was certainly not averse to involving himself in church affairs – he called church councils, instructed clergy on duties and matters of faith and made appointments of abbots and bishops in France. In the short term the papacy certainly did well: Charlemagne was a deeply pious man who was happy to accept the prime position of Rome, but his successors would not all be cooperative in this regard. The seeds were sown that would bear fruit in the tumultuous struggles for precedence between the pope and the Holy Roman Emperor.

Left: Pope Stephen II anoints Frankish king Pepin III 'the Short' in July 754. Through an alliance with the Franks, the papacy freed itself from the emperor in Constantinople. Grants of land from Pepin and his son Charlemagne established the papal states.

GREGORY I 'THE GREAT', 590–604
THEOLOGIAN AND AUTHOR WHO SENT MISSION TO ENGLAND

The first monk to become pope, Gregory is celebrated as The Great for his prolific and profound writings as well as his papal rule. In the Middle Ages he was known as the 'Father of Christian Worship' because of his efforts to revise the forms of worship. He is often seen as standing at the end of the Roman era, looking forward to and playing a significant role in shaping, the Church and Christian faith of the Middle Ages.

Diligent, learned, thoughtful, he was widely and enduringly admired for his qualities: he was acclaimed a saint on his death and is also considered a saint in the Eastern Orthodox Church – where he is known as Gregory Dialogus ('Gregory the Dialogist') on account of his authorship of the *Dialogues* (594), a collection of saints' lives. Even Protestant reformer John Calvin admired Gregory – he declared him the last good pope.

Below: Gregory is traditionally said to have standardized Western plainchant. This 13th-century illuminated manuscript shows him dictating the chant.

FACT BOX
Original name Gregorius
Born 540
Origin Roman
Date elected pope 3 September 590
Died 12 March 604
Key fact Only pope apart from Leo I and Nicholas I to be called 'The Great'

FOUNDED A MONASTERY

Gregory came from a wealthy and deeply religious family. He was the great-great grandson of Pope Felix III (483–92); when his father died, his mother Silvia became a nun, and three of his aunts also took monastic vows. Gregory himself retired from the world in 574 – after a good education that may have included legal training. He established a monastery named for St Andrew on his family's land on the Caelian Hill in Rome.

In 579 he became a deacon under Pope Pelagius II, who sent him as a legate to Constantinople. There he tried to drum up military support against the Lombards in Italy.

Back in Rome by 586 he reluctantly agreed to become pope on 3 September 590 after the death of Pelagius II in the plague that swept the city. In traditional accounts, Gregory led a penitential procession through the streets of the city and had a vision of the Archangel Michael that convinced him the city would be spared further suffering; according to some accounts, he wrote seven penitential psalms to be sung on this procession, but in fact these psalms date from the 11th century, around 500 years after his death.

WRITINGS – AND MUSIC

According to historian Gregory of Tours (538–94), Pope Gregory was second to none in rhetoric, grammar and argument; he was well versed in mathematics, music,

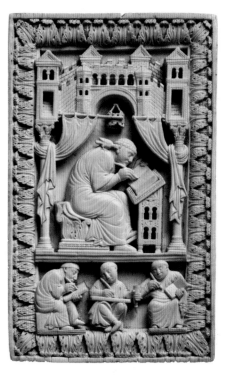

Above: An exquisite 10th-century ivory panel shows Gregory at work on his voluminous writings – with a dove (symbol of the Holy Spirit) dictating at his ear.

history, law and natural science and had read the Latin authors. In addition to the *Dialogues* (594), a collection of saints' lives, he wrote: more than 60 homilies, including 40 on the Gospels and 22 on the Book of Ezekiel; *Pastoral Rule* (591), a book of guidance for rulers; and the *Magna Moralia*, a 35-book interrogation of the Book of Job.

In addition Gregory is credited with standardizing Western plainchant, which was known as Gregorian chant. However, the chant was not standardized until the 8th century. Moreover, the first source to attribute this to him is the biography of the pope by John the Deacon written in 873, so nearly 300 years after his death. Historians agree that Gregory did not invent the chant; some suggest that 'Gregorian' rightly refers to a later pope and namesake, Gregory II (715–31).

ST AUGUSTINE OF CANTERBURY

Augustine (or Austin) was Prior of the Benedictine monastery of St Andrew in Rome when Pope Gregory chose him to lead a mission of 40 monks to convert pagan England to Christianity. The mission landed in 597 on the Isle of Thanet and was given a place to stay in Canterbury by King Aethelbert of Kent, whose wife Bertha was already a Christian. The mission converted Aethelbert and on Christmas Day 597 thousands of his people. Gregory sent further missionaries with the pallium (symbol of spiritual authority) for Augustine, who founded the Cathedral of Christ Church, Canterbury, and the Benedictine monastery of saints Peter and Paul just outside the city (now known as St Augustine's Abbey). In 604 Augustine consecrated two bishops of the English Church: Mellitus as Bishop of London, and Justus as Bishop of Rochester.

'SERVANT OF THE SERVANTS OF GOD'

Gregory promoted the moral primacy of the pope as descendant of St Peter, but did not argue that the bishop of Rome was above other bishops. When a bishop had done wrong, he should be subject to the pope, but otherwise 'all are equal by the law of humility'.

Like his predecessor, Gregory disputed the right of the patriarch of Constantinople to use the title 'ecumenical patriarch'. He felt that this title worked against the equality of all bishops and undermined the moral primacy of the pope as the inheritor of the power of St Peter. He was committed to humility and called himself 'Servant of the servants of God'.

ENGLISH MISSION

According to English monk the Venerable Bede (673–735), Gregory was inspired to send a mission to England by an encounter with fair-skinned Angles (English boys) in the slave market in Rome. He reputedly said *Non Angli, sed angeli* – 'they're not Angles, they're angels!'

Above: 'They're not Angles, they're angels!' Seeing English boys for sale at the slave market in Rome reputedly inspired Gregory to send Augustine on his mission to England.

Below: According to a medieval legend, while celebrating Mass Gregory was granted a vision in which blood poured directly from Christ's side into his chalice.

SABINIAN TO BONIFACE V, 604–25
POPE ADEODATUS I ISSUES FIRST PAPAL BULLS

In these years the papacy in Rome was overshadowed by Constantinople. There were frequent turnovers of pope, with many short reigns: each new elected pontiff had to wait for confirmation of his elevation from the Byzantine emperor before he could be consecrated. Often the confirmation was slow in coming, for frequently the emperor had pressing problems in the East: for example, Boniface V had to wait 13 months for imperial approval in 618–619, because Emperor Heraclius was fighting the Persian Sassanian empire.

Below: The Column of Phocas in the Roman forum once held a gilded statue of Emperor Phocas, erected in 608 in the reign of Boniface IV – probably as a symbol of the emperor's continuing sovereignty over Rome.

Pope Sabinian (604–6) presented quite a contrast to his imposing predecessor Gregory the Great. Where Gregory had promoted monks to key positions, Sabinian gave precedence to secular clergy and while Gregory had been praised for distributing grain at no cost from the papal granaries, Sabinian raised money by selling it at high prices – even in a famine.

His rule was unpopular and the people suffered not only from food shortages but also from southward incursions by the Lombards from their kingdom in northern Italy.

POPE IS 'UNIVERSAL BISHOP'

Boniface III had served Gregory I as a deacon and was, according to that great pontiff, 'a man of tried faith and character', but he lasted less than nine months in office, from his election on 19 February to his death on 12 November 607. While a deacon he had been sent to Constantinople by Gregory and had established a close relationship with Emperor Phocas; as pope he received from Phocas a decree recognizing Rome as the head of all churches and granting the pope the title of 'Universal Bishop'.

Boniface also made changes to rules governing papal elections – declaring it illegal, on pain of excommunication, to discuss a pope's successor while the pope was alive, and establishing that the process of finding a new pope should not be started until three days after a pope's death.

SANTA MARIA DELLA ROTONDA

Boniface IV (608–15) took a great interest in the English Church. He convened a council in Rome to restore monastic discipline at which he received the first Bishop of London, Mellitus, and he helped Mellitus settle matters concerning its organization. Boniface also

Above: In Rome, Boniface IV oversaw the conversion of the Pantheon into a church dedicated to the Blessed Virgin Mary and martyrs – now Santa Maria della Rotonda.

converted the Pantheon in Rome into a Church dedicated to the Virgin and Martyrs, now often known as Santa Maria della Rotonda.

In c.615 Boniface received a letter from the Irish missionary St Columban challenging him and accusing the papacy of heresy because of its acceptance of the decision of the 553 Second Council of Constantinople against the Three Chapters. This controversy played on and on.

In the tradition of Pope Gregory the Great, Boniface IV lived as a monk after

---

SANCTUARY

Pope Boniface V established the right of asylum in churches for criminals, determining that no one who had taken refuge there should be handed over to the authorities until his or her case was heard. This applied at first to the altar and choir but was later extended to the nave and finally the whole church enclosure.

Above: Coin of Emperor Phocas who gave the Pantheon to Boniface IV.

his election and appointed many monks to administrative positions. He subsequently converted his house into a monastery and retired there.

FIRST PAPAL BULLS

As Sabinian had reacted against the monastic appointments of Gregory I, so Adeodatus I (615–18) turned against the practice of his predecessor and set out to fill administrative positions with secular clergy rather than monks. Tradition has it that Adeodatus was the first pope to issue papal bulls – documents finished with lead seals (*bullae*). One bull survives from his reign, signed *Deusdedit Papae*, a version of the name Pope Adeodatus. He was an energetic and charitable man who won great admiration for his conduct in helping the victims of an earthquake and outbreak of leprosy that struck Rome in his pontificate.

REBELLION FOILED

In 619, before Boniface V (619–25) was consecrated, the Byzantine regent in Italy (Eleutherius, Exarch of Ravenna) launched a rebellion against Emperor Heraclius. He marched from Ravenna to Rome intending to make the new pope crown him, but was murdered by his own troops en route, at a fort on the Flaminian Way.

Boniface was known and loved for his gentle and mild demeanour and his charity – he distributed his wealth in gifts to the needy. He also carried Adeodatus's practice of preferring clergy to monks for official positions and accounts of his life stress his love for and support of the clergy.

Like his namesake a few years earlier, Boniface was engaged with the English Church. According to the writings of the Northumbrian monk the Venerable Bede (672–735), Boniface wrote to Mellitus, first bishop of London, and to Justus, first bishop of Rochester, when they were successively made Archbishop of Canterbury in 619 and 624 respectively, and also to King Edwin of Northumbria, and Edwin's Christian consort, Ethelburga of Kent, encouraging Edwin and his people to convert to Christianity.

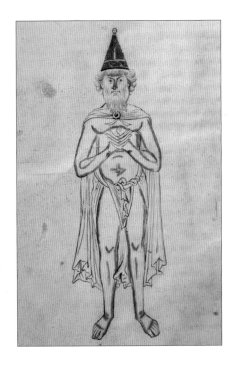

Above: The Venerable Bede, a monk from Jarrow in the English kingdom of Northumbria, reported that Boniface V urged the English to engage with Christianity.

Below: A detail of carving on an altar in the Basilica of San Nicola di Bari, Apulia represents Pope Adeodatus I, reckoned to be the first pope who issued papal bulls.

HONORIUS I TO MARTIN I, 625–53
PROLONGED CONTROVERSY OVER MONOTHELITISM

Bitter doctrinal disputes over Monothelitism – the idea that Jesus Christ did not have both divine and human wills, but a single will exercised through his divine and human natures – had a negative impact on relations between the papacy and Constantinople for many years. The controversy was associated with the decades-old disagreements between Monophysiticism (the contention that in Jesus a single, divine nature was dominant) and the orthodox teaching that Jesus had coexistent human and divine natures, separate but not divisible.

SINGLE WILL

Honorius I (625–38) became embroiled in the row when he made a statement apparently showing support for Monothelitism. Honorius issued his controversial teaching in response to a call in 634 from Patriarch Sergius of Constantinople for the Church to unite

behind the doctrine that Jesus had one will. Honorius declared that the confession of faith agreed at the Council of Chalecedon of 451 stated that Christ's dual natures could not be divided and that he understood this to mean that Jesus had a single will. Honorius attempted to outlaw further debate on the matter, but the controversy rumbled on.

HOW COULD THE POPE BE WRONG?

In later years Honorius's reputation suffered greatly. The Third Council of Constantinople (680–1), called by Byzantine emperor Constantine IV Pogonatus to try to put an end to the row, denounced Honorius's teaching as being heretical since it appeared to support heretical Monophysiticism. Pope Leo II condemned Honorius in 682, saying his teaching was outside the 'apostolic tradition' and was a stain on the 'immaculate faith'.

Above: Honorius I. Was he infallible when he apparently supported Monothelitism? His teaching was later denounced as a 'stain' on the Christian faith.

Many centuries later still, Honorius's teaching and its later rebuttal were used by opponents of the idea of papal infallibility – the notion a pope's official announcements were divinely inspired and so could not be mistaken – during the First Vatican Council in 1869–70. Those who defended Honorius attempted to argue that his response to Patriarch Sergius was not an official pronouncement.

ECTHESIS – PRO-MONOTHELITE STATEMENT

In 638 Emperor Heraclius issued a letter, the *Ecthesis*, giving official backing to Monothelitism and refused to endorse the election of the new pope, Severinus, unless the pontiff gave his approval to the letter. When Severinus refused, the Byzantine representative in Italy, the Exarch Isaac of Ravenna, looted the

Left: In the imposing Archbasilica of St John, the Lateran Council under Martin I decisively rejected Monothelitism in 649. Martin paid a dear price – humiliated at the hands of Emperor Constans II.

Right: This mosaic from Ravenna shows the baptism of Christ. The orthodox position was that Christ had dual divine and human wills working in tandem. Supporters of Monothelitism argued he had a single will.

Lateran Palace to try to force the issue. In the end imperial approval was forthcoming, but as soon as Severinus had been consecrated on 28 May 640, he delivered a ringing endorsement of the orthodox position – that Christ had dual divine/human nature and two wills.

However, the new pope survived the saga of his on/off consecration by just over two months and died on 2 August 640. He was remembered as a kind and mild man, generous to the clergy and to the needy, but clearly also of strong convictions and will.

John IV (640–2) maintained the official line and wrote to the new emperor, Constantine III, in 641 attempting to explain Honorius's apparent lapse from the true faith – claiming that when Honorius spoke of one will in Jesus Christ he meant merely that Jesus was never conflicted, that he had never had

Below: Martin I. Arrested by Emperor Constans II in the controversy over Monothelitism, he died in exile in the Crimean Peninsula, although the Roman Church later celebrated him as a martyr.

two wills working against one another. He also held a synod that reiterated papal condemnation of Monothelitism.

John IV was from Dalmatia (now part of Croatia) and, when he received news of attacks on Christians in that region by invading Slavs, sent an abbot named Martin into the region with substantial funds to help victims. He also arranged for the relics of various Dalmatian saints to be brought back to Rome for safekeeping and to honour them built an oratory, which still stands.

Theodore I (642–9), a Greek who was born in Jerusalem, was noted for his generosity to the needy but otherwise dedicated himself to carrying on the fight against heresy. He put pressure on Emperor Constans II to revoke the *Ecthesis* and excommunicated Pyrrhus and Paul, patriarchs of Constantinople, for their support of the heresy. Enraged, Paul imprisoned the papal nuncios in Constantinople.

IGNOMINIOUS END IN EXILE

Martin I (649–53), a learned and virtuous man who had served as nuncio himself in the past, presided over a Lateran Council in 649 that condemned Monothelitism. Emperor Constans II ordered the pope's arrest and Martin, although he was confined to bed through sickness, was seized in the

Lateran Palace and dragged via Greece to Constantinople, where he was tried and flogged and then finally dispatched into exile in Chersonesos Taurica in the Crimean Peninsula (now in southern Ukraine). He died in exile and is celebrated by the Church as a martyr.

PATRIARCH OF THE WEST

Theodore I was the first pope to use the title 'Patriarch of the West'. In the 5th and 6th centuries, while the four established patriarchies of the Eastern Church – Constantinople, Alexandria, Antioch and Jerusalem – were quite clearly demarcated, the territory of the pope was rather harder to delineate. The ecclesiastical system under Emperor Justinian (527–65) listed the pope as patriarch of the West alongside the four Eastern patriarchies given above. After Theodore began the official use of the title, it occurred only intermittently until the 16th–17th centuries, when it became established at a time when the pope was using several official titles. It remained popular until it was dropped by Pope Benedict XVI in 2006. The Pontifical Council for Christian Unity explained that year that the title had become 'obsolete and practically unusable'.

EUGENIUS I TO AGATHO, 654–81
VITALIAN MAKES PEACE WITH CHURCH IN THE EAST

The controversy over Monothelitism that had brought Pope Martin I to a humiliating end in Crimean exile almost saw to his successor Eugenius I (654–7), also. Initially Eugenius seemed inclined to compromise on the issue, and a letter from Patriarch Peter of Constantinople, a Monothelite, arrived urging reconciliation. But when the letter was read aloud to clergy and people in the Basilica di Santa Maria Maggiore, they were outraged and refused to allow Eugenius to leave the basilica until he pledged to maintain papal opposition to the heresy.

Eugenius subsequently refused to recognize Peter as patriarch. Emperor Constans II threatened him with arrest, but in the event the emperor was busy dealing with attacks by the rampant armies of Islam – who captured Rhodes in 654 and the following year defeated Constans himself at the naval Battle of the Masts fought off Phoenix (modern Finike, Turkey) – and the pope died before the threat was put into force.

Below: This is the underground crypt of the medieval Cathedral of San Leopardo, Osimo, built in 1191 by Mastro Filippo.

PEACE AT A COST
Vitalian (657–72) managed to restore peace between West and East, largely by avoiding direct discussion of controversial doctrinal matters, and Emperor Constans even visited Rome in 663 – the last Eastern emperor to do this for seven centuries. He was very well received, dined with the pope and twice attended Mass in St Peter's Basilica, making a gift to the pope of a pallium (robe) enriched with gold.

However, Constans took the opportunity of being in Italy to make a statement of his power – he confiscated all the bronze artworks and ornaments in Rome (and even the bronze roof tiles of the Pantheon) and ordered that the see of Ravenna, the base for the imperial administration in Italy, be recognized as independent of Rome's control.

ENGLISH DECISIONS
In Vitalian's reign the Synod of Whitby (663–4) in northern England decided that the English Church would follow Roman rather than Celtic Christianity, a decision of the greatest importance for the future of the faith in England. The English sent a priest, Wighard, to Rome

Above: Pope Agatho. Under his rule the Third Council of Constantinople established that Monothelitism was a heresy. He is celebrated as a saint in both Roman and Eastern churches.

for consecration as Archbishop of Canterbury but he died of the plague on arrival and in 668 Vitalian consecrated the learned monk Theodore of Tarsus in his place and sent him to England. Theodore was the seventh Archbishop of Canterbury and the first to govern the whole English church.

Vitalian also attempted to enforce papal authority as a judge of affairs in the Eastern Church. He held a synod in Rome to hear an appeal by Bishop John of Lappa, in Crete, who had been deposed by the Metropolitan Paulus. Vitalian found John innocent and ordered his reinstatement, adding that two monasteries that had been taken from his control should be returned.

CENTURION POPE
Adeodatus II (672–6) was a Roman-born Benedictine monk, and already elderly on his election as pope. Little is known of his pontificate save that he worked to improve monastic discipline and was known for his generous care of the needy – and especially of pilgrims.

Above: Christ delivers a miraculous haul of fish. Pope Agatho reputedly followed his Lord in being a miracle worker.

Below: Agatho's authority did not carry to England. He backed Wilfrid of York in his dispute with Theodore, Archbishop of Canterbury, but on his return Wilfrid was imprisoned, then banished.

His successor Donus (676–8) was celebrated especially for his commitment to restoring churches – including the Basilica Papale di San Paolo fuori le Mura and the Church of St Euphemia on the Appian Way.

Agatho (678–81) was a Sicilian, a Benedictine monk from Palermo, said to have been more than 100 years old when he became pope. He was known for his kindness and friendly nature and was dubbed *Thaumaturgus* ('miracle worker') on account of the many miracles he reputedly performed.

It seems something of a miracle that he also persuaded the Byzantine Emperor Constantine IV to lift the imperial tax levied on the consecration of each new pope. On the matter of the Monothelite controversy, Agatho replied with enthusiasm to a letter sent by Constantine suggesting a church conference to set the matter finally to rest, and sent delegates bearing a statement of orthodox doctrine to the Third Council of Constantinople (the Sixth Ecumenical Council), which met in 680–1.

HONORIUS CONDEMNED

Agatho died on 10 January 681 before the Third Council reached its decision. But it was a momentous ruling since the bishops at the council determined to outlaw Monothelitism as a heresy – and in so doing labelled Pope Honorius, who had made a pro-Monothelite statement, a heretic.

PAPAL OATH

Some traditionalist Catholics believe that Agatho was the first pope to swear an oath on coronation not to change what had been handed down as tradition. According to this argument, popes from Agatho right down to Pope Paul VI (1963–78) swore this oath at their coronation, but there is no concrete evidence that the popes did so. None of the popes after Paul VI – John Paul I, John Paul II, Benedict XVI and Francis – have had a papal coronation, so they could not have sworn the oath.

LEO II TO CONSTANTINE, 682–715
PROLONGED STRUGGLE WITH EMPEROR JUSTINIAN II

Leo II (682–3) was a worthy holder of exalted office: a learned man, fully at home in Greek and Latin, thorough in his knowledge of Scripture and a skilled and eloquent preacher, he was known also for his interest in music and the beauty of his chants and psalmody. Nevertheless he had to wait 19 months for imperial confirmation of his election as the successor to Pope Agatho because he initially resisted ratifying wording in the decrees of the Third Council of Constantinople that denounced Pope Honorius I as a heretic.

In the end Leo accepted the wording and endorsed the council's forthright rejection of the Monothelite position (which held in the Incarnation Jesus Christ had a single will rather than, as explained in orthodox doctrine, human and divine wills working together). Like his predecessor Agatho, Leo was a Sicilian. In his reign the Archbishop of Ravenna, independent since Vitalian's time, returned to Roman control.

Below: Saint Kilian, sent by Pope Conon to Franconia, was killed by soldiers on the orders of a local noblewoman, Geilana. He had offended her by preaching against the widow's marriage to her brother-in-law.

Above: Pope Constantine. He had had got to know Justinian, then a prince, during two visits as papal legate to Constantinople. As pope he visited the city again.

Benedict II (684–5) had to wait 11 months for imperial confirmation but in his brief reign got Emperor Constantine Pogonatus to lift the requirement that the election of a new pope must be confirmed in Constantinople. To mark this new harmony between the authorities of Rome and Constantinople Benedict agreed symbolically to adopt Constantine's sons, Heraclius and Justinian – and received in Rome a lock of hair belonging to each of the boys.

EASTERN POPES

John V (685–6) was a Syrian, born in Antioch, and was the first of eleven consecutive popes with a background in the East. He had been a deacon in the service of Agatho at the Third Council, but by the time he was elected pope he was seriously ill and unable to achieve much in his short pontificate.

Conon (686–7), the son of a Thracian soldier, was a compromise candidate for the papacy after the clergy and military

factions in Rome disagreed heatedly over who should be John V's successor. But he was well educated and humble, and supported by Emperor Justinian II. He consecrated the Irish missionary Kilian and sent him to preach the Gospel in Franconia (now a region in northern Bavaria, Germany). He was an old man and in poor health when he was elected, and died just 11 months later.

QUINISEXT COUNCIL

Sergius I (687–701) had a murky beginning to his reign in which he finally prevailed over two antipopes, Theodore and Paschal.

In matters of liturgy Sergius introduced the Agnus Dei ('Lamb of God') into the Mass before the eucharistic rite. Some authorities credit him with establishing at Rome the celebration of the festival of Candlemas, held on 2 February and marking the Purification of the Virgin Mary, 40 days after the birth of Jesus.

EMPEROR JUSTINIAN II

Born in *c*.669, Justinian became emperor aged 16 on the death of his father Constantine IV in 685. He called the Quinisext Council of 692 to agree disciplinary measures related to the second and third councils of Constantinople (553 and 680–1); these were the fifth and sixth ecumenical councils, which explains the name Quinisext. Justinian's attempts to get the papacy to ratify these measures led to conflict with popes from Sergius I to Constantine. Justinian was ousted from power in 695 and his nose was cut off; after a decade in exile he recaptured power in 705. Then in 711 he was deposed a second time and killed: an Armenian named Bardanes took power as Emperor Philippicus.

Right: Leo II. Lombard raids forced him to transfer the remains of several martyrs from their burial places in catacombs to churches within the walls of Rome.

In 692 the Quinisext Council called in Constantinople by Emperor Justinian II issued 102 directives, many aimed against practices in the Western Church: these would have put Constantinople on an equal ecclesiastical footing with Rome.

Despite the fact that neither the pope nor any of his representatives were at the council, Justinian demanded that Sergius endorse the directives. When Sergius declined, the emperor ordered his arrest and forcible removal to Constantinople, but the people of Rome and Byzantine troops in Italy stood firm against Justinian, who was deposed shortly afterwards and driven into exile.

John VI (701–5), a Greek, was clearly a good diplomat for he twice maintained the peace when violence threatened, first by intervening in 701 to prevent Exarch Theophylactos of Ravenna, who had marched into Rome, getting into a fight with local soldiers, and second in 705 by persuading Gisulf, the Lombard duke of Benevento, to retreat after he had made a military foray southwards and set up camp within sight of Rome.

Below: Coin of Emperor Justinian II. He had early military success recapturing areas in Thrace and Macedonia that had been taken by Slavs, but he lost imperial possessions in Armenia to Arabs.

DEVOTED TO THE VIRGIN MARY

John VII (705–7), also a Greek, faced a renewed demand from Emperor Justinian II (now restored to power) to endorse the directives of the Quinisext Council to which he responded only by returning the official documents without comment. He was devoted to the Virgin Mary and built an oratory to her as *Theotokos* ('Bearer of God') within the Old St Peter's Basilica – remnants survive in the Vatican grottoes; he also commissioned an icon, Madonna della Clemenza, now in the Basilica di Santa Maria in Trastevere.

Sisinnius, a Syrian, was elected pope on 15 January 708 and died less than three weeks later on 4 February. He suffered terribly from gout. In his short reign he did little except consecrate the Bishop of Corsica and order works to reinforce the walls of Rome.

PAPAL VISIT TO CONSTANTINOPLE

Sisinnius was succeeded by Constantine (708–15), who succeeded in making peace with Emperor Justinian II. He visited Constantinople in 711 – he was to be the last pope to travel to that great city until Pope Paul VI visited in 1967. When Constantine and Justinian met the emperor prostrated himself to kiss the pope's foot and then received communion from his hands.

GREGORY II TO ZACHARIAS, 715–52
CONTROVERSY OVER SACRED USE OF ICONS

In the reign of Gregory II (715–31) a dispute began between Constantinople and Rome over the making and veneration of icons or sacred images that would run on and off until 843, intermittently causing bitter conflict and emphasizing the differences between Eastern and Western churches.

Iconoclasts ('breakers of images') – those who opposed the making and use of icons – believed that the practice was akin to idolatry; those who supported it held that the images were only symbolic. The religious use of images had been opposed in the early church but had become popular in the 6th and 7th centuries.

When Emperor Leo III became a convinced iconoclast and issued an edict against the use of sacred images in 726, Gregory sent a stern rebuttal in which he emphasized that the faithful did not worship the images but used them for 'remembrance and encouragement' and declared, 'Church dogmas are not a matter for the emperor, but for bishops.'

Leo and Gregory had already clashed when Gregory defied the emperor's attempts to increase the taxes levied on

papal territories in Italy. Now Leo planned to have Gregory killed by the imperial representative in Italy, the Exarch of Ravenna; the Exarch, Eutychius, allied himself with the Lombards and marched on Rome. However Gregory was able to break up the alliance and restore peace.

BIRTH OF THE PAPAL STATES
As part of his these negotiations Gregory met the Lombard king, Liutprand, at Sutri outside Rome and received a donation of Lombard-held lands to the papacy. This – known as the Donation of Sutri – was the first expansion of papal lands beyond the Duchy of Rome, and marks the initial establishment of the eventually sizeable and powerful papal states.

Left: Pepin III's likeness is on his tomb in the Basilica of Saint-Denis, France. Pope Zacharias backed his claim to the throne at the expense of the final Merovingian king, Childeric III.

Left: According to tradition, Boniface – sent by Pope Gregory II to convert Germanic tribes – cut down a revered oak tree and used the wood to build a chapel dedicated to St Peter.

MIRACLE AT TOULOUSE
Born in Rome, Gregory carried out refortifications to the walls of the city. There was rising anxiety in this period at the seemingly unstemmable tide of military successes achieved by the armies of Islam (see box), and a fear that they might try to attack Rome herself.

Gregory is associated with a miracle at the Battle of Toulouse in 721 won by a Christian army under Duke Odo of Aquitaine against a Muslim army from Al-Andalus (Islamic Spain). According to this tradition, Gregory sent Odo three baskets of bread to be distributed before the battle and no soldier who ate the bread was killed or even wounded.

SPREAD OF ISLAM
The Prophet Muhammad, founder of the faith of Islam, died in 632 in Medina (now in Saudi Arabia) during the reign of Pope Honorius I. In the hundred-odd years that followed, Islamic warriors created an immense empire that stretched from Spain in the west to parts of China and India in the east, taking in North Africa, Palestine, Syria and Mesopotamia. Rome and Constantinople were left the pre-eminent cities in the Christian world – their historical rivals Antioch, Jerusalem and Alexandria were conquered. Tensions were high between the two centres of power. Constantinople increasingly had to concentrate on defending its eastern possessions. Rome set herself to come to terms with the rising powers of Europe.

Above: Pope Zacharias backed the seizing of the Frankish throne by Pepin. His successor Stephen II blessed Pepin and his sons Charlemagne and Carloman in Paris in 754.

Gregory also promoted missionary work in what is now Germany, sending Corbinian and Boniface to work as missionaries there.

Gregory III (731–41), a Syrian by birth, carried on the work of his predecessor both on sacred images – convening a council in Rome in 731 that issued a forthright statement against the iconoclasts – and in missionary work in Germany, in which context he appointed Boniface as metropolitan bishop of Germany.

APPEAL TO THE FRANKS

Then in 739 after the Lombards sacked the Exarchate of Ravenna and appeared set to attack Rome, he appealed for help to the Franks, the Germanic tribe who would later become essential allies of the papacy under their great king

Charlemagne. This time, however, the Franks declined to come to the pope's aid on the grounds that the Lombards had been allies in the battles against the Muslim armies of Al-Andalus. Rome was left vulnerable to attack, but survived.

Below: Emperor Leo III. Gregory II survived the trouble that arose after he blocked Leo's efforts to ban the use of sacred images in worship.

LOMBARDS TAKE RAVENNA

Zacharias (741–52), born of Greek descent in southern Italy, was a man of letters and a highly effective diplomat. He made peace with the Lombards although in his reign they captured the remaining Byzantine territories in Italy, the Exarchate of Ravenna, in 751.

He also patched up relations with Constantinople, despite the fact Emperor Constantine V Copronymus was a committed iconoclast, and developed the papal alliance with the Franks. He supported the claim of Pepin III as king of the Franks, and the deposition of the last Merovingian king, Childeric III – so inaugurating the birth of a close relationship between Rome and the new Carolingian royal house.

In Rome he built the church of Santa Maria sopra Minerva on the site of the pagan temple to Minerva and donated it to a group of nuns from Constantinople. He is remembered also for translating the *Dialogues* of Gregory the Great into Greek.

STEPHEN II TO STEPHEN III, 752–72
POPE BECOMES TEMPORAL RULER, HEAD OF THE PAPAL STATES

Two men called Stephen were elected to the papacy in 752. The first, elected on 23 March, survived just three days; a stroke despatched him before he could be consecrated. He is listed as Pope Stephen II in some sources, but was removed from the official listing of popes under Pope John XXIII (1958–63). The second, who ruled from 26 March 752 to 26 April 757, is therefore Stephen II. However, in some books he is listed as Stephen III – or as Stephen II (III).

This pope Stephen II distanced the papacy from Constantinople and moved closer to the Franks. His reign saw a seismic shift: the pope, no longer under imperial authority exercised from Constantinople, established himself as a sovereign prince, ruler of the papal states, with the King of the Franks as his protector.

LOMBARDS THREATEN ROME

The year before Stephen's election, the Lombards had captured Ravenna, capital of the Byzantine territory in Italy, the

Below: Pharamond is elected king of the Franks. A legendary figure, he was first mentioned in an eighth-century history that set out to link the Franks to Ancient Troy.

Exarchate of Ravenna. There was no escaping the conclusion that they were now a threat to Rome.

Stephen could not expect help from Constantinople: relations were strained because of the continuing bitter controversy over iconoclasm, and in any case the Byzantine Empire had its hands full coping with the threats of the Islamic Abbasid Caliphate based in Baghdad.

DONATION OF PEPIN

Stephen tried negotiations, meeting Lombard king Aistulf at Pavia in the autumn of 753, but when this proved fruitless he turned to the Franks, crossing the Alps and travelling to Paris, where he met King Pepin III 'the Short' of the Franks. In July 754 Stephen anointed Pepin – and his sons Charlemagne and Carloman – as kings of the Romans. In return Pepin promised to drive off the Lombards and return to the papacy lands in Italy that had been seized by the Lombards. This promise – subsequently known as 'the Donation of Pepin' – does not survive in written form but later documents of the 8th century refer to it.

Pepin swept into Italy at the head of his Frankish army and pinned Aistulf back into his capital, Pavia; Pope Stephen

Above: Stephen III overcame two rivals amid street fighting to claim the papacy. The establishment of the papal states had made it highly desirable to be pope.

THE FRANKS

The Franks were first known to history as Germanic tribes living near the River Rhine in around the 3rd century AD. After the collapse of the Roman Empire they were ruled by the Merovingian dynasty. The family that gave rise to the great kings Pepin III and Charlemagne were mayors of the palace under the Merovingians – administrators who increasingly were de facto rulers. Pepin III rose to power in alliance with the papacy and was crowned King of the Franks in November 751 by Bishop Boniface with the knowledge and backing of Pope Zacharias: the last Merovingian king, Childeric III, was deposed and despatched to a monastery. Pepin was succeeded by his sons Charlemagne and Carloman ruling side by side. On Carloman's death in 771, Charlemagne annexed his territory and became sole ruler of the Franks.

travelled back to safety in Rome. But when the Franks returned to their homeland the Lombards marched southwards once more and in January 756 surrounded Rome. Stephen called for aid again and Pepin, Carloman and Charlemagne did not fail him: they led their forces to the rescue a second time. With the Lombards humbled, the Franks bestowed on Pope Stephen the basis of the papal states – lands in the Exarchate of Ravenna, the Duchy of Rome, Istria and Venetia.

Stephen II's younger brother was to succeed him as Pope Paul I in 757. He faced an alliance between the Lombards under their new king Desiderius and Emperor Constantine V Copronymus, who invaded the papal states. Pepin acted as a mediator and most of the pope's territories were safeguarded.

MONKS TAKE FLIGHT

In the Eastern Church, Constantine launched a new wave of iconoclasm; Paul protested strongly and repeatedly. He gave refuge to waves of Greek monks who had fled persecution in Byzantine territories. Paul transferred the bones of several saints from the catacombs damaged by the Lombards in 756 to churches in the city. Among these were the remains of St Petronilla, who was then believed to be the daughter of St Peter.

After Paul died, Pope Stephen III (768–72) was immediately embroiled in a bloody succession crisis. First a Tuscan nobleman, Duke Toto of Nepi, tried to install his brother as pope, and he was briefly in power as antipope Constantine II. Then a Lombard faction had Toto killed and Constantine deposed and installed their own candidate, Philip. He,

Above: Lands in the Exarchate of Ravenna, site of the beautiful Basilica of Sant'Apollinare Nuovo, were part of the territory transferred to Pope Stephen II. This mosaic shows the Magi guided by a star.

too, was ousted and Stephen III was elected by an assembly of clergy, military and the people of Rome.

ALLIANCE IN THE BALANCE

Stephen initially trusted the Franks as his protectors, but was horrified when the Lombards and Franks entered into an alliance in which the Lombard princess Desiderata wed Charlemagne. Stephen made an alliance with the Lombards in 771, and in machinations surrounding this agreement Franks were murdered in Rome. The papacy's relationship with the Franks was hanging by a thread.

HADRIAN I, 772–95
POPE WHO FORGED A CRUCIAL ALLIANCE WITH CHARLEMAGNE

When Pope Stephen III chose alliance with the Lombards over loyalty to the Franks the decision could have been disastrous for Rome, but his successor Hadrian I (772–95) – a man of great ability and deep piety – extricated the papacy from these problems and rebuilt the alliance with the Frankish kings. This resulted in Charlemagne crushing the Lombards.

LOMBARD AMBITIONS
At the start of Hadrian's reign, the Lombard king Desiderius was ambitious to extend his rule throughout Italy. He saw that the Frankish king Charlemagne

Below: A momentous encounter. The 15th-century Chronicles of France depicts Hadrian greeting Charlemagne in Rome to cement the alliance between the papacy and Franks.

> **FACT BOX**
> **Original name** Hadrian
> **Also known as** Adrian I
> **Born** 700
> **Origin** Roman
> **Date elected pope** 1 February 772
> **Died** 25 December 795
> **Key fact** Established the papacy as a temporal power

had his hands full fighting the Saxons, and hoped to foster dissension among the Frankish people. The previous year Charlemagne's brother and co-ruler Carloman had died, leading Charlemagne to annexe his brother's lands and set himself up as sole king; Desiderius had Carloman's exiled widow and sons in the Lombard capital, Pavia,

and hoped to get Hadrian to back their claim to a share in Frankish power.

But Hadrian would not cooperate and instead ordered the arrest of Desiderius's agent in Rome, Paul Afiarta, and demanded the return of papal territories that the Lombards had seized. Desiderius threatened Rome. Hadrian refortified the city and called on Charlemagne for military help.

FAST AND FURIOUS RESPONSE
At this critical moment there was a lull in the Saxon war that enabled Charlemagne to strike in support of the pope. In autumn 773 he swept across the Alps, captured Verona and besieged Desiderius in Pavia.

Then, leaving his troops to carry on the siege, Charlemagne marched to Rome. He arrived on Holy Saturday at

> **ICONOCLASM**
> The controversy over whether it was permissible to make and venerate images of Jesus Christ and the saints caused bitter division in the 8th and 9th centuries. The religious use of images had been opposed in the early Church but had become popular in the 6th and 7th centuries. Byzantine Emperor Leo III prohibited the use of icons in 730 and persecution of those who revered icons became severe. Then in 787 the Second Ecumenical Council at Nicaea, convened by the Empress Irene, condemned iconoclasm and backed the use of images. Iconoclasm would return in 814 with the accession of Emperor Leo V and the use of icons was to be banned in 815. Finally in 843 Empress Theodora, widow of Emperor Theophilus, would restore the sacred use of icons – an event celebrated as the Feast of Orthodoxy in the Eastern Orthodox Church today.

Above: In Rome, Pope Hadrian constructed the Basilica of Santa Maria in Cosmedin on the site of an earlier church, de Schola Graeca, and an ancient food distribution centre.

Easter, was warmly welcomed and solemnly celebrated Easter with Hadrian at St Peter's.

DONATION OF CHARLEMAGNE

For three days the Roman and Frankish parties celebrated Easter, then on the following Wednesday met to settle affairs of state. This was a momentous encounter that transformed the face of Italy for centuries to come.

In the celebrated 'Donation of Charlemagne', the Frankish king gave Hadrian and his successors possession of great swathes of territory in the Italian peninsula. Two months later, Pavia fell to Charlemagne's army. The Lombard era was at a close.

CLASH OVER ICONS

Hadrian also intervened in the bitter rows over iconoclasm (see box), supporting the efforts of Byzantine Empress Irene (widow of Leo IV and co-ruler with her son Constantine VI) to end the

dispute. He despatched legates bearing a treatise that explained the doctrinal justification of venerating icons to the Second Council of Nicaea (787), which outlawed iconoclasm. This briefly caused a rift with Charlemagne, who rejected the council's decrees, perhaps because he was suspicious of this revival of co-operation between Rome and Constantinople and also, it is thought, taking offence because he had been invited to send bishops himself. His theologians issued the *Libri Carolini*, which defied Nicaea by declaring in favour of iconoclasm, but the difficulty passed and was explained on the grounds that Charlemagne had seen a poor Latin translation of the council's decrees that wrongly spoke of 'adoration' rather than the more restrained 'veneration' of images in worship.

Hadrian also fought against the heresy of Adoptionism in the Spanish Church, condemning the teaching of Archbishop Elipandus of Toledo on the dual natures of Jesus Christ. The teaching had this name because Elipandus argued that the human Jesus Christ was the 'adopted son' of God while the divine Jesus was God's son by nature.

In Rome, Hadrian rebuilt the churches of Santa Maria in Cosmedin and San Marco and also carried out restoration works on some of the old aqueducts.

LONG SERVICE

Hadrian reigned for 23 years, ten months and 26 days. His was the longest papal rule to date, and was not surpassed until Pope Pius VI's 24-year reign in 1775–99. In the whole history of the papacy only three other popes – Pius IX (1846–78), Leo XIII (1878–1903) and John Paul II (1978–2005) – have had longer reigns.

When Hadrian died aged 95 on 25 December 795 Charlemagne reputedly wept as if he had lost a close relative, and he celebrated this great pope in a verse epitaph written by the scholar Alcuin and inscribed on a marble monument that he sent to Rome. In the epitaph, which can still be viewed in St Peter's Basilica, Charlemagne called Hadrian 'father'.

Below: After the negotiations in Rome at Easter 774, Charlemagne returned to Pavia and directed the end of the siege. The citizens opened their gates to the Frankish army.

CHAPTER FOUR

CONFLICT IN THE CHURCH

LEO III TO LEO IX, 795–1054

The reign of Pope Benedict IX in the mid-11th century is one of the most degrading in the history of the papacy. He was linked to murders and rapes; he even sold the position of pope to his father-in-law John Gratian, who became Pope Gregory VI. Here was the offence of simony writ as large as could be. The papacy's alliance with the Frankish throne brought with it the gift of lands on the Italian peninsula that made the pope a temporal prince. In the 10th and 11th centuries the position of pope was a glittering prize disputed amidst violence, bribery and politicking by the Roman nobility.

Benedict IX was not only put on the throne by his father and briefly succeeded by his father-in-law, but was also the nephew of popes Benedict VIII and John XIX and related to popes Sergius III and John XI. These men were all associated with the Tusculani family, placed in power by various counts of Tusculum (near Rome in central-western Italy). Their bitter rivals were the Crescentii family, who provided one pope in Giovanni Crescentius (John XIII; 965–972) and controlled most of the pontiffs from c.950–1012, when their puppet Sergius IV died in the same year as the *patricius* (leader) of the clan.

Increased worldly power and the alliance with Frankish kings and subsequent Western emperors made the papacy independent of its former masters, the Byzantine emperors in Constantinople. In the mid-11th century the reforming pope Leo IX emphasized repeatedly the primacy of the pope over the whole Church. The ensuing conflict with church authorities in Constantinople led to a schism between the Western and Eastern churches that has not been healed to this day.

Left: The old order passeth. By tradition the papacy was established in authority over Rome and the Western Roman Empire by the 'Donation of Constantine', here celebrated by Renaissance master Raphael in his work for the Vatican Palace. The alliance with Charlemagne and the Franks set the papacy free from Constantinople.

LEO III, 795–816
POPE WHO CROWNED CHARLEMAGNE

Pope Leo III consolidated the already highly profitable relationship between the papacy and Franks by crowning Frankish king Charlemagne the first Holy Roman Emperor.

DRIVEN FROM ROME

Pope Hadrian's associates and family members initially made life almost impossible for his successor, Leo III (795–816). Some had perhaps expected to succeed Hadrian, and began to spread rumours to undermine the new pope. Hadrian's nephew Pascalis led a brutal attack on Leo as the pope toured the city on 25 April 799, trying without success to make him unfit for office by blinding him and cutting his tongue out, but Leo escaped intact and fled to Paderborn, Germany, seeking the protection of Charlemagne.

At the same time, Leo's enemies sent messengers to Charlemagne, accusing the pope of perjury and sexual offences. Could Charlemagne pass judgement on an elected pope? However his advisers, who included the learned monk Alcuin of York – the great scholar of Charlemagne's revival of learning – assured him

FACT BOX

Original name Not known; son of Atyuppius and Elizabeth

Born 750

Origin Roman; Greek or possibly Arab ancestry

Date elected pope 27 December 795

Died 12 June 816

Key fact Built key relationship with the Franks

Above: On Christmas Day, 800, Leo III crowns Charlemagne Emperor of the West – 'great and pacific emperor, governing the Roman Empire'. This view was painted by Raphael in 1516–17.

that there was no precedent for him to do this. He sent the pope back to Rome with a Frankish escort for protection.

Trouble continued in Rome, however, and in the autumn of 800 Charlemagne himself travelled there to attempt to settle matters. On 23 December of that year, Leo solemnly swore his innocence on the Gospels at the high altar of St Peter's before a synod of abbots, bishops and members of the Frankish and Roman nobility that was also attended by Charlemagne himself. The synod duly accepted his word and cleared him of all charges.

IMPERIAL CORONATION

Two days later at Christmas Day Mass in St Peter's, Leo crowned Charlemagne Emperor of the West. Charlemagne is generally viewed as the first Holy Roman Emperor, although he did not use this title – he was styled 'most serene Augustus, crowned by God, great and pacific emperor, governing the Roman Empire'. The coronation consolidated Leo's still precarious position, and clarified the basis on which Charlemagne had taken a role at the synod that cleared Leo of charges just two days earlier.

According to the Frankish account, Leo prostrated himself in front of Charlemagne, kissing the ground before his feet – the accepted act of adoration due to an emperor. This act of homage was not recorded by the papal chronicler, who stated that Leo anointed Charlemagne.

Afterwards Charlemagne claimed that he had been taken by surprise and would not have entered St Peter's on that day had he known what Leo intended, but it is impossible not to believe that the two men had planned this act of high visual drama in advance, perhaps even as early as their meeting in Paderborn the previous year.

Above: The coronation of Charlemagne. In this unprecedented act, which had no legal basis, Leo attempted to establish the right of the pope to anoint and crown the emperor.

At the Lateran, Leo commissioned two mosaics that provide a commentary on the coronation. In one, Jesus Christ hands St Peter the pallium and gives Constantine the labarum or Chi-Ro symbol of Christ's name; in a second Peter hands Leo the pallium and gives Charlemagne a banner and spear.

FILIOQUE

The ceremony sought to establish Charlemagne as protector of the papacy. The coronation would surely not have taken place if there had been a male emperor ruling in Constantinople. But there was not, for the Empress Irene, widow of Leo IV, was in power, having seized the throne from her son Constantine V with whom she had been co-ruler. In the eyes of many in the West, who believed in a male line of succession, the imperial throne was empty. In this sense the papacy – indeed, the whole Christian world – had no protector.

In 810 these co-rulers came into conflict over Charlemagne's support for adding the word *Filioque* ('and the Son')

Left: At the Lateran, Leo commissioned mosaics that comment on the coronation. In one, Christ hands Leo the pallium (a robe, symbol of spiritual authority) and gives Charlemagne a banner and spear.

to the creed. The proposed addition signified that the Holy Spirit derived from the Father and the Son (Jesus Christ) together, and did not come solely from the Father. Having first appeared in Spain as early as the 6th century, use of the *Filioque* wording had spread widely through the Western Church, but its use was opposed in the Eastern Church.

Leo accepted the doctrine but rejected the notion that the Church of the Franks could make changes to the creed that had been agreed by the ecumenical councils of Nicaea and Constantinople and so was a unifying factor for Eastern and Western churches. 'For safeguarding of the true faith', he had the creed (without *Filioque*) engraved in both Latin and Greek on silver panels and attached these to tombs of Saints Peter and Paul in Rome.

CHARLEMAGNE

Charlemagne was King of the Franks (768–814), King of the Lombards (774–814) and Emperor of the West (800–14). When he was born in April 747, his father Pepin was mayor of the palace under the Merovingian kings – notionally an administrator, but in fact a position of great power. With the backing of Pope Zacharias (741–52) Pepin seized the throne and ousted the final Merovingian king, Childeric III, who was despatched to a monastery. On Pepin's death in 768 the kingdom was divided between Charlemagne and his younger brother Carloman, then when Carloman died in 771 Charlemagne became sole ruler of the Franks. He was 24 years old. In alliance with the papacy, he went on to build a great empire, defeating the Lombards, the Saxons and the Avars. He promoted Christianity, education and the arts, commerce and agriculture in his vast realms, building many splendid churches and palaces, and his era is called the 'Carolingian Renaissance'.

STEPHEN IV TO SERGIUS II, 816–47
EMPERORS EXERT POWER OVER PAPACY

In the first half of the 9th century the descendants of Charlemagne exercised increasing power over the papacy. Initially popes Stephen IV and Paschal I held quite a strong position and sought to emphasize the papal role in anointing the emperor, but popes from Eugenius II to Sergius II lost ground and had to make concessions regarding imperial approval of and sovereignty over new popes.

Stephen IV (816–17) travelled to Reims to crown and anoint Charlemagne's successor, Louis the Pious, as Holy Roman Emperor. Louis had previously been crowned by his own father, Charlemagne, in 813, but Stephen's action underlined the papacy's role in establishing each new imperial ruler in power. Stephen and Louis confirmed their alliance and the pope's possession of the papal states. Stephen died shortly after his return to Rome, on 24 January 817.

His successor Paschal I (817–24) had his coronation almost immediately after his election, perhaps to prevent any interference in the process by Louis. When Paschal sent news of the event to Louis, he received in return a celebrated document, the *Pactum Ludovicianum,* which congratulated Paschal, recognized his right over the papal states and guaranteed that future popes could be freely elected and need only inform the emperor after being crowned. Some historians doubt the authenticity of this document, however, which was so highly favourable to the papacy.

In 823 Paschal crowned and anointed Louis's son Lothair I as co-emperor with his father in Rome. This was the first coronation ceremony in which the pope handed the emperor a sword as a symbol of temporal power that was to be used to banish evil.

SIMONY

Simony means selling ecclesiastical positions or church sacraments. The name comes from Simon Magus, a sorcerer from Samaria who according to the biblical book Acts of the Apostles (8:18) tried to buy from the Apostles the knowledge of how to transmit the Holy Spirit. The oldest surviving statement against simony is the second canon of the Council of Chalcedon of 451. Simony became a major and widespread problem in the European Church in the 9th–10th centuries.

POPE MUST SWEAR FEALTY TO EMPEROR

Eugenius II (824–7) owed the Holy Roman Emperor gratitude from the first day of his pontificate. He was elected by Roman nobles with imperial support and in opposition to the candidate favoured by the clergy in Rome. As a result Frankish control of the papacy reached a high point in this reign: Eugenius did not resist a new constitution imposed by Lothair I on a visit to Rome in 824, under which the emperor had sovereignty over Rome and each pope elect had to swear fealty before he could be elected.

'FATHER OF THE PEOPLE'

On matters of church discipline and organization, Eugenius established that priests should not wear secular clothing or have secular occupations, and took various measures to promote learning. He was known for humility and love of

Left: Pope Stephen IV crowns Louis the Pious – as depicted in the 14th-century manuscript 'Grandes Chroniques de France'. Stephen wanted to restate that the papacy's blessing was necessary for an imperial succession.

simplicity, and his generosity to the poor, especially widows and orphans, won him the title 'father of the people'.

Pope Valentine lasted only 40 days in August–September 827. At the start of the reign of his successor, Gregory IV (827–44), the pope was reprimanded by Louis for having attempted to arrange his consecration before receiving the emperor's approval of the election. Subsequently Gregory attempted to mediate in the quarrels between Lothair and his father Louis in the course of which Lothair led a rebellion and briefly deposed his father in 833. Then, following the death of Louis in 840, war broke out between Lothair and his brothers and in the end the great empire of Charlemagne was broken up by the Treaty of Verdun (843).

CORRUPTION

Sergius II (844–7) was elected by the Roman nobility and had to contend with an antipope, John, popular with the people of Rome. He managed to overcome this challenge but rushed his consecration to end the issue. This

Above: Paschal I honours the Virgin Mary. He built or renovated several churches in Rome as part of the Carolingian Renaissance associated with Charlemagne – a programme of artistic and theological rebirth.

Below: Money could not buy Simon Magus secret knowledge about the Holy Spirit from the Apostles. Italian Renaissance artist Filippino Lippi imagined the scene.

brought on another show of imperial strength, and Lothair sent his son Louis to Rome at the head of an army to punish the pope for having failed to wait for emperor's approval of his election. Sergius was forced to accept that no pope could be elected without the emperor's approval, and that each papal consecration must be in the presence of an imperial representative.

Because he suffered so badly from gout, Sergius delegated much of his power to his brother, Bishop Benedict of Albano. Between them they carried out major rebuilding in Rome, but won an unwanted reputation for financial misdemeanours and simony.

SARACEN ATTACK

For many years, since they had captured Palermo in Sicily in 831, Muslim Arabs had been a force to fear in southern Italy. In 846 a Muslim fleet sailed up the Tiber and unleashed 500 horsemen who sacked Rome, even tearing silver from the doors of St Peter's. Many saw it as a judgement of God on the financial wrongdoing under Pope Sergius.

LEO IV TO LEO V, 847–903
POPE'S CORPSE EXHUMED AND PUT ON TRIAL

Leo IV (847–55) responded with fortitude and energy to the challenge laid down by the Saracens when they sacked Rome in the last days of Pope Sergius II. Leo built a coalition against the common enemy, and himself taking command of a fleet combining the navies of Amalfi, Gaeta and Naples, defeated the Arab navy in a sea battle off Ostia in 849.

LEONINE WALL
He then set several hundred prisoners to work alongside locals to improve Rome's fortifications, raising the great Leonine Wall – 40ft/12m high, 12ft/3.6m thick, 1.8 miles/3km long and with 40 towers – around the Vatican and St Peter's. Another tradition about this great defender of the faith and of Rome holds that when a blazing fire threatened to engulf the Borgo district adjacent to St Peter's Square, Leo stopped the flames by making the sign of the cross.

Benedict III (855–8) was elected after another candidate, Hadrian, had refused to become pope, and faced an antipope, Anastasius, who had the backing of Emperor Louis II. Remarkably, however, the popular backing for Benedict proved too strong for the imperial candidate and after Louis dropped his opposition

Above: When Leo IV made the sign of the cross it was sufficient to turn back flames that had threatened the Borgo district. A Vatican Palace fresco by Raphael celebrated the event.

Benedict was consecrated. He acted with authority in disciplining Frankish bishops and restating the primacy of Rome over Constantinople. In his reign, the Christian King Aethelwulf of Wessex made a pilgrimage to Rome with his son, the future King Alfred the Great.

VIGOROUS AUTHORITY
Nicholas I the Great (858–67) was a more forthright proponent still of papal authority and Rome's jurisdiction over the church; he challenged the Western emperor's right to legislate on ecclesiastical matters, and restated the pope's inheritance of priestly and royal authority from St Peter. This vigorous leader made three great statements of papal authority. He refused to accept the deposition of

Left: 'Pope Joan' gives birth in mid-procession. An anti-Catholic pamphlet of 1675 imagines the scene, describing Rome as 'the whore of Babylon'.

Patriarch Ignatius of Constantinople by Byzantine emperor Michael III and excommunicated his replacement, Photius, causing a new schism between Eastern and Western churches. He excommunicated the archbishops of Cologne and Trier in finding against their decision to allow King Lothair of Lorraine to divorce his first wife and remarry. And he reinstated the Bishop of Soissons, France, overriding the Archbishop of Reims's decision.

A relative of two previous popes, Stephen IV and Sergius II, Hadrian II (867–72) had twice declined to become pope before he finally accepted in 867. He was an ineffective pontiff. His five-year reign included the fourth Council of Constantinople (869–70), which deposed Patriarch Photius of Constantinople.

FIRST POPE TO BE MURDERED
John VIII (872–82) was the first pope to be assassinated – he was poisoned and clubbed to death as a result of a local dispute. This rather sordid end followed an active and effective pontificate in which in alliance with the Franks he defended Italy against Muslim raiders.

He clashed with and excommunicated the Bishop of Porto, Formosus, who later became pope.

Marinus I (882–84) was Bishop of Caere (modern Cerveteri) when elected pope – the first bishop of another diocese to be made Bishop of Rome. Among his few acts of note as pontiff was to absolve Formosus and restore him to his bishopric in 883.

Hadrian III (884–5) likewise achieved little. By now Charlemagne's once great empire was in decline, and Pope Stephen V (885–91), finding no help from the Franks, was forced to turn once more to Constantinople in seeking aid against Arab raids on Italy.

Formosus (891–6) was a highly effective pontiff and skilled diplomat, a deeply pious man and a very fine preacher, but one who made many enemies. His name means 'good-looking' – and he

Above: The infamous 'Cadaver Trial'. Stephen VI had the corpse of his predecessor Boniface VI dug up to face accusations of wrongdoing while pope.

was accused of vanity. He allied with Arnulf of Carinthia, King of the Eastern Franks, against Emperor Guy III of Spoleto and his son Lambert, and crowned Arnulf Emperor in Rome in 896. Arnulf fell ill and became paralysed and the alliance came to nothing, but it earned Formosus the hatred of the House of Spoleto and cast a long shadow over the following years.

THE CADAVER TRIAL

The next two years saw four popes, one of whom was imprisoned and murdered, and a scandalous trial. Boniface VI (896) died after 15 days. His successor Stephen VI (896–7) was one of Formosus's many

bitter enemies, and in the gruesome 'Cadaver Trial' he had the former pope's body exhumed, dressed in full papal regalia and propped up on the throne to face trial for alleged offences committed while pope. Formosus was found guilty, stripped and had the three fingers of his right hand that he had used for giving blessings cut off; then the corpse was cast into the river Tiber. These events caused a scandal and Stephen was imprisoned and strangled in captivity.

Romanus reigned for four months in August–November 897 but was deposed and ended his life as a monk and Theodore II died after being pope for 20 days in December of the same year. In his very brief reign Theodore had the body of Formosus, which had been recovered by a hermit from the Tiber, reburied.

John IX (898–900) tried to rehabilitate Formosus's reputation and held synods at Rome and Ravenna to this end. Bitter struggles over the memory of Formosus dominated the reign of Benedict IV (900–3) and Leo V (August/September 903). Leo was imprisoned by an antipope, Christopher, and probably murdered in captivity.

Below: Church Triumphant. Defeated pagans are dragged before Pope Leo IV after his victory at sea over the Saracens in the Battle of Ostia (849).

POPE JOAN

Tradition – usually dismissed as legend – has it that a woman held the reins of papal power in 855–7, between Leo IV and Benedict III. According to the story that circulated in chronicles through the Middle Ages, she went by the name of John VIII, and was English by birth; after coming to Rome via Athens and building a great reputation as a master of the liberal arts in the disguise of a man, she was unanimously elected pope. When she became pregnant by a companion, she tried to conceal it but gave birth while in the midst of a procession from St Peter's to the Lateran, in a lane between the Colosseum and St Clement's Church. One version claims she reigned in 1099–1106 between Urban II and Paschal II. It is also said that for 600 years each newly elected pope had to submit to an intimate examination – he sat in a specially designed chair with a section cut away so that a junior cleric could touch the pope's genitals to verify that he was a man.

SERGIUS III TO GREGORY V, 904–99
PAPACY ENDURES A 'DARK AGE'

In these years the papacy was a prize bitterly contested by noble families in Italy. Sergius III (904–11) owed his time in the limelight to the support of Count Theophylact of Tusculum and was little more than his puppet. According to one account, Sergius was the lover of Theophylact's daughter Marozia and had an illegitimate son by her who went on to become Pope John XI.

MURDEROUS POWERPLAY

Sergius had in fact been elected pope in 898 by supporters of Stephen VI and enemies of Formosus, but he had been driven from Rome by John IX. When the antipope Christopher ousted John IX's successor Leo V, Sergius moved in with the support of Count Theophylact. He defeated Christopher and seized power for himself. It is said that he ordered the murder by strangling of both Christopher and Leo.

Popes Anastasius III (911–13) and Lando (913–14) were both Count Theophylact's men and did his bidding – indeed, all the popes down to John XII were in the pocket of Theophylact or his descendants. One note of interest about Lando is that he was the last pope – until Pope Francis in 2013 – to use a papal name that had not previously been chosen by a pontiff.

To combat Saracen raids in Italy, John X (914–28) built an anti-Muslim Christian alliance that pointed forward

Above: Pope John X. To combat Saracen raiders, he built an anti-Muslim Christian alliance that pointed forward to the crusader armies of 1096 and afterwards. His army won the Battle of Garigliano (915).

to the crusader armies of 1096 and afterwards. John himself led the army to victory over the Saracens at the Battle of Garigliano in June 915. He rewarded King Berengar of Italy for his participation by crowning him Holy Roman Emperor, with Theophylact's backing, on 3 December 915.

DANGEROUS MISTRESS

John was reputedly the lover of Marozia's mother Theodora, to whom he granted the title *senatrix* (senatoress) of Rome. In 924, following the assassination of Berengar and the death of Theophylact he tested the patience of his noble backers by seeking an alliance with Hugh of Provence. Marozia – now married to Guy, Margrave of Tuscany – had the pope cast in prison and later smothered to death.

Leo VI (928) and Stephen VII (928–31) were both Marozia's appointments, and both may have been killed; John XI (931–35/6) was her son by Sergius III. He was loyal to her but was deposed and imprisoned by another of her sons, his half-brother Duke Alberic II of Spoleto.

Leo VII (936–939), Stephen VIII (939–42), Marinus II (942–6) and Agapitus II (946–55) were all appointed by Alberic and entirely dominated by him. They all took an interest, encouraged by Alberic, in reforming Italian monasteries. Leo invited Odo, abbot of the Cluniac order of reforming monks, to Rome.

WHEN THE VATICAN WAS LIKE A BROTHEL

On the death of Agapitus, Alberic's illegitimate son Octavian succeeded as pope John XII (955–64). He may have been as young as 17 years old and was entirely unsuited to lead the Church, for he led a wildly dissolute life – and in his time the Vatican was described as a brothel.

He relied on the support of Otto I of Germany, who had marched into Italy in 951 and declared himself King of the Lombards, and John consolidated his position by crowning Otto and his wife Adelaide as Roman Emperor and Empress on 2 February 962. John and the Roman nobles swore an oath of loyalty to Otto who issued a guarantee of the independence of the papal states.

Below: Benedict V: a medal dated 964. He was pope for just one month, 22 May–23 June, before he was ousted by Emperor Otto I and his preferred candidate, Leo VIII.

POPES OF THE DARK AGE

For half a century from Sergius III in 904 to John XII in 955, popes were under the influence of the Roman Theophylacti family. The Latin name *Saeculum obscurum* ('dark age') was first given to these years by the 16th-century Vatican librarian and papal historian Caesar Baronius.

Above: John XII oversees the punishment of those who plotted against him – his confessor, Benedict, is blinded and a deacon has his right hand cut off.

But when Otto left Rome to impose his authority on Berengar II, King of Italy, John began to plot behind his back, provoking the fury of the emperor who replaced him with Pope Leo VIII (963–5). Briefly in 964, after Otto had left Rome, John engineered his own reinstatement but then he died suddenly while having sexual relations with one of his concubines – the word in Rome was that he died after being struck on the head by the devil himself.

On his death the Romans refused to accept Leo and elected Benedict V (964) as their own candidate. But Otto returned to Rome, removed Benedict from the papal throne and reinstalled his own man.

John XIII (965–72), another candidate imposed by Otto, followed Leo. At Christmas 967 he crowned the emperor's 12-year-old son as co-Emperor Otto II. His unpopularity among the Romans was a political matter rather than a judgement on his character, for he was learned and pious, and an expert in canon law. His nickname was 'the white hen', on account of his very fair hair.

Otto died shortly after the election of Benedict VI (973–4) and while his son Otto II was distracted imposing himself in Germany, Roman nobles strangled Benedict and replaced him with antipope Boniface VII. Otto II's candidate Benedict VII (974–83) prevailed after a struggle and the antipope Boniface was excommunicated. Benedict and Otto worked harmoniously and kept the peace in Rome for nine years, promoting monasticism and church reform.

On Benedict's death Otto II offered Majolus, abbot of Cluny, the chance to be pope but he refused it. One of Otto's ministers, Pietro Canepanova, stepped into the breach as John XIV (983–4).

However, he was left isolated and vulnerable when Otto died on 7 December 983 and the antipope Boniface VII returned from exile and deposed the pope, throwing him in prison where he starved to death. Boniface held power until his death in July 985.

FIRST CANONIZATION

John XV (985–96), another pope controlled by the Roman nobility, was not inactive – in 993 he solemnly canonized Bishop Ulrich of Augsburg (died 973) in the first recorded ritual of this kind. When he died of fever in March 996, the new German king Otto III chose his cousin Bruno of Carinthia as Gregory V (996–9). Within three weeks of his consecration on 3 May 996, Gregory crowned Otto emperor. Then when Otto returned to Germany a revolt in Rome drove Gregory to flee and installed an antipope, John XVI. Furious, Otto marched on Rome, captured the antipope and reinstalled Gregory. However, Gregory died in February 999 after contracting malaria before his 30th birthday.

Below: The Benedictine Abbey of Cluny was widely seen as a leading light of monasticism in Europe. So Leo VIII turned to its abbot, Odo, for advice on monastic reform in Italy.

SYLVESTER II, 999–1003
POPE WHO WAS ACCUSED OF BEING A MAGICIAN

The French-born Gerbert of Aurillac was Archbishop of Ravenna when with the support of Emperor Otto III he was elected to become pope. He chose the name Sylvester II to honour Pope Sylvester I (314–35), who had been pontiff in the era of the great Emperor Constantine I (324–37). He aimed to position himself and Otto as the Sylvester and Constantine of the 10th–11th century, leaders of a renewed Christian empire.

PREMATURE END TO PROMISING PARTNERSHIP

They worked closely together, seeking to consolidate papal–imperial authority and to eliminate abuses in the Church such as simony and the practice of some priests living with women as if married. In 1001 they were driven from Rome

Below: Stephen I, the first king of Hungary, reputedly received his crown from Sylvester. Some historians think this a legend; if it did happen, it must have been with the blessing of Otto.

by a revolt among the nobility and took refuge in Ravenna. Otto died of malaria the following year, bringing their highly promising cooperation to a premature end. Sylvester was allowed to return to Rome, but died himself not long afterwards.

THE MOST BRILLIANT MAN OF HIS TIME

Sylvester was a very great scholar and author who engaged with and promoted the study of mathematics and astronomy. He reintroduced to Europe the abacus and the armillary sphere (an astronomical instrument), which had been out of

Below: Sylvester II. The first French pope was so learned that legends sprang up alleging he had made devilish pacts to acquire specialist knowledge.

use there since the classical era of ancient Greece and Rome.

He was receptive to the learning of the Arabs of Al-Andalus (the Muslim state on the Spanish peninsula), elements of which were drawn from classical texts that had been translated into Arabic but otherwise lost to history. He learned of Hindu–Arabic numerals (the numerals with which we are familiar today) and used them on his abacus at a time when most Europeans were using Roman numerals – I, V, X, C and so on. He was also a gifted teacher, who before he became pope taught at the Cathedral School at Reims and was tutor successively to the young men who became emperors Otto II and Otto III.

MAGUS?

After his death in 1003, many legends circulated about Sylvester and his great learning. While a young man he had studied at the monastery of Santa Maria de Ripoli in Spain and people spread rumours that he had travelled to the Islamic cities of Cordoba and Sevilla.

Right: Sylvester was open to the learning of Arab scholars and brought the armillary sphere (an instrument used in astronomy) back into use in Europe.

William of Malmesbury recounted the story that Sylvester stole an invaluable book of spells from its Islamic keeper and fled through the night; when he was pursued he hid by hanging beneath a wooden bridge over a river and because he was not touching water or land he could not be discovered. Afterwards he fled and reached a beach where he made a pact with the devil to carry him across the sea to safety.

CONTROLLED BY A FEMALE DEMON?

Other sources claimed that Sylvester carried about an artificial head, Meridiana, that gave him the answer 'yes' or 'no' to any questions he asked; Meridiana told him that he would be seized by the devil if he ever read Mass in Jerusalem. According to this tradition, Sylvester

Below: Otto III receives homage. He had a close relationship with Sylvester, who had been his tutor before he became emperor. Sadly, both died prematurely.

misunderstood the warning. He cancelled a planned trip to Jerusalem, but did not scent danger when he agreed to read Mass in the Church of Santa Croce in Gerusalemme ('The Holy Cross of Jerusalem') in Rome: he was dismembered by the devil who scraped out his eyes and threw them to demons to play with. He was also said to be in alliance with a female demon or was schooled directly by the devil. In one account he won the papacy by playing dice with the pope. Another legend has it that his bones (in a tomb in St John Lateran) rattle to signal when a pope is about to die.

ANTICHRIST

At the end of the first millennium people were looking for signs that the Last Days and God's Final Judgement were imminent. A monastic reformer and Benedictine abbot named Adso of Montier-en-Der wrote a treatise on the Antichrist for Queen Gerbera (wife of Louis IV of France) that became widely popular in the Middle Ages. Adso was well connected and, aside from Gerbera, had friendly contact with Sylvester II before he became pope when he was Bishop Gerbert of Aurillac. In Adso's account, which takes the popular form of a saint's life, the Frankish empire would endure to the end of time, which would be ushered in by the Antichrist, born in the Jewish tribe of Dan in Babylon and filled with wickedness by the devil himself. He would travel to Jerusalem, rebuild the Temple and claim to be the Son of God – performing miracles, raising the dead and gaining followers among the world's rulers. For three and a half years he would persecute good Christians. Then in a final battle on the Mount of Olives, Christ (or the archangel Michael) would defeat the Antichrist in a spot opposite where Jesus ascended into heaven, and bring about a time of peace and repentance for the faithful followed by the Last Judgement. This book later circulated under various names, including those of Alcuin and St Augustine.

JOHN XVII TO DAMASUS II, 1003–48
THE TUSCULANI FAMILY AND THE FIGHT FOR THE PAPACY

John XVII (1003), John XVIII (1003–9) and Sergius IV (1009–12) were candidates elected by and dependent on the Roman Crescentii family. However the influence of this family – which had largely controlled the papacy in the second half of the 10th century – was waning, and Pope Benedict VIII (1012–24) was loyal to their great rivals the Tusculani.

Below: In this miniature, Henry receives his crown from Christ himself. In fact, he was crowned by Pope Benedict VIII in 1014.

EARLY CRUSADING ZEAL

Johns XVII and XVIII and Sergius IV achieved little of note. John XVIII is remembered as a pope who abdicated and ended his life in a monastery, while Sergius IV is linked to a papal bull calling for the forces of Islam to be driven from the Holy Land; he reputedly issued this in 1009 following the destruction of the Church of the Holy Sepulchre in Jerusalem by the Fatimid caliph al-Hakim bi-Amr Allah, but many historians consider it to be a forgery.

Above: The Church of the Holy Sepulchre in Jerusalem was destroyed by a Fatimid caliph in 1009. Did Sergius IV call for Islam to be driven from the Holy Land?

Benedict VIII was a layman who came to power by force. Initially he was challenged by an antipope, Gregory VI, and was driven from Rome, but he attained power with the backing of King Henry II of Germany and afterwards crowned Henry Holy Roman Emperor on 14 February 1014. But he proved an effective pope.

The two men held a synod at Pavia that passed clauses outlawing simony and lack of self-restraint among the clergy. Benedict also supported his friend Odilo, abbot of Cluny, in his monastic reforms. In Italy the pope built an alliance with Norman settlers against Muslim Saracens in Sardinia and then dealt with the increasing threat of Byzantine troops in southern Italy by travelling to Germany in 1020 to seek the Emperor's military backing.

While there, Benedict consecrated the Cathedral of Bamberg, visited the monastery of Fulda and received from Henry a charter confirming the gifts to the papacy of Charlemagne and Otto I. Then in 1022 the pope and the emperor imposed imperial authority on southern Italy.

Right: Conrad II, crowned by Pope John XIX in 1027, founded the Salian dynasty that – through Conrad, Henry III, Henry IV and Henry V – ruled the Holy Roman Empire until 1125.

FIRST INDULGENCE

Benedict was succeeded by his brother Romanus, who took the name of Pope John XIX (1024–32). Following the death of Emperor Henry II in 1024 he was crowned Emperor Conrad II in a lavish ceremony at St Peter's at Easter 1027. King Canute of Denmark and England was in Conrad's party on this trip. John XIX is also remembered as the first pope to grant an indulgence (statement that a person's sins can be pardoned) in return for money.

FEAST OF IMMORALITY

In these years the papacy was a family affair – and an utterly scandalous one, at that. John XIX's nephew Theophylactus succeeded as Pope Benedict IX; according to some accounts, he was just 12 when he was elected. He had no qualifications as pope apart from the backing of a powerful family: he led a dissolute life and was said by the reforming monk

Below: Benedict VIII was a highly effective pope. He allied with the Normans against the Saracens in Italy and got imperial support to counter the Byzantines.

Petrus Damiani (1007–73) to have feasted on immorality. His reign came in the three parts: 1032–44, 1045 and 1047–8. In 1045 he was briefly replaced by Bishop John of Sabina who took the name Sylvester III, but then Benedict regained power by force. In 1048, either through greed or because he wanted to marry, he sold the papacy to his godfather John Gratian and abdicated. Gratian became Pope Gregory VI (1045–6).

THREE-WAY STRUGGLE

Benedict regretted his resignation and returned to seize the papal throne. At one point in 1046 all three figures – Benedict IX, Sylvester III and Gregory VI – were claiming to be the rightful pope. King Henry III of the Germans declared the first two deposed and stated that Gregory should resign because he had paid for the office of pope. Bishop Suidger of Bamberg was elected as Pope Clement II (1046–7) and on the same day Henry was crowned as Holy Roman Emperor.

Yet even this was not the end of the scandals visited on the papacy by Benedict IX. On Clement's death in October 1047, Benedict grabbed power

a third time; enraged, Henry III despatched German troops to Rome to remove Benedict by force. Bishop Poppo of Brixen was elected as Pope Damasus II. But he died after just 23 days (reigning 17 July–9 August); some accounts suggest that Damasus was poisoned by an associate of Benedict, but more reliable sources suggest he died after contracting malaria. He was succeeded by Pope Leo IX (1049–54).

SHORTEST PAPAL REIGNS

The rule of Damasus II, at 23 days, is only the seventh shortest papal reign. He comes after Urban VII (13 days, 15–27 September 1590); Boniface VI (16 days in April 896); Celestine IV (17 days, 25 October –10 November 1241); Theodore II (20 days in December 897); Sisinnius (21 days, 15 January–4 February 708); and Marcellus II (23 days, 9 April–1 May 1555). The shortest reign of the modern era – that of John Paul I (34 days, 26 August– 28 September 1978) is only the 11th shortest across the whole history of the papacy.

THE GREAT SCHISM OF THE TWO CHURCHES

The schism or split between Western and Eastern churches – subsequently known as the Roman Catholic Church and the Eastern Orthodox Church – began in a bitter exchange of excommunications in 1054 and has endured right into the 21st century.

On 16 July 1054 Cardinal Humbert of Silva-Candida dramatically laid a bull of excommunication against Patriarch Michael Cerularius of Constantinople on the high altar of the Cathedral of Hagia Sophia in Constantinople in the middle of the celebration of the Mass. Patriarch Cerularius responded by issuing his own excommunication of Cardinal Humbert and of the pope.

There was no way of knowing at the time that this split would endure, as it has, for more than 900 years, for it was one of many disagreements between the churches in the East and in the West.

Below: Iconoclasm – the breaking of sacred images – was a major issue. The Eastern Church often viewed images as idolatrous, but popes defended their use in worship. The Theodore Psalter of 1066 shows Nicephorus the Patriarch and the pope examining iconoclasts breaking an image.

Above: The Hagia Sophia in what is now Istanbul was the seat of the Patriarch of Constantinople, the counterpart of St Peter's in Rome.

Over previous centuries there had been theological disputes and ecclesiastical arguments over matters including the pope's claim to have primacy over other bishops, the use by Western churches of unleavened bread in the Eucharist and the relative status of Rome and Constantinople – the city of Constantinople (modern Istanbul, Turkey) had been founded by Emperor Constantine in 330 as a new capital for the Roman Empire, but Rome claimed prime importance as the place in which saints Peter and Paul were martyred and buried and the historic home of the Church.

Many popes including Gregory I 'the Great' (590–604) challenged the assumption by the Patriarch of Constantinople of the title 'ecumenical patriarch' since they felt it undermined the primacy of the pope as the inheritor of the power of St Peter. Another major matter of dispute was over whether the Holy Spirit derived from God the Father or from God the Father and God the Son together; the Latin word *filioque* ('And from the Son') was widely included in

the Creed in Western churches from at least the 8th century in a phrase specifying that the Holy Spirit 'proceeds from the Father and the Son', but was strongly opposed in Eastern churches, where the accepted form of the Creed stated that the Holy Spirit proceeds 'from the Father'.

There had even been schisms before: for example, after Pope Felix III (483–92) excommunicated Patriarch Acacius of Constantinople in 484 a schism between the two churches lasted until 519, when Pope Hormisdas (514–23) and Patriarch John II of Constantinople agreed a reconciliation. A second schism arose in 863 when Patriarch Photius of Constantinople and Pope Nicholas I the Great (858–67) exchanged excommunications after Photius attacked the papal claim to supremacy and the Western churches' use of *filioque*. The schism

Above: Gregory I the Great, third from the left in this carving from the south portal of Chartres Cathedral, emphasized the pre-eminent position of the pope above all other Christian leaders as the inheritor of the authority granted to Saint Peter.

ended in 867 on the death of Nicholas I, the assassination of Byzantine emperor Michael III and the seizing of power by Emperor Basil I who wanted to restore relations with Rome.

IMMEDIATE BACKGROUND TO THE 1054 SCHISM

Pope Leo IX (1049–54) strongly asserted the primacy of the pope over the whole Church. He also provoked the ecclesiastical authorities in Constantinople by intervening in Byzantine territories in southern Italy in an ill-fated campaign against the Normans there that ended with his being in captivity for several months. During this intervention he held a synod and appointed Cardinal Humbert Archbishop of Sicily. In 1053 Patriarch Michael Cerularius of Constantinople ordered the closing of all Latin churches in Constantinople.

In 1054 Leo wrote a forthright letter to the patriarch, in which he cited the Donation of Constantine – a forged document, then thought to be genuine, that was reputedly written in 315 or 317 by Emperor Constantine to give the pope, Sylvester I (314–35), and his successors imperial authority to govern Rome and the Western empire, power over the world's churches and primacy over the bishops of Constantinople, Antioch, Alexandria and Jerusalem. In his letter Leo claimed authority over Constantinople, which he decried as a source of heresy. Patriarch Michael replied with a letter in which he claimed the disputed title of ecumenical patriarch.

Leo sent Cardinal Humbert to Constantinople as his legate, but the patriarch refused to meet him – provoking the excommunication. In the time between Leo sending the legation and Cardinal Humbert making his dramatic gesture, Leo died in Rome; technically the excommunication, which relies on the authority of a reigning pope, was not valid.

MOVEMENTS TOWARDS RECONCILIATION

Over the ensuing centuries there were various attempts at reconciliation between the two churches, but none had a lasting effect. Pope Gregory X (1271–76) and Byzantine Emperor Michael VIII Palaeologus agreed a reunion at the Council of Lyon in 1274 but while the emperor supported the agreement the Eastern clergy would not accept it.

In 1369, also, Byzantine emperor John V Palaeologus submitted to the authority of Pope Urban V (1362–70) and the Latin Church during a visit to Rome, but the initiative came to nothing. Another reconciliation was agreed by Pope Eugenius IV (1431–47) and Byzantine Emperor John VIII Palaeologus at the Council of Ferrara in 1439 but again did not result in a reunion of the churches.

Modern efforts seem to be making genuine progress, however. In January 1964 Pope Paul VI (1963–78) met Ecumenical Patriarch Athenagoras I on the Mount of Olives in Jerusalem. The following year, on 7 December 1965, the two leaders issued a joint statement that withdrew the excommunications exchanged in 1054.

The movement towards reconciliation was further strengthened when in 2013 Patriarch Bartholomew I of Constantinople attended Pope Francis's inauguration mass. This was the first time the ecumenical patriarch of Constantinople had attended a papal installation since 1054.

Below: Leo IX justified his position by referring to the 'Donation of Constantine', the forged document in which Constantine allegedly gave the papacy imperial authority in the West.

LEO IX, 1049–54
POPE WHO LAUNCHED GREAT REFORM PROGRAMME

During the papacy of Leo IX (1049–54) the Western and Eastern churches came to the brink of the Great Schism or split that began just three months after his death and would last with only brief interruptions right through into the modern era.

BAREFOOT IN ROME

Leo IX was a great reforming pope. His driving desire was to attack and eliminate what he saw as the scourges of the church in the mid-11th century – clerical marriage, simony (the sale of spiritual benefits and church offices) and the practice of lay rulers having control of church appointments. He was himself elevated to the papacy by a lay ruler – Emperor Henry III – but he insisted that he would only accept the position if he were also freely elected by the people and clergy in Rome. He travelled to Rome and, arriving in pilgrim's clothing and barefooted, was acclaimed and elected by the people and crowned pope on 12 February 1049.

BAND OF REFORMERS

His companion on the journey to Rome was Hildebrand, a fellow reformer and a monk from Cluny, better known to history as Pope Gregory VII (1073–85). Leo brought to the centre of church affairs a small band of reformers, all gifted scholars and great administrators. In addition to Hildebrand, these included Humbert of Moyenmoutier, who became Cardinal Humbert of

Left: Leo IX flexed the muscles of the papacy in the clash with Constantinople. He believed the Donation of Constantine, which he cited, to be genuine.

Silva-Candida (see box); Frederick of Lorraine, who became the reforming pope Stephen IX; and Hugh of Remiremont, a significant figure in the reigns of Leo's successors.

One unusual feature of Leo's papacy was that the pope travelled widely as part of his programme of reform, chairing more than ten councils in France, Germany, Sicily and Italy outside Rome to reinforce strictures against simony, the marriage of clergy and other offences. In his first year in office he held a celebrated synod in Rome at Easter 1049 that renewed the requirement of celibacy for priests, then presided in person over further synods and councils at Pavia, Reims in France and Mainz in Germany. He was back in Rome for another Easter synod in 1050. In these travels he maintained contact with local churchmen and gave physical expression to the pope's primacy as leader of Christ's Church.

Below: Leo came from Eguisheim – then in Upper Alsace and part of the Holy Roman Empire, now in the Haut-Rhin department in northeastern France. His statue stands in the village square. His father, Count Hugh, was a cousin of Emperor Conrad II.

FACT BOX

Original name Bruno of Egisheim
Born 21 June 1002
Origin German — from Alsace
Date elected pope 12 February 1049
Died 19 April 1054
Key fact Oversaw build-up to Great Schism of 1054

PRISONER OF THE NORMANS

But Leo's itinerant papacy was brought to a shuddering halt when he suffered a humiliating defeat at the hands of the Normans in the Battle of Civitate in southern Italy and was then held as their prisoner for nine months.

The Normans, initially useful allies for the papacy in combatting Byzantine Greeks and Muslim Saracens in southern Italy, had begin to pose a threat to the papal states. Leo had planned to attack them in alliance with Henry III and the Byzantines but when both dropped out was left to face the Norman army with an inadequate force bolstered by Swabian mercenaries. After the battle on 18 June 1053, the pope was captive at Beneveto until March 1054.

THE GREAT SCHISM

Leo's assertion of the primacy of the pope as leader of the whole Church provoked conflict with the Eastern Church, worsened by his military intervention in the Byzantine territories of southern Italy – during which he held a synod and appointed Cardinal Humbert as Archbishop of Sicily.

Below: Leo's Easter Synod of 1050 was occupied with the controversial teaching of Berengara of Tours, who denied the doctrine of transubstantiation – according to which the bread and wine of the Mass become the body and blood of Christ.

Patriarch Michael Cerularius of Constantinople closed the Latin (that is, Western) churches in Constantinople and issued a condemnation of points of Western dogma. Leo wrote a forthright letter to Cerularius in 1054 citing the Donation of Constantine, then believed genuine, as showing that the pope should be honoured as spiritual and temporal leader of the empire.

In April 1054 he despatched to Constantinople a legatine mission under Cardinal Humbert of Silva Candida to negotiate over these differences. The pope died in Rome that same month, and did not live to see the dramatic result

Above: Pope Leo IX is taken prisoner by the Normans. He is celebrated as a saint in the Roman Catholic Church. He died before the outcome of his clash with Patriarch Michael Cerularius was known.

of the mission. For after unsatisfactory negotiations Humbert took matters into his own hands and placed a bull of excommunication against Patriarch Michael Cerularius on the altar of the Church of Hagia Sophia in Constantinople; in retaliation, the Patriarch excommunicated Humbert and his party. The split between Rome and Constantinople was made concrete.

CARDINAL HUMBERT – THE MAN WHO MADE THE EXCOMMUNICATION

Cardinal of Moyenmoutier was born in *c*.1000 in France. He joined the Benedictine monastery of Moyenmoutier in Lorraine aged 15 and rose to become its abbot. He worked with his friend Bruno of Toul to effect church reform and when Bruno became Pope, Leo IX was summoned to Rome. He was appointed Archbishop of Sicily and then Cardinal-Bishop of Silva-Candida – possibly the first Frenchman to be made

a cardinal. After serving Leo IX on a legatine mission to Constantinople – during which he delivered the bull of excommunication of Patriarch Michael Cerularius of Constantinople that effected the Great Schism between Eastern and Western Churches – he returned to Rome and served under popes Victor II and Stephen IX, for whom he was librarian of the Roman Curia. He died in Rome on 5 May 1061.

CRUSADES AND THE REFORMATION

In almost 500 years from 1054 to 1534 the papacy unleashed the crusades – holy wars principally against Muslim power in the Middle East and heretic Christians in Europe; survived almost three-quarters of a century in exile from Rome during the Avignon papacy of 1309–77; and as patrons brought the Italian Renaissance in art, architecture and learning to its full flowering. The names of Urban II, the pope who launched the First Crusade, Gregory XI, the pope who returned the papacy to Rome in 1377, and papal patrons such as Sixtus IV or Julius II resound through history. Other popes such as Paul II and Alexander VI – notorious for corruption, overweening ambition or licentiousness – demeaned the institution of the papacy and drove the church on to the rocks of the Protestant Reformation.

Left: In this period the papacy was a major patron and had the finest artists of the Italian Renaissance at its disposal. Michelangelo, Raphael and Donato Bramante discuss work on the Vatican and St Peter's Basilica with Pope Julius II, in this painting by Emile Jean Horace Vernet (1789–1863).

CHAPTER FIVE

BIRTH OF THE CRUSADES

VICTOR II TO CLEMENT III, 1055–1191

The Great Schism of 1054 between Eastern and Western churches looms large in history. Its significance is greatly enhanced for historians by its longevity – the split has lasted with minor interruptions to the 21st century. Yet in the mid-11th century there was little to distinguish this from previous fallings out between Rome and Constantinople and so for the papacy in 1054–5 it was business as usual – which meant initially a continuation of the programme of reform begun by Emperor Henry III and popes Clement II and Damasus II and carried forward with great energy by Leo IX and his successor Victor II.

Political manoeuvrings included the negotiation of a crucial alliance between the pope and the Normans in southern Italy – to protect the independence of the papacy and the Church in the face of the claims of the Holy Roman Empire. One of the greatest reforming popes, Gregory VII, stood up defiantly against Holy Roman Emperor Henry IV in the celebrated 'Investiture Controversy'. Gregory's reign was transformational in the long term: his assertion of the pope's supremacy laid the groundwork for the development of the papal monarchy in the 12th and 13th centuries. Indeed he gave his name to the whole programme of 'Gregorian Reform'.

This period also saw the birth of the crusading era: Pope Urban II called the First Crusade, resulting in the establishment of a Christian kingdom of Jerusalem and associated territories in Outremer, and this was followed before 1191 by the less successful Second and Third Crusades. By the end of this period popes were committed to using crusades as an instrument not only of holy war against Muslims in the Holy Land but also of papal policy closer to home.

Left: Entrance of the pope and Emperor Frederick I Barbarossa into Rome. Popes Hadrian IV (1154–59), Alexander III (1159–81) and successors played out their own chapters in the long-running battle between papacy and imperial power.

VICTOR II TO ALEXANDER II, 1055–73
CHURCH REFORM UNDER LEO'S SUCCESSORS

The popes who succeeded Leo IX pressed on with the programme of church reform he had begun in association with Emperor Henry III. Victor II (1055–7) was Henry's choice to succeed Leo: a German noble, he had risen to become Bishop of Eichstatt and then the emperor's chief adviser. After his consecration he shared the top table with the emperor at a council in Florence that took further measures to prevent simony and clerical marriages and he afterwards presided at synods in Lyon and Toulouse in 1055–6. On Henry's death in 1056 Victor became guardian of the infant Henry IV and adviser to the regent, Empress Agnes.

ASSOCIATION OF REFORMERS
Stephen IX (1057–8) was one of the group of reforming churchmen associated with Leo. Known as Frederick of Lorraine before becoming pope, he was the brother of Duke Godfrey of Lorraine and Leo's cousin; he had served as papal

Below: The use of fortified hilltop castles to dominate a region was key to the Normans' success across Europe. They built this castle at Caccamo, Sicily, in 1093.

Right: Norman lord Robert Guiscard, conqueror of southern Italy and Sicily, allied with Pope Nicholas II, who made him Duke of Apulia, Calabria and Sicily.

legate to Constantinople and afterwards become abbot of the major Benedictine abbey of Monte Cassino, then been made cardinal priest by Victor II. He became pope in 2 August 1058 but was already dying and survived only eight months, until 29 March 1058.

In this brief period he zealously opposed simony and clerical marriage. He worked closely with cardinals and fellow reformers Peter Damian, Humbert of Silva-Candida and Hildebrand, a monk from Cluny and important associate of Leo IX who went on himself to become a great reforming pope, Gregory VII.

When he died, the Tusculani family moved to take the papacy back from the reformers, attempting through bribery to install their own candidate John Mincius, Cardinal Bishop of Velletri, as pope. John was in power as antipope Benedict X for nine months, but cardinals loyal to the reform movement elected Gerard of Lorraine, Bishop of

Florence, as pope in his place. The antipope took to his heels and Gerard was consecrated on 24 January 1059.

LATERAN SYNOD
As Pope Nicholas II he had a short but profoundly important papal reign. Among his first acts as pope was to attempt to eliminate bribery and aristocratic manoeuvring from papal elections. He issued a decree at an Easter synod at the Lateran on 13 April 1059 to the

NORMANS IN ITALY
The Normans were originally Vikings (known as 'Northmen' and subsequently Normans). After the unsuccessful Viking siege of Paris in 886 their chieftain Rollo or Robert settled in what is now western France and established the feudal Duchy of Normandy.

Rollo's descendants' use of heavy cavalry and fortified castles, together with natural daring, cunning and ruthlessness, made them a supremely effective military force and they spread out through Europe on missions of conquest. They arrived in southern Italy and Sicily in the early 11th century, initially fighting as mercenaries in the service of local Lombard princes against Muslim Arabs and Greek Byzantine troops.

The sons of Tancred de Hauteville established themselves as major landholders in the region – Pope Nicholas II's ally Robert Guiscard was Tancred's sixth son. Guiscard built a great military reputation: he was celebrated in chronicles, and by the poet Dante in *La Divina Commedia* ('The Divine Comedy') as one of the greatest of Christian warriors, with a place in the 'Heaven of Mars'.

Right: Choral miniature of Pope Alexander II celebrating Mass at the Abbey of Cassino, Italy.

effect that each new pope should initially be chosen by the seven cardinal bishops, then approved by the other cardinals. The clergy and people would then give their assent; the emperor would confirm the election, but his right to do so was not hereditary and was subject to confirmation by each new pope at the start of a new imperial reign.

The same synod also promoted several reforms, banning simony, clerical marriage and clerical concubinage (priests living with a woman as if married); gave papal protection to pilgrims and papal backing to the *Pax Dei* ('Peace of God') movement that sought to protect church property, priests, women, merchants and pilgrims from violence.

NORMAN ALLIANCE

Nicholas's other major engagement was to make an alliance with the Norman leader Robert Guiscard, whom he invested as Duke of Apulia, Calabria and Sicily at the Council of Melfi in August

Below: The papal reign of Alexander II saw William of Normandy invade England. Alexander instructed English clergy to back his claim to the throne of England.

1059. In return Robert swore an oath of fealty to the pope and promised to help Nicholas regain lost papal territories and to maintain Nicholas in power. This new alliance provoked a clash with the German imperial court since it undermined the Emperor's claim to protect the pope and hold these parts of Italy himself. In 1060 German bishops voted that Nicholas's decrees were void and declared that he should be deposed.

The following year Nicholas died, and an antipope, Honorius II, was established in Basel with the support of the Empress Agnes. But in Italy Bishop Anselm of Lucca was elected and consecrated as Pope Alexander II with the backing of Roman troops and the support of Hildebrand. Honorius II marched on Rome but in the end lost the support of the imperial court and was deposed at a council in Mantua. Alexander held power.

NORMAN CONQUEST

As pope Alexander II pressed on with the campaign of reform, he also issued an early papal call for a crusade, against the Islamic Moors in Spain, and in 1066 gave papal blessing to Duke William of Normandy's invasion and conquest of England – issuing an edict to the English clergy that they should back William's claim to the throne.

GREGORY VII, 1073–85
THE GREAT REFORMER

Remembered as one of the most important popes of the medieval church, Gregory VII gave his papal name to the Gregorian Reform, the improvement programme begun by his close associate and mentor Leo IX (1049–54) aimed at preserving the morality of the clergy and the independence of the Church. In the 'Investiture Controversy' – a dispute over the right to appoint abbots and bishops and invest them with the symbols of their office – he twice excommunicated Emperor Henry IV in a bold statement of the papacy's renewed authority.

'HOLY SATAN'

Hildebrand was the son of a Tuscan peasant, short and unprepossessing, with a paunch belly, a thick regional accent and poor verbal delivery. He was not a great theologian or scholar, but he had immense ability and character – he could impose himself on a group by strength of his single-minded purpose. The reforming monk Peter Damian called him a 'holy Satan'.

On becoming pope he took the name Gregory as tribute to Gregory I. He brought to the position a forthright conception of the authority of the pope and the primacy of the papacy over secular governments as well as archbishops, bishops and other members of the church hierarchy. In his view, the pope could judge all and was answerable only to God. All popes, as spiritual descendants of Peter the Apostle, were saints.

FACT BOX

Original name Hildebrand
Born c.1025
Origin Tuscan
Date elected pope 22 April 1073
Died 25 May 1085
Key fact First pope to depose a crowned ruler

Above: Gregory VII. Before his election as pope he had been a major presence at the papal court through the reigns of Leo IX, Stephen IX, Nicholas II and Alexander II, pursuing their reform programme against simony, clerical marriage and concubinage.

He asserted the primacy of the pope over the kings of countries throughout Europe; many rulers – including William I of England – refused when Gregory demanded they swear an oath of fealty. His determination that he as pope rather than the ruling monarch should have authority over Investiture (appointment) of abbots and bishops brought conflict with Philip I of France and, more seriously and enduringly, with Emperor Henry IV.

CHALLENGE TO PAPAL AUTHORITY

In 1075 after Henry made appointments to the bishoprics of Milan, Fermo and Spoleto, Gregory wrote forcibly to Henry demanding that he undo the appointments and cease contact with five counsellors whom Gregory had earlier excommunicated. In January 1076 a synod in Worms declared that Gregory had forfeited his right to be pope; the bishops renounced their obedience to him and Henry declared Gregory deposed, calling on the Romans to choose a new pope.

Gregory responded by excommunicating and deposing Henry, and declaring Henry's subjects absolved of their oath of fealty. This bold act sent shock waves through the Christian world and had major consequences in Germany, where rebellious nobles met at Tribur to elect a new ruler. In the event they could not agree on a new king so decreed that Henry must promise obedience to the pope and that if he had not reconciled himself to Gregory by the first anniversary of his excommunication his throne would be considered vacant; they invited Gregory to Augsburg to determine the way forward.

PENANCE AT CANOSSA

Henry saw that he needed to act. He travelled in person to Italy and intercepted the pope at the Castle of Canossa,

Below: Papal supremacy. An 18th-century engraving imagines the moment in which Henry pays homage to Gregory at Canossa.

This proved to be nothing more than a brief truce; emperor and pope were soon at each other's throat once more. The rebels in Germany elected Rudolf of Rheinfelden as the new king on 15 March 1077, and he was crowned in May that year; then in 1078 Gregory issued a formal prohibition against lay investiture. In 1080 Gregory excommunicated Henry a second time and recognized Rudolf as his successor, but Rudolf was mortally wounded in the course of defeating Henry in a battle at the Elster river.

Henry hit back against Gregory, presiding as the synod of Brixen in south Tyrol that deposed Gregory a second time in June 1080, and nominated Archbishop Wilbert of Ravenna as the new pope. Henry gathered an army and marched on Rome, and took the city in March 1084. Wilbert was enthroned as antipope Clement III and crowned Henry emperor.

'LOVED RIGHTEOUSNESS'

Gregory, meanwhile, took refuge in Castel Sant'Angelo, from where he was rescued by his Norman ally Robert Guiscard and helped to escape into exile at Salerno. There he died, on 25 May 1085, defiant in what looked like defeat: tradition has it that on his deathbed he paraphrased words from Psalm 44, 'I have loved righteousness and hated iniquity, therefore I die in exile.' He was buried in the cathedral there.

Above: The Castle of Canossa, outside which Henry waited to do penance, is now a ruin. In the 12th century it was one of Italy's most formidable fortresses.

where he was staying with Countess Matilda of Tuscany en route to Augsburg. Gregory refused Henry entry to the castle for three full days – and the emperor, according to tradition, waited outside the whole time, barefoot in winter and wearing a penitent's hair shirt.

When he was finally admitted, Henry knelt before Gregory and begged forgiveness; Gregory absolved him and readmitted him to the Church.

INVESTITURE

The central matter in dispute between Henry and Gregory was the right to appoint or invest bishops or abbots. It had become established custom for kings and nobles to make the appointments in question, and church positions – since they often brought with them wealth and possession of land – were commonly sold. As part both of the church reform campaign against simony (the sale of church positions and spiritual benefits) and his own promotion of papal supremacy, Gregory claimed the right of investiture for the pope.

Below: A kneeling Henry IV asks Matilda and Abbot Hugh of Cluny to intervene on his behalf in his dispute with Gregory VII.

VICTOR III AND URBAN II, 1086–99
BIRTH OF THE CRUSADING ERA

Popes Victor III and Urban II had to deal with the chaotic aftermath of the era of Gregory VII. After Victor's brief rule, conducted in the face of antipope Clement III, Urban occupied the papal throne for over a decade, a reign remembered most of all for his preaching a holy war to liberate Jerusalem – and the enduring effects of the cycle of crusades that he launched.

NORMAN POWER

Gregory's reign had ended in bloodshed and disorder on the streets of Rome. Threatened by the prospect of Henry IV ensconced in the Eternal City with a puppet pope in the form of antipope Clement III, Robert Guiscard and a formidable Norman army had marched on Rome. Henry fled back to Germany

Right: Before becoming pope, Urban was prior of the abbey of Cluny in France. He consecrated the third rebuilding of the abbey.

even before Guiscard arrived; the Normans then attacked and took the city – amid scenes of brutal violence in which Rome was badly damaged by fire. Then after Gregory fled, with Guiscard's help, to Salerno and shortly afterwards died there, Desiderius – abbot of Monte Cassino – was elected pope, against his will.

POPE VICTOR III

He did not last long. Driven from Rome by supporters of antipope Clement III, he returned to the Abbey of Monte Cassino, whose development he had made his life's work. Desiderius was an

Below: Various preachers took up Urban's crusading call. Peter the Hermit, a priest from the French city of Amiens, electrified his listeners, inspiring crowds of peasants to follow him in the People's Crusade – distinct from the main crusading groups of royals and noblemen.

MONTE CASSINO

The Abbey of Monte Cassino was founded on a hilltop near the town of Cassino around 80 miles (130km) southeast of Rome by St Benedict of Nursia in 529. It was the cradle of the Benedictine Order. The Lombards sacked the abbey in 581, and the monks fled to Rome for more than 100 years. The abbey was re-established by Abbot Petronax in 718, but sacked by the Saracens in 884. Rebuilt again, it was at the height of its glory under Desiderius (Pope Victor III), who while abbot in 1058–87 presided over manuscript illumination of high quality celebrated throughout the Western World. He also oversaw grand rebuilding and exquisite mosaic work by Byzantine artists. Pope Alexander II consecrated the abbey in 1071. The abbey was again sacked by Napoleon Bonaparte's army in 1799 and severely damaged by Allied bombers in World War II, rebuilt after the war and reconsecrated by Pope Paul VI in 1964.

Below: A 13th-century fresco in the Monastero of San Benedetto in Subiaco honours the founder of the Rule of St Benedict. Benedict's monks began at Subiaco before settling at Monte Cassino.

immensely able man, who had greatly extended the abbey's territory and vastly improved its library (see box) and abbey church, and had also negotiated the highly significant alliance between the papacy and the Normans.

In the second year of his reign he emerged from Monte Cassino in a flurry of activity: he excommunicated the antipope, sent an army to Tunis where it defeated the Saracens, and with the support of the seemingly invincible Norman army marched to Rome, drove Clement III to flight and was crowned. But then he returned hastily to his abbey, where he died on 16 September 1087.

URBAN AND THE FIRST CRUSADE

The continuing struggle with Clement III delayed the election of a successor but eventually a French cardinal, Odo of Châtillon-sur-marne, was elected Pope Urban II on 12 March 1088. For some years Urban had to tread carefully in the face of the emperor's hostility but was finally established in Rome by 1094. Like his predecessors he vigorously pursued the agenda of church reform and in a series of synods passed measures against simony and clerical marriage and to reinforce papal authority in the Investiture Controversy.

One of his concerns was to improve relations with Constantinople and in time restore unity to the church and he invited Byzantine Emperor Alexius I Comnenus to send delegates to the Council of Piacenza in 1095. There Urban and the delegates heard heartrending tales of the threat to Christian holy places in the east from the Seljuk Turks. These accounts inspired Urban to call for a crusade, a holy war led by the flower of chivalric Europe to protect Christians and sacred sites in the East.

Urban made his dramatic call to arms a few months later, at a different church council, at Clermont in central France. He had originally intended to speak in the cathedral at Clermont, but after he issued a statement that he wished to

Above: Urban's sermon at Clermont unleashed a flood of violence and ushered in the crusading era that transformed relations between East and West.

speak on a matter of importance for all Christendom, the crowd that gathered was too large to fit in and he delivered his epochal sermon in a field outside the city.

On 27 November 1095, he called on the Christian warriors of the west to ride to the aid of the brothers in the east and liberate them from Turks and Arabs; he promised remission of sins (forgiveness) as a reward. According to one account of his sermon, by Robert the Monk, Urban personified the city of Jerusalem: 'From you,' he declared, 'she begs help… Take on this journey for the remission of sins, in confidence of the undying glory of God's kingdom.'

'GOD WILLS IT!'

At once a shout went up in the crowd: 'God wills it! God wills it!' Adhemar, bishop of Le Puy, stepped forward and knelt before Urban, asking to be allowed to take part in a voyage to the east: Urban appointed him leader of the crusade. Many came forward in response to his example. Thus was launched the First Crusade. Its armies captured Jerusalem on 15 July 1099, a fortnight before Urban's death in Rome.

PASCHAL II AND GELASIUS II, 1099–1119
INVESTITURE CONTROVERSY RUMBLES ON

In the pontificates of Paschal II (1099–1118) and Gelasius II (1118–19) the main issue was the continuing dispute over whether the pope or secular rulers should have the right to appoint or invest abbots and bishops. In addition – following the success of the First Crusade launched by Urban II – there were manoeuvrings over whether Jerusalem and other territories captured in the Holy Land should be papal territory or a secular state.

GENTLE CHARACTER

The antipope Clement III had hung around throughout Urban's reign, but he died shortly after Paschal was elevated to the papacy. Paschal, a gentle and good-natured man but by no means a pushover, then had to face down no fewer than three further antipopes raised by King Henry IV and his supporters – Theodoric in 1100, Aleric in 1102 and Sylvester IV in 1105 – but none of them caused significant trouble. When Henry IV again refused to budge on the

Below: Pisa Cathedral in Italy. Gelasius II consecrated the cathedral in 1118; later in the century Pope Gregory VIII was buried there.

Above: Paschal delivers the papal bull establishing the religious order of the Knights Hospitaller to the order's founder, Gerard Thom, in 1113. The first knights in the order kept a hospital in Jerusalem to care for pilgrims.

investiture issue, Paschal excommunicated him and the emperor died in Liege on 7 August 1106.

PASCHAL FAILS TO HOLD A FIRM LINE

Paschal reached a settlement on investiture with Philip I of France and Henry I of England in 1107 but the matter continued to poison relations with the German crown. The new emperor, Henry V, was every bit as intransigent as

KINGDOM OF JERUSALEM

Archbishop Daimbert of Pisa, papal legate on the First Crusade, tried to claim Jerusalem and associated lands captured in the First Crusade for the papacy. Daimbert was sent to Jerusalem in 1099 to replace the original papal legate, Adhemar of Le Puy, who had perished after contracting the plague in Antioch; he won for himself the position of Patriarch of Jerusalem. The first ruler of Jerusalem, the crusading knight Godfrey of Bouillon, was elected to power by the crusaders on 22 July 1099, but refused to be named king in the city that was the rightful possession of Jesus Christ and took the title of 'Defender of the Holy Sepulchre'. Daimbert won Godfrey's promise that on his death the territory would pass to the papacy. But when Godfrey unexpectedly died Daimbert was outmanoeuvred by Godfrey's brother Baldwin (formerly of Boulogne, now of Edessa) who seized power. Daimbert had no choice but to crown him King Baldwin I of Jerusalem on Christmas Day 1100.

his father had been, but equally was determined to be crowned emperor by the pope in Rome.

After Pope Paschal issued a formal condemnation, Henry crossed the Alps with an army and a cadre of lawyers. Pope and emperor met at Sutri, near Rome, and thrashed out an agreement under which Henry renounced his right to investiture, Paschal promised to make the German church return to the emperor all lands and rights they held from the crown and Henry would have his longed-for coronation.

When this agreement was made public there was uproar among German bishops and a popular uprising in Rome.

Above: The knights of the First Crusade capture Jerusalem in July 1099. According to the Gesta Francorum *chronicle, 'there was so much killing that the blood came up to our ankles'.*

Henry took flight and carried Paschal off as his prisoner; two months in captivity broke Paschal's resolve entirely and he gave in – restoring Henry's rights of investiture and agreeing to the coronation, which was performed in Rome on 13 April 1111.

This settlement, too, provoked a row. A papal council declared it invalid, the emperor was excommunicated by Archbishop Guido of Vienne (later Pope Callistus II) and then in 1112 Paschal tore up the agreement and in 1116 once again issued a condemnation of investiture by secular rulers. But he had lost his authority and the issue rumbled on through the pontificate of Gelasius II and into that of Callistus II (1119–24).

KNIGHTS HOSPITALLER

Amongst all these difficulties, on 15 February 1113, Paschal gave papal backing to the establishment of one of the greatest and most enduring of the chivalric orders, the Knights Hospitaller. The religious order of St John of Jerusalem had been founded under the Benedictine rule in Jerusalem in 1099, immediately after the First Crusade, by a knight or merchant named Gerard Thom – later 'Blessed Gerard'. Its members were initially guardians of a long-standing hospital for pilgrims to Jerusalem that had been founded in 600, destroyed by the Fatimids in 1010 and rebuilt by merchants from Amalfi and Salerno in 1023.

Paschal decreed that the members of the order – which his papal bull called the Hospitallers of St John of Jerusalem – should be subservient to the papacy not the King of Jerusalem. Its members soon began to offer armed escort to pilgrims and the order was established as a major military force by its second Grand Master, Raymond du Puy of Provence in the years 1120–60.

ALONE IN A COUNTRY FIELD

Gelasius II (1118–19) was never properly established as pope. He had to face an antipope, Gregory VIII, raised by Henry V; he was imprisoned and brutally beaten by Henry's supporter Censius Frangipani and was later forced by another Frangipani attack to flee Rome on horseback – after which he was found sitting alone in a country field, still wearing his papal vestments. Gelasius took to his heels and died in exile at the monastery of Cluny on 29 January 1119.

Below: The ruins of the Hospitallers' castle of Belvoir (known as the 'Star of the Jordan') stand near the Sea of Galilee in northern Israel. The castle was built by Grand Master Gilbert of Assailly in the 12th century.

CALLISTUS II, 1119–24
WELL-CONNECTED ARISTOCRAT WHO TAMED EMPEROR HENRY V

Before his election as Pope Callistus II, Guido was well established as a church reformer and forthright opponent of lay investiture (the claim by lay rulers that they had the right to appoint abbots and bishops) – as Archbishop of Vienne, he had himself excommunicated Emperor Henry V over the issue. The major achievement of his pontificate was to bring the long-running investiture dispute between pope and emperor to a successful conclusion with the signing of the Concordat of Worms in 1122.

WELL CONNECTED

Guido was an aristocrat, born the fourth son of Count William I of Burgundy and related to the German, French, Danish and English royal houses. Nominated by Pope Gelasius as his successor, Guido was elected by the cardinals who had followed the pope into exile at Cluny and then crowned Callistus II at Vienne on 9 February 1119 – and afterwards unanimously approved by the cardinals in Rome.

Below: Callistus issued the bull Sicut Judaeis *('As the Jews') in 1120. Its aim was to protect the Jews in Europe, who in the era of crusading vigour were frequently being attacked and killed.*

HENRY EXCOMMUNICATED

At once Callistus called a Church Council in Reims and sent an embassy to Henry V at Strasbourg: the emperor withdrew his support for the antipope Gregory VIII and agreed to meet Callistus at Mousson in France. But when Henry arrived at Mousson with a large army, Callistus – fearing he would be forced to make concessions – declined to meet, and then excommunicated Henry and the antipope Gregory.

Afterwards he travelled to Rome, where he was joyfully received. The antipope Gregory fled to Sutri, but with the support of a Norman army Callistus dragged the fugitive antipope from hiding and carried him back to Rome, where he was humiliated by being forced to ride through the streets

Above: Louis VI of France watching the construction of a church. At the start of Callistus's reign, Louis and most of the French barons attended the church council called by the pope at Reims.

mounted backwards on a camel. Afterwards Callistus imprisoned Gregory near Salerno and used the power of the

FACT BOX

Original name Guy/Guido of Burgundy

Born Unknown

Origin Burgundy

Date elected pope 2 February 1119

Died 14 December 1124

Key fact Settled Investiture controversy at Concordat of Worms

Above: Indulgences (guarantees that sins would be forgiven) granted to crusaders were renewed by the First Lateran Council in 1123.

Below: Emperor Henry V. Under the compromise of the Concordat of Worms he invested bishops and archbishops with secular authority; their spiritual authority came from the pope.

Normans to eliminate the threat of the Frangipani family, staunch supporters of Henry V and the imperial party.

CONCORDAT OF WORMS
Securely established in Rome, Callistus was happy to reopen negotiations on the investiture issue. These were started at Wurzburg in October 1121 and continued at Worms in September 1122. Callistus sent Cardinal Lambert of Ostia (the future Pope Honorius II) as his legate to Worms, and the papal party won a significant victory in the agreement that was finally signed off as the Concordat of Worms on 23 September 1122: the pope would invest bishops and archbishops with spiritual authority (he would invest them with ring and crosier, symbols of spiritual authority); the emperor would invest them with secular authority (he would invest them with a sceptre, a symbol of secular power). This was derived from a compromise arrangement that had been earlier established in Norman England.

In addition, the emperor guaranteed freedom of election for bishops and archbishops, while the pope granted such elections in Germany should be held in the emperor's presence and the emperor would have the right of arbitration where an election was disputed.

BASILICA OF SANTA MARIA IN COSMEDIN
Callistus called the First Lateran Council to confirm the Concordat of Worms. After this triumph, he worked to restore the territorial holdings of the papacy in Italy and to combat the power of nobles in the Campagna region. In Rome his aim was to restore peace after years of unrest dating back to Gregory VII. He worked on St Peter's and rebuilt the Basilica of Santa Maria in Cosmedin.

He settled a number of disputes in the French church, which he knew and understood so well, and ruled that his own See of Vienne should take primacy over that of Arles, ending an old dispute. He also despatched Gerard of Angouleme as papal legate to Brittany. He imposed his authority on King Henry I of England, forcing Henry under threat of excommunication to accept Thurstan as Archbishop of York.

In Germany he canonized Conrad of Constance, a 10th-century German bishop and ally of Otto I, in 1123, and sent Otto of Bamberg as his papal legate to the churches of Pomerania on the Baltic Sea, where Otto achieved many conversions and founded 11 churches.

HONORIUS II, 1124–30
SWORD-WIELDING THUGS OVERTURN A PAPAL CORONATION

Honorius II came to power amid uproar. Members of the powerful Frangipani family refused to accept the election of Cardinal Teobaldo Buccapeco, the favoured candidate of their rivals the Pierleoni family, as Celestine II: they burst into his coronation service with swords drawn and forcibly brought about the elevation to the papacy of their own

candidate, Cardinal Lamberto of Ostia. Celestine II was injured in the struggle and resigned the papacy on the spot; he is usually counted as an antipope.

The conflict did not end there. There was infighting between the factions, but at length support for Celestine dwindled and Honorius was left the only viable candidate. At this point he resigned, but was unanimously re-elected and acclaimed pope, then consecrated on 21 December 1124.

CONCORDAT OF WORMS
Cardinal Lamberto, the new Pope Honorius II, was no mere puppet candidate but an established churchman who had been made cardinal bishop of Ostia by Pope Paschal II in 1117, and accompanied Pope Gelasius II to Cluny before playing a key role in the negotiations for the Concordat of Worms as Callistus II's envoy.

Above: St Norbert of Xanten by Peter Paul Rubens. Honorius gave approval in 1126 to Norbert's founding of the Premonstratensian order – or 'White Canons'.

Unlike his aristocratic predecessor, however, he was of peasant origin, having been born in a rural community near modern Imola in the Emilia-Romagna region of Italy. He had risen through the church hierarchy through application and a forceful character, as well as great natural ability – he deserves a great deal of credit for the success of the negotiations that brought about the Concordat of Worms.

GERMAN SUCCESSION
The death of Emperor Henry V on 23 May 1125 led to a power struggle for the succession. Henry, childless, nominated his nephew Frederick Hohenstaufen but a faction of German

FACT BOX
Original name Lamberto Scannabecchi
Born 9 February 1060
Origin Romagna
Date elected pope 21 December 1124
Died 13 February 1130
Key fact Backed Lothair of Supplinburg in German succession crisis

Above: Honorius granted papal recognition to the Knights Templar, established by Hugues of Payens and Godfrey of Saint-Omer, at the Council of Troyes in 1129.

princes elected Lothair of Supplinburg, while Frederick's brother Conrad was also put forward for the succession.

Conrad marched over the Alps and was crowned King of Italy by Archbishop Anselm of Milan, but Honorius supported Lothair and backed German bishops in their excommuni-

Below: Cluny Abbey. Honorius intervened in the dispute between Pons of Melgueil and Peter the Venerable at Cluny. Peter collected materials on Islam and defended the theologian Peter Abelard.

cation of Conrad. In the end both Frederick and Conrad were forced to acknowledge Lothair as emperor.

ROGER II OF SICILY

Another succession struggle in Apulia brought Honorius into military conflict with Duke Roger II of Sicily. On the death of Duke William II of Apulia in July 1127, Roger landed from Sicily and claimed his cousin's lands, declaring that he had been nominated William's heir, but Honorius contested this, saying that William had left his territory to be part of the papal states.

Honorius built an alliance of local nobles and excommunicated Roger and even, on 30 December 1127, preached a crusade against him. In July 1128 Roger's troops and Honorius's army encountered one another on the banks of the river Bradano. Although there was no proper battle it was clear Roger had the victory: amid desertions by his own troops, Honorius secretly agreed to make Roger Duke of Apulia in return for his oath of fealty. The deal was made public the following month at Benevento.

Determined to impose his authority throughout the church, Honorius had significant conflicts with the abbots of Monte Cassino and Cluny. At Cluny he deposed the worldly Pons of Melgueil as abbot and invested the reformer Peter the Venerable in his place.

At Monte Cassino he took on the unruly abbot Oderisio di Sangro, an old enemy who reputedly made fun of Honorius's peasant origins when his back was turned: three times without success he summoned Oderisio to Rome, then finally deposed him in 1126.

TEMPLARS

In 1129 Honorius approved the establishment and rule of another major chivalric brotherhood, the Knights Templar. French knights Hugues of Payens and Godfrey of Saint-Omer had established the brotherhood to protect pilgrims in *c*.1120 and were given space by King Baldwin II of Jerusalem in the former al-Aqsa mosque on Temple Mount in Jerusalem – because this was then believed to be the site of the biblical Temple of Solomon, they took the name 'Poor Knights of Christ and the Temple of Solomon'. In 1126 Hugues of Payens came to Europe to seek backing and after drawing up a rule for the brotherhood with the help of Bernard of Clairvaux, received the Church's official blessing at the Council of Troyes in 1129.

Below: The Knights Templar kept Temple Church, near Fleet Street, London, as their headquarters. It was consecrated in 1185.

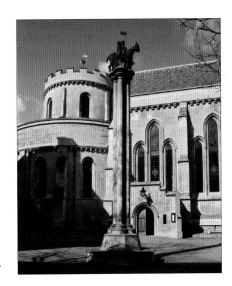

INNOCENT II TO LUCIUS II, 1130–45
PAPAL SCHISM AS RIVAL POPES DIVIDE EUROPE

The church under Innocent II (1130–43) endured a long and extremely difficult schism, with European monarchs split between backing Innocent and supporting his persistent rival, the antipope Anacletus II who ruled in direct opposition to Innocent in 1130–38.

Innocent – known before he became pope as Gregorio Papareschi, Cardinal-Deacon of St Angelo – was raised to the papacy by the power and manoeuvrings of the Frangipani clan in Rome. On the very night of his predecessor Honorius's death on 13 February 1130, the Frangipani family arranged for him to be elected by a minority of cardinals. But when they tried to present this as a *fait accompli*, the majority of cardinals – as well as many Roman nobles and people – declared it uncanonical and elected their own candidate, Papal Chancellor Cardinal Aimeric, as pope: he took the name Anacletus II.

Anacletus and his supporters – many of whom were associates of the rival Pierleoni clan – took control of the Lateran and St Peter's. Anacletus was consecrated at St Peter's while Innocent II received the same honour at a rival ceremony in the basilica of St Maria Novella. Pierleoni bribes won more and more of the city to Anacletus's side and in the end Innocent had to flee – creeping away to safety in two chartered galleys down the river Tiber.

'WELCOMED BY THE WORLD'
With the help of Bernard of Clairvaux and Norbert of Magdeburg, however, Innocent won the support of the

Above: Celestine II. In his early life he was a pupil of Peter Abelard. He backed the Knights Templar and Hospitaller, giving the latter control of a Jerusalem hospital.

monarchs of France, England and Germany to his cause – in Bernard's words, 'expelled from the City, he was welcomed by the world.' Anacletus allied himself with Roger II Duke of Apulia, whom he recognized as King of Sicily; he also had backing in Scotland, Aquitaine and the northern Italian cities.

In 1132–3 Innocent and Emperor Lothair invaded Italy and took control of all of Rome save the section occupied by Anacletus. Innocent crowned Lothair Holy Roman Emperor in the Lateran, but when Lothair returned to Germany the pope's support dwindled very quickly and he was forced to flee Rome to Pisa, where he summoned a council to condemn the antipope.

END TO THE SCHISM
Still the schism continued. Lothair invaded southern Italy in 1137 and imposed his authority – in the short term at least – on Roger II of Sicily but then, by now feeling his 71 years and keen to return home, he set off once more for Germany. He died on the way home in a peasant's hut in the Tyrol on 3 December 1137.

PETER ABELARD

A great philosopher, theologian, poet and teacher, Peter Abelard provoked great opposition in the Church and his teachings were condemned by Pope Innocent II. Abelard was also celebrated for his involvement in one of history's most resonant and tragic love affairs – his doomed entanglement with his former pupil Heloise. The son of a knight from Brittany, he gave up his inheritance and the chance of a military career to become an itinerant scholar of philosophy and theology. As a teacher in Paris, he fell in love with his pupil Heloise and together they had a son, Astrolabe, and married secretly; but then they were forced by Heloise's family to separate and enter monastic life – Abelard was even castrated. Later he became abbot of the order of nuns Heloise had founded, the Paraclete, and drew up a rule for the nuns; the couple collected their amorous and religious correspondence. Abelard became a celebrated teacher at Mont-

Above: The remains of doomed lovers Abelard and Heloise were reburied side by side in the Père Lachaise Cemetery, Paris, in the 19th century.

Saint-Genevieve near Paris, attracting pupils from all over Europe, and his wide-ranging revisions of traditional theology led to his condemnation.

Lothair's death was followed in January 1138 by that of Anacletus himself – and this more than anything brought the schism to a close. For although a replacement was elected in the form of antipope Victor IV, he was persuaded to resign by the formidable Bernard of Clairvaux just weeks later, on 29 May 1138. The Second Lateran Council in April 1139 ended the schism and excommunicated Roger of Sicily.

INNOCENT HUMBLED

But then Innocent, overconfident at these developments, almost threw it all away. After the resignation of Victor IV, Roger of Sicily had recognized Innocent as rightful pope, but Innocent refused to accept reconciliation and marched south to confront Roger in battle. On 22 July Innocent was captured at Galluccio with his cardinals and treasure. Three days later he was forced to recognize Roger as King of Sicily.

Innocent's reign was dominated by the long schism, but he did rebuild the ancient Roman basilica of Santa Maria in Trastevere, incorporating Ionic capitals taken from the ruins of either the Baths of Caracalla or the Ancient Roman Temple of Isis. During the restoration he demolished the recently completed tomb of his foe Anacletus II and replaced it with one for himself. He died in Rome on 24 September 1143.

CELESTINE II AND LUCIUS II

Before his death Innocent had quarrelled with Louis VII of France over Louis's rejection of Pierre de la Chatre as Archbishop of Bourges, and placed an interdict on the French kingdom. His successor Celestine II's brief reign (1143–4) was distinguished chiefly by the end of this difficulty – he lifted the interdict and absolved Louis, who accepted the papal candidate. Lucius II (1144–5) attempted to challenge Roger II of Sicily but was forced to accept a

Below: Innocent rebuilt the ancient Roman basilica of Santa Maria in Trastevere, and appears in this mosaic in the church at the far left.

Above: Lucius II. He backed the cause of the Empress Matilda in the English civil war known as the Anarchy. Closer to home he had to sign a humiliating truce with Roger of Sicily in 1144.

demeaning truce, and as a result of this humiliation faced an uprising in Rome led by the brother of antipope Anacletus II, Giordano Pierleoni, who declared a secular republic independent of the papacy. Lucius took arms against the rebels, but died after being hit by a heavy stone during the fighting.

EUGENIUS III, 1145–53
POPE WHO CALLED THE SECOND CRUSADE

Eugenius III was elected pope on the same day his predecessor Lucius II died, 15 February 1145, with Rome in turmoil as rebels against papal authority attempted to establish a secular republic. He was a surprising choice – a gentle, self-effacing man, a former monk of Clairvaux and pupil of the formidable Bernard of Clairvaux and subsequently abbot of the Cistercian monastery of Saints Vincent and Anastasius near Rome.

'A MERE RUSTIC'?

Bernard of Clairvaux was not impressed: he wrote to the Curia, 'May God forgive you for what you have done!' and castigated them for picking 'a mere rustic'. However, the pope was later to be roundly praised for his character by Peter the Venerable, abbot of Cluny: 'Never,' wrote Peter, 'have I found a truer friend,

Below: Louis VII of France receives Eugenius's blessing in the Basilica of St-Denis (Paris) prior to embarking on the Second Crusade. Eugenius called the crusade in 1145.

FACT BOX
Original name Bernardo da Pisa
Born not known
Origin Pisa
Date elected pope 15 February 1145
Died 8 July 1153
Key fact First Cistercian to become pope

a more sincere brother, a purer father.' It is said that throughout his pontificate he wore a Cistercian monk's habit beneath his pontifical robes.

When Eugenius tried to make his way to St Peter's to be consecrated pope he found the route blocked by the secularist rebels. Within three days he had fled Rome and thereafter spent the majority of his eight-year pontificate (1145–53) in exile.

He set about raising a new crusade to the Holy Land. On Christmas Eve 1144 the Turkish general Imad ed-Din Zengi had captured the capital of the crusader state the County of Edessa from its

Above: Inspiration pours into Hildegard of Bingen from above. Mystic, composer, author and Benedictine abbess, she was at the height of her powers in Eugenius's reign. In October 2012 Pope Benedict XVI declared her a Doctor of the Church.

Christian garrison. The news – carried to Rome by Bishop Hugh of Jabala in Syria – stunned the pope and the Christian world.

OUTREMER AND TURKISH RESURGENCE

The First Crusade had resulted in the creation of four crusader states: the County of Edessa, which was based on the city of that name (now Urfa in Turkey) and founded by Baldwin of Boulogne in 1098; the Principality of Antioch, which was founded by Bohemond of Taranto in the same year; the Kingdom of Jerusalem, which was established in 1100 when Baldwin (formerly of Boulogne, now of Edessa) was crowned King of Jerusalem; and, finally, the County of Tripoli, which was formed by Raymond of Toulouse in

1102. The four states together tended to be known as Outremer, from the French for 'overseas'.

On 1 December 1145, after less than a year on the papal throne, Eugenius issued a papal bull entitled *Quantum praedecessores* calling on Louis VII of France and his people to wage a holy war against the Turks, offering remission (forgiveness) of sins for those who took up the cross of Christ. That same Christmas Louis announced his intention to lead a crusade and won the pope's enthusiastic blessing: Eugenius reissued his papal bull on 1 March 1146 and authorized his mentor Bernard of Clairvaux to preach the crusade throughout Europe.

'CRUSADERS BEYOND COUNTING'

Bernard preached a famous sermon on 31 March 1146 at Vézelay in central France, whipping the crowd into a frenzy of enthusiasm. He wrote to Eugenius: 'I opened my mouth; I preached; and the crusaders have multiplied beyond counting.' On Christmas Day 1146 his sermon before Conrad III of Germany reduced the king to tears:

Below: The Cistercian Abbey of Sénanque in Provence, France, was founded in 1148. Eugenius was the first Cistercian to become pope and reputedly wore his monk's habit beneath his papal robes at all times.

Right: Holy Roman Emperor Frederick I Barbarossa. Eugenius agreed an alliance with him under which the exiled papacy would regain Rome but died before it could be put into effect.

Conrad, Frederick of Swabia (later Emperor Frederick I Barbarossa) and many Germans also took the cross.

Less than a quarter of a century after his death, Bernard was canonized, on 18 January 1174, by Pope Alexander III – he became the first Cistercian saint. Then in 1830 he was declared a 'Doctor of the Church' by Pope Pius VIII.

The crusade was a star-studded affair: in addition to Louis VII and Conrad III, Louis's wife Eleanor of Aquitaine (later, after her first marriage had been dissolved, Queen consort of England alongside King Henry II) and brother Robert I of Dreux also travelled along with William of Warennes, 3rd Earl of Surrey, William II, Count of Nevers and other notables. But it ended in humiliating failure, with a botched siege of Damascus, and badly damaged the reputation of Bernard of Clairvaux.

Eugenius was denounced as a 'man of blood … [and] oppressor of the innocent' by religious reformer Arnold of Brescia, a former associate of Peter Abelard and long-term enemy of Bernard of Clairvaux. After many travels, Arnold had allied himself with the secular radicals in Rome and preached

enthusiastically against the pope and cardinals. Eugenius excommunicated him in July 1148.

GERMAN ALLIANCE

Towards the end of his life Pope Eugenius formed an alliance with Emperor Frederick I Barbarossa that promised to restore Rome to the pope. In the Treaty of Constance (1153) Frederick also promised to oppose any attempts by the Byzantines to re-establish a foothold in Italy; in return, Eugenius would crown Frederick emperor in Rome. However Eugenius died, at Tivoli on 8 July 1153, before the emperor could honour his promise.

BERNARD OF CLAIRVAUX

Bernard of Clairvaux was a fervent and energetic French abbot, a major force behind the growth of the Cistercian order, an ally and key supporter of popes Innocent II and Eugenius III and a staunch opponent of what he saw as heresy. He did much to promote a personal Christian faith, with devotion to the Virgin Mary prominent. The son of Burgundian nobles, Bernard joined the Cistercian order aged 19 on the death of his mother Aleth of Montbard. In 1115 he founded a new abbey in a clearing initially named Claire Vallée (later 'Clairvaux'). In 1128 he helped formulate the rule of the chivalric order of the Knights Templar at the Council of Troyes, then in the 1130s was an indomitable force in support of the exiled Pope Innocent II. In 1146 he preached the Second Crusade with the blessing of Pope Eugenius III. Bernard died at the age of 63 on 20 August 1153. He was canonized in 1174.

HADRIAN IV, 1154–9
THE ONLY ENGLISH POPE

After the brief reign of Anastasius IV (1153–4), the extremely able Englishman Nicholas Breakspear came to the papal throne as Hadrian IV (1154–9). He built an important alliance with Emperor Frederick I and with his help finally eliminated that long-term enemy of the papacy, Arnold of Brescia.

FROM ST ALBANS TO ROME

Hadrian IV (1154–9) is the only English pope to date. Born Nicholas Breakspear, he grew up near St Albans in Hertford-shire, southeast England, and became a canon regular of St Rufus near Arles, southern France, eventually becoming abbot. Known as a strict disciplinarian, he was a very good speaker and also it is said, an extremely good-looking man. Eugenius III appointed him cardinal bishop of Albano in 1150 and then sent him as papal legate to Scandinavia in 1152, where he won such a great repu-tation that on his return to Rome he was elevated to the papacy.

Once in power he moved quickly against Arnold of Brescia, who remained a thorn in the side of the papacy. He ordered Arnold to leave Rome, then when Arnold ignored the order and

Above: England's only pope – to date. Hadrian IV was born Nicholas Breakspear in Abbots Langley, Hertfordshire. He acted swiftly and ruthlessly against Arnold of Brescia.

Cardinal Guido of Saint Pudenziana was killed by Arnold's followers, placed the city of Rome under an interdict. It was just before Palm Sunday 1155. All the churches of Rome would be closed over Easter, depriving Rome of the income generated by countless pilgrims. The people protested; Arnold and his cronies were expelled; the interdict was lifted. On Easter Sunday Pope Hadrian cele-brated Mass at the Lateran.

ALLIANCE WITH FREDERICK

Hadrian next sent legates to Frederick I Barbarossa, who had crossed from Germany into Italy and been crowned King of the Lombards at Pavia. The legates asked for help in apprehending Arnold of Brescia. Frederick delivered the rebel into their hands: Arnold was hung, then his body was burned and his ashes flung into the Tiber.

Hadrian and Frederick then met at Campo Grosso near Sutri. The meeting was almost over before it began: Frederick refused the traditional act of respect, whereby the emperor led the pope's

> **FACT BOX**
> **Original name** Nicholas Breakspear
> **Born** *c.*1100
> **Origin** Abbots Langley, Hertfordshire
> **Date elected pope** 4 December 1154
> **Died** 1 September 1159
> **Key fact** Made alliance with Frederick I

horse by the bridle and held his stirrup while the pope dismounted; in retalia-tion, Hadrian refused to give Frederick the traditional kiss of peace. A brief stand-off ended when Frederick gave way. They agreed an alliance that essen-tially reiterated the terms of the Treaty of Constance of 1153: Frederick would defend papal interests; the pope would excommunicate enemies of the empire; neither side would negotiate independ-ently with the Byzantines, Sicily or the Senate of Rome; and Hadrian would crown Frederick Emperor in Rome.

Below: Byzantine Emperor Manuel Comnenus invaded Italy during Hadrian's reign, in 1155. Papal forces allied with the Byzantines against Norman Sicily.

> ### ANASTASIUS IV – PEACEMAKER
>
> Anastasius IV (1153–4) was already around 80 years old when he was elected pope on the death of Eugenius III. He lasted less than 18 months. He was a peacemaker. Roman-born and formerly the cardinal bishop of Sabina, he had served as Innocent II's vicar in Rome during that pope's long exile; he used his local experience to estab-lish some much-needed amity in relations with the republicans. He spent freely on restoring the Lateran Palace and the Pantheon.

Above: Frederick I rides into Rome. Hadrian IV crowned Frederick Holy Roman Emperor on 18 June 1155 in St Peter's Basilica.

CORONATION VIOLENCE

They acted quickly to forestall opposition from the Senate in Rome to the coronation. Hadrian performed it with little fanfare early in the morning of Saturday 18 June 1155. It was followed by brutal fighting between Frederick's German troops and the republicans that left 1,000 Romans dead and 600 captive; even so, parts of the city remained barricaded against the emperor, so Frederick and Hadrian – not prepared to mount a siege – retreated.

FRIENDS NO MORE

Relations between emperor and pope began to sour over the Normans of southern Italy. Hadrian hoped that Frederick would march south to humble King William I 'the Bad' of Sicily, who had succeeded Roger II in 1154, but Frederick returned to Germany. When Hadrian refused to recognize William as king and then excommunicated him, the Normans flexed their military muscles in the south. The treaty that brought peace, signed at Benevento in June 1156, granted William greatly increased

territory and papal recognition of his kingship in return for swearing on oath to acknowledge the pope as feudal suzerain (overlord), and agreeing to pay an annual tribute.

Granting William territories that Frederick viewed as his own further aggravated the imperial-papal relationship, which came almost to breaking point after a letter from Hadrian, read aloud in the emperor's presence at the Diet of Besançon in 1157, appeared to suggest that the emperor held his lands from the pope as a feudal vassal from his lord. Historians disagree as to whether this was deliberate or a slip of the pen;

in any case, Hadrian was forced to backtrack – or, at least, explain his meaning more carefully – but the row rumbled on; he even prepared to excommunicate Frederick, but died unexpectedly at Agnani on 1 September 1159 before he could implement his decision.

Below: Arnold of Brescia, a reforming canon who denounced Eugenius III as 'an oppressor of the innocent', is viewed as a precursor of the Reformation. Hadrian oversaw his capture and execution. He had Arnold's ashes thrown into the Tiber to prevent his burial place from becoming celebrated.

ALEXANDER III TO CLEMENT III, 1159–91
STRUGGLES AGAINST FREDERICK I AND HIS SON HENRY VI

The poor relationship between the papacy and the Holy Roman Empire caused many difficulties in the reigns of the popes who succeeded Hadrian IV – from Alexander III (1159–81) to Clement III (1187–91).

The first, Alexander III, faced the challenge of a series of antipopes backed by Emperor Frederick I from the start of his reign. He fled to France, where in 1162–5 he won the recognition of Louis VII of France and Henry II of England. Whilst in Paris, he laid the foundation stone for one of the world's greatest and most evocative buildings, the Cathedral of Notre Dame.

LOMBARD LEAGUE

Alexander returned to Rome briefly in 1165, but the following year he was forced into exile again in Benevento; from his base there, he oversaw the formation of the Lombard League, an alliance of northern Italian cities against the emperor. This alliance won a major victory over Frederick at Legnano in 1176, paving the way for the Peace of Venice (1177) under which Frederick finally recognized Alexander as pope.

Above: Pope Lucius III. Lucius took a tough line with heretics in 1184 in Ad abolendam ('On Abolition').

LAWYER-POPE

In 1179 Alexander presided over the Third Lateran Council (1179) that condemned heresies, promoted education and extended to all cardinals the right to elect popes (see box). Before becoming pope Alexander had been a professor of law at the University of Bologna. He was a shrewd and intelligent diplomat, the first of a series of lawyer-popes.

Lucius III (1181–5) also endured difficult relations with Frederick I and in 1185 refused to crown Henry VI as Frederick's designated successor. Lucius presided over the Synod of Verona in 1184 that imposed excommunication on all heretics and those who protected them.

Under Urban III (1185–7) conflict with the emperor became more open. In 1186 Frederick's son Henry VI married Constance, daughter and heir of Roger II of Sicily, at a stroke undoing the papacy's strategy of building an alliance with Norman Sicily against the empire. The marriage was performed in Milan by the Patriarch of Aquileia, who also afterwards crowned Henry King of Italy; outraged, Urban excommunicated the patriarch and the bishops who had assisted him.

When Urban also clashed with Frederick over elections to the archbishopric of Trier, Frederick sent Henry to

Below: In the Battle of Hattin in July 1187 Salah al-Din Yusuf ibn Ayyub (Saladin) delivered a crushing blow to the army of the Kingdom of Jerusalem. In the same year Saladin took Jerusalem herself.

CARDINALS

The name 'cardinal' comes from the Latin *cardo*, meaning 'pivot', and was first applied to the priests serving the 28 titular churches of Rome, who were also attached to the papal basilicas – of St Peter's, St John Lateran, S Paolo fuori le mura and S Maria Maggiore; they were seen as pivots between the pope and the parishes of Rome. A synod of 769 established that only a cardinal could become pope and then in 1059 under Pope Nicholas II cardinals were granted the right to elect the pope. Under Urban II (1088–99) the cardinals were organized in

a college and accepted as second only to the pope in three ranks – cardinal-priests, cardinal-deacons and cardinal-bishops. The right of election – in practice limited to cardinal-bishops – was extended to all cardinals in 1179 at the Third Lateran Council. A two-thirds majority was required. The right to wear a red hat would be granted to cardinals in 1245 by Pope Innocent IV. Only the pope can create a cardinal. Today cardinals are granted the title 'Eminence' and are considered to be princes of the church. They are the pope's main counsellors.

Above: Alexander III presents a sword representing political power to Sebastiano Ziani Doge of Venice. Ziani hosted Alexander, Frederick I Barbarossa and William II of Sicily for the signing of the Treaty of Venice in 1177.

invade the papal states. Urban prepared to excommunicate the emperor but died before he could carry it through.

WAR IN THE EAST

Also in Urban's reign, on 4 July 1187, the Christian knights of the Kingdom of Jerusalem suffered a devastating defeat at the hands of the Ayyubid general Salah al-Din Yusuf ibn Ayyub – or Saladin – that effectively wiped out the kingdom's military capability and made inevitable Saladin's capture of Jerusalem later that year. Urban reputedly died of grief on hearing the news.

In the course of his very brief reign (21 October to 17 December 1187) Gregory VIII preached a Third Crusade, issuing on 29 October 1187 the bull *Audita tremendi*. This was in response to the defeat at Hattin and before the

news of Saladin's capture of Jerusalem came through.

Under Clement III (1187–91) crusading sermons won the support of Henry II of England, Philip II of France and Frederick I himself for the holy war. Frederick departed first, in May 1189, won a major victory over the Seljuk Turks but then died on 10 June 1190 crossing the river Saleph (now called the Göksu, in Turkey) and the German arm of the crusade petered out. Henry II died before he could honour his vow but Philip II and Henry's son Richard I did embark in July 1190. Richard inflicted a major defeat on the previously invincible Saladin at the Battle of Arsuf, but the crusade ended in a negotiated settlement that did not deliver possession of Jerusalem.

PEACE IN ROME

Clement was a Roman by birth and in his pontificate succeeded in making peace with Roman republicans, ending a decades-long dispute with the papacy. Under the agreement the citizens of Rome elected their own magistrates but

the pope could nominate the governor of the city. At the end of his reign, conflict with the empire flared up again after Clement bestowed Sicily on Count Tancred of Lecce, in defiance of Henry VI who claimed the territory through his wife Constance. Henry led an army into Italy but Clement died before the issue could be resolved.

Below: An image from the 15th-century Le Miroir Historial by Vincent de Beauvais shows Thomas a Becket meeting Alexander III in France. Becket was murdered in Canterbury in 1170 and canonized by Alexander in 1173.

CHAPTER SIX

BIRTH OF THE MENDICANT ORDERS

CELESTINE III TO BENEDICT XI, 1191–1304

The Fourth Lateran Council of November 1215 issued no fewer than 72 canons against heresy, while also clarifying crusading privileges, encouraging education and establishing standards for the clergy. The defence of the faith and fight against heresy was at the forefront of papal activity in these years, and lay behind successive popes' enthusiasm for crusading. The fight to maintain orthodoxy also inspired the foundation by Gregory IX of the papal inquisition to combat heresy and the support of Innocent III and Honorius III for the mendicant orders of the Dominicans and the Franciscans.

By the start of Innocent III's pontificate in 1198 the papacy had despatched two crusades to the Holy Land: the First Crusade, called by Urban II, had resulted in the capture of Jerusalem and establishment of the crusader territories known collectively as Outremer; the Second, called by Eugenius III after the capture by Turks of the capital of the crusader territory of the County of Edessa, had been a disastrous failure. Despite this disappointment, Innocent III was committed to the use of crusading as an instrument of papal policy, not only calling the Fourth Crusade but also launching a whole series of crusades within Europe – against Muslims, heretics and even fellow Christians who were opponents of papal policy. Innocent called crusades against Markward of Anweiler who was challenging papal policy in southern Italy and Sicily; against pagans in the Baltic region; against Cathar heretics in southern France; and against the Muslim Almohad caliphs in Spain. Then in 1213 he called a Fifth Crusade to the Holy Land. He reiterated the call at the Fourth Lateran Council in 1215 and when he died in Perugia the following year he was trying to promote the crusade.

Left: Innocent III grants approval of the regula prima *for the new Franciscan order to Francis and his first group of monks in 1210. The fresco by Giotto is in the Upper Church at Assisi.*

CELESTINE III, 1191–8
CROWNED THE TROUBLESOME EMPEROR HENRY VI

Like many of his predecessors, Celestine III endured a turbulent relationship with the Holy Roman Emperor – particularly difficult in his case because he was dealing with the ruthless and violent Henry VI. Remarkably, he prevailed upon Henry to support his call for a new crusade, although Henry did not travel on the crusade and it petered out to nothing. However the pope was successful in supporting the chivalric orders and confirmed the new order of the Teutonic Knights.

LONG CHURCH CAREER

The first member of the Orsini family of Rome to become pope, Giacinto Bobo-Orsini had been a cardinal for 47 years when he was elected to the papacy as Celestine III on 30 March 1191. He was in his 85th year. As a young man, he had been a student and friend of that remarkable monk and teacher Peter Abelard, and had then been a legate to Germany, Spain and Portugal.

Above: Celestine grants the Ospedale di Santa Maria della Scala of Siena its independence in 1442. The fresco commemorating the event was painted by Domenico di Bartolo.

Below: England's great crusading king: Richard I. Henry VI's imprisonment of Richard caused an international incident and led to Henry's excommunication.

Archbishop Thomas a Becket – King Henry II of England's obdurate opponent – held Bobo-Orsini to be his most trustworthy friend in the Roman Curia.

Despite this long ecclesiastical service, Giacinto was only a deacon and so was ordained a priest shortly after his election, on Holy Saturday 13 April 1191, and then was consecrated a bishop on Easter Day 14 April.

CORONATION

He inherited a pressing problem with Emperor Henry VI who had marched into Italy to enforce his claim to Sicily through his wife Constance (daughter and heir of Roger II of Sicily). This was despite the fact that Celestine's predecessor Clement III had granted Sicily to Constance's nephew Count Tancred of Lecce (an illegitimate son of Constance's brother Roger). In Rome on 15 April 1191 Celestine crowned Henry and Constance emperor and empress.

Pressing southwards to put Tancred in his place, Henry besieged Naples, but a revolt in Germany by Henry the Lion,

---

FACT BOX

Original name Giacinto Bobone
Born *c.*1106
Origin Rome
Date elected pope 30 March 1191
Died 8 January 1198
Key fact Confirmed military order of the Teutonic Knights

Above: A miniature from the Liber ad honorem Augusti *('Book in Honour of the Emperor') by Peter of Eboli shows Henry VI entering Rome and being crowned as emperor by Celestine.*

Duke of Saxony and Bavaria, forced him to lift the siege and march home. Henry later got his way: in 1194 after the death of Tancred left the crown of Sicily in the hands of a boy, William III, Henry met scant resistance as he surged into Palermo and was crowned King of Sicily on Christmas Day.

EXCOMMUNICATED

In the interim, Henry went far beyond accepted boundaries of behaviour in imprisoning King Richard I of England who had been captured by Duke Leopold of Austria (an enemy of the English king after a quarrel on the Third Crusade at Acre) as he was making his way home from the Third Crusade. Henry kept Richard in jail for months before ransoming him for the vast amount of 150,000 silver marks. In 1193

Right: Celestine III, seen here consecrating the first bishop of Viterbo, excommunicated both Henry VI and Alfonso IX of Leon.

Celestine excommunicated Henry for this unprecedented act in imprisoning a returning crusader and set about trying to enforce repayment of the ransom.

ENTHUSIASM FOR A CRUSADE

In 1195 Celestine called a new crusade. According to an account by English chronicler Ralph of Diceto, Clementine declared that the limited success of the most recent holy war should not prevent Christians from staying strong in their faith that God would 'instruct their hands in battle'; he promised a plenary indulgence (full forgiveness of sins) 'and afterwards eternal life'.

Surprisingly Henry VI acted on this call. According to some sources, he wanted to win Celestine's favour so that the pope would crown Henry's son Frederick II. Whatever the reason, a German crusade departed – but without Henry – in spring 1197. The troops landed at Acre and occupied Beirut and Sidon but Henry VI did not join them because he died while campaigning in Sicily in September 1197, aged 32, and the crusade faded away. This minor campaign is not given a crusade number by historians.

Celestine was forthright in his support of the crusading orders, notably the Knights Templar and the Hospitallers. Moreover in 1192 he approved the establishment of a new military order, the Teutonic Knights, who had established a brotherhood at Acre.

In his last years Celestine attempted to abdicate and to nominate Cardinal Giovanni di San Paolo as his successor but the cardinals would not permit this and Celestine continued as pope until his death in Rome on 8 January 1198 at the age of around 92.

INNOCENT III, 1198–1216
THE MOST POWERFUL POPE OF THE MIDDLE AGES

Innocent III was the most important pope of the Middle Ages, a major church reformer who presided over the Fourth Lateran Council of 1215, a notable legal mind who developed significant teachings on papal authority and expanded the pope's power in the papal states, a forthright defender of the faith who called both the Fourth and the Fifth Crusades as well as a series of holy wars against pagans, heretics and Muslims in Europe.

A nephew of Pope Clement III, Lothar of Segni (the future Innocent III) was from an aristocratic Roman family. As a young man he studied in Paris under Peter of Corbeil and Peter the Chanter, the leading theologians of the day, and alongside Englishman Stephen Langton, whom he later appointed Archbishop of Canterbury. Afterwards he studied law at the University of Bologna. He was

Below: Innocent had a dream in which he saw two men – said to be Francis of Assisi and Dominic Guzman – holding up the Basilica of St John Lateran in Rome. He understood the Franciscan and Dominican orders would support the Church.

intelligent, learned, serious-minded and a theologian of some merit. His theological tract *De miseria condicionis humane* ('On the Misery of the Human Condition') was widely popular.

MARKED BY THE HOLY SPIRIT
He was still relatively young, aged 37, when he was elected pope – on the very day that his predecessor, the 92-year-old Celestine III, died. Tradition has it that when he was elected three doves (symbols of the Holy Spirit) were flying around the room, and that the whitest of the three flew to the newly elected pope and landed alongside his right hand.

Innocent moved quickly to re-establish papal authority in Rome, building a military fort in the city, the Torre dei'Conti, and asserting his precedence over the leading nobles and ministers. He also set out to safeguard and expand the papal states, taking advantage of the opportunity presented by the death in 1197 of Emperor Henry VI. He despatched papal legates to cities of central Italy, many of which declared loyalty to the papacy.

SUN AND MOON
A letter he sent in 1198 to the rectors of these cities contained a striking image of papal authority: he likened secular princes to the Moon and the papacy to the Sun. Both are created and maintained by God: in the same way that the Moon reflects the light of the Sun, secular authorities draw their dignity and status from the authority of the pope.

In expanding and consolidating the papal states, Innocent established the pope as a major secular prince in central Italy. Following the death of Henry VI his widow Constance ruled Sicily on behalf of her son and Henry's heir, the

Above: Otto of Brunswick is expelled. Innocent withdrew his backing of Otto in the imperial succession dispute and plumped for the eventual emperor, Frederick II.

Above: This fresco of Innocent III is in the Lower Church of St Benedict's Monastery in Subiaco. Innocent donated funds to the monastery in 1203.

four-year-old Frederick II. Constance died in 1198 but before her death appointed Innocent Frederick's guardian. Innocent regained papal rights in Sicily that had been lost to William I of Sicily in the time of Pope Hadrian IV.

Two candidates disputed the succession – Philip of Swabia and Otto of Brunswick. Innocent backed Otto's claim but after Philip was murdered in a feud, Otto backtracked on an earlier agreement with Innocent and attempted to retake former imperial territory in Italy and Sicily. Innocent excommunicated him and gave his full backing to Frederick.

In 1214 Otto's claim evaporated after he and his ally King John of England were defeated in the Battle of Bouvines against King Philip II Augustus of France. Frederick was now the sole candidate. Innocent took advantage of this dispute to make a statement of the pope's right to judge candidates in a disputed imperial election, a statement that became part of canon law.

CRUSADES

The Third Crusade had not resulted in the reconquest of Jerusalem, and in August 1198 Innocent issued a new call

to arms, promising a papal indulgence (for the forgiveness of sins) and imposing a tax on clergy of one-fortieth of their annual revenue for a year to help raise funds. But the resulting Fourth Crusade (1202–4) spiralled out of Innocent's control, diverting first to Zara in Hungary (modern Zadar in Croatia) and then to Constantinople. The city was sacked amid degrading scenes of murder, rape and looting in April 1204.

But this did not deter Innocent from crusading. He launched a whole series of crusades within Europe – against opponents of papal policy as well as against heretic Christians and Muslims. In the course of the holy war of 1212 against the Muslim Almohad caliphs in Spain, crusader knights fought alongside the armies of Sancho VII of Navarre, Peter II of Aragon and Alfonso VIII of Castile to win victory over the Muslims at the Battle of Las Navas de Tolosa. Then in 1213 he called a Fifth Crusade.

REFORM

Innocent reformed the curia and the papal judicial system, centralizing church institutions and reinforcing the pope's supremacy within the church hierarchy: he reiterated the subordination of bishops to the pope, and insisted only the pope could agree movements, resignations and removals of bishops. He encouraged the Franciscans and Dominicans. Among the

measures of the Fourth Lateran Council of 1215 was one defining the Real Presence in the Mass, another requiring Christians to confess their sins and receive Holy Communion at least once a year and another banning clerics from taking part in trial by ordeal. Less than a year after the close of the Council, Innocent died suddenly, aged just 55, from malaria in Perugia on 16 July 1216.

Below: Francis of Assisi. Innocent gave his backing to Francis's new monastic order – which became the Franciscans – in an audience on 16 April 1210.

CRUSADES AGAINST ENEMIES OF THE PAPACY

For five centuries, beginning in 1096 and lasting until the end of the 16th century, popes sent Christian armies to battle in crusades (holy wars) against Muslims, pagans and heretic Christians.

Historians number nine crusades, beginning with the First Crusade (1096–9) that resulted in the capture of Jerusalem from Fatimid Muslims, and ending with the Ninth Crusade (1271–2) in which the future King Edward I of England made a few territorial gains. These were principally fought against Muslim power in the region of the Holy Land and in Egypt.

In addition to the nine numbered crusades, there were many other smaller crusades in the years 1096–1271 and several other campaigns promoted as crusades after 1271 – at least until the Battle of Lepanto (1571), a victory for the Christian 'Holy League' (of the papal states, Spain, Venice, Genoa, the Duchy of Savoy and the Knights of Malta) over the Ottoman Empire's fleet; the triumph was attributed to the Blessed Virgin Mary and celebrated by Pope Pius V (1566–72) with the declaration of the Feast of Our Lady of Victory.

NINE CRUSADES

When he called the First Crusade at Clermont in France in November 1095, Pope Urban II likened the possession of Jerusalem by Seljuk Turks to the taking 'into slavery of the holy city of Christ'. (The Seljuk Turks held the city at this time, but in 1098, while the crusaders were en route from Europe, were ousted by Fatimid Muslims so that when the crusaders took Jerusalem it was from the Fatimids.) He personified Jerusalem and declared 'from you, she asks for help!' His sermon produced a wildly enthusiastic response – the crowd chanted 'God wills it!' 'God wills it!' and surged forward to volunteer.

Two expeditions embarked – one popular, known as the People's Crusade; and one noble, the Princes' Crusade, consisting of no fewer than five armies led by (among others) Godfrey, Lord of Bouillon and Raymond, Count of Toulouse. The survivors of these groups joined forces in Constantinople and eventually after many trials, battles and sieges captured Jerusalem.

In the wake of the crusade, four Christian states were established in Palestine and Syria, in what came to be known as Outremer (from the French for 'overseas'): the County of Edessa, the Principality of Antioch, the Kingdom of Jerusalem and the County of Tripoli. This territory survived in various forms until 1291 and was the inspiration for a whole series of crusading expeditions to the Holy Land and to North Africa.

SECOND TO NINTH CRUSADES

The Second Crusade (1147–9), called by Pope Eugenius III (1145–53) following the capture of Edessa by Muslim forces, ended with a humiliating failure to capture Damascus. The Third Crusade (1189–92) was called by Pope Gregory VIII (pope 21 October to 17 December 1187) after the army of the Kingdom of Jerusalem suffered a heavy defeat in the Battle of the Horns of Hattin that led to Muslim general Saladin's subsequent capture of Jerusalem. It ended in a negotiated settlement that did not deliver the hoped-for retaking of Jerusalem.

The Fourth Crusade (1202–4) was called by Pope Innocent III (1198–1216) with the intention of assaulting the Holy Land by way of Egypt, but the city of Venice – which provided the crusaders' fleet – diverted the campaign against its enemies in the Christian city of Zara and the campaign afterwards degenerated into the sacking of Constantinople. The Fifth Crusade (1217–21) attacked Muslim power bases in Egypt but achieved little; however, the Sixth Crusade (1228–9) – led by Holy Roman Emperor Frederick II after he had been excommunicated by Pope Gregory IX (1227–41) following a quarrel – succeeded, through diplomacy and

Left: Pope Urban II preaching the First Crusade to Philip I and assembled knights, noblemen and cardinals in France, 1095.

not through military campaigning, in regaining possession of Jerusalem, Nazareth and Bethlehem.

Jerusalem fell to the Khwarazmian Turks in 1244, and King Louis IX of France led the Seventh Crusade (1248–54) in response: another attack on Egypt and another desperate humiliation in which Louis was captured and ransomed at vast expense. Louis then led the Eighth Crusade in 1270: embarking for Syria, it diverted to attack Tunis in North Africa and there Louis died either of dysentery or bubonic plague; the crusade petered out. The Ninth Crusade (1271–2) led by Prince Edward of England (the future King Edward I) achieved very little.

CRUSADE INDULGENCES

In calling the First Crusade, Pope Urban II promised those who took part a plenary indulgence that freed them from all temporal punishment for their sins. In the medieval church an individual who had sinned could gain God's forgiveness through genuine repentance and confession but still faced a temporal punishment for the sins; the tradition had developed by which the Church could offer a partial indulgence (waiving part of the punishment) to those who gave money, supported the poor through alms giving or performed a required amount of penance but Urban's speech now offered a plenary or full indulgence. He said, 'Take on this journey for the remission of sins, in confidence of the undying glory of God's kingdom.'

In the ensuing centuries, many popes called wars that offered full crusade indulgences for those who took part in a holy war, and a case can be made that all these wars should be counted as crusades. They include campaigns against Muslims in Europe: in the long struggle against Islamic power in the Iberian Peninsula, the Reconquista – which lasted from the arrival in Spain of Muslim Arabs and Berbers in the late 8th century until 1492, when the armies of Ferdinand and Isabella of Aragon and

Castile conquered the city of Granada, the last territory in the peninsula held by Muslims – a succession of campaigns were declared crusades.

They include wars against Christians viewed as heretics – Pope Innocent III (1198–1216) called a crusade against the Cathars or Albigensians of southern France and no fewer than five crusades were launched in 1430–2 in Bohemia against the followers of university lecturer and preacher Jan Hus; Pope Sixtus V (1585–90) offered crusading privileges to the sailors of the Spanish Armada of 1588 – since he viewed the war of Roman Catholic Spain against Protestant England as a crusade.

CRUSADES AGAINST PAGANS

Others were called against pagans in northern Europe – in 1147 Eugenius III (1145–53) offered full crusade indulgences to those fighting against the pagan Wends in the Baltic region. Crusades were also called to further papal interests closer to home – for example in 1127

Above: Gregory IX quarrelled with, and indeed excommunicated, Emperor Frederick II at the time of the Sixth Crusade.

Pope Honorius II (1124–30) called a crusade against King Roger II of Sicily and in 1199 Pope Innocent III (1216–27) declared a crusade against Markward of Anweiler in Sicily.

Below: Carcassonne in southern France was besieged in 1209, early in the Albigensian Crusade against the Cathars.

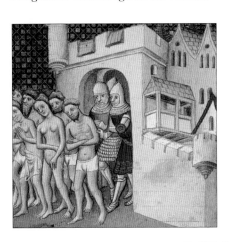

HONORIUS III, 1216–27
CRUSADING POPE WHO LAUNCHED THE MENDICANT ORDERS

Following the death of Innocent III at Perugia on 16 July 1216 a new pope was quickly elected. Cencio Savelli was consecrated Pope Honorius III in Perugia on 24 July and crowned in Rome on 31 August. Before becoming pope, Savelli had served under Clement III and Celestine III as treasurer of the Roman Church and had compiled in 1192 the *Liber Censuum Romanae Ecclesiae* ('Census Book of the Roman Church'), an eight-volume record of ecclesiastical revenues since the year 492. Historians rely on this as a key resource for the economics of the Church in the Middle Ages. Savelli had served as tutor to the future Holy Roman Emperor Frederick II. He was already elderly and rather weak when elected pope.

FACT BOX
Original name Cencio Savelli
Born 1148
Origin Roman
Date elected pope 18 July 1216
Died 18 March 1227
Key fact Launched Fifth Crusade; approved Dominicans and Franciscans

CRUSADING FERVOUR

Pope Honorius set about bringing to fruition his predecessor Innocent III's plans for a new crusade to the Holy Land. The first armies, under Leopold VI of Austria and Andrew II of Hungary, departed for Acre on schedule but their campaign achieved little beyond the capture of a few sacred relics, and the main contingent of crusaders diverted to attack the territories of the Muslim Ayyubids – descendants of Saladin – in Egypt in 1218. Meanwhile Honorius was frustrated by the refusal of his former pupil, Frederick, to honour his promise to go on crusade to the Holy Land.

The campaign in Egypt got off to a promising start, and at one point Ayyubid sultan al-Kamil offered the crusaders possession of Jerusalem, its associated kingdom and the Relic of the True Cross (on which Christ was said to have been crucified), which had been in Ayyubid hands since Saladin took it in the Battle of the Horns of Hattin (1187). But the crusaders did not accept the offer because the papal legate Pelagius determined Jerusalem could not be bartered over. In the end the campaign petered out in abject failure.

Honorius crowned his former pupil Holy Roman Emperor in Rome in 1220. He continued to put pressure on Frederick to lead a crusade, and in 1223 reached an agreement under which the

Below: Francis was known for his preaching and for demonstrating his faith in the way he lived. He reputedly said 'Preach the gospel at all times; when necessary, use words.'

Left: Francis of Assisi preaches a sermon to Honorius III. Honorius gave formal approval to the Franciscans' code in 1223. This magnificent Giotto fresco can be seen in the Upper Church of the Papal Basilica of St Francis of Assisi.

widowed Frederick took the 11-year-old heir to the crown of Jerusalem, Isabella, as his new wife and promised to lead a crusade – as King of Jerusalem – in 1225. Yet still Frederick delayed, and Honorius III died in Rome in March 1227 before he could see his plans bear fruit. Frederick did finally embark for the Holy Land in June 1228 and in the course of the Sixth Crusade regained control of Jerusalem.

COMBATTING ENEMIES

Honorius also carried on his predecessor's crusading work in fighting Muslim Almohads in Spain and heretic Cathars (later called Albigensians) in southern France. In Spain Honorius called a crusade in 1218-19 to build on the success of Innocent III's 1212 crusade. In southern France a military campaign against the Cathars had been under way since 1209, but after initial successes had suffered setbacks at the hands of resurgent rebels; Honorius persuaded the French king, Louis VIII to lead a new campaign in 1226 that recaptured many towns and castles including Avignon.

THE MENDICANT ORDERS

Honorius III engaged a new force in the fight against heresy with his approval of the Order of Preachers (later called the Dominicans), founded by Spanish priest Dominic Guzman to preach the Gospel and combat heretical beliefs. Honorius gave members of the new order, which was officially approved on 22 December

1216 under papal bull *Religiosam vitam*, a place of residence in Rome, first at the convent of San Sisto Vecchio and then at the Basilica of Santa Sabina.

On 29 November 1223 another bull, *Solet annuere*, gave papal approval to the rule of the Franciscans. Francis of Assisi had established the Order of the Friars Minor (Franciscans) and drawn up a primitive code for his early members in 1209; this won the approval of Innocent III. Later, he appealed to Honorius for help and the pope appointed Cardinal Ugolino (later Pope Gregory IX) protector of the order. Francis then drew up a fuller code, which Honorius approved in 1223. Three years later Honorius approved the Carmelite Order under his bull *Ut vivendi normam* of 30 January

Above: Honorius gives his blessing to Dominic Guzman and his newly formed Dominican monastic order, in 1216.

1226. The Dominicans, Franciscans and Carmelites were the first of a new breed of monastic organization that did not own property and relied on charity for their survival: the mendicant orders.

AS AN AUTHOR

Renowned as the compiler of the *Liber Censuum Romanae Ecclesiae*, Honorius is also remembered as the author of biographies of popes Celestine III and Gregory VII, 34 sermons and a volume of church ceremonial and ritual, the *Ordo Romanus*. He is also associated with a *grimoire*, or magic textbook.

CATHARS

The Cathars – or Albigensians, from the French town of Albi, which was mistakenly identified as their base – were dualists, who believed in two gods – one higher and purely good, and a lesser second divinity who was evil and had created the material world; they held that the human soul was pure and good but trapped in the material creation, and that humans should seek salvation through a life of chastity, poverty and asceticism. The crusade against the Cathars or Albigensians, launched by Innocent III in 1209, largely ended with a peace treaty in 1229 but the Church's fight against the Cathars' beliefs was carried on by the Dominican Inquisition, established in 1233. Many Cathars fled to Italy and were not heard from after the end of the 14th century. In France, following further intermittent Cathar rebellions, a royal army besieged the Castle of Montségur – said to be the Cathars' final stronghold in 1243–4. Around 220 Cathars were burned at the stake, but a handful reputedly escaped with a treasure that, according to esoteric tradition, had been handed down by the Knights Templar – and may have been the Holy Grail itself.

GREGORY IX, 1227–41
POPE WHO FOUNDED THE PAPAL INQUISITION

Gregory IX was a stern and profoundly spiritual man, friend both of Dominic Guzman and Francis of Assisi and adviser to Clare of Assisi, who founded the Poor Clares. Already over 80 years old on his election to the papacy, he had a harsh side and could be swift to anger, finding it difficult to be patient with those who opposed him. He founded the papal inquisition to fight heresy, but is also remembered for promulgating the *Decretals* in 1234, used by the Church as a legal codebook until after 1918.

STUDENT IN PARIS

Before becoming pope, Ugo di Segni was a student of theology at the University of Paris and had a long career as a highly valued diplomat under his uncle Pope Innocent III and Pope Honorius III. In these years he was on good terms with the young Emperor Frederick II. But after his enthronement as Gregory IX, he quickly fell out with Frederick, whose failure to depart on crusade as promised had already enraged Honorius. Just three days into his reign he ordered Frederick to embark for the Holy Land.

Frederick had taken the cross in 1215 in response to Innocent's call to arms of 1213 and then renewed his vows in 1220 after Honorius III crowned him Holy Roman Emperor. He had repeatedly been on the verge of embarking on the Fifth Crusade, and sent an advance party of his force in 1221, but he himself

Above: Emperor Frederick II took Jerusalem in 1229. This miniature shows him reaching an agreement with al-Kamil, the Sultan of Jerusalem.

had not departed – and his absence was a major factor in the abject failure of that crusade in Egypt. He finally departed for the Holy Land in 1227 but then an outbreak of plague on his fleet forced him to turn back to Brindisi.

FREDERICK AND THE SIXTH CRUSADE

Seeing this as further evidence of Frederick's dishonesty and unreliability, Gregory excommunicated the emperor. Frederick issued a condemnation of the pope's actions, then blithely embarked for the Holy Land despite the fact that technically an excommunicate could not lead a crusade. Gregory issued another forthright condemnation of the emperor. In Frederick's eyes he was leading the crusade on his own terms as emperor rather than as an instrument of papal power.

In the Sixth Crusade of 1228–9 Frederick regained possession of Jerusalem under a treaty signed with Ayyubid sultan of Egypt, al-Kamil, on 18 February 1229. Frederick crowned himself Lord

of Jerusalem the following month on 17 March, then returned to Italy, where he defeated papal troops that Gregory had sent into Frederick's Italian territories.

Gregory lifted the excommunication but renewed it in 1239 after Frederick had embarked once more on military activity in Italy. Gregory called a general council of the church for Easter 1241 in Rome, but Frederick forbade bishops to travel to Rome and captured a number of those who did. He invaded the papal states and surrounded Rome – at which point Gregory died, already more than 90 years old. Frederick withdrew his troops.

CHURCH REFORMS

In the 1230s – temporarily at peace with the emperor – Gregory focused on spiritual matters and church organization. He established the papal inquisition to

---

FACT BOX

Original name Ugo/Ugolino di Segni
Born c.1145
Origin Roman
Date elected pope 19 March 1227
Died 22 August 1241
Key fact Promulgated *Decretals* (1234), code of canon law

Below: Because Frederick had been excommunicated, no bishop would crown him in Jerusalem. He performed the ceremony himself.

fight heresy. In 1231 he enacted a law under which heretics should be handed over to secular authorites for due punishment – meaning burning at the stake.

In 1234 he tried to end the Schism with the churches of the East, but despite a series of meetings in Nicaea in January 1234 this attempt came to nothing. The same year he promulgated the *Novo Compilatio decretalium* ('New Collection of Decretals'), a book of canon law drawn up by canon lawyer Raymond of Peñafort on the basis of papal letters and conciliar rulings.

'FATHER OF ALL NATIONS'

Before becoming pope, while Cardinal-Bishop of Ostia, Gregory (then called Ugo) would adopt the monastic robes

Above: Cardinal Ugolino di Segni (later Gregory IX) consecrates St Gregory's Chapel at St Benedict's Monastery, Subiaco.

of a member of the Order of Friars Minor established by Francis of Assisi and walk barefooted with Francis, discussing matters of faith. Francis viewed Ugo as a father, and called him 'the bishop of the whole world and the father of all nations'; it was at Francis's request that Honorius III appointed Ugo protector of the order in 1220. Gregory was also a friend of Dominic Guzman and promoted the Dominican movement; on Dominic's death in 1221 Ugo held the funeral service. As pope he canonized both Francis (in 1228) and Dominic (in 1234).

CELESTINE IV TO CLEMENT IV, 1241–68
POPES WHO OPPOSED FREDERICK II AND HIS DESCENDANTS

The five popes from Celestine IV to Clement IV (1241–68) fought tirelessly against Frederick II and his Hohenstaufen descendants Conrad IV, Manfred and Conradin. In Clement IV's reign the Hohenstaufens were finally brought low by the papacy in alliance with King Louis IX of France's brother Charles of Anjou, who became King of Naples and Sicily in 1266.

CONCLAVE

Celestine IV (1241) was the first pope to be elected in a conclave. Gregory IX's death had come in the midst of a fierce conflict with Frederick II with the emperor's army encamped near Rome, and the cardinals could not agree on the best candidate to deal with the emperor. After a deadlock of 60 days, a group of cardinals was confined by Roman senator Matteo Rosso Orsini; they elected the elderly and frail Goffredo da Castaglione as pope. Born in Milan, and a nephew of Urban III, he was pope for 17 days from 25 October to 10 November 1241.

RECONCILIATION?

It took the cardinals a year and a half to find a successor, but they finally elected Sinibaldo Fieschi as Innocent IV on 25 June 1243. He was one of the leading authorities on canon law of his day and had taught the subject at the University of Bologna before being called to the Roman Curia in 1226 and made a cardinal in 1227.

He seemed the right man to manage Frederick for the emperor was known to respect Fieschi's learning and the two men had been on good terms – and had remained so after the emperor's excommunication. Frederick joked that he had lost the friendship of a cardinal and gained the enmity of a pope.

Left: Queen Margaret of Scotland was canonized by Pope Innocent IV in 1290 in recognition of her personal holiness and fidelity to the Church.

Above: Innocent IV approved the rule of the Poor Clares, in 1253. The founder of the order, Clare of Assisi, kneels before the pope. This painted wood image is from Nuremberg, c.1360–70.

Innocent and Frederick entered negotiations, principally over lifting Frederick's excommunication and the return of Lombardy to the papal states. But these came to nothing and Innocent, aware imperial agents were instigating plots against him, fled Rome and escaped via his birthplace Genoa to Lyon. The possibility of reconciliation was lost.

There in 1245 he called the First Council of Lyon, which solemnly condemned and deposed Frederick on the grounds of perjury, sacrilege and suspicion of heresy, freeing his subjects from their oath of loyalty to him. Innocent called on German princes to elect a new emperor and they named first Henry

Raspe, landgrave of Thuringia, and then after Henry's death in 1247, William of Holland.

Frederick died on 13 December 1250 but the papal-imperial conflict rumbled on, first against Frederick's son Conrad IV then after Conrad's death in May 1245 against another this time illegitimate son, Manfred, who was regent for Conrad IV's infant son Conradin. Manfred took power in Sicily, despite the fact that Innocent had granted the kingdom to King Henry III of England's nine year-old son, Edmund. Manfred defeated the papal army at Foggia on 2 December 1254.

BEYOND EUROPE

Innocent called for a new crusade after Jerusalem, regained by Frederick II in the Sixth Crusade (1228–9), fell to Khwarazmian Turks in 1244, and King Louis IX of France embarked on the Seventh Crusade in 1248. This was a failure and ended with Louis in chains and facing a ransom demand of 800,000 gold bezants.

Innocent sent a mission to the Mongols in 1245, calling on their leader to convert to Christianity and stop the slaughter of Christians. The Third Great Khan Guyuk, grandson of Genghis Khan, replied demanding that the pope and all other European rulers submit to his authority. The letter, written in Persian, is still in the Vatican Library.

Alexander IV (1254–61) carried on Innocent's policies, excommunicating Manfred and investing Edmund with Sicily. He tried without success to organize a crusade against the Turkic Tatars who had raided Poland.

CORPUS CHRISTI

The French-born pope Urban IV (1261–4) established the Feast of Corpus Christi to celebrate the Real Presence of Christ in the Eucharist, on the Thursday after Trinity Sunday. Urban had been a professor of canon law at Paris and served as Patriarch of Jerusalem under Alexander IV, but had returned to Europe to seek help for the Christians in the East when Alexander died and he

Above: Pope Clement IV negotiated with the Mongol ruler Abaqa. This illustration shows Abaqa on horseback next to Arghun and his young son Ghazan Khanz.

was elected to the papacy on 29 August 1261. He tried to solve the problem of Sicily by offering the crown to Charles of Anjou, brother of Louis IX of France, whilst negotiating with both Charles and Manfred to try to launch a new crusade.

His crusading aim was to refound the Latin Empire of Constantinople: this had been established during the Fourth Crusade, but ended when a Byzantine force under Michael VIII Palaeologos retook the city from its last Latin emperor, Baldwin II, in 1261. Urban died in Perugia on 2 October 1264 before Charles arrived to receive the crown or the crusade could be brought about.

Clement IV (1265–8) carried the plan to fruition, crowning Charles who then defeated Manfred and captured and beheaded Conrad IV's son Conradin. His reign also saw the humiliating failure of the Eighth Crusade, again led by Louis IX of France, which got no further than Tunis in North Africa, an action planned as a preliminary to an attack on Egypt prior to a campaign in the Holy Land. Louis died – reputedly crying 'Jerusalem!' with his last word – and the crusaders failed to take Tunis.

FISHERMAN'S RING

The earliest known reference to the Fisherman's Ring, which was used until 1842 to seal papal documents, is in a letter written by Pope Clement IV in 1265. Initially the ring was used to seal the pope's private documents and a different seal was used for official letters, but in the course of the 15th century popes began to use the Fisherman's Ring for official letters. A new ring is cast for each pope, who receives his Fisherman's Ring during his papal coronation. Also known as the *Annulus Piscatoris* and 'Piscatory Ring', it traditionally bears a relief of the Apostle Peter fishing from a boat; however, the gold-plated silver ring that Pope Francis was given during his installation mass in St Peter's Square in the Vatican on 19 March 2013 bore the image of Peter holding the keys that represent papal authority over the church. It was a design made by Enrico Manfrini for Pope Paul VI but not previously made into a ring.

GREGORY X, 1271–6
POPE WHO ISSUED NEW RULES FOR PAPAL ELECTIONS

Clement IV died at Viterbo on 29 November 1268. The cardinals – split into a French and an Italian camp and unable to reach the necessary two-thirds majority to approve a candidate – took three years to find a successor. In the end they were locked in the papal palace in Viterbo and threatened with having their supplies of food withdrawn; finally, six cardinals were designated to make the decision and lighted on a compromise candidate, Tedaldo Visconti, archdeacon of Liege. Visconti satisfied both camps because, while Italian-born, he had spent most of his career to date outside Italy and so was not caught up in Italian factional disputes.

'IF I FORGET THEE O JERUSALEM…'

Visconti was not a cardinal or even a priest. He had accompanied Cardinal Jacopo of Palestrina on a mission to

Below: Maffeo and Niccolo Polo deliver a message to Pope Gregory X from the Mongol emperor, Kublai Khan. Niccolo was the father and Maffeo the uncle of the celebrated Venetian traveller Marco Polo.

> **FACT BOX**
> **Original name** Tedaldo/Tebaldo Visconti
> **Born** *c*.1210
> **Origin** Lombardy
> **Date elected pope** 1 September 1271
> **Died** 10 January 1276
> **Key fact** Promoted rules for papal elections used until the 20th century

England, and at the time he was elected he was far away in the Holy Land – in Acre with Prince Edward of England (the future King Edward I), on the Ninth Crusade. Throughout his pontificate he was a keen promoter of crusading and the interests of the Christians in the Holy Land. Famously in his final sermon before departing Acre for Italy to become pope, he quoted Psalm 137: 'If I forget thee, O Jerusalem, let my right hand forget her cunning.'

Elected on 1 September 1271, Visconti arrived back in Viterbo on 12 February 1272, was ordained a priest in Rome on 13 March 1272 and consecrated Pope Gregory X on 27 March

Above: A stained glass window in Vienna Cathedral depicts Rudolf I of Habsburg (left), whom Gregory backed in a dispute over the imperial succession.

1272. On the fourth day after coronation Gregory called a general council of the church to meet at Lyon on 1 May 1274. He set to work to organize a new crusade to the Holy Land. The Council of Lyon determined that one-tenth of church benefices for six years be collected to support Christians in the Holy Land and fund a new crusade. The money was collected, but the crusade did not take place.

GERMAN SUCCESSION

In the 1250s Pope Alexander IV had backed Richard, Earl of Cornwall, against Alfonso X of Castile for power in Germany, and following Richard's death in 1272 Gregory resisted Alfonso's attempts to take control, instead advising the German princes to elect a successor, and then backing their chosen candidate Rudolf of Habsburg.

Gregory invited Rudolf to Rome to be crowned emperor. In fact Gregory

ALBERTUS MAGNUS AND THOMAS AQUINAS

Albertus Magnus (Albert the Great) was a Dominican bishop and teacher of theology, one of the great scholars of the Middle Ages. He wrote copiously on the Bible and on the works of the Ancient Greek philosopher Aristotle, who had recently been rediscovered by way of Spanish Arab scholars. Albert, who died in 1280 in Cologne and was canonized in 1931, established that nature could legitimately be studied by Christians; in 1941 he was declared patron saint of the natural sciences. His greatest pupil was his fellow Dominican Thomas Aquinas who studied under Albert from 1245 onwards. Aquinas is celebrated as the greatest of the medieval scholastics or 'schoolmen' who based their teachings on the Christian Fathers and Aristotle; as author of the masterpieces *Summa theologiae* and *Summa contra gentiles* that systematized theology; and as founder of the school known as 'Thomism'. Aquinas was taken gravely ill while travelling to the Council of Lyon after receiving a personal invitation from Gregory X. He

Above: The great scholars Albertus Magnus and Thomas Aquinas have a vision of St Paul as they work in their study. Aquinas surpassed his teacher, Albertus, to become the greatest of the medieval scholastics. Painting by Alonso Antonio Villamor.

took refuge in the Cistercian abbey of Fossanova and died there on 7 March. He was canonized in 1323.

and Rudolf met at Lausanne in October 1273, where Rudolf swore to defend the Church, renounced imperial claims to possessions in Rome and the papal states and, at Gregory's insistence, took the cross and committed himself to lead the planned crusade.

Gregory invited the Byzantine Emperor Michael VIII Palaeologus to send ambassadors to the council at Lyon and at the fourth sitting on 6 July 1274 they agreed a reconciliation of the Eastern and Western churches, accepting the creed as used in the Western church (with the *Filioque* ('and the Son') clause), as well as the Roman doctrine of purgatory and the pope's supremacy over the whole Christian world. However the Byzantine Emperor found it difficult to implement the agreement and the apparent end of the Great Schism soon came to nothing.

UBI PERICULUM

Another significant result of the Council of Lyon was the agreement of new rules to govern the conclave of cardinals at a papal election, designed to prevent in future the long delay that had blighted the start of Gregory's own reign. Under these rules, gathered in the papal bull *Ubi periculum* ('Where danger'), cardinals would in future be required to gather within ten days of a pope's death at the location of his death and be locked away in conditions growing more and more uncomfortable with reducing food supplies, until they elected a candidate. These rules were in place for more than 700 years until the reforms

Right: Thomas Aquinas. As well as writing masterpieces of theology, he was author of a series of profoundly beautiful eucharistic hymns (sung during Mass).

of Pope Paul VI (1963–78), although in several elections they were suspended or disregarded.

A CITY EXCOMMUNICATED

In Italy, Gregory set out to bring peace between the Guelphs and Ghibellines, factions who had been in conflict in northern Italy all through the 12th and 13th centuries. In the long-running struggle for primacy of the papacy against the German emperor, the Guelphs were supporters of the papacy and the Ghibellines supporters of the emperor. Gregory excommunicated the city of Florence, a hotbed of Guelph/Ghibelline violence, when its leading figures were obstructive of his attempts at pacification.

On the way back from the Council Gregory died at Arezzo on 10 January 1274. He is buried in Arezzo Cathedral.

INNOCENT V TO BENEDICT XI, 1276–1304
POPES WHO TRIED BUT FAILED TO LAUNCH A NEW CRUSADE

Innocent V, the first Dominican monk to be elected pope, lasted one day over six months as supreme pontiff. He made it the custom for the pope to wear a white cassock, the Dominican habit. He pressed on towards the main aims of Gregory X's pontificate, in particular trying to bring about a new crusade.

Innocent was succeeded by Hadrian V, pope for just five weeks until his death on 18 August 1276. During his pontificate he revoked the conclave measures contained in Gregory X's bull *Ubi periculum*.

Below: Honorius approved the rule of the Carmelites (the Brothers of the Blessed Virgin Mary of Mount Carmel) in 1286. The order is traditionally said to have been founded on Mount Carmel, Israel.

DOCTOR POPE

Pope John XXI (1276–7) was a learned scholar and medical doctor, who wrote a medical textbook *Liber de oculo* ('Concerning the Eye'), the psychological *De anima* ('On the Soul') and a highly prized medieval book on logic *Summulae logicales* ('Small Logical Sums'). Born in Portugal, he had taken a master's degree at the University of Paris and then taught medicine at the newly established University of Siena.

After being elected to the papacy he continued to dedicate himself to his research and writing – working in a study he had constructed at the papal palace at Viterbo – and left the public and political side of being pope to his adviser, Cardinal Orsini (the future Pope

Nicholas III). John died of injuries sustained when the makeshift study in which he was working collapsed.

RESIDENT OF THE VATICAN

Cardinal Orsini became pope as Nicholas III (1277–80). In Rome he restored St Peter's Basilica and the Vatican, being the first pope to use it as his official residence. He was not averse to favouring his own family for preferment in the church and was lampooned for nepotism; in *The Divine Comedy*, Dante placed him in the Eighth Circle of Hell for the sin of simony.

Martin IV (1281–5) was more or less a puppet of Charles of Anjou, king of Sicily and Naples. He appointed Charles Roman Senator and in order to facilitate

UNAM SANCTAM

On 18 November 1302 Boniface VIII issued his celebrated papal bull *Unam Sanctam* ('The one holy', a reference to the Church). This declared that spiritual salvation depended on being subject to the Pope. It declared: 'outside the Church there is no salvation nor the remission of sins… of the one and only Church there is one body and one head… we declare, we proclaim and we define as a truth necessary for salvation that every human being must be subject to the Roman pontiff.'

Charles's plan to recreate the Latin Empire of Constantinople that had been established after the Fourth Crusade, he excommunicated Byzantine Emperor Michael VIII Palaeologus.

PEACE IN ROME

Honorius IV (1285–7) was already around 75 years old and the veteran of a long diplomatic career when he was elected on 2 April 1285. Roman-born and the brother of a Roman senator, Pandulf, he brought peace to the city, which had been in constant uproar under Martin IV.

Below: John XXI was renowned as a scholar. This is the title page of Copulata Omnium Tractatuum, *his treatise on logic.*

Above: Pope Celestine V resigned on 13 December 1294. He was a Benedictine hermit, Pietro del Morrone, who had been elected only on 5 July that year.

Under Nicholas IV (1288–92) the last Christian territorial holding in Holy Land, Acre, was lost to Sultan Khalil of Muslim Egypt in 1291. Outremer was no more; Nicholas called without success for a crusade. The first Franciscan to be elected to the papacy, he promoted missionary work, notably in China, Serbia, Bulgaria, Armenia and Ethiopia; in 1289 he sent the Franciscan missionary John of Montecorvino to Kublai Khan, the Mongol ruler of China, and John went on to found the first missions in China and India and become Archbishop of Peking.

After Nicholas's death in Rome on 4 April 1292, the papal throne was vacant for 2 years 3 months while cardinals wrangled. Benedictine hermit Pietro del Morrone wrote a letter warning of God's anger if the authorities did not make a quick election – and ended up being elected himself as Pope Celestine V on 5 July 1294. The saintly founder of a monastic order later called the Celestines, he proved unequal to the demands of his high office and abdicated after just five months.

BONIFACE VIII

He was succeeded by Benedetto Caetani as Pope Boniface VIII (1294–1303). Dedicated to learning, he founded

the University of Rome in 1303 and reorganized the Vatican archives, and was a patron of artists, notably Giotto di Bondone.

Learned, impulsive, quick to anger, Boniface had a very strong sense of his own authority and was drawn into violent conflict with those who challenged him. He fell out seriously with King Philip IV of France over the pope's intervention in a dispute between France and England and Philip's efforts to exercise royal authority in the French church.

He issued the bull *Unam Sanctam* (see box) as a statement of papal power and authority, but was then challenged and even attacked by French minister Guillaume de Nogaret and Sciarra, head of the Colonna clan. Confronting him at Anagni, the pair demanded Boniface resign; when he refused, they struck him in the face and stripped him of his crown and vestments. But then they fell to arguing themselves, allowing the pope to escape and his supporters to drive them off. Boniface died shortly afterwards.

Benedict XI (1303–4) excommunicated Nogaret and the others who had taken part in the attack. He died suddenly on 7 July 1304, after only eight months as pope. Some accused Nogaret of having poisoned him.

Below: In an illustration to Dante's Divine Comedy, *the poet meets Pope Nicholas III. He condemned Nicholas for simony.*

CHAPTER SEVEN

AVIGNON EXILE AND PAPAL SCHISM

CLEMENT V TO EUGENIUS IV, 1305–1447

French pope Clement V, who was effectively controlled by King Philip IV of France, began the papacy's long exile from Rome by settling as pope in Avignon in 1309. The 'Avignon Exile' lasted more than 67 years, 1309–77. Popes in this period established a splendid court at Avignon, and Clement VI in particular lived in the grandest style of a prince at the Palais des Papes there. Nevertheless several pontiffs looked to return to Rome, and Urban V did achieve a temporary return to the city, in 1367–70, but was driven out by unrest. The papacy was not returned permanently to Rome until the reign of Gregory XI.

The Avignon Exile was followed by the Papal Schism (or Great Western Schism) – the period 1378–1417, in which two and sometimes three popes reigned at the same time and in opposition to one another. This Schism began with the election in 1378 by the same cardinals of two popes – Urban VI, who reigned in Rome, and Clement VII, who established his own papal court and returned to Avignon. It was resolved at the Council of Constance (1414–18), which accepted the resignations of John XXIII and Gregory XII and excommunicated a third pope, Benedict XIII, who refused to stand down, while electing a new pontiff, Oddone Colonna, as Pope Martin V.

The standing of the papacy was at a very low point and the delegates to Constance passed resolutions declaring that the council had superior authority to the pope. Adherents of the 'conciliar movement' thereafter posed a major problem for a succession of popes. When the council elected a new antipope Felix V, the recklessness of this action undermined the conciliarists' own authority and restored the standing of the papacy to a significant degree.

Left: Clement VI built a splendid new papal palace in Avignon to replace the older palace of Benedict XII (1334–42). The new building contained a grand chapel 170 feet (52 metres) long. This view was painted by 19th-century French artist Jules Romain Joyant.

CLEMENT V, 1305–14
POPE RESPONSIBLE FOR BEGINNING THE AVIGNON EXILE

In addition to being the pontiff who settled the papacy in Avignon, and began the 67-year 'Avignon exile' from Rome, Clement V is remembered as the pope who, at the insistence of Philip IV of France, oversaw the dissolution of the Knights Templar military order in 1312 and the seizure of some of their vast assets.

After the death of Benedict XI from dysentery, cardinals were in dispute for 11 months at Perugia over a suitable successor, and eventually through the machinations of Philip IV selected Archbishop Bertrand of Bordeaux in June 1305. Informed of his election in Bordeaux, he was consecrated on 14 November of that year in Lyon, in a very grand ceremony at which Philip was present. In his whole pontificate Pope Clement V did not once visit Rome.

'SHEPHERD WITHOUT LAW'
For the first four years of his pontificate the papal court moved between Poitiers, Lyon and Bordeaux, but in 1309 pope and courtiers settled in the Dominican priory at Avignon. Throughout his years as pope Clement suffered terribly from stomach cancer. He was a clever and

FACT BOX
Original name Bertrand de Got
Born *c.*1260
Origin French
Date elected pope 5 June 1305
Died 20 April 1314
Key fact Acquiesced in Philip IV's dissolution of the Knights Templar

adept pope, but lacked the ability to stand up to Philip; he was also guilty of unashamed nepotism in promoting members of his family within the Church and built up a secret hoard of wealth by simony (the sale of ecclesiastical positions and favours) as well as other means. The poet Dante placed him in Hell and denounced him as 'a shepherd without law'.

From the start of his pontificate Clement did the bidding of Philip IV. At the French king's prompting, he annulled Boniface VIII's *Unam Sanctum* bull,

Below: Consecrated pope in Lyon, France, Clement never made it to Rome. In 1309 he settled the papacy in Avignon, where it would stay for more than 67 years.

which had made such a ringing statement of papal authority, and the same pope's *Clericis Laicos* bull, which had outlawed the payment by clergy of subsidies to secular authorities. He was also swept along by Philip's intense desire to do away with the military order of the Knights Templar, to whom the French king owed very substantial debts.

MOVE AGAINST TEMPLARS
The Templars were under public attack because of the lavish lifestyle of some members and on account of charges of heresy made by former Templar knights. One proposal was for the Templars to merge with the Knights Hospitaller and to this end Clement invited the Grand Masters of the two orders to Poitiers to discuss the matter. The Templar Grand Master, Jacques de Molay, arrived in 1307 but the Grand Master of the Hospitallers, Fulk de Villaret, was delayed.

Philip moved against the order, issuing secret commands by which 5,000 Templars in France – including Jacques de Molay – were seized in dawn raids and arrested on charges of heresy, blasphemy and sodomy. Under torture most of the Templars admitted to allegations

Below: From the start of his pontificate Clement did the bidding of Philip IV of France. In 1305 he created ten cardinals, including nine from France (and four who were his nephews).

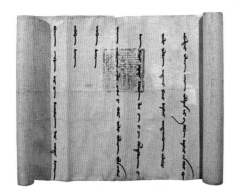

Above: This letter from Mongol leader Oljeitu to Clement was part of negotiations between the papacy and Mongol empire over a potential alliance against Muslims.

including that they spat on the cross and denied Christ during their initiation rites, that they were not permitted to refuse to have sexual relations with other knights and that they worshipped a pagan idol. (Some historians have argued that the allegation about spitting on the cross, which was widely confessed, may have been true – and been part of an initiation rite that demanded a loyalty to the order so complete that it even overrode religious faith.)

On 22 November 1307 Clement demanded that all Christian rulers arrest Templars and seize their assets. In hearings before a papal committee, senior Templars retracted the confessions they had made under torture but this did not save them.

EDUCATIONAL AND LEGAL LEGACY

Clement was committed to education and founded the universities of Orleans and Perugia, while also establishing chairs of Arabic and other oriental languages at Bologna, Oxford, Paris and Salamanca. He also played a role in the development of canon law: his collected decretals combined with those of the Council of Vienne were promulgated in 1317 by his successor as pope, John XXII.

At the Council of Vienne in 1312 Clement dissolved the Templars and transferred the majority of their assets to the Knights Hospitaller; Philip, however, seized the order's French assets. Then at a trial in Paris on 18 March 1314 Jacques de Molay and leading Templar Geoffrey de Charney again retracted their confessions and were sentenced to death by burning at the stake. According to legend, Jacques cried out as he gave up his spirit that both Pope Clement and King Philip would soon meet him before the Throne of God – and indeed both men were dead before the end of 1314.

MONGOL CONTACT AND CRUSADING INITIATIVE

Clement entered into tentative negotiations with the Mongol empire in the hope of building an alliance against the Muslims in the Holy Land. Mongol embassies in 1305, 1307 and 1313 made

Above: Last days of the Templars – they make their case before Clement and Philip IV. Clement dissolved the brotherhood in 1312 and Philip seized their assets.

contact with Clement and European monarchs, but nothing came of them. Then in 1312 at the Council of Vienne, Clement called a crusade to the Holy Land. Philip IV took the cross, but died – in a hunting accident – in November of the same year before he could enact his promise.

STRUCK BY LIGHTNING

Clement himself died at Roquemaure in Provence on 20 April 1314. According to tradition, lightning struck the church in which his body lay on the night after his death, causing a great fire that almost entirely destroyed the body. He was buried, as requested in his will, at Uzeste in southwestern France, close to his birthplace of Villandraut.

JOHN XXII, 1316–34
THE SECOND AVIGNON POPE

There was a delay of more than two years between the death of Clement V on 20 April 1314 and the election of Jacques Duèse as John XXII on 7 August 1316 due to disagreements between factions of cardinals. The election was brokered by Count Philip of Poitiers (later King Philip V of France), who arranged a conclave of 23 cardinals at Lyon. John XXII settled the papacy permanently at Avignon, where he founded the papal library.

A short, thin man with a pale complexion, John was strong-willed and sometimes impetuous, but also serious-minded with a keen intelligence. Aged 67 on his election as pope, he was a fine administrator who, after studying theology and law in Montpellier and Paris, had served as chancellor to Charles II of Naples before being made Cardinal Bishop of Porto in 1312.

FRANCISCAN DISPUTE

John tried to end a long-running and bitter division within the Franciscan order between the majority (the Conventuals) and the *Fraticelli* or Spirituals, who argued that monks should observe absolute poverty on the grounds that Christ and the Apostles had owned nothing. In 1317, after clashes in which Spirituals drove Conventuals out of abbeys and took local control, John condemned the Spirituals and announced that those who continued to resist would be treated as heretics; some were burned at the stake.

Above: The longest-reigning of the Avignon popes, John XXII consolidated the close links with the French crown. He canonized Thomas Aquinas on 18 July, 1323.

When in 1322 the Franciscan chapter of Perugia declared it a valid position to argue that Christ and the Apostles had no property either individually or collectively, John denounced this position and the following year issued a papal bull that pronounced it 'heretical'.

ANTIPOPE NICHOLAS V

John clashed with Holy Roman Emperor Louis IV and as a result faced the challenge of an antipope, Nicholas V, set up in Rome by Louis. The trouble began when Louis came to power after overcoming the challenge of Frederick of Austria and John warned him not to act as emperor until he as pope had deliberated on the disagreement.

Louis issued the Sachsenhausen Appellation of 22 May 1324 that denied that the papacy had authority over imperial elections; he also attacked John's denunciation of the Spiritual Franciscans. John then excommunicated Louis and Louis marched into Italy where he set up a Franciscan Spiritual, Pietro Rainalducci, as antipope Nicholas V and had a straw effigy of John XXII burned in the streets of Rome; Michael of Cesena, the general of the Franciscans, argued that a church council should sit in judgement on John.

Thereupon John excommunicated Nicholas V and deposed Michael. Subsequently, after Louis returned to Germany, Nicholas submitted to the pope who allowed him to live out his days in peace, with a small pension, in the palace at Avignon.

DECLINING STATUS

John's close relationship with the French crown contributed to a growing distrust of the papacy. He was guilty – like many of the other Avignon popes – of nepotism and showing favouritism to fellow Frenchmen. He created three of his nephews cardinals and out of the 28 cardinals he created no fewer than 20 were from southern France.

Below: Holy Roman Emperor Louis IV was a difficult opponent for John, who had to face down the challenge of antipope Nicholas V, set up by Louis.

FACT BOX

Original name Jacques Duèse
Born 1249
Origin French, born in Cahors
Date elected pope 7 August 1316
Died 4 December 1334
Key fact Restored papal finances and settled papacy permanently in Avignon

Above: An English friar from Surrey, William of Ockham protested against John's move against the Spirituals, or Fraticelli, backers of absolute poverty, within the Franciscan order.

MEISTER ECKHART

The German philosopher, theologian and mystic Meister Eckhart was condemned by John XXII in a papal bull of 27 March 1329. Johannes Eckhart was born in *c.*1260 in Hochheim, Thuringia (now part of Germany), joined the Dominicans aged 15 and studied – possibly under the great Albertus Magnus – in Cologne, before teaching theology and taking a master's degree in Paris. He held official Dominican positions in his native Thuringia, in Saxony and Bohemia and after 1314 was dedicated to preaching, based in Strasbourg. He viewed God as the inner being of all things – an 'uncreated and uncreatable' light in the soul – and gave instructions on how the human soul can establish union with God. He was accused of heresy while a professor in Cologne later in life, and his case was heard before a papal court in Avignon. He told them that his teachings were based on religious experience: 'What I have taught is the bare truth.' Pope John's condemnation came after Eckhart's death – probably in 1327 or 1328 – in Avignon.

Yet he also had positive attributes. A great proponent of missionary activity, he established bishoprics in India, Iran, Armenia and Anatolia. He also reorganized church administration and control of finances – in particular, issuing a tax document that set fees for work done by the papal chancery. He established a university at Cahors in France.

BEATIFIC VISION

John was embroiled in a controversy over his views on the blessed soul's encounter with God after death. In sermons in 1331–2 he reiterated the idea, which he had also expressed before becoming pope, that the souls of the blessed would not access full experience of God's glory (the beatific vision) until the Last Judgement – whereas most theologians argued that blessed souls would

Above: John supported missionary work and created bishoprics as far afield as India. This illustration of building at Jerusalem is from the John XXII Bible in the Palais des Papes.

not have to wait but would be in full communion with God after death. A committee at the University of Paris condemned John's position and Cardinal Napoleone Orsini even tried to establish an ecumenical council to sit in judgement on the pope. John tried to find a common position with his opponents before his death on 4 December 1334, aged 84.

Church historians do not consider John a heretic because the doctrine of the beatific vision was not formally defined at the time of his pontificate. His successor Benedict XII did issue that definition in the encyclical *Benedictus deus* (1336).

EXILE OF THE PAPACY TO AVIGNON IN THE SOUTH OF FRANCE

For a period of over 67 years, from 1309 to 1377, the papacy was exiled from Rome in the city of Avignon, southern France. French-born pope Clement V (1305–14) settled the papacy in Avignon under the influence of Philip IV of France. Some of his successors, notably Clement VI (1342–52), lived in fine style there in the Palais des Papes ('Palace of the Popes'). Urban V (1362–70) returned to Rome in 1367–70 but was forced by unrest there to retreat to France, before Gregory XI (1370–8) brought the papacy back to Rome in 1377.

Below: Italian poet Petrarch spent much of his youth in Avignon. He called on Urban V to return to Rome.

Right: The Widow of Rome. A 13th-century allegorical image shows Rome mourning the loss of the papacy to southern France.

BACK IN AVIGNON DURING THE PAPAL SCHISM

In the Papal Schism of 1378–1417 that followed the Avignon Exile, two and sometimes three leaders of the Church set themselves up to reign in opposition to one another: a succession of these, starting with antipope Clement VII (1378–94), ruled in Avignon but were opposed by popes resident in Rome. Church historians identify the leaders of the Church in Rome as popes and the others, in Avignon (and later also in Pisa), as antipopes.

The 'Avignon Exile' refers to the period 1309–77, when there was a single line of popes, resident in Avignon rather than Rome, and does not include the years in which antipopes ruled in Avignon while popes ruled in Rome.

'A SEWER'

When Clement V settled in Avignon the city belonged to the Duke of Anjou, who was a vassal of the pope. Its appeal lay in the fact that it offered refuge from the highly unsettled situation in Rome and the papal states; it could also be said that it was located more centrally in Christian Europe than Rome; but the main reason Clement settled there was that he was effectively under the thumb of the French king, Philip IV. To begin with, the city was unappealing, especially to Italian courtiers forced to move there. The poet and humanist Petrarch – who spent part of his youth there after his family had to relocate to follow Clement V – was scathing about the place: he called it 'a sewer where all the muck of the universe collects'.

PALAIS DES PAPES

But over the years in which the popes and the papal court were resident in Avignon, the city was greatly developed. The formidable eight-towered Palais des Papes was raised on a rock some 190 feet (58 metres) above the main city, alongside a 12th-century Romanesque cathedral, Notre Dame des Doms. The cathedral contains the elaborate Gothic tomb of Pope John XXII (1316–34), the second Avignon pope, who added several chapels to the building.

The palace consists of two main parts. The first, the Palais Vieux ('Old Palace') was built in 1334–42 by Pope Benedict XII (1334–42) on the site of the old episcopal palace used by the bishops of Avignon. It was largely plain and heavily fortified, its four wings flanked by towers. The second, the Palais Nouveau ('New Palace'), was erected by pope Clement VI, with additions by Innocent VI (1352–62) and Urban V (1362–70). The building, which contains the vast Grand Chapel (170 feet/52 metres) in

Below: Urban V. He made several additions to the new papal palace begun by his predecessor Clement VI – in particular, completing the palace courtyard.

Above: The Palais des Papes dominates the city. Six papal conclaves were held in Avignon, from the election of Benedict XII in 1334 to that of the antipope Benedict XIII in 1394.

length, was lavishly ornamented and decorated with wooden ceilings, stained glass, golden ornamentation, frescoes and paintings, tapestries and sculpture. When finished, the complex covered 118,400 square feet (11,000 square metres).

In 1348 Clement VI purchased Avignon and the surrounding area, the Venaissin, from Queen Joan I of Naples who had come by the land through her husband Andrew, a member of the Hungarian branch of the House of Anjou.

CITY TRANSFORMED

Avignon expanded, its population growing to around 30,000, and became established as a centre not only of religion but also of intellectual life, trade and banking. The School of Theology and the University Law School were internationally renowned. The papal library – with its remarkable collection of 2,000 books including Hebrew, Greek, Latin and Arabic manuscripts – was the largest in Europe at the time, and a treasure trove for the first humanists. The finest musicians and singers

came to perform in the Grand Chapel. The merchants of Avignon grew rich catering to a population including bishops and cardinals who lived in great style in mansions and palaces. With such a magnificent headquarters, the Curia or papal administration was expanded during the Avignon period. Avignon remained the property of the papacy until the time of the French Revolution, when it was annexed by the French National Assembly in 1791. The palace was used as a military barracks and its interior was badly damaged.

BLACK DEATH IN AVIGNON

In 1348 the Black Death struck Avignon, killing roughly three-quarters of the people – around 62,000; one-quarter of the papal staff died. Pope Clement VI bought a large field for use as a cemetery and took part in processions to ask God to spare the city, until he decided these increased the risk of infection and cancelled them. People blamed the Jews for this visitation, and there were riots in Narbonne and Carcassonne in which all the local Jews were murdered. Clement issued two bulls condemning these attacks and threatening with excommunication any Christians who continued to attack Jews. He was the first pope to defend the Jews and he welcomed them to Avignon.

BENEDICT XII TO URBAN V, 1334–70
POPES BUILD AND EXPAND PAPAL PALACE IN AVIGNON

The popes from Benedict XII to Urban V (1334–70) established the papal court at Avignon and built the grand Palais des Papes there. Clement VI kept a lavish court like a secular prince but the popes to either side of his pontificate, Benedict XII and Innocent VI, were more austere figures dedicated to reform.

Benedict XII (1334–42) was a Cistercian monk, a tall and bulky former Inquisitor known for his loud voice who had built his reputation rooting out the Cathar heresy in the south of France. He was elected on 20 December 1334, within three weeks of the death of John XXII. He was a stern figure, who set to

Below: Benedict XII (right) confirms the rule in Bologna of Taddeo of the Pepoli banking family. As part of his drive to return to Rome, Benedict proposed a move to Bologna. In the end he did not leave Avignon.

work to root out nepotism and corrupt clerical practices and insisted on stricter observance of monastic rule, drawing up new constitutions for the Benedictines, Cistercians and Franciscans.

He largely failed on the international stage. His attempts to keep the peace between England and France did not succeed, and the long conflict that became known as the Hundred Years' War began in 1337 during his pontificate (see box).

PALAIS DES PAPES

Early in his reign Benedict seemed set on returning to Rome, and spent money on the restoration of St Peter's and the Lateran, but French cardinals and Philip V pressured him to remain in Avignon. He set to work building the Palais des Papes (the Papal Palace) there, on a site south of the cathedral. Alongside a 150ft/45m tower that housed the papal

HUNDRED YEARS' WAR

The prolonged conflict between England and France known as the Hundred Years' War in fact lasted more than a century, from 1337 to 1453. It began when King Edward III of England – a nephew of Charles IV, who died in 1328 – laid claim to the French throne in opposition to Count Philip of Valois who took power as King Philip VI. The wars included celebrated English victories such as those at Crécy in 1346, Poitiers in 1356 and Agincourt in 1415 as well as famous French triumphs such as relief of the siege of Orléans in 1428 by a force led by Joan of Arc. The conflict is generally said to have ended with the French victory at the Battle of Castillon in 1453. The English were left with possession only of Calais.

Above: Urban V was a reformer and educational patron. Austere and pious, he wore the habit of the Benedictine order to which he belonged even after becoming pope. He was beatified in 1870.

Above: Pope Clement VI – an extravagantly gifted but reportedly worldly man – here delivers to the bishop of Ferrara an ultimatum to the Visconti of Milan.

Ottoman Turks – he received in 1369 a visit from Eastern emperor John V Palaeologus, who submitted to Latin Christianity and to the pope; however, John was not able to win the support of his clergy and the reunion of the churches did not come about.

In the meantime, unrest in Italy arising in part from disputes with the powerful Bernabo Visconti of Milan led Urban to decide to return to Avignon in 1370. Before the end of the year he had died, on 19 December 1370 while standing before the high altar of Avignon Cathedral during Mass.

Below: The reliquary cross of Urban V was said to contain a fragment of the cloth used by St Veronica to wipe Christ's blood-and sweat-stained face on His way to Calvary.

treasury and the pope's own apartments, he built a two-storey chapel and the palace's northern section.

EXTRAVAGANCE AND VICE

Clement VI (1342–52) greatly enlarged the papal palace and lived in great comfort, in the style of a worldly prince with fabulous robes and being extravagantly generous to crowds of hangers-on. He declared, 'My predecessors did not understand how to live as pope.'

Before becoming pope, as Pierre Roger, he had an astonishing career: with doctorates in canon law and theology, he had been appointed Archbishop of Sens and then of Rouen before the age of 30, and served as Chancellor of France for Philip VI. He was charming, brilliantly intelligent and was said to be the finest preacher of his time. He was not without vices, however, and there were rumours of sexual affairs – most of all with the beautiful Countess Cecile of Turenne. The poet Petrarch claimed that the Avignon churchmen under this pope consorted with prostitutes and misused their wealth to seduce the wives and daughters of indignant local menfolk.

Not only did he spend lavishly on the papal palace, but in 1348 he also purchased Avignon and its county of Venaissin for 80,000 gold florins. The seller was Queen Joan I of Naples, who was also Countess of Provence and who had fled to Avignon begging for her name to be cleared at a papal trial after she had been accused of murdering her husband Andrew and Naples had been invaded by King Louis I of Hungary. In the trial Clement found her not guilty before buying her local landholdings.

STERN REFORMER

The pontificate of Innocent VI (1352–62) came as a shock in Avignon after the extravagance of Clement VI. Innocent was a stern clerical and monastic reformer. He spent money fortifying the papal palace and city against marauding gangs but was keen to effect a return to Rome and attempted to prepare the ground there for papal governance. But he died before his plans bore fruit.

BRIEFLY BACK IN ROME

Urban V (1362–70) did achieve a temporary return to Rome, in 1367–70. While in residence there – as part of attempts to arrange a crusade against the

GREGORY XI, 1370–8
THE LAST OF THE AVIGNON POPES

Gregory XI succeeded in returning the papacy to Rome in 1377 and so ending the near-68-year exile in Avignon.

A nephew of Pope Clement VI, Gregory received many benefits from his uncle who created him cardinal deacon in 1348 aged only 19. He was well educated – he studied at the University of Perugia, and gained a reputation as a leading theologian and canon lawyer. He was not a priest when he was elected pope at Avignon on 30 December 1370, but was ordained within a week and then crowned pope on 5 January 1371.

MYSTIC PIETY

Gregory was deeply religious, pious with a mystical strain, known for his purity of heart, ascetic character and humble bearing. He felt that the papacy belonged in Rome, and that the unrest in the papal states must be dealt with. He also knew and liked the Italian peninsula, after his spell in Perugia when he learned the language and became acquainted with many of the leading humanist scholars. Among his first acts was to attempt – without success – to broker peace between England and

Left: Born Pierre-Roger De Beaufort in Limoges, Gregory XI was the last French pope and the last to govern the Church from Avignon. In returning the papacy to Rome, he had to face down the opposition of his own country and several cardinals.

France, for hostilities had broken out again in what was later called the Hundred Years' War. Gregory also tried – again unsuccessfully – to arrange a new crusade and bring about reconciliation between the Eastern and Western churches. He embarked upon church reform.

Early in his pontificate, on 9 May 1372, he announced his intention to return the papacy to Rome. But he knew that this might be a challenging task – not least because fighting against unrest in the papal states and the attempt to move back to Rome under Urban V had severely weakened the papacy's finances. He borrowed from Louis I, Duke of Anjou and King Charles II of Navarre to bridge the gap.

ATTEMPTS TO TAME VISCONTI

Then he turned his attention to unrest in Italy. He excommunicated the troublesome Bernabo Visconti of Milan, who had seized papal territory in Reggio and other locations. Visconti was supremely unbothered – and showed it by forcing the legates who carried the excommunication to eat the parchment on which it was written. Gregory declared war on him in 1372. He built an alliance of the Holy Roman Emperor Charles IV, Queen Joan I of Naples and King Louis I of Hungary and sent English condottiere John Hawkwood into battle on behalf of the papacy, but achieved only an unsatisfactory peace signed on 6 June 1374.

ST CATHERINE'S PLEA FOR A RETURN TO ROME

Visconti carried on causing trouble, allying with Florence and stirring up insurrection in the papal states. In response Gregory placed an interdict on the city of Florence, excommunicating all its inhabitants and outlawing their possessions (which could therefore legally be seized) on 31 March 1376. The mystic Dominican nun, Caterina Benincasa – known to history as St Catherine of Siena – travelled to Avignon and called on the pope to arrange a new crusade against the Muslims and to return the papacy to its true home, the city of Rome.

DIFFICULT HOMECOMING

The journey to Rome was extremely prolonged and difficult. Gregory and his cardinals departed from Avignon on 13 September 1376 and left France from

Below: English condottiere or mercenary John Hawkwood fought both for and against the papacy. Italian artist Paolo Uccello painted this mounted portrait of Hawkwood, originally as a fresco.

FACT BOX

Original name Pierre-Roger De Beaufort

Born 1329

Origin French, born in Limoges-Fourches

Date elected pope 30 December 1370

Died 26–7 March 1378

Key fact Ended the Avignon papacy, returned to Rome

Marseilles on 2 October. The voyage at sea was interrupted by severe storms in which several ships were lost. Over several months the papal party reached Corneto, then made their way down to Ostia and sailed up the river Tiber to the monastery of San Paolo. Gregory did not arrive in Rome until 17 January 1377. The pope did not receive a friendly welcome. Feelings were running high against the papacy as a result of prolonged unrest and dissension in the papal states and a massacre in Cesena in February – which was ordered by papal legate Cardinal Robert of Geneva (the future antipope Clement VII) and was carried out by John Hawkwood and his 'White Company' of mercenaries – only served to make matters even worse. Riots in Rome forced Gregory

Above: St Catherine of Siena travelled to Avignon to ask Gregory to return the papacy to Rome and call a new crusade against Islam.

to retreat to Anagni in May 1377, but he returned to Rome on 7 November 1377 and died there in March 1378 while negotiations were under way to bring peace to the papal states.

JOHN WYCLIFFE

Pope Gregory issued five bulls condemning the work of English church reformer and theologian John Wycliffe on 22 May 1377 – and took energetic measures against the Lollards who were Wycliffe's followers. Born in Yorkshire, northern England, in *c.*1330, Wycliffe studied at Oxford University and gained a doctorate in divinity before becoming a prominent churchman. He called for the Church to abandon its worldly wealth and attacked the doctrine of Transubstantiation (that the bread and wine in the Mass are transformed into the body and blood of Christ), arguing that the bread remained bread while also containing the Real Presence of Christ. He also translated the Bible into English. He and the Lollards were increasingly attacked in England after the Peasants' Revolt of 1381. Wycliffe was condemned at a synod in London in 1382 and expelled from Oxford University. He died, after suffering a stroke, in December 1384. Wycliffe can be seen as a forerunner of Martin Luther and other thinkers of the Protestant Reformation.

Right: English cleric John Wycliffe, translator of the Bible into English, was an outspoken critic of Transubstantiation, the Requiem Mass and the papacy itself.

URBAN VI TO MARTIN V, 1378–1431
THE PAPAL SCHISM

During the Papal Schism of 1378–1417 a succession of popes and antipopes ruled in opposition to one another, principally in Rome and Avignon. At times there were three rival popes all claiming authority as leader of the Church at once, each one with a college of cardinals and supporting court in tow. The split – caused by political rather then theological disputes – was brought to an end by the Council of Constance of 1414–18.

URBAN VI VS CLEMENT VII

After Gregory XI died in March 1378 – shortly after returning the papacy to Rome from its near-68-year exile in Avignon (1309–77) – an unruly crowd of Romans unhappy at the succession of French popes surrounded the cardinals in conclave and tried to force them to elect a Roman as pope. In the event the cardinals chose an Italian (although not a Roman) – Bartolomeo Prignano, Archbishop of Bari and a native of Naples. He took the name Urban VI.

Below: Coronation of the antipope. The illustrator of this manuscript had no doubt that the powers of evil were behind those who challenged the authority of the papacy.

Above: Pope Martin V (centre) was elected at the Council of Constance in 1417. He backed Sigismund (kneeling) to end the unrest caused by Jan Hus in Bohemia.

Before his election a well-liked and able administrator in the papal chancery, Prignano proved unpredictable and irascible once in power. He did not treat the cardinals well and so, encouraged by the French king, they fled to Anagni and elected a Frenchman, Robert of Geneva, as a rival pope, Clement VII. They annulled the first election on the grounds that it had been made under duress. Antipope Clement VII established his own papal court, returning to Avignon.

A DIFFERENT ANTIPOPE

This was a new development in the history of papal elections. When previous popes and antipopes had been established in power, they had been elected and backed by rival groups, but in this case the same group of cardinals had elected two popes. Neither candidate backed down, and Europe was divided in support of the two popes.

The Holy Roman Empire, Portugal, England, Flanders, Ireland, the Republic of Venice and the northern Italian city-states were among those who supported the Roman pope Urban VI. France, Naples, Burgundy, Savoy, Aragon, Castile, Scotland and others supported the Avignon pope, Clement VII.

The schism was disastrous for the standing of the papacy and undermined peace in Europe. The divisions along national lines tended to foster conflict between countries. There were wars in the Iberian Peninsula over the schism.

POPE AND ANTIPOPE

The split endured after the pontificates of the initial candidates. In terms of papal history the Roman pontiffs are considered popes – Urban VI (1378–89), Boniface IX (1389–1404), Innocent VII (1404–6), Gregory XII (1406–15) and Martin V (1417–31); the others – Clement VII (1378–94), Benedict XIII (1394–1417), Alexander V (1409–10) and John XXIII (1410–15) – are seen as antipopes.

MISSED OPPORTUNITY

There were attempts to end the crisis. On the death of Boniface IX in 1404 eight cardinals in conclave at Rome

---

POPES AND ANTIPOPES OF THE PAPAL SCHISM

Popes
Urban VI 1378–89
Boniface IX 1389–1404
Innocent VII 1404–6
Gregory XII 1406–15
Martin V 1417–31

Antipopes
Clement VII 1378–94
Benedict XIII 1394–1417
Alexander V 1409–10
John XXIII 1410–15

HUS AND THE HUSSITES

The Council of Constance that effected an end to the Papal Schism condemned and burned as a heretic Czech church reformer Jan Hus. A university lecturer and preacher who was influenced by Englishman John Wycliffe's forthright proposals for church reform, Jan Hus made his name as a church reformer through his sermons in Czech at the Bethlehem Chapel in Prague. He had been excommunicated by Alexander V for defying a papal ban on preaching in private chapels and was summoned to the Council of Constance with a promise of safe conduct. Despite this promise, however, he was condemned as a heretic and burned at the stake on 6 July 1415. Afterwards, no fewer than five crusades were called against his followers, the Hussites, in Bohemia in the years 1420–32.

Above: Duke Frederick IV of Austria smuggled antipope John XXIII away from the Council of Constance along the Rhine in a boat. John later returned to Constance, where he was deposed and imprisoned.

offered to refrain from electing a successor if Benedict XIII would stand down, but his representatives refused, so the cardinals elected Innocent VII.

Below: Church authorities promised Jan Hus he would be safe at Constance, but he was burned at the stake after being denounced as a heretic.

At various points, diplomats and leading churchmen called for a church council to solve the issue, but this solution was initially rejected on the grounds that a church council could not be called by anyone save a reigning pope. As seen in the calls for a council to sit in judgement on John XXII and again here, there was a growing conciliar movement in Europe arguing that a general church council had greater authority than an individual pope.

THIRD RIVAL POPE

In 1409 a third pope was elected. Representatives of Benedict XIII and Gregory XII had come to an agreement that the two popes would meet but when the two pontiffs in fact failed to do so, the cardinals elected Alexander V in Pisa. He reigned briefly in 1409–10 and was succeeded by John XXIII (1410–15).

In 1409–15 Gregory XII in Rome, Benedict XIII in Avignon and first Alexander V then John XXIII in Pisa were all claiming to be pope at the same time.

COUNCIL OF CONSTANCE

In the end the issue was resolved at the Council of Constance (1414–18), called by Pisan pontiff John XXIII and backed by Roman pope Gregory XII. The council accepted the resignations of John and Gregory and excommunicated Benedict XIII, who refused to give way, then elected an Italian, Oddone Colonna, as Pope Martin V (1417–31). This is generally taken as ending the Papal Schism, although Avignon refused to accept the new appointment and continued to recognize Pope Benedict XIII and on his death in 1417 two more antipopes were elected – some archbishops elected Benedict XIV and others elected Clement VIII.

EUGENIUS IV, 1431–47
INITIAL STEPS IN RESTORING PAPAL AUTHORITY

Augustinian monk Gabriele Condulmaro – a tall, thin and good-looking nephew of Pope Gregory XII – was unanimously elected pope by a conclave of cardinals in Rome on 3 March 1431. He was crowned in St Peter's eight days later on 11 March 1431. His pontificate was dominated by issues arising from the reign of his predecessor Martin V – in particular, clashes between the pope and the Council of Basel, which had been called by Martin then postponed, in the course of which the pope's authority faced very serious challenges.

Martin V had been wary of general church councils and the conciliar movement whose adherents argued that a council had greater authority than the pope. Among his first acts had been a condemnation of the 'conciliar theory' and a statement that no appeal could be made from the pope's judgement on any matter of faith. He had called a church council at Pavia in 1423 but then arranged its postponement for seven years, and he died in 1431 before the delegates met in Basel. This council loomed over the reign of Eugenius IV.

COUNCIL OF BASEL

Within five months of the council starting, Eugenius attempted to wind it up: on 18 December 1431 he issued a bull dissolving the council and proposing that it should meet again at the end of 18 months, in Bologna. But the delegates refused to disperse, and reissued resolu-

Above: Last of the antipopes: Amadeus VIII, Duke of Savoy, was elected as antipope Felix V at Ferrara in 1439. He resigned in 1449, and was a cardinal at the end of his life.

tions made at the Council of Constance in 1414–18 to the effect that a general council had greater authority than the pope. Then they ordered Eugenius to appear before them in Basel.

A compromise was reached through the intervention of Holy Roman Emperor Sigismund, whom Eugenius crowned in Rome on 31 May 1433, under which Eugenius withdrew his order of dissolution and recognized the

Below: Scenes from the life of Eugenius IV were sculpted in the central door of St Peter's Basilica, decorated by Antonio Filarete.

council while also rejecting the resolutions that elevated its authority above that of the papacy.

ANTIPOPE FELIX V

Then in 1438 Eugenius called a second council at Ferrara and excommunicated the delegates still sitting in Basel. In retaliation the Basel council suspended him on 24 January 1438 and then denounced him as a heretic and deposed him on 25 June 1439 before in the following November electing Duke Amadeus VIII of Savoy as antipope Felix V.

Further afield the pope's authority was in tatters – in France, Charles VII issued the Pragmatic Sanction of Bourges, which supported freedom for the French church and limitations on papal authority, while in Germany the Diet of Mainz similarly limited the pope's authority in the Holy Roman Empire.

CHURCH UNITY?

However, in Italy Eugenius gained a much-needed boost to his standing when he agreed a reunification of Western and Eastern churches on 5 July 1439 at the council he had called, which had been forced by an outbreak of plague to move from Ferrara to Florence. Byzantine Emperor John VIII Palaeologus was happy to agree to the reunification as part of negotiations for a crusade against the Ottoman Turks. However, it was no more lasting than previous attempts to patch up the Great

---

FACT BOX
Original name Gabriele Condulmaro
Born *c.*1383
Origin Venetian
Date elected pope 3 March 1431
Died 23 February 1447
Key fact Defeated the conciliar movement

Schism of 1054, and the resulting crusade ended in a heavy defeat at the Battle of Varna on 10 November 1444.

In the end antipope Felix V and the remaining delegates at Basel were left isolated. Sigismund's successor as Holy Roman Emperor, Frederick III, backed Eugenius over the antipope and when Eugenius recognized the claim of King Alfonso V of Aragon to the crown of Naples, Alfonso, too, gave his support and so consolidated Eugenius in power.

TROUBLE IN ROME

Early in his reign, Eugenius – a committed opponent of nepotism – had taken on several members of the Colonna family, relatives of Martin V whom that pope had showered with positions, territories and lands. This plunged him into a conflict with the powerful Colonna. In 1434, with the papal states in uproar following attacks against the pope by rebel condottieri, the Colonna set up a republic in Rome, and in June that year Eugenius had to flee in the disguise of a Benedictine monk: he was rowed down the centre of the Tiber while his enemies hurled stones at him from both banks, and escaped to Florence.

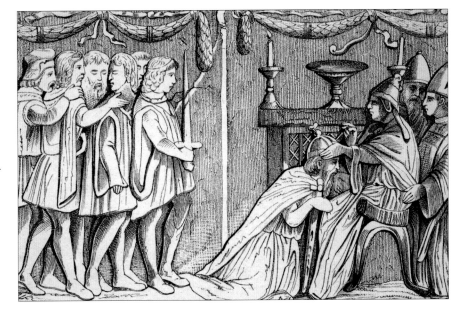

Above: Eugenius IV crowned Sigismund – King of Germany, Bohemia and Italy – as Holy Roman Emperor in 1433.

Given a great ovation on arrival, he took refuge in the Dominican convent of Santa Maria Novella, and sent Giovanni Vitelleschi, Bishop of Recanati, to restore order in Rome; Vitelleschi, in consort with the papal condottiere Francesco Sforza, retook most of the papal states.

Before the end of his reign, Eugenius was able to return to Rome after an exile of almost a decade – on 28 September 1443. He died there on 23 February 1447 at the end of a pontificate so clouded by trouble and conflict that he is said to have regretted on his deathbed that he ever left his monastery.

His pontificate went some way to re-establishing the standing of the papacy and reasserting its authority over the conciliar movement. He may have been lacking in tact, but he was genuinely pious and committed to the welfare of the poor: as a young man, he distributed a great part of his inheritance to the needy before entering the Augustinian monastery of St George in Venice. Among his other achievements were the re-establishment of the University of Rome and the consecration of Florence Cathedral, complete with dome by Filippo Brunelleschi, on 25 March 1436.

FRANCESCO SFORZA

Francesco Sforza, an illegitimate mercenary commander's son who rose to become Duke of Milan, was foremost among the condottieri active in Eugenius IV's reign. These were mercenaries who switched sides in conflicts in the papal territories. At different times he fought both for and against the pope and Sforza's on-off patron Filippo Maria Visconti, Duke of Milan. Born in 1401, he married Visconti's only child, the illegitimate Bianca Maria, in 1441. He became Duke of Milan in 1450 after a long struggle following Visconti's death and established a dynasty that remained in power for almost 100 years. He died in Milan on 8 March 1466. He was famed for his ability to bend metal bars with his hands alone. He was mentioned admiringly in Niccolo Machiavelli's *The Prince* (1513).

Left: Francesco Sforza, mercenary, Duke of Milan and dynastic founder. When Renaissance miniaturist Bonifacio Bembo painted this portrait, Sforza insisted on wearing his battered campaigning hat.

CHAPTER EIGHT

RENAISSANCE AND REFORMATION

NICHOLAS V TO CLEMENT VII, 1447–1534

The Renaissance – the period of European history marked by a magnificent flowering of the arts and a new interest in learning, as people rediscovered the values and culture of the classical world – found its first expression in 14th-century Italy. The first of the Renaissance popes to value the arts as an expression of God's glory reigned in the mid-15th century: Nicholas V, who founded the Vatican Library and began the recreation of Rome as a Renaissance city. Later popes enthusiastically carried this work on. Sixtus IV restored some 30 churches in Rome and began the decoration of the magnificent Sistine Chapel. Perhaps the greatest of papal art patrons, Julius II, began the rebuilding of St Peter's Basilica, and commissioned masterpieces from Raphael in the Vatican and Michelangelo on the Sistine Chapel ceiling. Leo X was a patron of learning who expanded the Vatican Library, reformed the University of Rome and supported printers, scholars and poets. Himself an excellent musician, he invited the finest musicians to Rome and the papal choir became famous.

Rome became the centre of the Italian Renaissance.

These years were a high point for the pope as patron of the arts, but also witnessed a nadir in terms of the pontiff's spiritual standing. The Renaissance popes included men who degraded the papacy through their corruption and self-indulgence. Paul II wore extravagant robes with rouge on his face. Alexander VI used any means to advance his four illegitimate children, who included Cesare and Lucrezia Borgia. It could scarcely have been clearer that reform was needed. German theologian Martin Luther's disgust at the sale of indulgences to fund the rebuilding of St Peter's launched the Protestant Reformation.

Left: The Creation of Adam takes centre stage in the Sistine Chapel ceiling, painted in 1508–12 by Michelangelo at the behest of Pope Julius II. Italian painter and historian Giorgio Vasari said it contained 'every perfection possible'.

NICHOLAS V AND CALLISTUS III, 1447–58
NICHOLAS V FOUNDS THE VATICAN LIBRARY

Nicholas V (1447–55) embarked on the architectural regeneration of Rome, was a patron of many artists and humanist scholars and founded the Vatican Library. He also ended the clash with the Council of Basel and the conciliar movement and rebuilt peace in the papal states and throughout Italy. He brought about peace in papal states; rejecting the previous policy of using mercenary armies and instead built strategically placed castles with able governors. His successor Callistus III (1455–8) was the first of a line of Spanish popes, a Borgia from the Kingdom of Valencia.

HUMANIST ENCOUNTER
As a young man the future pope Nicholas V – then called Tommaso Parentucelli – had to break off his studies in Bologna due to lack of money, and found employment as a tutor in the Strozzi and Albizzi families in Florence, where he met many of the leading

Above: The Transfiguration *by Bellini:* 'He was transfigured before them … His face did shine as the sun' (Matthew 17). Nicholas V made the Transfiguration (on 6 August) a universal feast.

humanist scholars of the day. He returned to Bologna and took a master's degree in theology before serving Niccolo Albergati, Bishop of Bologna, for 20 years. When elected pope on 6 March 1447 he took the name Nicholas V after the bishop; he is the last pope to date to take the name Nicholas.

Nicholas was cheerful and pious, pale with dark eyes and a piercing gaze. He set out to restore peace in the church, the papal states and throughout Italy and to make Rome, so long neglected and so many times battered and damaged, a city rich in architecture and the arts – and so a worthy centre for the Christian world.

Left: Nicholas V honours the memory of Francis of Assisi. Nicholas established peace in the papal states, moving away from using mercenaries and building castles with able governors.

POLITICAL/ECCLESIASTICAL ACHIEVEMENTS

Nicholas ended the schism within the Church by bringing about the resignations of the antipope Felix V on 7 April 1449 and his own recognition as pope by the remnant of the Council of Basel. He called a Jubilee in 1450 and as many as 100,000 pilgrims came to Rome – attracted by the offer of a plenary indulgence (the remission of temporal punishment for their sins); the offerings they made helped pay for the reconstruction of the city. On 19 March 1452 he crowned Holy Roman Emperor Frederick III in St Peter's – a statement of renewed papal authority and the last such coronation to take place there.

He restored peace to the papal states and negotiated the Peace of Lodi in 1454 between Venice, Milan, Florence and Naples. His intention was to organize a crusade against the Ottoman Turks for on 29 May 1453 the one great negative event of his reign had occurred: at the head of an army of around 80,000, 21-year-old Ottoman Sultan Mehmet II captured Constantinople, wiping out the Christian Byzantine Empire. Nicholas tried but without success to generate enthusiasm for a holy war.

VATICAN LIBRARY AND REGENERATION OF ROME

Highly intelligent and a gifted scholar, Nicholas was devoted to learning; he read very widely and collected books – some of his volumes, with marginal notes in his fine handwriting, still survive. He was a Renaissance man in the sense we use that term today – he knew all that was worth knowing; as his friend Aeneas Silvio Piccolomini (later Pope Pius II) said, 'what he does not know is outside the scope of human knowledge'.

In Rome he founded the Vatican Library containing 1,200 volumes and including rare Greek manuscripts brought by refugees from the Fall of Constantinople. He had a team of 45 copyists at work, and the finest scholars

JOAN OF ARC

Over the course of these two pontificates Joan of Arc was cleared of heresy. After her exploits inspiring the French army against the English during the Hundred Years' War – inspired she claimed by God and the voices of saints Michael, Catherine and Margaret – she had been found guilty of witchcraft and heresy and burned at the stake in Rouen in 1431. In 1449 Nicholas V ordered her retrial and this carried on for seven years and heard 115 witnesses until in 1456 Callistus III declared her innocent. Her rehabilitation would be complete when Pope Benedict XV canonized her on 16 May 1920.

Above: Joan of Arc announces the Liberation of Orléans to Charles VII at Loches. Callistus declared her innocent of the charges of witchcraft that had led to her execution in 1431.

including the humanist Lorenzo Valla set to work making Latin translations of Greek works.

He rebuilt the Leonine Walls, paved several streets, carried out much-needed work on the aqueducts and restored the Castel Sant'Angelo. He rebuilt the Vatican, using architects Leon Battista Alberti and Bernardo Rossellino, and hiring artist Fra Angelico to paint frescos of saints Stephen and Lawrence in his study and chapel.

FIRST OF THE BORGIAS

Callistus III, the first Borgia pope, was aged 78 at his election on 8 April 1455. He had gout and spent the great part of his reign in bed. Callistus was notorious for his nepotism, and he appointed several relatives to key positions; in 1456 he raised his nephew Rodrigo Borgia (later the corrupt Pope Alexander VI) to the rank of cardinal.

He did succeed in raising a crusade of sorts – a papal fleet that won a few minor victories. His pontificate also saw the 'miracle of Belgrade' – when a makeshift army inspired by the sermons of Italian-born Franciscan friar Giovanni da Capestrano drove off a vast Ottoman besieging force some 70,000 strong, and saved the city of Belgrade from capture. To mark the event, Callistus made the Transfiguration of Jesus a universal feast to celebrate the victory. It is celebrated on 6 August, the day on which news of the Battle of Belgrade – which seemed to evoke the glories of the First Crusade – arrived in Rome.

Left: The Virgin Mary appeared to Pope Callistus III to ask him to save Siena from the ravages of famine. Callistus was the first Borgia pope and the uncle of Pope Alexander VI.

PIUS II, 1458–64
POPE WHO PUBLISHED AN EROTIC NOVEL

Pius II rose to the papacy from relatively humble beginnings and by way of a colourful church career in which he was secretary to an antipope, fathered several illegitimate children, was excommunicated and almost lost his life on a secret international mission. He was a humanist and gifted writer of international renown, author of novels, poetry, geography and history, and a skilled diplomat; but he failed in the main endeavour of his pontificate, to call a crusade against the Ottoman Turks who had not only captured Constantinople in 1453 but were posing a threat to the whole of Europe.

Born Aeneas Silvio Piccolomini in the Republic of Siena, he was one of 18 children in a once wealthy family that had fallen on hard times. He managed eight years of humanistic study and embarked on a church career as secretary to cardinals including Cardinal Niccolo Albergati, the Bishop of Bologna for whom Tommaso Parentucelli (Pope Nicholas V) had worked.

Below: As Aeneas Silvio Piccolomini, the future Pius II receives his cardinal's hat in December 1456. He had a long church career before becoming pope in his 50s.

FACT BOX
Original name Aeneas Silvio Piccolomini
Born 18 October 1405
Origin Corsignano [now Pienza], Siena
Date elected pope 19 August 1458
Died 14 August 1464
Key fact Unable to launch the crusade he longed for

SAVED BY THE VIRGIN MARY?
In the service of Cardinal Albergati, Piccolomini went on an extraordinary secret mission. His task was to persuade King James I of Scotland to invade England, as part of a scheme to bring the Hundred Years' War to an end. His first attempt was stymied by the refusal of the English, who seemingly suspected skulduggery, to allow him to land; so he returned to Sluys, in Flanders (now in the Netherlands), and took ship again directly to Scotland. This voyage was almost his last, for a great storm sent him towards the coast of Norway; fearing for his life, he vowed that if he survived he would walk barefoot to the nearest shrine of the Blessed Virgin Mary. When he finally landed, in Dunbar, he honoured his promise but nearly lost his feet in tramping without shoes across frozen miles to the nearest shrine, at Whitekirk. He suffered from the effects throughout his life.

EXCOMMUNICATED
Subsequently he became an official of the Council of Basel, the church council that caused such difficulties for Eugenius IV, and then secretary to the antipope Felix V. He was excommunicated. In 1442 he became poet laureate and private secretary in the service of King Frederick IV of Germany (later Holy Roman Emperor Frederick III); the ban

of excommunication was lifted. In these years, he lived a dissolute existence and fathered several illegitimate children. He became ill, mended his ways and became a priest in 1446.

Thereafter he played an important role in reconciling Frederick with the papacy. He was made Bishop of Trieste in 1447, Bishop of Siena in 1450 and Cardinal Bishop of Santa Sabina in 1456. He was elected pope on 3 September 1458.

CRUSADING DRIVE
At once he set to work trying to raise a crusade against the Turks. He called a council to this end for Christian rulers at Mantua in June 1459, but it was a failure; indeed, none of his efforts as pope to launch the crusade he had pronounced on 14 January 1460 came to anything. In 1461 he even wrote to the Ottoman Emperor Mehmet II, giving a detailed criticism of the Koran and of Islam and urging him to embrace Christianity and to become Christian

Below: A fresco in Siena Cathedral by Bernardino Pinturicchio shows Pius II's coronation. He launched himself into a campaign to raise a crusade.

Above: Pius, too sick to stand, arrives in Ancona borne on a litter. For all his determination he did not manage to launch the crusade he longed for against the Turks.

also wrote a 13-book autobiography, *Commentaries*, and made a collection of his letters. The earlier works were written during his dissolute youth, but the *Commentaries* dates from his time as Pius II and as such is the only autobiography written by a reigning pope.

Below: Mehmet II. He tried to claim the Roman title 'Caesar' after he captured Constantinople in 1453. Pius wanted him to become Christian ruler of the former Eastern Roman Empire.

Emperor of the East, but this letter achieved nothing; some historians doubt whether it was ever sent to Mehmet, but it certainly circulated in Europe.

Eventually, in June 1464, Pius took the cross himself and set out in the hope of leading the crusade himself. He declared, 'Our call to "go forth" had not been listened to; perhaps if we say "Come along with me" this will have more impact'. But it was a doomed enterprise: he was already so sick that he

had to travel on a litter; and when he arrived at Ancona, from where the crusade was due to embark, he found very few assembled crusaders and the promised Venetian fleet missing. On 12 August a paltry twelve ships arrived in place of the promised fleet. This was too much for Pius and he died at Ancona, his plans in tatters, just two days later on 14 August 1464.

FROM EROTIC VERSE TO PAPAL AUTOBIOGRAPHY

Among Pope Pius II's many writings were several erotic works in Latin: poems, a comedy called *Chrysis* and a novel entitled *The Tale of Two Lovers*. He

PAUL II, 1464–71
A LOVER OF SHOW – AND MELONS

Celebrated for his love of extravagant show, Paul II (1464–71) wore lavish robes and lived while pope in the magnificent Palazzo San Marco (now called Palazzo di Venezia), which he built at vast expense to the papacy in Rome. He is remembered for dissolving the Roman Academy on the grounds that it promoted the pagan values of the classical world; in doing so, he made enemies of many leading humanists including Bartolomeo Platina, who later wrote *The Lives of the Popes* – and some of the more colourful tales about Paul's misdemeanours can be attributed to this enmity.

'OUR LADY OF PITY'

A nephew of Pope Eugenius IV, he was born Pietro Barbo in a family of wealthy Venetian merchants, and became a cardinal at the age of just 23. He was very ambitious – and free with his money, which made him popular: he once boasted that if he became pope he would buy every cardinal a summer villa.

Before the age of 30 he was archpriest of the Vatican Basilica and was already known for his love of ecclesiastical robes

and emotionality. The then pope, Pius II, said of Barbo that he should be called 'Our Lady of Pity' because he was quickly reduced to tears when pleading his case; Pius may also have been making a nod towards Barbo's love of fine robes, his wearing of rouge on his face – and perhaps, also, his taste for sexual relations with handsome young men.

By all accounts Barbo thought himself handsome and when he was elected on 30 August 1464 he wanted to call himself Formosus II (the name, used by a handsome pope in 891–6, which means 'good-looking'), but the cardinals dissuaded him and he took the name Paul II.

Paul had won the election by agreeing a number of conditions with the cardinals – (a 'capitulation'), including that the number of cardinals would not be increased beyond 24, that the creation of new cardinals and certain important church appointments would be made

Below: Bartolomeo Platina, author of The Lives of the Popes, *is installed as director of the Vatican Library. He had a highly troubled relationship with Paul II.*

Above: The coronation of Paul II. He won election by agreeing conditions with the cardinals – a 'capitulation'.

only with the approval of the College of Cardinals and that within three years of taking office he would call an ecumenical council. But once pope he declared that he was not obliged to stand by these commitments.

LEARNING AND ANTIQUITIES

Paul endured a serious falling out with leading humanists, resulting from his dissolution of both the Roman Academy, and the College of Secretaries in the papal chancellery where many found employment. He was not uncultured

FACT BOX

Original name Pietro Barbo

Born 23 February 1417

Origin Venice

Date elected pope 30 August 1464

Died 26 July 1471

Key fact Dissolved the Roman Academy

---

and was a significant patron of scholars; he did a great deal for the advancement of learning by permitting the establishment of the first printing presses in the papal states, first in Subiaco in 1464 and then in Rome in 1467.

He loved fine things, and collected hangings, bronzes and jewels, antiquities and art objects for his palazzo – now known as the Palazzo di Venezia in central Rome. His papal tiara was decorated with diamonds, emeralds, pearls, sapphires, topaz and other gems; when, after Paul's death, Pope Sixtus IV and various cardinals inspected his hoard of jewels they found more than 50 shells filled with pearls, altogether worth more than 300,000 ducats, as well as a single diamond that alone was worth 7,000 ducats. According to some stories he even took fine gems to bed with him.

Right: In 1467 Paul allowed carnival horse racing along the Via Lata in Rome; it became known as the Via del Corso.

ROME RESTORED

Paul restored several ancient monuments in Rome, including the Pantheon, the equestrian statue of Marcus Aurelius (now in the Capitoline Museums) and the arches of Titus and Septimius Severus. As part of Carnival festivities, he allowed the running of a horse race down the Via Lata (subsequently known as the Via del Corso).

He decreed Jubilee Years, in which pilgrims were called to pay their respects at the shrines and churches of Rome, should be held four times a century rather than twice every hundred years.

BOHEMIAN EXCOMMUNICATION

Paul moved against the Hussites (followers of the Bohemian reformer Jan Hus) when he excommunicated the pro-Hussite Bohemian king, George of Podebrady, and called on King Matthias I Corvinus of Hungary to invade. After Matthias conducted a successful campaign, Paul crowned him King of Bohemia in March 1469.

Around this time, in 1468, he tried without success to persuade Holy Roman Emperor Frederick III to launch a crusade against the Ottoman Turks; as part of these negotiations he laid on the

Above: In 1466 Paul excommunicated George of Podebrady who supported the Hussites, deposing him as king of Bohemia.

most lavish of welcomes for Frederick when the emperor made the second visit of his reign to Rome.

Paul died of a stroke at the age of 54, on 26 July 1471. Self-indulgent in all things, Paul was known for his extravagant love of melons, and according to one account his death came as a result of serious overindulgence in the fruit. Another account had it that his stroke hit while he was having sexual relations with a pageboy.

SIXTUS IV, 1471–84
POPE WHO CHANGED THE FACE OF ROME

Sweeping away medieval alleys and creating elegant piazzas and broad streets, renovating churches and spanning the Tiber with the beautiful Ponte Sisto, Sixtus IV transformed Rome into a fine Renaissance city. He built and began the decoration of the Sistine Chapel, but was also responsible for the establishment of the infamous Spanish Inquisition.

Francesco della Rovere was a Franciscan monk who served as minister general of the order from 1464 and was a highly regarded theologian known for his piety and unworldly character. Made a cardinal in 1467, he was elected pope on 9 August 1471 and straight away embraced extravagance and nepotism.

He spent more than one-third of the papacy's annual income on his coronation tiara, which cost 100,000 ducats. One of his first acts was to raise two of his nephews to be cardinals – one of these, Pietro Riario, was believed actually to be the pope's son by his own sister and lived such a degenerate life that he died of his excesses aged just 28. Among his other appointments were an eight-year-old boy as Bishop of Lisbon and an eleven-year-old boy as Bishop of Milan. There were even allegations that he handed out ecclesiastical positions in return for sexual favours from young men. These may be the work of Protestant propagandists.

PLOT AGAINST THE MEDICI

Sixtus allowed the papacy to become embroiled in a dispute with the Medici of Florence and a rather sordid assassination plot against Lorenzo de'Medici that severely damaged the moral standing of the Holy See. The Medici was a

> **FACT BOX**
> **Original name** Francesco della Rovere
> **Born** 21 July 1414
> **Origin** Republic of Genoa
> **Date elected pope** 9 August 1471
> **Died** 12 August 1484
> **Key fact** Built and named the Sistine Chapel

Above: Sixtus IV was notorious for nepotism. This portrait of the pope in c.1475 is by Joos van Gent (Joos van Wassenhove).

Below: Rome beautified. Sixtus gave his name to the elegant Ponte Sisto and to the Sistine Chapel, both built in his reign.

SPANISH INQUISITION

Under a papal bull of 1 November 1478 Sixtus created the notorious Spanish Inquisition at the request of King Ferdinand II and Queen Isabella I, to combat the threat these monarchs believed was posed to Catholicism in Spain by converts from Judaism (Marranos) and from Islam (Moriscos). Isabella's former confessor Tomas de Torquemada was appointed as Grand Inquisitor. Sixtus later sent out a papal brief that reprimanded Spanish inquisitors for failing to follow procedures and being too zealous in treating alleged heretics.

Above: Sixtus was a patron of artists including Perugino, Botticelli and Pinturicchio. The Giving of the Keys to St. Peter, *a fresco in the Sistine Chapel, was painted in 1481 by Perugino.*

celebrated banking family: when they refused to loan Sixtus the money he needed to buy the town of Imola, which he wanted to give to his nephews, he had switched to their great rivals the Pazzi and threatened Lorenzo de'Medici with excommunication. It appears that Sixtus gave his backing to a plot in which agents of Sixtus's nephew Girolamo Riario attacked Lorenzo de'Medici and his brother Giuliano during Mass in Florence Cathedral: they struck blasphemously at the moment when the Host was elevated, stabbing and killing Giuliano and seriously injuring Lorenzo, who escaped to safety in the sacristy. Afterwards Sixtus placed an interdict on Florence and prevailed upon King Ferdinand I of Naples to declare war on the city. This lasted two years.

Sixtus made attempts to raise a crusade against the Turks with very limited success: an expedition in 1472 led by Cardinal Olivero Carafa captured Smyrna but a second attempted crusade in the following year failed. Then in 1480 the Turks captured Otranto on the Italian mainland and Sixtus, fearing that Rome might be next, called again for a crusade – a Christian army led by Alfonso II of Naples besieged the city; the death of Sultan Mehmet II and a disputed succession in Istanbul probably prevented the Ottomans from sending reinforcements and the episode ended with the invaders withdrawing and Otranto restored to freedom.

ROME REMADE

However, in terms of the rebuilding of Rome and endowment of Church buildings and institutions Sixtus's pontificate was a golden one. He built the first bridge across the Tiber since the classical era – the elegant Ponte Sisto, named after him – and laid out the Via Sistina (later called the Borgo Sant'Angelo), which links the Castel Sant'Angelo and St Peter's. He restored 30-odd churches, including Santa Maria del Popolo, San Vitale and Santa Maria della Pace, as well as the Acqua Vergine aqueduct.

SISTINE CHAPEL

He famously built the Sistine Chapel and hired major Renaissance artists including Pietro Perugino, Sandro Botticelli and Domenico Ghirlandaio to decorate it. (Michelangelo's work on the Chapel ceiling was under Pope Julius II in 1508–12.) Sixtus consecrated the chapel and dedicated it to the Virgin Mary on 15 August 1483, on which occasion he celebrated the first mass in the chapel.

He also brought the Roman Academy back to life and restored the foundling hospital, the Ospedale di San Spirito. He made a major investment in the Vatican Library, increasing his size threefold: Bartolomeo Platina recovered from his disgrace under Pope Paul II to be named librarian. A papal bull gave bishops authority to give unidentified corpses and the bodies of executed criminals to doctors to be cut up and studied; this helped make possible the anatomist Vesalius's masterwork *De humani corporis fabrica* ('The Fabric of the Body'), written in 1543 and perhaps the most important anatomy book in history.

He died on 12 August 1484 and is commemorated by one of the finest of all papal tombs, a magnificent bronze in the Vatican by Florentine sculptor, goldsmith and painter Antonio del Pollaiuolo.

Below: Tomas de Torquemada, Grand Inquisitor of the Spanish Inquisition. The seated figure in this painting by Pedro Berruguete is believed to be Tomas.

INNOCENT VIII, 1484–92
POPE WHO KEPT AN OTTOMAN PRINCE CAPTIVE IN THE VATICAN

A weak and self-indulgent character, Innocent VIII was promoted to the papacy through the influence of Cardinal Giuliano della Rovere (the future Pope Julius II) and throughout his pontificate was under the cardinal's thumb. His reign was a disaster: he failed to impose authority on Rome, where the Orsini and Colonna families competed violently for the upper hand, or on the papal states, which descended into near-anarchy.

PUPPET POPE

Born Giovanni Battista Cibo in Genoa, he was of Greek ancestry. He was made Bishop of Savona under Paul II and – thanks to della Rovere's manoeuvrings – became a cardinal under Sixtus IV. The conclave from which he was elected pope, in 1484, was strongly divided, and was held while the people of Rome were rioting in the streets. Both della Rovere and Cardinal Rodrigo Borgia (the future Alexander VI) had their eye on the main prize, but neither – despite

Left: Innocent VIII. An inscription on his tomb suggests the New World was found in his reign; some historians suggest that Columbus's voyage to the Americas took place earlier than generally thought.

vast bribes – could garner enough support in the Sacred College, and so della Rovere settled in the short term for being the power behind the throne: he brought about the election of the utterly second-rate Cibo, whom he knew he could control.

Once pope, Innocent enthusiastically embraced the nepotism that was now taken for granted by many pontiffs. He already had two children by a mistress from Naples, and these he openly acknowledged and showered with benefits. He arranged the marriage of his son Franceschetto to Maddalena, daughter of Lorenzo de' Medici; Lorenzo's reward was the elevation of his own son Giovanni (the future Pope Leo X) to cardinal at the age of 13.

CAPTIVITY OF PRINCE CEM

Sixtus IV had virtually bankrupted the papacy and Innocent – whose own expenditure was also lavish – was not averse to indulging in simony to try to restore papal finances. He even resorted to inventing new ecclesiastical posts in order to charge large sums for their sale.

He was fortunate in that he chanced upon an unexpected and substantial source of income when he agreed to keep the rival claimant to the Ottoman sultanate, Prince Cem, in captivity in Rome. Following the death of Sultan Mehmet II, his successor Bayezit had

Left: End of the Reconquista. An altarpiece in the royal chapel of the Cathedral of Granada depicts the last Muslim ruler of Granada leaving the city in 1492.

FACT BOX

Original name Giovanni Battista Cibo

Born 1432

Origin Republic of Genoa

Date elected pope 29 August 1484

Died 26 July 1492

Key fact Reign saw the end of the 700-year-long Reconquista in Spain

---

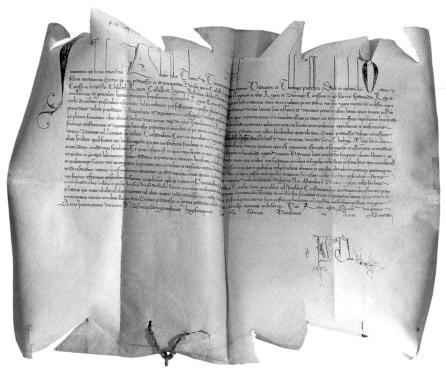

Above: Turkish sultan Bayezit II. Innocent kept Bayezit's brother Prince Cem in captivity in Rome. From Bayezit he received a relic – the lance that pierced Christ's side at His crucifixion.

Above: Innocent VIII issued a bull in 1487 appointing Tomas de Torquemada Inquisitor General of Spain. Spanish chronicler Sebastian de Olmedo called Torquemada 'the hammer of heretics'.

been challenged by his brother Cem; when Cem's bid for power failed, he had fled. Cem had then been taken into captivity on the island of Rhodes by the Grand Master of the Knights Hospitaller, Pierre d'Aubusson, who was handsomely remunerated by Bayezit for guarding the prince. Cem was later moved to France and in 1489 came into the care of Pope Innocent. In return for the vast sum of 120,000 ducats, Innocent agreed to keep Cem in Rome; the pope also received the gift of a treasured sacred relic, the Holy Lance that had pierced Christ's side on the cross. Cem and his travelling party were housed in the Vatican in a splendid apartment, where they lived in great comfort.

BULL AGAINST WITCHCRAFT

At a time of some agitation in Western Europe about the presence of witches in communities, Innocent issued a papal bull on 5 December 1484 that gave backing to belief in witchcraft, issued a condemnation of it and supported the activities of Inquisitor Heinrich Kramer in trying to root out witches in Germany. In Italy he was drawn into a conflict with Naples after its king, Ferdinand I, refused to pay papal dues. He excommunicated Ferdinand in 1489, and also condemned Italian philosopher Giovanni Pico della Mirandola, whose *900 Theses* had been published in 1486.

YEAR OF REMARKABLE EVENTS

For the last year of his life, Innocent was seriously ill: he kept to his bed but somehow found the energy to eat large meals when he awoke, and grew very fat; an attempt to give him a blood transfusion shortly before his death sadly resulted in the death of the three blood donors.

Before he died, however, he was cheered to receive the news that Ferdinand and Isabella had driven the Muslim Moors from Granada and so brought to a triumphant conclusion the 700-year holy war of the Reconquista. He survived another six months or so and died on 25 July 1492. One week later Innocent's compatriot and fellow-Genoan, the explorer Christopher Columbus, set sail from Palos de la Frontera, Andalusia, on a voyage of exploration partly funded by Ferdinand and Isabella that resulted in the European discovery of the Americas.

RECONQUISTA

The Reconquista ('reconquest') was the struggle by Christians to reclaim control of the Iberian Peninsula from Muslims. It lasted over 700 years from the early 8th century when Muslim Arabs and Berbers captured the land from the Visigoths, to 1492, when the armies of Aragon and Castile took Granada, the last Muslim territory. The final stage was a ten-year war waged by Ferdinand and Isabella and financed by crusade taxes and the sale of crusade indulgences. Sultan Boabdil surrendered Granada at the end of 1491 and Ferdinand and Isabella took control on 2 January 1492. They reconsecrated the main mosque as a church; and there were great rejoicings in the Vatican. Innocent, close to death, gave Ferdinand the title of 'Catholic Majesty'.

ALEXANDER VI AND PIUS III, 1492–1503
RENAISSANCE POPE MOST NOTORIOUS FOR SINFULNESS

The corruption and excess of Pope Alexander VI's pontificate fed calls for the Protestant Reformation. He was vastly ambitious and worldly, openly acknowledging his several illegitimate children, notably the four he had by Roman noblewomen Vannozza dei Cattanei – Juan, Cesare, Goffredo and Lucrezia – and stopped at nothing to advance them through nepotism, marriage and diplomatic intrigue.

Rodrigo de Borgia himself had had a church career of many decades when he was elected pope on 11 August 1492, at around the age of 61. He had received his first ecclesiastical benefices while still a teenager, from his uncle Alonso de Borgia, then Bishop of Valencia and subsequently Pope Callistus III. He served as vice-chancellor of the Church and used the position to build up a vast personal wealth.

Below: Alexander takes a humble position at the feet of the Virgin Mary. His name may be a byword for self-serving corruption but he was deeply read in Holy Scripture.

Above: Rodrigo de Borgia – Pope Alexander VI – at prayer. He was a highly talented man, but not at all pious – happy to use bribery and indulge in nepotism.

Physically impressive and highly intelligent, Rodrigo was a gifted conversationalist, skilled at getting his own way. He loved playing cards. He lived in the expansive – and expensive – style of a Renaissance prince and after scandalous conduct in Siena was reprimanded by Pius II in 1460. He was also undeniably a skilled administrator and good diplomat, as shown by many of his dealings under pressure as pope.

PAPACY FOR SALE

In the papal conclave of 1492 Rodrigo spent freely and lavishly to persuade cardinals to vote for him – in effect, he bought the position of pope; he famously bribed Cardinal Ascanio Sforza, whose vote delivered the required two-thirds majority, with four mule-loads of silver. But his election was popular in Rome and celebrated by the locals with bonfires and torchlit processions and even a bullfight in the square before St Peter's; and on the procession to his coronation he received a great ovation.

He set to work to restore peace and justice in a Rome troubled by squabbles among adherents of noble families, and kept Tuesdays as a day on which those with grievances could make them heard before the pope himself.

FRENCH INVASION

Just two years into his pontificate Alexander faced the crisis of King Charles VII of France's invasion of Italy with a 30,000-strong army. Charles wanted to press his claim to the throne of Naples against that of King Alfonso II, whom Alexander had backed. Alexander's rival Cardinal Giuliano della Rovere (the future Pope Julius II) gave his support to Charles, who threatened to depose Alexander and call an ecclesiastical council.

Fearing for his future, Alexander briefly attempted an alliance with the Ottoman sultan Bayezit II, but in the end used all his diplomacy to negotiate a settlement with Charles in Rome. The French king got his way and crowned himself King of Naples on 12 May 1495.

By that date Alexander had formed a Holy League of the Holy Roman Emperor Maximilian I, Venice, Milan and King Ferdinand of Spain – notionally against the Turks but principally to drive the French from Italy. Charles, alarmed, retreated quickly to France and in due course Alfonso's son Ferdinand II was installed on the throne of Naples.

FACT BOX ALEXANDER VI
Original name Rodrigo de Borgia
Born 1431
Origin Jativa near Valencia
Date elected pope 11 August 1492
Died 18 August 1503
Key fact Libertine pope with six sons and three daughters

PAPACY AND AMERICAS

When Alexander VI was asked to arbitrate in disputes between the Portuguese and Spanish over New World territory, his decision favoured Spain. In 1493 he issued the bull *Inter caetera* ('Among other things'), according to which Spain had the right to lands and seas west, and Portugal the right to territories and seas east of a line drawn from north to south 100 leagues (320 miles/515km) west of the Cape Verde islands. In the Treaty of Tordesillas in 1494 between Spain and Portugal the principle was agreed but the line moved to 370 leagues (1,185 miles/1,900km) west of the Cape Verde islands. Pope Julius II agreed this change in 1506.

BORGIA MURDER

In June 1497 Alexander was plunged into mourning when his eldest son, the 20-year-old Juan (or Giovanni) – who had already through his father's machinations married Maria Enriquez, King Ferdinand IV of Castile's cousin, and became Duke of Gandia in Spain – was found murdered in Rome. His body was hauled from the Tiber, his throat cut and showing evidence of nine stab wounds.

Alexander took refuge in the Castel Sant'Angelo and did not eat or drink for three days. The likely murderer was Juan's brother Cesare – according to rumours, they were both pursuing the sexual favours of the same woman, either their own sister Lucrezia or their sister-in-law Sancia, wife of their brother Goffredo.

Alexander was shocked into piety for a short while, and declared, 'We loved the Duke of Garcia more than any other person in the world. God has done this as a punishment for our wrongdoings. We on our account are determined to mend our own life and to begin reform of the Church.' He drew up a draft bull containing measures to outlaw simony and concubinage (priests living as if married with women) but it was never enforced.

Right: In Florence Dominican friar Savonarola denounced church corruption. Alexander silenced him – he was excommunicated and burnt alive.

Alexander had made his son Cesare a cardinal at the age of 18, but following his brother Juan's assassination, on 17 August 1498 he became the first person to resign from the cardinalate and was named Duke of Valentinois by Louis XII of France. Thereafter Alexander set him up as an Italian prince with territories carved from the papal states. In 1499 he married Charlotte d'Albret, sister of King John III of Navarre.

Alexander died of a fever contracted on 12 August 1503 in a Rome that was in the grip of a heatwave, where malaria and the plague were on the prowl. The story that he died after mistakenly eating the poisoned confectionery he had intended for a cardinal when the plates were switched is probably no more than a legend. But it is true that the pope's body decayed and swelled in the heat,

Below: Alexander with his daughter Lucrezia Borgia. She was said to be a great beauty. He shamelessly made use of his position to advance his family.

the face discoloured and the nose and tongue swelled horribly – and that when they came to put his body in its coffin the coffin was too small: Alexander's corpse was rolled in a carpet and battered and beaten until it could be squeezed into its final container.

PIUS III – A MAN OF INTEGRITY

Alexander's successor Pius III reigned for just 26 days from his election on 22 September to his death on 18 October 1503. A nephew of Pius II, he was a man of integrity who looked to bring about much-needed reforms but died before he could achieve anything.

JULIUS II, 1503–13
GREATEST OF PAPAL ART PATRONS

The remarkable Julius II is remembered as a warrior pope for his exploits in the field in reuniting the papal states and driving the French out of Italy, but also – and above all – as a patron of the arts, the pontiff who began the rebuilding of St Peter's and commissioned both Raphael's extraordinary frescoes in the Vatican and Michelangelo's immortal ceiling painting in the Sistine Chapel.

A nephew of Pope Sixtus IV – and the third consecutive pope to be the nephew of a previous pontiff – he had an extensive ecclesiastical career and had attempted to manoeuvre and bribe

---

FACT BOX

Original name Giuliano della Rovere
Born 5 December 1443
Origin Albisola, Republic of Genoa
Date elected pope 1 November 1503
Died 21 February 1513
Key fact Began rebuilding of St Peter's Basilica

Below: Michelangelo succeeded triumphantly in his commission for the Sistine Chapel ceiling. In four years, 1508–12, he painted more than 300 figures and covered more than 5,000 sq ft (500 sq m).

his way to the papal throne before. He spent most of the reign of his predecessor and enemy Alexander VI in exile at the French court and twice took part in French invasions of Italy with Charles VIII in 1494 and with Louis XII in 1502.

Julius was unscrupulous. Short-tempered and frequently rude, he often leapt into action without full thought for the consequences and was not good at organization or judging character. Yet he was powerful, brave and never gave up – in some ways, as his achievements show, he was an impressive man. The epithet 'terrible' was applied to him.

He was devoted over many years to Francesco Alidosi, whom he raised to the cardinalate, defended and protected despite many failures and mourned deeply and extravagantly – to the extent where many have speculated that the

Above: Raphael painted this moving portrait of Julius in c.1512, around a year before the pope's death. Julius wore a beard in 1511–12 in mourning for the loss of Bologna from the papal states.

men may have been lovers. Alidosi served as go-between for Julius and the artist Michelangelo and signed on the pope's behalf the contract for Michelangelo's paintings of the Sistine Chapel ceiling.

SECOND JULIUS CAESAR

On his election as pope on 1 November 1503 – after another conclave in which bribes flowed like water – he set to work to restore order to the papal states and northern Italy. Often taking to the field at the head of the papal troops in full armour, he regained control of Perugia

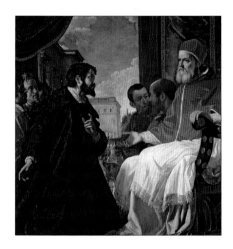

Above: Artist and patron: Michelangelo explains ideas to Julius. The pope began to commission Michelangelo after seeing the artist's magnificent sculpture of the Pietà.

Above: One of the frescoes Raphael painted for the papal apartments in the Vatican shows Emperor Constantine's victory at the Battle of the Milvian Bridge in 312.

and Bologna and as part of an Anti-Venetian League of Cambrai (with France, Milan, the Holy Roman Empire and Spain) defeated Venice in 1509. In his vision he was an emperor as well as a pope, a second Julius Caesar.

Formally reconciled with Venice after a ceremony in February 1510 at which he granted the republic absolution, he turned on his former ally, France. In the ensuing war of 1510–12 Julius had many severe setbacks and faced an ecclesiastical council in Milan called by Louis XII of France that denounced him and declared him suspended from office; but he built a new Holy League of Venice, Henry VIII of England, Ferdinand II of Spain and Naples and eventually Holy Roman Emperor Maximilian II, and called in Rome the first Lateran Council, which declared the rulings of the Milan council void and excommunicated all associated with it. This, combined with uprisings in northern Italy against the French, led to the withdrawal of the French army and the gain for the papal states of Piacenza and Parma.

PATRON OF THE ARTS

Even before becoming pope Julius II was a great artistic patron who commissioned the magnificent bronze tomb by Antonio Pollaiuolo for his uncle Sixtus

IV. As pope he was patron of the finest artists of his day, including Michelangelo, Donato Bramante and Raphael.

In 1503 Julius determined to rebuild St Peter's Basilica. He appointed one of Italy's leading architects, Donato Bramante, to design it and in 1506 laid the foundation stone of the new basilica. Bramante worked on the new St Peter's from 1506 to his death in 1514 when Raphael succeeded him as principal architect. Bramante also built the Belvedere Courtyard at the Vatican for Julius.

Julius was a friend of Michelangelo, whom he commissioned to paint the extraordinary ceiling of the Sistine Chapel, to design the dome of the new St Peter's and to build Julius's own monument. This tomb was originally intended to be 36ft/11m in height and to contain no fewer than 40 life-size statues; it was to be housed in the new St Peter's – according to the art historian Vasari, one of the principal reasons for rebuilding St Peter's was to create a suitable setting for the tomb. In the end a much-reduced tomb was completed in 1545, 32 years after Julius's death – and stands today in San Pietro in Vincoli, where before becoming pope Julius had been cardinal-priest; only the statue of Moses is by Michelangelo – but that statue is a masterpiece. Julius and Michelangelo had a

close and often fiery relationship and Julius had a significant input to master-works such as the Sistine Chapel ceiling.

Raphael produced exquisite frescoes for the pope's new apartments in the Vatican. Julius famously declared that he would not occupy the same papal apartments as his enemy, the Borgia pope Pope Alexander VI, and declared that all paintings commissioned by the Borgias should be covered with black crepe. Raphael also painted a masterful portrait of Julius as a pensive old man, one of the finest portraits in art history, now in the Uffizi Gallery, Florence.

Another artist to benefit from his patronage was Pinturicchio, who painted the frescoes in the apse of the Church of Santa Maria del Popolo; Julius also commissioned several cardinals' sepulchres for the church from Sansovino.

SWISS GUARD

Julius founded the Pontifical Swiss Guard in 1506. At the time Swiss mercenary regiments served in many armies and before becoming pope Julius II had fought alongside Swiss mercenaries in Charles VIII's invasion of Italy. The first guard consisted of 150 men commanded by Captain Kasparvon Silenen, who were blessed by Julius on 22 January 1506. Julius granted the guards the title 'Defenders of the Church's freedom'. The Guard is still responsible for the pope's safety.

LEO X AND HADRIAN VI, 1513–23
POPE DENOUNCED BY MARTIN LUTHER

Leo X made Rome the centre of European cultural life and was another very great papal patron of the arts and learning; he famously said 'God has given us the papacy, now let us enjoy it.' However, he did not make an adequate response to the first stirrings of the Protestant Reformation and so failed to protect the Church from its later dissolution.

Born Giovanni de'Medici, he was the second son of Florentine ruler Lorenzo de' Medici and was made a cardinal-deacon at the age of 13. At the Medici court he had the finest available humanist education – one of his tutors was philosopher Pico della Mirandola – and also studied law and theology at the University of Pisa. After the expulsion of the Medici from Florence in the course of the French invasion of Italy in 1494 he travelled in northern Europe.

He was not good-looking, with a big head and wide, red face, but he was charming and likeable – a sophisticated and highly cultured man, peace-loving and good-natured.

As a patron of the arts he accelerated the rebuilding of St Peter's and built the Church of San Giovanni dei Fiorentini on Via Giulia. He supported Raphael, who worked on papal rooms in the Vatican, and Michelangelo (whom he had known since they were both boys in Florence). Leo chiefly used Michelangelo on projects in their hometown to aggrandize the Medici.

FACT BOX LEO X
Original name Giovanni de'Medici
Born 11 December 1475
Origin Florence
Date elected pope 9 March 1513
Died 1 December 1521
Key fact Humanist education made him great patron of learning

Above: Big-headed. Leo had a wide head and unprepossessing looks but he had a sophisticated intelligence. This striking portrait, in chalks, is by early Mannerist artist Giulio Romano.

He was a great patron of learning who, in addition to expanding the Vatican Library as well as reforming the University of Rome, supported the printer Aldo Manuzio in publishing editions of the Roman and Greek classics and employed one of the great Greek scholars of the Renaissance, Janus Lascaris (who is sometimes called John Rhyndacenus), while encouraging many of the leading writers of the day, especially poets.

Leo is widely believed to have been homosexual and to have enjoyed close relations with some of his chamberlains. His court was colourful, with jesters and panthers – and a pet white elephant named Hanno, which he had received as a gift from King Manuel I of Portugal. He loved to go hunting, accompanied by as many as 300 in his entourage, and gave vast and indulgent banquets.

All this was very expensive – and to defray expenses Leo relied on raising money through the sale of cardinals'

Above: Leo issued his bull Exsurge Domine *('Arise O Lord!') 'against the erroneous Martin Luther and his followers' on 15 June 1520, threatening the German with excommunication.*

hats and in particular the sale of indulgences. In 1517 alone he named 31 new cardinals.

The preaching in Germany of an indulgence to raise money for the construction of St Peter's provoked an attack by the German reformer Martin Luther that led to a bitter dispute in which Luther denounced Leo as 'antichrist' and Leo excommunicated Luther – and this is seen as the beginning of the Protestant Reformation.

FAILED DIPLOMACY
Leo had to deal with the ambitions of French kings Louis XII and Francis I in Italy: after Francis won the Battle of Marignano in September 1515 Leo had little choice but to make a peace that allowed the French crown to nominate all the leading bishops, abbots and priors in the French Church. In 1519 Leo then attempted to prevent the accession of Charles I of Spain as Holy Roman Emperor Charles V but in the end allied

with Charles against Francis. His attempts to raise a crusade against the Turks failed.

On 1 December 1521 he died unexpectedly ten days before his 46th birthday. He may have had malaria or bronchopneumonia, but because his corpse became swollen and discoloured, contemporaries whispered that he had been poisoned. He left the Church virtually bankrupt – having spent more than 5 million ducats in his pontificate, and for all his worth as a patron the reputation of the papacy was at a very low ebb.

Left: Desiderius Erasmus by Quentin Massys. His editions of the New Testament were important for the Protestant Reformation, but he never lost his respect for the Roman Catholic Church and the papacy.

Above: Raphael painted this portrait of Leo X, his cousin Giulio de' Medici (left) and Cardinal Luigi de' Rossi in 1518. Giulio de' Medici became Pope Clement VII in 1523.

POPE HADRIAN VI

Born Hadrian Florenszoon Boeyens in Utrecht, Hadrian VI (1522–3) was a former professor of theology at the University of Louvain and tutor to Holy Roman Emperor Charles V; he had even acted as Charles's regent in Spain. Elected pope on 9 January 1522, he was unable to win the backing of the Romans and although he set out to reform the Church and tame the Ottoman Turks he achieved very little towards either goal before his death on 14 September 1523 in Rome.

Hadrian VI is the only Dutch pope to date and the last non-Italian to be pope until the Polish pontiff John Paul II in 1978.

THE PAPACY AND THE PROTESTANT REFORMATION

Beginning in the early 16th century Protestant Reformers denounced the papacy as 'antichrist' and established their own religious groups to replace the Church of Rome.

There had been plenty of attempts to reform abuses in the Roman Catholic Church before the advent of the Protestant Reformation. These went all the way back to Peter Waldo or Valdes, founder (c.1140–1218; founder of the Waldensians) and St Francis of Assisi (1181–1226; founder of the Franciscans) and also included Englishman John Wycliffe (1330–84) and Bohemian Jan Hus (1378–1417).

The controversy generally seen as the start of the Reformation was between Pope Leo X (1513–21) and German theologian Martin Luther. It was over the pope's sale of indulgences (granting remission of the temporal penalty for a person's sins), principally to raise money for the construction of St Peter's. Popes had been granting indulgences for many

Below: A woodcut shows church discipline being enforced as Leo X supervises the burning of Martin Luther's books after the first Diet of Worms, in 1521.

centuries, and abuse of this mechanism had been strongly criticized before. However, by the early 16th century the time was ripe for reform – and revolt. The Papal Schism of 1378–1417 – a time when two and sometimes even three popes had set up in opposition to one another – had undermined the standing of the papacy and had been followed by a period in which popes such as Innocent VIII (1484–92) and Alexander VI (1492–1503) had through nepotism, self-indulgence, corruption and sexual promiscuity brought their office to its nadir. The spiritual authority of the papacy and the Church was severely weakened.

LEO X UNDER ATTACK

Shortly after becoming pope, Leo X had affirmed a special indulgence previously issued by Julius II (1503–13) to raise money for the construction of St Peter's; the preaching of this indulgence by Dominican friar Johann Tetzel in Germany provoked Luther, a professor at the University of Wittenberg and a pastor, to pin his 95 theses on the door of Wittenberg Cathedral on 31 October 1517. (This is the traditional account, accepted for centuries; modern scholars suggest that while Luther certainly circulated his theses, he did not actually pin them to the cathedral door.)

Above: The power of the word: Martin Luther's Sermon – a detail from a triptych painted in 1547 by German artist Lucas Cranach, the Elder, a friend of Luther and enthusiastic supporter of the Reformation.

The theses, which Luther intended as topics for debate on the sale of indulgences – spread quickly throughout Germany and beyond in Europe.

On 15 June 1520 Leo issued a papal bull *Exsurge Domine* ('Arise O Lord') that condemned 41 of Luther's propositions, called on him to recant and threatened excommunication. Luther defied him, burning a copy of the bull and denouncing the pope as 'antichrist sitting in the Temple of God'; Leo issued a second bull *Decet Romanum Pontificem* ('It pleases the Roman pontiff') on 3 January 1521 that excommunicated him.

'PROTESTANTS'

In April 1521 Luther appeared before the Diet or Assembly of Worms, in Germany, to answer charges of heresy. He was asked to repudiate his works, but refused unless he could be convinced that he was wrong using reason or Scripture. He declared, 'Here I stand; I can do no other.' He left Worms and went into hiding; the following month, in the Edict of Worms, the Diet declared him an outlaw whose writings should be forbidden and who should be pursued and handed to the Holy Roman Emperor to be disciplined.

In 1526 the Diet of Speyer determined that each ruler should be free to decide whether or not to enforce the Edict of Worms; in 1529 Emperor Charles V had withdrawn this provision, and at another diet in Speyer, in 1529, six Lutheran princes and 14 cities of Germany made a protest against Charles's decision. They – and supporters of the Reformation protest generally – became known as 'Protestants'.

SCRIPTURAL AUTHORITY

These Protestants challenged the teaching authority of the Church and declared that each Christian could have an individual relationship with God, reliant only the Word of God as revealed in the Scriptures. They emphasized the importance of translating the Bible into vernacular languages. Luther published a translation of the New Testament into German in 1522; Englishman William Tyndale published a translation of the New Testament into English in 1525.

JUSTIFICATION BY FAITH

Luther attacked the Church's teaching on redemption, the necessity of doing good works to be saved and the action of God's grace. He declared Scripture alone was authoritative, and people were justified (that is freed from sin and made righteous) by God's grace through faith alone – good works were not necessary.

French lawyer John Calvin was converted to Protestantism and, after taking refuge in Basel, Switzerland, wrote the *Institutes of the Christian Religion* (1536), the Protestants' first systematic work of theology. He followed Luther on justification by faith alone, and developed the doctrine of predestination, according to which one group of souls (the Elect) were eternally chosen for salvation while another were eternally marked out for damnation. Like Luther he denounced the pope as 'antichrist'.

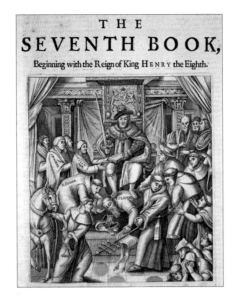

The Reformation spread widely through Europe. By *c*.1550 northern Europe was dominated by Lutheranism. Italy and Spain remained untouched, and they became the centre of the Church's fightback in the Counter-Reformation.

THE CHURCH OF ENGLAND

King Henry VIII of England was initially a friend to the papacy. In 1521 he wrote a pamphlet entitled *A Defence of the Seven Sacraments* in response to Luther and Pope Leo X awarded him the title *Fidei Defensor* ('Defender of the Faith'). But

Left: The title page of John Foxe's Seventh Book shows Henry VIII trampling on Pope Clement VII with the help of Cranmer.

in little over a decade king and pope were at loggerheads and the English Church split from the Church of Rome.

From 1527 Henry VIII pestered Clement VII with requests that Henry's marriage to Catherine of Aragon be annulled; Clement was unwilling to provoke Catherine's nephew Charles V by granting the annulment. Clement said Henry could not marry until a papal verdict had been announced but Henry married Anne Boleyn in 1533 and at a trial in England, Archbishop Thomas Cranmer determined Henry's first marriage was annulled. In 1533 Clement excommunicated Henry and Cranmer. In 1534 the English Act of Supremacy made the king supreme head of the English Church. Henry confiscated for the crown the wealth of the Church in England in the Dissolution of the Monasteries.

Below: Martin Luther in the Circle of Reformers. At the table are John Wycliffe (extreme left), Luther (centre) and Jan Hus (extreme right). Facing the table figures include a cardinal, the pope and a Franciscan.

CLEMENT VII, 1523–34
INEFFECTIVE WHILE PROTESTANT REFORMATION GATHERS PACE

Clement's attempts to challenge the authority of Holy Roman Emperor Charles V led to the ignominious Sack of Rome in 1527 by Charles's unpaid, mutinous troops. They also contributed to the unwanted progress of the Protestant Reformation because while the pope and emperor were quarrelling they could not act to defend the Church.

Clement was born Giulio de'Medici in 1478 one month after his father Giuliano's assassination in Florence Cathedral in a plot hatched by Pope Sixtus IV's nephew Girolamo Riario. He was raised by his uncle Lorenzo the Magnificent, then after Lorenzo's death in 1492 by his cousin, Lorenzo's son Giovanni (who became Pope Leo X).

Giulio gained valuable experience in administration and diplomacy: he was vice-chancellor under Leo and a major director of papal policy in Leo's pontificate. He served as cardinal protector of England.

Below: This imperious marble Moses was the only part of the tomb of Julius II that Michelangelo completed. Giorgio Vasari said it was 'unequalled by any modern or ancient work'.

FACT BOX
Original name Giulio de'Medici
Born 26 May 1478
Origin Florence
Date elected pope 19 November 1523
Died 25 September 1534
Key fact Helpless during Sack of Rome by Emperor Charles V

Elected pope on 19 November 1523 aged 48, he was pious, thin-lipped and rather haughty; and while he was also intelligent, learned and hardworking, he was poor at making decisions. For all his diplomatic experience he failed dismally to find a good line in dealing with the international struggle for power between King Francis I of France and Holy Roman Emperor Charles V.

Clement's frequent shifts of allegiance led eventually to the Sack of Rome by Charles's mutinous troops in May 1527. Having supported Charles up to the Battle of Pavia in 1525, in which Charles triumphed and Francis was taken prisoner, he then allied with Francis (along with Milan, Venice and Florence) in the 1526 League of Cognac against the Empire.

'HELLISH' SACK OF ROME
In 1527 Charles's troops in Italy ran amok after finding that there were no funds available to pay them: they moved on Rome, then after the death of their commander, Duke Charles III of Bourbon, stormed the city. Only the bravery of the Pontifical Swiss Guard, who lost 147 of their number in the fighting, enabled the pope to escape to safety in the Castel Sant'Angelo. Looting, raping and stealing went on for eight terrible days – the greatest indignity suffered by Rome since the invasion of the Visigoths. One stunned eyewitness wrote, 'Hell cannot compare to the current condition of Rome'.

Above: Portrait of Clement VII: he was pious and haughty, but poor decision-making led to his humbling in the Sack of Rome by Charles V's troops.

Clement surrendered in June, then remained in the Castel Sant'Angelo for six months, until he finally managed to escape by night in the guise of a gardener. He fled to Orvieto and then Viterbo – and was not to return to Rome until October 1528. Under the terms of the peace, agreed in summer 1529, Charles agreed to return Florence to the Medici, who had been expelled again in the fighting. It took a siege of 11 months before the city was taken, in 1530, and Clement made his son Alessandro de'Medici Duke of Florence. Clement did not challenge Charles's authority again; in Bologna on 24 February 1530 Clement crowned Charles Holy Roman Emperor – the last time a pope would crown a Holy Roman Emperor.

MICHELANGELO

Sculptor, architect, painter and poet Michelangelo Buonarroti was born in 1475 in Caprese, part of the Republic of Florence. After his sculptures of the *Pietà* (1498) and of *David* (1501–4), he was hired by Julius II to design and make the pope's tomb (only the statue of Moses was completed, 1513–15) and paint the ceiling of the Sistine Chapel (1508–12). For Pope Leo X he worked largely in Florence, particularly on the Medici Chapel in the new sacristy of the Church of San Lorenzo. After 1534 he lived in Rome, working as an architect on the Capitoline Square and the dome of St Peter's Basilica, as well as painting the Sistine Chapel's *The Last Judgement*. He died on 18 February 1564 in Rome.

HENRY VIII AND THE ENGLISH CHURCH

Clement's disastrous pontificate also saw the separation of the English Church from Rome, a major development in the Protestant Reformation. From 1527 onwards Henry VIII was asking the pope to annul his marriage to Catherine of Aragon, widow of his deceased brother Arthur, on the grounds that marrying a brother's wife was forbidden and so the marriage had not been blessed by God with a male offspring. After the humiliation of the Sack of Rome, Clement was no longer willing to risk the anger of Holy Roman Emperor Charles V – and Charles supported Catherine's cause because of their familial connection: she was his aunt.

In March 1530 Clement announced that Henry was forbidden to marry until the papal verdict had been reached.

Right: Commissioned by Clement VII, Michelangelo painted The Last Judgement *on the altar wall of the Sistine Chapel in 1536–41. The Risen Christ divides the saved (rising to heaven, left) from the damned (falling to hell, right).*

However, Henry would not wait. In January 1533 he married Anne Boleyn and a trial in England at which Archbishop of Canterbury Thomas Cranmer presided found that the king's first marriage was annulled.

In 1533 Clement finally acted – determining that the marriage to Catherine of Aragon was valid and excommunicating Henry and Cranmer. It was too late. The following year saw the English Act of Supremacy, which made the king, not the pope, the head of the English Church.

THE LAST JUDGEMENT

Like his forerunners in the Renaissance papacy, Clement was a lavishly generous patron of the arts and learning. He was a friend of Erasmus and the goldsmith and sculptor Benvenuto Cellini and a patron of Machiavelli and Guicciardini;

Above: This delicate ink drawing by Dutch artist Maarten van Heemskerck shows the interior of the basilica of St Peter's with the new building under construction, c.1532.

from Michelangelo, considered the greatest living artist in his day, Clement commissioned the peerless painting of *The Last Judgement* on the east wall of the Sistine Chapel.

PART THREE

INTO THE MODERN ERA

In the mid-16th century Pope Paul III led the Church in the Counter-Reformation – an energetic response to the Protestant revolt. The teaching decrees of the Council of Trent, the outreach of the Jesuits and the severity of the Inquisition in stamping out heresy were supplemented by the glories of Baroque art and architecture as Rome was made beautiful to demonstrate the greatness of God and his Church and by the energy and spiritual force of reformers such as Teresa of Avila, John of the Cross and Francis de Sales. As the political influence of the papacy waned and disappeared, popes focused energy on being teachers and examples. Pontiffs such as John XXIII and John Paul II connected forcefully with the faithful and have both been canonized saints. Their successor, Pope Francis, is the first pope to be appointed from the Americas.

Left: Pope Francis, elected on 13 March 2013, took his papal name to honour St Francis of Assisi, whom he called 'the man of poverty, the man of peace, the man who loves and protects creation'. Here he is mobbed by the faithful in St Peter's Square on 16 September 2015.

CHAPTER NINE

THE COUNTER-REFORMATION

PAUL III TO INNOCENT X, 1534–1655

Pope Paul III is celebrated as the first pope of the
Counter-Reformation – the Roman Catholic Church's efforts to
renew itself and fight back against the Protestant Reformation. He
appointed leading humanist churchmen to a commission tasked with
analyzing the Church's problems and devising reforms. Paul drove
reform forward. He called the Council of Trent, whose decrees clarified
doctrine and brought in many organizational improvements, and
approved the establishment of new and revitalizing Catholic orders
such as the Jesuits. His successors carried the work on. Julius III
approved the creation and founding of the Jesuits' Collegium
Romanum for training priests to serve in Germany. The ascetic and
authoritarian Paul IV established the Index of Prohibited Books
and strongly backed the work of the Roman Inquisition in stamping
out heresy. Pius IV, Pius V and Gregory XIII in particular implemented
the reforms of the Council of Trent. Various popes also supported
military action against the Protestants of northern Europe – notably
Pius V and Gregory XIII, who sent aid to French regent Catherine
de'Medici in her struggles with the French Huguenots.
Rome was beautified to reflect the greatness of Church and papacy. By
the close of the 16th century, 30 new streets had been laid out, three
aqueducts splendidly restored and scores of fountains and fine parks
created; under Sixtus V the long rebuilding of St Peter's Basilica, begun
in 1506, was brought to a triumphant conclusion in 1590. Then in the
early 17th century, particularly under the artistic patronage of Urban
VIII, the city was further improved with the full and gorgeous
flowering of the baroque architectural and sculptural style in Rome.

Left: The Council of Trent (1545–63) embodied the Counter-Reformation.
The Tridentine Creed and the Tridentine Mass resulted from its work. It had
25 sessions under three popes, Paul III, Julius III and Pius IV.

PAUL III, 1534–49
FIRST POPE OF THE COUNTER-REFORMATION

Paul III (1534–49) may be the first pontiff of the Counter-Reformation, but in many respects he was also the last of the Renaissance popes. While he was responsible for calling the Council of Trent (1545–63), whose decrees ushered in reform and clarified doctrinal matters, and for approving the formation of reforming Catholic orders such as the Jesuits, he also – like many of his forerunners in the Renaissance papacy – spent lavishly on the arts, lived like a secular prince in fathering four children and enthusiastically embraced nepotism as a way to advance his family interests.

'PETTICOAT CARDINAL'

Alessandro Farnese was a brother of Giulia Farnese, mistress of Pope Alexander VI: Alexander appointed him

Below: Paul spent lavishly on his family's palace, the Palazzo Farnese, in Rome. This allegory of Paul between Peace and Fertility, is from a fresco in the palace by Cecchino Salviati.

FACT BOX
Original name Alessandro Farnese
Born 29 February 1468
Origin Canino, papal states
Date elected pope 13 October 1534
Died 10 November 1549
Key fact Called the Council of Trent

treasurer of the Roman Church and made him a cardinal deacon in 1493. Because he owed his advancement in the Church to his sister's position, he was known as the 'petticoat cardinal'.

Exploiting his position, he grew wealthy and spent lavishly on the Palazzo Farnese in the Via Giulia. He travelled on diplomatic missions and was known for his love of the hunt and of grand ceremonial. He kept a mistress in Rome and fathered four children – Pierluigi, Paolo, Ranuccio and Costanza.

As pope he was a shameless nepotist – he famously raised his two grandsons to be cardinals at the ages of 14 and 16.

Above: Paul III (Alessandro Farnese) was descended from a family that had served the papacy since the 12th century. His grandfather, Ranuccio the Elder, was a leading condottiere whom Pope Martin V made a Roman senator. This celebrated portrait is by the great Titian.

His son Pierluigi was well known for his wildly dissolute lifestyle and his love of homosexual antics, but this did not stop Paul raising him to be Captain-General of the Church and later in 1545 establishing him as Duke of Parma and Piacenza.

Paul was 67 when elected pope on 13 October 1534. Pageants and chivalric tournaments were held in Rome, as smiles returned to Roman faces following the tragedy of 1527; later, in 1536, Paul announced the revival of the Carnival, and the Romans enjoyed balls, feasts, firework displays, horseraces and bullfights.

Paul commissioned Michelangelo not only to work on the Palazzo Farnese, but also to refashion the Campidoglio

Right: Nicolaus Copernicus. He may have felt that dedicating the work to Paul III would give him some protection. This statue is in Warsaw, Poland.

and move the equestrian statue of Marcus Aurelius to be its centerpiece, to work as architect on the new St Peter's Basilica and to design his tomb – it was erected in St Peter's by Guglielmo della Porta. He also drove the great artist on to finish *The Last Judgement* in the Sistine Chapel and to complete his final frescoes in the Capella Paolina (the Pauline Chapel) in the Vatican.

He was a patron of the artist Titian who made a series of magnificent portraits of the pope – including one, in *c.*1545–6 of the pope with his grandsons: a symbol of the corruption of a Renaissance papacy that was devoted to nepotism and dynastic politicking.

PIOUS AND CHARMING
Yet for all his extravagance and his many faults, Paul III was also devout and serious about reform of the Church. Sensitive and intelligent, he was very well educated: in his youth, he had a human-

Below: The opening session of the Council of Trent took place in December 1545 – eight years after Paul first proposed it. He did not attend in person; he was represented by a papal legate.

ist education under Pomponio Leto and was associated with the Medici in Florence, where he made friends withGiovanni de'Medici, the future Pope Leo X. As pope, Paul was known for his immense charm and shrewdness: he spoke fine Italian and Latin and in negotiations was a wary negotiator, highly skilled at deferring a decision until an issue was fully worked out. Then he acted decisively.

COUNTER-REFORMATION
Shortly after his accession Paul summoned a general church council to meet at Mantua. After many delays it convened in Trent in December 1545. It would meet 25 times over the next 18 years, to 1563, and laid the groundwork for the Church's Counter-Reformation, making practical reforms and issuing definitions on key points of doctrine such as original sin, purgatory, the Seven Sacraments and justification (the means by which people should seek salvation – the principal means usually were either through good works or by faith).

He gave military and financial support to Holy Roman Emperor Charles V in his military campaign of 1546–7 against the Schmalkaldic League of Protestant princes. He also issued a second and final excommunication against King Henry VIII of England in December 1538.

COPERNICUS
Among the fields of learning encouraged at the papal court by Pope Paul III was astronomy and Polish mathematician and astronomer Nicolaus Copernicus dedicated his groundbreaking *De revolutionibus orbium coelestium* ('On the Revolutions of the Heavenly Spheres') to Paul in 1543. Copernicus's understanding that the Sun and not the Earth was at the centre of the solar system and that the Earth, rotating daily on its axis, circuits the Sun paved the way for the scientific revolution of later centuries. Born in Thorn (modern Torun) in Poland in 1473, he studied at the universities of Krakow, Bologna and Padua and visited Rome in the Jubilee year of 1500. He died on 24 May 1543, the year in which his book was published. The Church did not condemn Copernicus until 1616, in the era of Galileo Galilei.

REFORMING ORDERS
Under Paul the establishment and consolidation of new reforming religious orders, which had had its first beginnings under his predecessor, continued apace. The Theatines and Barnabites, given papal approval by Clement VII in 1524 and 1533 respectively, thrived – as did the Capuchins, an offshoot of the Franciscans Clement had approved in 1528. The Ursulines, an order of teaching nuns, were founded in Paul's pontificate in 1535. In 1540 Paul issued his bull *Regimini militantis ecclesiae* ('For government of the militant Church'), which gave formal approval to the Society of Jesus (or Jesuits). In July 1542 he set up the Holy Office of the Inquisition with significant reforming powers effective throughout Europe.

Paul died on 10 November 1549, still devastated after the assassination of his son Pierluigi two years earlier and after a violent row with Pierluigi's successor as Duke of Parma and Piacenza, Paul's own grandson Cardinal Ottavio Farnese.

JULIUS III, 1550–5
CHURCH REFORM CONTINUES DESPITE A WEAK POPE

The Counter-Reformation continued apace through the pontificate of Julius III, almost in spite of the efforts of the dissolute pope himself.

In 1551 Julius did briefly reconvene the Council of Trent, suspended in 1548, but he suspended it again two years later; he reconfirmed the order of the Jesuits and founded their Collegium Germanicum for training priests to defend the Catholic faith in Germany. But he directed most of his energy to his own pleasure, spending vast sums on entertainments devised for him by the Mannerist architect Giacomo Barozzi da Vignola at the pope's country house, Villa Giulia, and scandalizing Rome and the Church by the brazen promotion of his adopted nephew Innocenzo Ciocchi del Monte, a good-looking beggar he had picked up on the streets of Parma.

SKILLED ADMINISTRATOR

For all that he did not bring honour to the papacy once pontiff, Giovanni Maria Ciocchi del Monte was a renowned canon lawyer and an admired administrator before becoming pope. He had an excellent education under the humanist Raffaele Brandolini in Rome and studied law firstly at Perugia and then Siena.

He was twice made governor of Rome and during the Sack of Rome almost lost his life after being given up as a hostage by Pope Clement VII to the

Above: Julius liaised closely with the artists whose patron he was. Here Michelangelo presents a model of a building to the pope in a painting by contemporary artist Fabrizio Boschi.

Below: Julius appointed the great Giovanni Pierluigi da Palestrina, whom he knew from Palestrina's Book of Masses, *singing master to the papal choir. Before his death in 1594, Palestrina composed 105 masses.*

emperor's troops. Under Paul III he was appointed cardinal-bishop of Palestrina and he served as the first president of the Council of Trent. He came to the papacy as a compromise candidate.

INNOCENZO

On his election Pope Julius was already known for his infatuation with Innocenzo, the beggar boy he had selected from the streets of Parma and made his adoptive nephew. His first act as pope was to promote the young man to be a cardinal, and thereafter he was shameless in directing church positions and revenues

FACT BOX

Original name Giovanni Maria Ciocchi del Monte

Born 29 February 1468

Origin Rome

Date elected pope 7 February 1550

Died 23 March 1555

Key fact Founded the Germanicum, Jesuit college to train priests for Germany

---

Above: Before becoming pope, Julius had been first president of the Council of Trent. As pope he reconvened the council, which had been suspended in 1548. This statue, in bronze, is in Perugia.

Innocenzo's way. Wildly infatuated, he refused to change his ways even when cardinals Reginald Pole and Giovanni Carafa warned him that he was abusing his position and that tongues were wagging over the relationship.

These tongues were saying the lavish banquets held at the pope's country dwelling, Villa Giulia, degenerated into homosexual orgies. This of course was food and drink for Protestant pamphleteers and polemic authors such as English clergyman Thomas Beard, Cromwell's schoolmaster, who in his *Theatre of Judgement* described how, when Innocenzo was delayed, the pope waited like an impatient lover for his mistress – and also that he made indecent boasts about the young man's physique and performance.

COUNCIL OF TRENT

The Council of Trent had been suspended in 1548: initially an outbreak of plague in Trent had caused a move to Bologna, but when some prelates refused to leave Trent, Pope Paul had suspended the council rather than risk a schism with two rival councils in session.

Julius III reconvened the council to meet on 1 May 1551 and six sessions were held; but it was boycotted by French bishops and, although some Protestant theologians attended, its success was limited and Julius suspended it again on 15 April 1552 against a backdrop of conflict between Emperor Charles V and King Henry II of France over Parma.

On church reform he made various attempts to re-establish reform commissions, reconfirmed the Society of Jesus and in a papal bull of 31 August 1552 founded the Society's Collegium Germanicum and gave it a guaranteed annual income.

ARTS AND LEARNING

Julius brought the composer Giovanni Pierluigi da Palestrina to Rome to serve as *maestro di cappella* (singing master) for the papal choir at St Peter's. Before becoming pope, Julius had been cardinal bishop of Palestrina, near Rome – the composer's native city, from which he took his name; Palestrina had been organist of St Agapito there. Julius had been deeply impressed by Palestrina's first musical publication – a book of Masses, which was the first of its kind by an Italian composer.

Julius pressed on with the building of the new St Peter's. Michelangelo, appointed principal architect under Paul III in 1547, worked on the project until his death in 1564, refusing a fee because he said he was working for the glory of

VILLA GIULIA

Originally a country villa situated just outside the city wall, the Villa Giulia is now within Rome and houses the National Etruscan Museum. The house was mostly designed by Giacomo Barozzi da Vignola, with garden structures by Bartolomeo Ammanati – the whole supervised by painter, architect and pioneer art historian Giorgio Vasari. It is celebrated as one of the finest examples of Mannerist architecture. The villa was papal property until 1870 when it was taken over by the Kingdom of Italy and the museum was founded in 1889.

God and the Apostle Peter. The great artist also worked on the pope's country villa, the Villa Giulia, along with painter and architect Giorgio Vasari, author of the celebrated *Lives of the Artists*.

CATHOLICISM IN ENGLAND

In 1553 Catholicism was restored in England with the accession of Queen Mary I. Julius sent English cardinal Reginald Pole as papal legate to England. He served as Archbishop of Canterbury from 1556 to his death in 1558.

Below: Julius took a close interest in the design of his beautiful Villa Giulia on the edge of Rome. It could be reached from the Vatican by boat along the Tiber.

MARCELLUS II TO PIUS V, 1555–72
CHURCH RESURGENT AS COUNCIL OF TRENT RECONVENES

The years 1555–72 saw the reconvening and final sessions of the Council of Trent and the first attempts by the papacy to implement its decrees and decisions.

Cardinal Marcello Cervini, a leading church reformer, was elected to succeed Julius III as pope on 9 April 1555. He took the name Marcellus II. Experienced and well educated, he possessed integrity and was a humanist scholar of no small ability. His pontificate had a very promising start: he took a firm stand against nepotism, cut back the papal court and had an inexpensive coronation. But after only 22 days he died, aged just 53, from a stroke.

NO COMPROMISE

Paul IV (1555–9) was a fiercely ascetic authoritarian and reformer, whose uncompromising hatred of Charles V and Spain led the papacy to a damaging defeat. Before becoming pope, as Cardinal Gian Pietro Carafa, he was Pope Leo X's envoy to England and Spain, then in 1524 with Gaetano da Thiene cofounded the Theatines, an extremely ascetic clerical reform movement. He served on the ecclesiastical reform commission established by Paul III, and as cardinal after 1536 took responsibility for reorganizing the

PALESTRINA'S MISSA PAPAE MARCELLI

Perhaps the most celebrated mass by Giovanni Pierluigi da Palestrina, the *Missae Papae Marcelli* ('Pope Marcellus Mass') was written in honour of Pope Marcellus II, whose highly promising pontificate in 1555 lasted just three weeks. The work was traditionally sung at the papal coronation mass, up to and including the coronation on 30 June 1963 of Paul VI – the last pope to date to be crowned.

Above: Pius V. If he feared one thing, it was being too tolerant rather than too fierce. His reign was an austere period in which the Inquisition stamped out opposition. This insightful portrait is by Spanish artist El Greco (Domenico Theotocopuli).

Roman Inquisition. He was 79 on his election, and his pontificate brought conflict at every turn.

Paul knew his mind and would not compromise – or even listen to opposing arguments. In December 1555 he made an alliance with France in the hope of driving Spain from Italy; this provoked

war with Spain and led to a heavy defeat in August 1557, so Paul had to make peace from a position of weakness the following month. When Holy Roman Emperor Charles V abdicated and was succeeded by his brother as Ferdinand I, Paul refused to accept either decision on the grounds that he had not been asked for papal approval.

In his dealings with Protestant Europe, he had equally negative effects. He denounced the Peace of Augsburg of September 1555 that proposed an arrangement whereby Catholics and Protestants might live side by side in

Germany on the basis that in each state the ruler would determine the religion. In England he turned against Cardinal Pole and attempted to recall him to Rome on rather unconvincing charges of heresy – and his meddlings there served to pave the way for the return to Protestantism under Elizabeth I.

INDEX

In his rule the Roman Inquisition became a force to be feared – and he faithfully attended every one of its weekly meetings. He approved the drawing up in 1557–8 of the Index of Prohibited Books deemed too dangerous for the faithful to read, which included all the works of Erasmus. He turned ferociously on the Jews, creating a Jewish ghetto in Rome, and requiring Jews to converse only in Latin or Italian and to wear yellow hats on the street – measures that were to remain in force until the 19th century. Only one synagogue per city was permitted – and seven were destroyed in Rome.

On top of all this, Paul IV's reputation was badly damaged by the corruption and cruelty of his nephew Carlo Carafa, whom Paul had created cardinal. When

Below: The Blessed Virgin Mary, a painting by Francesco Zuccarelli. Pius V attributed victory in the Battle of Lepanto to her and declared the Feast of Our Lady of Victory to celebrate the triumph over the Turks.

Left: Pius supported Catherine de' Medici against the Huguenots (Calvinist Protestants). This portrait was painted by Catherine's contemporary, the French artist François Clouet.

Paul died on 18 August 1559, the news of his demise caused wild celebrations in Rome – crowds gathered to attack the Inquisition and set its prisoners free, and then felled and decapitated Paul's statue on the Capitol and hurled its head into the Tiber.

TRENT – FINAL SESSIONS

Pius IV (1559–65) retreated from many of these extreme positions – revising the Index, toning down the Inquisition and restoring peaceable relations with Spain. He reconvened the Council of Trent for its final session in 1562–3, and gave papal confirmation to its definitions and decrees in a bull of 26 January 1564, then on 3 November of the same year issued a summary of doctrine, *Professio Fidei Tridentina* ('The Tridentine Statement of Faith') that bishops were required to accept.

In Rome he built the Porta Pia (designed by Michelangelo) and the Villa Pia and rebuilt the church of Santa Maria degli Angeli. He died on 9 December 1565.

Pius V (1566–72) was another stern ascetic, a Dominican and a veteran of the Inquisition who as pope set about implementing the decisions and decrees of the Council of Trent. He often wore a hair shirt under his vestments and walked barefoot in penitential rites. He issued a catechism (1566), revised the

breviary (book of church services) in 1568 and missal (prayers and responses for celebrating Mass) in 1570, and established the Mass in the form in which it remained until the 20th century.

He excommunicated Elizabeth I in 1570; he sent financial and military aid to French regent Catherine de'Medici to attack the French Huguenots; he complained that Holy Roman Emperor Rudolf II was too tolerant of his subjects' religious behaviour. He joined the Catholic League that pitted Venice, Spain and the papacy against the Turks: this led to a major Catholic victory at the Battle of Lepanto in 1571. He declared the Feast of Our Lady of Victory to celebrate triumph in the Battle of Lepanto. Victory was attributed to the Blessed Virgin Mary.

Pius died in Rome on 1 May 1572 and this time there was no rejoicing. Indeed, he would be canonized on 22 May 1712 – the only pope between Celestine V in 1294 and Pius X (1903–14) to be declared a saint.

Below: This architectural study in brown ink by Michelangelo may be his design for the Porta Pia, which he built for Pius IV in the walls of Rome.

PAPACY AND THE COUNTER-REFORMATION

In the 1540s the papacy of Pope Paul III (1534–49) launched the Counter-Reformation, the Roman Catholic Church's fightback against the Protestant religious revolution.

Encompassing internal reform as well as energetic outreach, the movement was principally carried forward through the doctrinal teaching and decrees of the Council of Trent, through the education

Below: Pope Paul III launched the Counter-Reformation to revivify the Catholic Church, but his rule had many of the faults of the Renaissance papacy. This 1545 portrait by Titian shows him with his nephews.

and missionary work of new religious orders such as the Jesuits and a hard-hitting fight against heresy in the work of the Roman Inquisition.

This work was accompanied over decades by the redevelopment of the churches, streets and squares of Rome to create a city that would impress upon pilgrims the greatness of God and renewed vigour and glory of His Church. In 1600, Pope Pius IV presided over a Jubilee in which three million pilgrims came to Rome and they can only have been impressed by the major improvements to the city, which would carry on well into the early 17th century.

Above: The Jesuits were a driving force of the Counter-Reformation. Loyola received from Paul III the papal bull approving the foundation of the Jesuits in 1540.

ROLE OF PAPACY

In all these endeavours the papacy played a key role. Popes called the sessions of the Council of Trent and forcefully implemented its teachings and decrees, gave unwavering support to the Jesuits and other reforming orders and were energetic patrons and organizers of the improvements.

Despite being a worldly pontiff in many ways, Pope Paul III was the initial driving force of the movement. He called the Council of Trent, which met for its first session in 1545–7, gave papal backing to the formation of the Society of Jesus or Jesuits in 1540 and in 1542 set up the Holy Office of the Inquisition.

The first session of the Council of Trent agreed a whole series of enduringly important decisions. It defined the number of sacraments as seven and the doctrine on original sin. It established the canon of Old Testament and New Testament books. It fixed as authoritative

Right: Reformer St Philip Neri founded the Congregation of the Oratory, a society of secular clergy (those who are not monastics), in 1575. They had no formal vows.

the creed issued by the Council of Nicaea in 325 and the Council of Constantinople in 381. It rejected Luther's proposed justification by faith, arguing that a person was justified (moved from sin to salvation and righteousness) through the operation of the gratuitously given grace of God.

Julius III (1550–5) convened the second session of the council in 1551–2. This was boycotted by French bishops, but nevertheless defined the doctrine of transubstantiation (according to which the substance of bread and wine becomes wholly transformed into Christ's body and blood at the Eucharist).

Pius IV (1559–65) convened the Council of Trent a third time under a bull of 29 November 1560. The council met from 18 January 1562 to 4 December 1563 and agreed further reforms and doctrinal teachings including statements on purgatory, matrimony and the veneration of saints.

BORROMEO

In the preparation for and management of the council, Pius was highly reliant upon his nephew Charles Borromeo, one of the great figures of the Counter-Reformation. Pius had called Borromeo to Rome on his election and made him a cardinal; Borromeo then served as secretary of state to Pius and his principal adviser and afterwards was vital to the implementation of the decrees, which were confirmed in a papal bull of 26 January 1564 and summarized in the *Professio Fidei Tridentina* ('Tridentine Statement of the Faith') that Pius required all bishops to accept. He also played a key role in the development of the catechism brought out by Pius V (1566–72). Borromeo was canonized in 1610 and is celebrated as St Charles Borromeo on 4 November.

IMPLEMENTATION

The implementation of the decrees and teachings of the Council was continued by Pius V. As well as issuing a catechism (1566), he made a revision of the breviary (church service book) in 1568 and issued a missal (responses for Mass) in 1570.

Pope Sixtus V (1585–90) is seen as one of the key figures of the Counter-Reformation because he carried out major reforms of the Church's administrative system, notably establishing 15 congregations or departments in the Curia that remained largely unaltered until after the Second Vatican Council of 1962–5 and which were essential to the effective delivery of the reforms of the Council of Trent.

Sixtus also brought great drive and energy to the rebuilding of Rome intended to glorify God, the Church and the papacy. He was the pope under which the new St Peter's Basilica was completed in 1590, more than 80 years after the foundation stone had been laid by Pope Julius II (in 1506).

ROMAN CATHOLIC MYSTICISM

Another essential part of the Counter-Reformation was the spiritual renewal fostered by the poetic mysticism of Teresa of Avila and St John of the Cross and the devotional writings of Francis

de Sales. Spanish nun Teresa of Avila won the backing of Pope Pius IV in order to open the first Carmelite Reform convent (a reformed, more austere strain of the Carmelite order) in 1562. Her fellow Spaniard John of the Cross opened the first Carmelite reform monastery in 1568. Both wrote classic texts of contemplative faith – Teresa's works include *The Way of Perfection* (1583) and *The Interior Castle* (1588), as well as the autobiographical *Life of the Mother Teresa of Jesus* (1611); John wrote several celebrated poems on the process through which a soul might become united with God, including 'The Dark Night of the Soul' and 'The Living Flame of Love'. Born in what is now France, Francis de Sales served as Bishop of Geneva in 1602–22 and wrote *Introduction to the Devout Life* (1609), which declared that busy members of the laity could achieve spiritual perfection – and that this was not reserved for those who withdrew from the world.

Below: The Church fights back. Religion Overthrowing Heresy and Hatred was carved in c.1697 by Pierre Le Gros the Younger for the Jesuits' home church, the Gesù in Rome.

GREGORY XIII, 1572–85
BACKER OF THE JESUITS AND GREAT BUILDER OF SEMINARIES

Gregory XIII carried on the Counter-Reformation with energy, faith, enthusiasm and force – if anything, perhaps too much force. He took the fight to Protestantism and showed little mercy. But he is remembered above all for his commitment to the education of priests and missionaries, his strong support of the Jesuits and his reform of the Ancient Roman Julian calendar in the Gregorian calendar that he introduced in 1582.

Aged 70 on his election as pope, Ugo Boncompagni was nearing the end of a long and distinguished career as a canon lawyer and papal diplomat. After studying at the University of Bologna, he had taught canon law there for eight years, 1531–9, and was then sent by Pius IV to the Council of Trent. Made a cardinal in 1565, he was Pius's legate to Spain. He was elected pope on 14 May 1572.

EDUCATION AND MISSION
Gregory dedicated his pontificate to combatting Protestantism and to implementing the decrees of the Council of Trent. He established committees of cardinals to stamp out church abuses and revise the Index of Prohibited Books. He did not indulge in nepotism; although among the 24 cardinals he made, two

(Filippo Boncompagni and Filippo Vastavillano) were his nephews, these were generally considered worthy of their elevation to the cardinalate.

Above: An enthusiastic promoter of the Counter-Reformation, Gregory XIII was a major supporter of the Jesuits. He is remembered for his reform of the calendar.

Left: The Massacre of St Bartholomew's Day: Gregory called a Te Deum service of thanksgiving in St Peter's to celebrate the events of 24 August, 1572, in which 30,000 Huguenots were killed.

FACT BOX

Original name Ugo Boncompagni
Born 7 January 1502
Origin Bologna
Date elected pope 13 May 1572
Died 10 April 1585
Key fact Commissioned the Gregorian Calendar

Above: As part of his beautification of Rome, Gregory built fountains in three squares – including the Fontana de Moro, designed by Giacomo della Porta in 1575.

He especially responded to the council's call for the creation of seminaries to train a new generation of priests. In this area Gregory relied mainly on the Jesuits. He gave generously to the Germanicum college for training German priests, enlarged the Jesuit College in Rome, which became known as the Gregorian University, and backed the establishment of more than 20 Jesuit colleges in cities abroad, including Vienna, Douai, Graz, Augsburg and Prague. In Rome, colleges for Armenians, English, Greeks, Hungarians and Maronites were established.

Jesuit missionaries carried the faith out to east and west: to Japan, India, China and Brazil. In Rome, Gregory oversaw the building of the extraordinary Jesuit mother church, the Gesù, a magnificent example of the high Baroque style in architecture designed in 1568 by Giacomo della Porta.

He also gave official approval to a new religious order, the Congregation of the Oratory, founded in 1575 by Philip Neri as a community of priests who did not take monastic vows, but committed themselves to preaching and prayer. He also backed the reform of the Carmelites by St Teresa of Avila in 1580.

ST BARTHOLOMEW'S DAY

Gregory gave his backing to the use of military force against the Protestants of Europe, providing financial support for Roman Catholic rulers. He celebrated the Massacre of St Bartholomew's Day – the events sparked on 24 August 1572 in Paris, when as many as 30,000 French Huguenots (Calvinist Protestants) were killed in mob violence that may have been instigated by Catherine de'Medici – by calling a Te Deum service of thanksgiving in St Peter's. He commissioned Vasari to paint three frescoes in the Vatican commemorating the slaughter and issued a commemorative medal.

He provided troops and equipment to back rebellions in Ireland against the rule of Elizabeth I of England and may have been given his backing to a plot to assassinate her.

PALAZZO DEL QUIRINALE

Gregory built fountains in Rome in the Piazza del Pantheon, Piazza Navona and the Piazza del Popolo. His other building projects in the city included the Palazzo del Quirinale, built from 1574 onwards as a summer palace on the Quirinal Hill, the highest of the city's seven hills, well away from the summer humidity typical in the Lateran Palace. The new palazzo was designed by Ottaviano Mascherino; today it is the official residence of the Italian president.

Gregory also commissioned Giacomo della Porta to complete the magnificent Gregorian Chapel in St Peter's. This contains the extraordinary Altar of Our Lady of Succour (so called from a 12th-century fresco that Gregory had mounted there in 1578), celebrated for its amethysts, alabaster and columns of marble and porphyry. The chapel, sometimes claimed as the most beautiful anywhere in the world, also contains superb mosaics by Marcello Provenzale and Salvatore Monosilio.

ANARCHY IN THE PAPAL STATES

Gregory's enthusiasm as an artistic and educational patron brought the papacy close to penury. In an attempt to raise funds he attempted to confiscate territories and castles in the papal states, causing great unrest. Gregory died in Rome on 10 April 1585 with the papal states close to anarchy.

Below: Bernini's masterpiece depicts the Ecstasy of St Teresa of Avila. Her mystical work was a key part of the spiritual revival of the Counter-Reformation.

SIXTUS V, 1585–90
POPE SETS ROME ON PATH TO GLORY AS BAROQUE CITY

Sixtus V blew into the Vatican like a whirlwind. Impatient and choleric, he was willing to take draconian measures – and in just five years he reformed the Curia, repaired church finances and with brutal effectiveness restored peace in the lawless papal states. He also carried out major redevelopment in Rome.

He was an able, driven man who had risen on merit. Born in Ancona the son of a farmworker and himself a swineherd as a boy, he became a novice in the Franciscans at the age of 12, was ordained at Siena in 1547 and soon gained a reputation as a fine preacher: his Lenten sermons in Rome in 1552 won him the support of major figures of the Counter-Reformation including Ignatius Loyola, Philip Neri and the future popes Paul IV and Pius V.

His church career was assured, but his uncompromising approach led him into trouble early on: serving Pope Paul IV as inquisitor general in Venice, he was so high-handed in his dealings that he had to be recalled to Rome. Pope Pius V appointed him the Franciscans' vicar general and made him a cardinal in 1570 but, out of favour under Gregory XIII, he retired from church life to edit the works of Bishop Ambrose of Milan and build a villa on the Esquiline. The first volume of his edition of Ambrose was published in 1580, but his scholarship is said to be of indifferent quality.

CENTRALIZING POWER

Fittingly for a man of such personal force, when he was elected pope on 24 April 1585, the vote was unanimous. He set to work to curtail the power of the college of cardinals, under a papal bull of 3 December 1586 setting a limit of 70 on the number of cardinals – this was to remain the maximum until the pontificate of John XXIII (1958–63).

He created 15 congregations to govern the Church and administer its

Above: Sixtus the redeveloper of Rome. Moving the ancient Roman obelisk from the Circus of Nero to the centre of St Peter's Piazza before St Peter's took 800 men, 40 horses and 40 winches.

affairs – a set-up that remained largely unchanged until the reforms of the Second Vatican Council (1962–5). These included congregations to oversee the Index of Forbidden Books, the Sapienza (Roman University) and the Vatican Press and implement the Council of Trent.

He made a bold statement of papal authority over bishops: at the Council of Trent there had been some debate as to whether bishops derived spiritual authority from God or the pope, and

FACT BOX
Original name Felice Peretti
Born 13 December 1520
Origin Ancona, papal states
Date elected pope 13 May 1572
Died 27 August 1590
Key fact Oversaw completion of St Peter's Basilica

COMPLETION OF NEW ST PETER'S BASILICA

The new St Peter's Basilica was completed in 1590, the final year of Sixtus V's pontificate. It had been under construction since Pope Julius II had laid the foundation stone of the new basilica in 1506. Architects on the project included the great Raphael and Michelangelo; the final architects, who completed the building of the basilica's majestic dome, were Giacomo della Porta and Domenico Fontana, appointed by Sixtus in 1585. The lantern would be completed under Gregory XIV (1590–1) and the cross raised by Clement VIII (1592–1605).

Sixtus established that all bishops must submit to the pope in Rome and thereafter visit the city to make regular reports to the pope.

He transformed papal finances, cutting back on expenditure, imposing new taxes, extending public loans and raising vast sums through the sale of administrative and bureaucratic positions. Before the end of his short reign he had become immensely rich.

SHOW OF FORCE

Everywhere he acted at breakneck speed. It took him only two years to restore order in the anarchic papal states. No fewer than 7,000 outlaws were publicly executed in the course of his reign of terror; the heads of executed brigands were displayed on spikes on the Pont Sant-Angelo in the first year of his pontificate – and it was said that these outnumbered the melons for sale in the markets of Rome.

In foreign policy he supported military action against Protestant rulers. He pledged major backing for Philip II's planned attack on Protestant England –

Above: Both the façade of the Church of St John Lateran (background) and the Lateran Palace (left) were rebuilt by Domenico Fontana towards the end of Sixtus's pontificate.

and renewed the excommunication of Elizabeth I. In the event – after the failure of the Spanish Armada in 1588 – he did not pay. As a result of his support, the Catholic faith made great advances in Poland.

REBUILT TO GOD'S GLORY

Sixtus believed Rome should project the papacy's grandeur and spiritual power. Using his favourite architect, Domenico Fontana, he rebuilt the Vatican and the Lateran Palace, then oversaw the laying out of elegant new avenues and a

superb new aqueduct, the Acqua Felice, that carried fresh water a distance of 20 miles (32km) from Palestrina. Under his direction symbols of the city's pagan past were brought into the service of God and the papacy, as obelisks were raised in front of the Vatican, the Lateran, Santa Maria Maggiore and Santa Maria del Popolo, and statues of Saints Peter and Paul were placed atop the restored

Left: Pope Sixtus V rebuilt Rome to honour God. He used his energy and drive to complete the rebuilding of St Peter's Basilica in 1590.

Above: A gypsy predicts that Felice Peretti, the future Sixtus V, will become pope. Sixtus came from a poor background but showed great promise in his youth.

columns of Trajan and Antoninus Pius. His fierce will drove the long-term rebuilding of St Peter's Basilica to a triumphant conclusion.

Yet, for all this, he was deeply unpopular in Rome and following his death on 27 August 1590 crowds celebrated wildly in the streets and tore down the statue that had been erected in his honour on the Capitol.

URBAN VII TO GREGORY XV, 1590–1623
SUCCESSION OF PONTIFFS DIE AFTER VERY SHORT REIGNS

Seven popes governed the Church from 1590–1623, with three in the 16 months between 15 September 1590 and 30 December 1591 alone.

Urban VII was pope for just 13 days, 15–27 September 1590 – the shortest reign in the history of the papacy. Aged 69 on his election, he had served as papal ambassador to Spain and Inquisitor General and was known for his profound piety. He died before his coronation after contracting malaria on the very day after his election.

Gregory XIV (1590–1) carried on the church reform policies of his forerunners. He was elected with the backing of Philip II of Spain, a pretender to the French throne, and in international affairs promoted Philip's interests in excommunicating the Protestant King Henry IV of France and raising an army for invasion to support the French Catholic League.

Below: Clement VIII suffered from poor health towards the end of his life. He was visited by St. Philip Neri who attempted to cure him.

Curiously Gregory was afflicted with a tendency to laugh at inappropriate times – and this occurred during his coronation. He died of a gallstone that weighed 2.5oz (70g).

Innocent IX was pope for two months, 29 October–30 December 1591. He was 82 and in poor health when he was elected, towards the end of a career in which he had been papal nuncio to Venice and Patriarch of Jerusalem. During the reign of Gregory XIV he was largely in charge of the papal administration, due to Gregory's ill health, and so when he became pope himself policy continued without much change in supporting French Catholics against Henry IV.

KING BECOMES A CATHOLIC
The manoeuvrings over the French throne came to an end when Henry IV became a Catholic on 25 July 1593. The new pope, the able and hard-working Clement VIII (1592–1605), recognized Henry as French king and removed his excommunication in 1595. Clement also, through his papal legate Cardinal

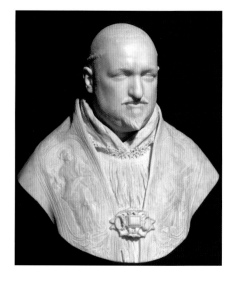

Above: Pope Paul V, by Bernini. Among Paul's acts were the canonization of Charles Borromeo and the beatification of Ignatius of Loyola, Teresa of Avila and Francis Xavier.

Alessandro de' Medici (later Pope Leo XI), negotiated peace between France and Spain at the Treaty of Vervins (a town in northern France) signed on 2 May 1598.

Clement committed himself to the work of the Counter-Reformation, expanding the Index of Prohibited Books and backing the Inquisition. In his pontificate the Inquisition condemned and executed the Dominican friar and polymath Giordano Bruno, who was burned at the stake on 17 February 1600 and has been much celebrated since for his original ideas on astronomy, God and the training of the memory. Bruno argued that the Sun is essentially a star as modern scientists understand that, and that the universe is infinite – with countless worlds containing intelligent beings.

That same year, 1600, saw a Jubilee in which as many as three million pilgrims visited Rome to pay their respects at the holy places of the city.

A probably apocryphal story involves Pope Clement in the history of the Western popularization of coffee.

BANK OF THE HOLY SPIRIT
The Banco di Santo Spirito was established by Paul V on 13 December 1605. It was the national bank of the papal states – and the first national bank in Europe. After two mergers it became the Banco di Roma in 1992 and after another merger became Capitalia in 2002. Capitalia was taken over by Unicredit in 2007.

According to this tale, Clement approved of the drinking of coffee when he was being urged to denounce it as 'the bitter invention of Satan' because of its popularity among Muslims.

Clement suffered from gout and spent the last part of his life in bed. He died on 3 March 1605 in Rome.

THE LIGHTNING POPE

When Cardinal Alessandro de'Medici became Leo XI aged 70, he survived less than a month, 1–27 April. He fell ill immediately after his coronation and was nicknamed 'the Lightning Pope' because his reign was so short.

Paul V (1605–21) was drawn into a serious dispute with Venice – principally over the use of a civil court to try priests

– that damaged the papacy's prestige. In May 1606 he placed an interdict on the republic with little effect, and the mediation of France was needed to bring the matter to a conclusion in April 1607. This made him cautious in international relations and he did not back German Catholics when violence broke out with Protestants at the start of the Thirty Years' War (1618–48).

In Rome, Paul restored the aqueduct of Trajan, which was renamed Aqua Paola in his honour, and built the Borghese Chapel (so called from his family name) in the Basilica of Santa Maria Maggiore.

SECRET BALLOT IN PAPAL ELECTIONS

Gregory XV (1621–3) carried out two major reforms. Firstly he introduced the procedures for papal elections that are

Left: Portrait of Pope Gregory XV and his nephew Ludovico Ludovisi by Domenichino (Domenico Zampieri). Gregory issued the last papal ordinance against witchcraft.

Above: Clement VIII appointed Francis de Sales (seated) Bishop of Geneva. Author of Introduction to the Devout Life, *Francis promoted Catholicism in Switzerland. He was canonized in 1665.*

largely still followed today – notably, the use of a written secret ballot in an election behind closed doors. These were contained in a papal bull of 15 November 1621. Secondly he established the Congregation for the Propagation of the Faith, a board to control missionary activity around the world. In 1622 he canonized Ignatius of Loyola, Francis Xavier, Philip Neri and Teresa of Avila.

In Rome he was a patron of the celebrated Baroque artist Guercino, who in 1623 painted the altarpiece 'The Burial of St Petronilla' for St Peter's Basilica, as well as of Gian Lorenzo Bernini and Alessandro Algardi, both of whom made his bust. He sat with his nephew, Ludovico Ludovisi (whom he made cardinal) for a fine double portrait by Domenichino (Domenico Zampieri).

Gregory died on 8 July 1623 in the Quirinal Palace.

URBAN VIII, 1623–44
FULL FLOWERING OF THE BAROQUE IN ROME

Urban's pontificate saw the fullest and most splendid flowering of the Baroque architectural and sculptural style in Rome. His reign is also remembered for the condemnation and imprisonment of astronomer Galileo Galilei by the Roman Inquisition.

The son of a Florentine nobleman, Maffeo Barberini came to Rome at an early age following his father's death. He was educated by the Jesuits in Rome and studied law at Pisa, then under Clement VIII was sent first as papal legate (1601) and then papal nuncio (from 1604) to Paris, where he became close to King Henry IV. Pope Paul V made him a cardinal in 1606 and he was elected pope, in succession to Gregory XV, on 6 August 1623.

COMBATTING THE HABSBURGS
Urban's pontificate saw the key period of the Thirty Years' War (1618–48) and the ministry of Cardinal Richelieu in

Below: Celebration, Baroque style – Glorification of the Reign of Pope Urban VIII *is a ceiling painting by Pietro da Cortona in the pope's Roman palace, the Palazzo Barberini.*

Above: Pope Urban VIII. He supported missionary work, revised the breviary and officially condemned slavery. He was a major patron of the sculptor Gian Lorenzo Bernini.

FACT BOX
Original name Maffeo Barberini
Born April 1568
Origin Florence
Date elected pope 6 August 1623
Died 29 July 1644
Key fact Did not defend his friend Galileo against investigations by the Inquisition

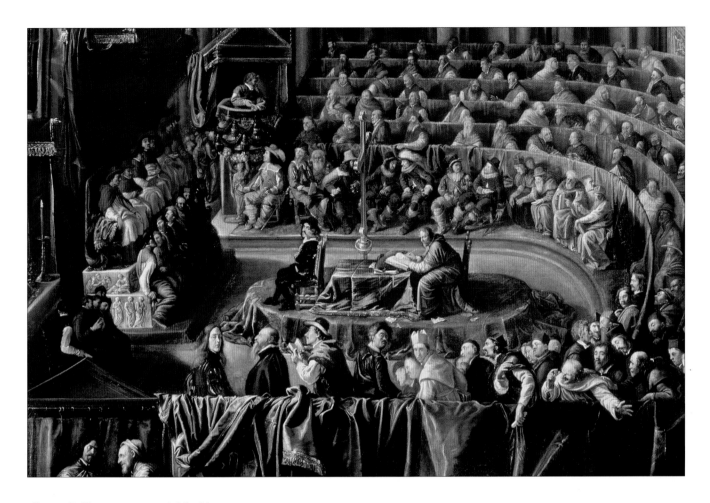

Above: Galileo was put on trial for his heliocentric theory because it challenged the biblical account of Creation. He was sentenced to life imprisonment (commuted to house arrest).

France. Urban tended to support French interests, partly as a result of his service as papal nuncio at the court of Henry IV but principally through a desire to combat the imperial ambitions of the Habsburgs of Spain and Austria.

He did not support the Habsburg Holy Roman Emperor Ferdinand II against the Swedish Protestant ruler Gustav II Adolf (better known as Gustavus Adolphus). After Cardinal Richelieu allied Roman Catholic France with Protestant Sweden and declared war on Roman Catholic Spain in 1635, the war – which had initially been between Catholics and Protestants – was no longer divided on religious lines but became a struggle between the royal houses of Bourbon and Habsburg.

GALILEO CONDEMNED

Italian astronomer, mathematician and natural philosopher Galileo Galilei was condemned by the Inquisition in 1633 and sentenced to life imprisonment (later commuted to house arrest) for advocating the heliocentric theory of the universe (according to which the Earth orbits the Sun) in his book of 1632, *Dialogue Concerning the Two Chief World Systems*. He was forced to recant on his support for the theory, which presented problems for the Church since it could not be reconciled with the biblical account of creation; heliocentrism had been proposed by Copernicus in his 1543 book *On the Revolutions of the Heavenly Spheres*, which was dedicated to Pope Paul III and

had drawn no papal condemnation, but it had later been condemned by Paul V in 1616. Urban was a friend of Galileo and had even written a Latin poem celebrating his achievement in identifying sun spots, but he did not defend the condemned man. Galileo was born in Pisa on 15 February 1564. He died aged 77 on 8 January 1642 near Florence.

Right: Galileo Galilei. According to legend, after the Church forced him to recant his theory that the Earth moves around the Sun, he muttered 'And yet it moves'.

Above: Bernini carved this bust of Urban's mother, Camilla Barbadori, and one of his father, Antonio Barberini, for the family vault at Sant' Andrea della Valle, Rome.

At home Urban looked to his defences. In Rome he fortified the Castel Sant'Angelo and built defences along the right side of the Tiber. He developed Civitavecchia as a successful military port, constructed Fort Urbano at Castelfranco and developed an arms manufacturing centre at Tivoli.

MISSIONARY OUTREACH

In church matters Urban gave substantial backing to missionary work. In 1627 he founded in Rome the Collegium Urbanum, a specialist training centre for overseas missionaries. He opened to all missionaries two countries – Japan and China – that Gregory XV had said were open only to Jesuits. Urban revised the breviary and issued a new edition in 1632. He himself wrote the Office of St Elizabeth and composed new hymns for the feasts of St Elizabeth of Portugal,

Left: A miracle in marble. Bernini's celebrated carving of the pope – with its extraordinary rendition in stone of the folds of cloth – is part of Urban's tomb in St Peter's Basilica.

Francesco Barberini to the cardinalate; he later appointed Francesco librarian of the Vatican. He made a second nephew, Antonio Barberini the Younger, first cardinal in 1627 then commander-in-chief of the papal troops and a third, Taddeo Barberini, Prefect of Rome. He made his own brother, another Antonio, cardinal and later granted him a position at the Vatican Library. Such appointments channelled wealth to the Barberini family.

ROMAN BAROQUE – AND BERNINI

Urban was a major patron of the great Baroque architect and sculptor Gian Lorenzo Bernini, from whom he commissioned the magnificent bronze canopy or baldachin above the high altar in St Peter's and Urban's own very grand papal tomb, also in St Peter's. Urban and Bernini were also responsible for the magnificent Triton Fountain in Piazza Barberini and the superb nearby Palazzo Barberini, the pope's family palace. Some of this work reused the bronze from the pantheon – and the Romans commented satirically, referring to the pope's family name, 'What the barbarians didn't manage, the Barberini achieved'.

Above: Directly beneath the dome of the basilica, St Peter's Canopy ('Baldacchino') covers the high altar. It was commissioned from Bernini by Urban close to the start of his reign in 1623 and completed in 1634.

RETURN TO NEPOTISM

His reign saw a return to the nepotism practised so enthusiastically by his predecessors. Only three days after his coronation, he raised his nephew

Below: Bernini also worked on the Palazzo Barberini, the pope's magnificently reconstructed family palace in Rione Trevi, Rome. He succeeded Carlo Maderno and Francesco Borromini on the project.

St Hermenegild and St Martina. He canonized Elizabeth of Portugal and Andrew Corsini and beatified several people, including John of God and Cajetan (Gaetano da Thiene), co-founder of the Theatines.

In Urban's bull of 22 April 1639 he condemned slavery in Paraguay, Brazil and the West Indies. Another bull, which was issued on 6 March 1642, condemned the *Augustinus*, a book on the theology of St Augustine by the late Bishop of Ypres, Cornelius Jansen, whose writings were the source of the movement of Jansenism.

INNOCENT X, 1644–55
POPE DOMINATED BY THE *PAPESSA*

Innocent X reversed most of the policies of his predecessor Urban VIII, supporting the interests of Spain rather than France in international affairs. He is remembered particularly for being dominated by his sister-in-law and perhaps lover Olimpia Maidalchini, who was notorious for her greed and avaricious self-interest.

SPANISH CONNECTION

Giambattista Pamphili studied in Rome and qualified as bachelor of laws. Under Gregory XV he served as papal nuncio to Naples and subsequently to Madrid. He was made cardinal-priest of Sant'Eusebio in 1626. He emerged victorious in 1644 from a troubled papal conclave in which the French and Spanish factions were at loggerheads; after rejecting the principal Spanish candidate, Cardinal Firenzola, the French members of the conclave accepted Pamphili as a compromise despite his known pro-Spanish sympathies.

Almost at once he set about unpicking the work of his predecessor, ordering an enquiry into the way Urban's relatives had enriched themselves and sequestering their wealth. Antonio and Francesco Barberini took to their heels, and sought refuge in Paris with Cardinal Mazarin,

FACT BOX
Original name Giambattista Pamphili
Born 7 May 1574
Origin Rome
Date elected pope 15 September 1644
Died 7 January 1655
Key fact Adopted pro-Spanish, anti-French policies

an Italian churchman who had succeeded Richelieu as chief minister of France. Innocent initially took a stern approach to this, but was forced to yield when the cardinal began to raise an army to invade Italy.

EUROPEAN INTERVENTIONS

He supported Spain in refusing to recognize Portugal's independence or accept its king, John IV of Braganza. When the Peace of Westphalia of 1648 brought an end to the Thirty Years' War, Innocent issued a bull declaring null and void any articles in the treaty that would have a negative impact on Catholic interests but his intervention was simply ignored by the parties involved.

In a papal bull of 1653 Innocent issued a further papal condemnation of Cornelius Jansen's *Augustinus*, to complement that issued by Urban VIII. Innocent condemned five propositions concerning God's grace and human free will from the *Augustinus*. The Jansenist controversy in France was to run for many decades.

'LADY POPE'

Although he attacked the relatives of Urban VIII for wrongfully appropriating church funds, Innocent was not above

Left: The finest portrait ever painted? Diego Rodriguez de Silva y Velázquez painted Innocent X in the midpoint of his pontificate, in 1650.

Above: Papal power: a bronze statue of Innocent by Alessandro Algardi. In the English Civil War (1642–49) Innocent sent his papal nuncio with troops to support the king and safeguard the Catholic faith in Ireland.

nepotism himself and funnelled wealth to members of his Pamphili family. In particular, he was dominated by his late brother's ambitious and worldly widow, Olimpia Maidalchini-Pamphili, who was in almost constant communication with the pope and appeared to hold a veto on his decisions. Said by a contemporary to be possessed of 'nauseating greed', and sometimes described as *papessa* ('lady pope'), she benefited from the sale of military and civil positions and of benefices.

The pope even appointed her Princess of San Martino in 1645, and some accounts claim that she used the expertise of her private pharmacist to poison cardinals in order to open positions that could then be sold for money. Some suggested she must have been Innocent's lover, although he was already

Right: Innocent was a major patron of the arts. The Palazzo Nuovo in the Piazza del Campidoglio was completed in his rule.

70 on his election and was 80 when he died. Her influence was only challenged by one of Innocent's relatives, Camillo Astalli, whom the pope made a cardinal and secretary of state, but she ousted him and he was removed from office.

PIAZZA NAVONA

In Rome, Innocent was responsible for the Baroque transformation of the Piazza Navona, which lay in front of his family palace, the Palazzo Pamphili. He commissioned the extraordinary 'Fountain of the Four Rivers' made in 1651 by Gian Lorenzo Bernini and the church of Sant'Agnese in Agone from father and son architects Girolamo and Carlo Rainaldi, together with Francesco Borromini. Girolamo Rainaldi also designed the magnificent family palazzo (1644–50), with its superb long gallery created by Borromini and decorated with frescoes by Pietro da Cortona.

Innocent was also a patron of the Spanish artist Diego Velázquez. When the artist visited Rome from Madrid in 1649–50 Innocent provided a warm welcome, presented him with a golden chain and medal and commissioned a superb portrait (see box). The picture captured a ruthless gleam in Innocent's eyes and some of those at the Vatican were afraid that Innocent would be unhappy with the result, but he reputedly declared 'All too true' when he first saw it and showed his appreciation by hanging the picture in the waiting room he kept for visitors.

Above: Archangel Michael tramples a Satan recognizable as Innocent. Guido Reni's painting of c.1636 is in the Capuchin church of Santa Maria della Concezione, Rome.

Innocent died on 7 January 1655 after an illness in which all his worldly wealth was stripped from him by hangers-on, especially his long-term adviser and intimate aide Olimpia Maidalchini-Pamphili. On his death Olimpia showed her true colours by refusing to meet the cost of his burial. The pope's body was left to lie in the corner of the sacristy at St Peter's for three days and was eventually given the simplest of burials, paid for by Innocent's former butler.

VELAZQUEZ PORTRAIT OF INNOCENT X

The portrait of Innocent X painted by Spanish painter Diego Velázquez in 1650 is considered by some to be the finest portrait ever painted. Now held in the gallery of the Palazzo Doria Pamphili, in Rome, it was the model for the 'Screaming Popes' series created by Irish artist Francis Bacon in the 1950s–60s.

CHAPTER TEN

PAPAL POWER AND INFLUENCE

ALEXANDER VII TO CLEMENT XIII, 1655–1769

In the mid-18th century Pope Benedict XIV won friends and admirers far and wide, even among opponents of the Roman Catholic Church. Voltaire wrote of him, in a couplet penned to accompany a portrait of the pope, 'Here is Lambertini, pride of Rome, and Father of the World, who instructs the whole world by his writings and honours all through his virtues.' This pope – admired for his moderation, intelligence and his support for the study of history and science – was rare in this era, for generally the popes from Alexander VII to Clement XIII struggled to come to terms with what became known as the age of reason and were unable to make their mark on the European stage.

In these years the pope was increasingly sidelined in international affairs. Clement XI attempted to position himself as a mediator in the War of the Spanish Succession but only succeeded in underlining the fact that the papacy no longer had a major role in the politics of Europe. Clement XIII was a saintly figure but despite being a firm supporter of Jesuits himself was unable to calm the chorus of demands for action against the society from the leaders of European countries and was close to dissolving the order when he died in 1769.

Yet these years also saw another succession of great papal artistic patrons who were responsible for beautifying Rome in the ornate and elaborate Baroque style. Under Alexander VIII, Bernini created the stately colonnade on St Peter's Piazza and the magnificent *Cathedra Petri* ('Chair of St Peter') in St Peter's Basilica. Bernini also reworked several squares. Clement X built the Palazzo Altieri and added a splendid fountain, designed by Bernini, to St Peter's Piazza.

Left: St Peter's Piazza was made elegantly beautiful by popes including Alexander VIII, who commissioned Gian Lorenzo Bernini's colonnade, and Clement X, who added the fountain – also by Bernini. This view is by 18th-century Italian artist Antonio Joli.

ALEXANDER VII, 1655–67
POPE WHO BUILT COLONNADE ON ST PETER'S PIAZZA

Alexander VII's 12-year pontificate saw the building of Gian Lorenzo Bernini's great masterpiece, the colonnade on St Peter's Piazza, and the religious conversion of Queen Christina of Sweden who settled in Rome as a Catholic.

Born into one of the grand families of Siena, Fabio Chigi was the grand-nephew of Pope Paul V (1605–21). Despite being unable to go to school as a child because of illness, he studied hard under the finest tutors and was awarded doctorates in theology, law and philosophy from Siena University. In a distinguished church career he served as vice-legate of Ferrara, Inquisitor of Malta and nuncio to Cologne, and attempted to defend the interests of the papacy in the negotiations that resulted in the 1648 Peace of Westphalia.

Thereafter he was made a cardinal by Innocent X (1644–55) and Bishop of Imola in 1652. He served as Innocent's secretary of state and was cardinal priest of the Church of Santa Maria del Popolo.

Below: Early in his rule, when he lived strictly and modestly, Alexander is said to have seasoned his meat with ashes. Later he reacquainted the papacy with the nepotism that had stained the reigns of earlier pontiffs.

The conclave that followed the death of Alexander's predecessor, Innocent X, lasted no less than eighty days because of the initial refusal of the French chief minister, Cardinal Mazarin, to accept Chigi, the preferred candidate, as pope; but in the end Mazarin backed down and the pious and learned Bishop of Imola became Pope Alexander VII.

MEMENTO MORI

Alexander was deeply devout. Initially he took a firm stand against nepotism and in the first year of his pontificate even banned his relatives from coming to Rome; in this period his papacy was

Above: Bernini was one of Alexander's preferred artists and devised a magnificent Baroque tomb (1672–78) for this pope in marble and gilded bronze in the north transept of St Peter's.

FACT BOX

Original name Fabio Chigi

Born 13 February 1599

Origin Siena, Republic of Florence

Date elected pope 1 April 1655

Died 22 May 1667

Key fact Reiterated condemnation of Jansenists

Above: Bernini restored the Scala Regia, the staircase to the Sistine Chapel, in 1663–66 during Alexander's pontificate.

notable for the simple life he led: he reputedly gave audience in a room containing human skulls and a coffin as a *memento mori* (reminder of mortality – from the Latin, 'remember you will die').

But in 1656 he reversed his position, seemingly persuaded by advisers that family ties made governance stronger, and appointed relatives to key ecclesiastical and civil positions.

LITERARY INTERESTS

He personally maintained a simple life and focused much of his interest on literature and learning. He published a book of Latin poems in 1656 and expanded the Vatican Library. He also issued a new edition of the Index of Prohibited Books and an apostolic constitution (or decree) stating the doctrine of the Immaculate Conception of the Blessed Virgin Mary.

FRENCH TROUBLE

Alexander had difficulty dealing with France. French king Louis XIV broke off relations, seizing Avignon and the surrounding area; Alexander was forced to acquiesce, and accepted a humiliating settlement in the Treaty of Pisa in 1664. In France the Jansenists claimed that

Innocent X's condemnation of their theology in 1653 was not just, since the propositions concerning divine grace and human free will he condemned were not found in the *Augustinus* of Cornelius Jansen; but Alexander, who advised Innocent on the initial document, reconfirmed the condemnation in his 1665 papal bull *Ad Sacram* ('To the Sacred'). He sent to France a 'formulary' – a document to be signed by all clergy and used as a means of identifying and disciplining those with Jansenist sympathies.

ROYAL CONVERT

Queen Christina of Sweden converted to Catholicism and abdicated her throne in 1654. She travelled to Rome and entered the city in a splendid sedan chair designed by Bernini that had been despatched to greet her by Alexander VII. On Christmas Morning 1655 Alexander confirmed her in the faith in a ceremony in St Peter's. She lived in exile in Rome in the Palazzo Farnese and then the Palazzo Corsini for the next 35 years, until her death in 1689.

Alexander died on 22 May 1667 in Rome. Gian Lorenzo Bernini designed a magnificent marble tomb for him erected in St Peter's Basilica in 1672–8.

Below: Queen Christina in Sweden by Pierre-Louis Dumesnil the Younger. She converted to Catholicism and made her way to Rome to live as a guest of the papacy.

THE PAPACY AND BAROQUE ART AND ARCHITECTURE

The spectacular Baroque style began as the art of the Counter-Reformation. The popes and other Church patrons set out to create sacred architecture and art that made a direct appeal to the emotions and senses of the faithful.

Under a succession of popes, Rome was transformed, the city's churches made beautiful to the glory of God and in the service of the Counter-Reformation. The city was remodelled, the old huggermugger of medieval alleys and roads replaced with straight streets that terminated in vistas of grand buildings and fine squares with fountains, obelisks and columns. The purpose of Baroque art for the papacy and the

Below: The drama of space and light that typified Baroque church architecture is on display in the interior of St Peter's, Rome – pictured here in 1750 by Giovanni Paolo Pannini.

ecclesiastical hierarchy was to energize the faithful and impress them with the greatness of God and His Church. Baroque artists made both a sensuous and a spiritual appeal to worshippers, often combining naturalistic and dramatic treatments of a subject.

COLOUR AND DRAMA

In promoting these styles, the papacy and Church were also countering in a dramatic and engaging fashion the call for plainness made by the churches of the Protestant Reformation. While many Protestants denounced religious art as idolatrous, worshipped in plain chapels and even embarked on iconoclastic sprees in which they painted over frescoes with whitewash and destroyed statues and stained glass windows, the art of the Roman Catholic Counter-Reformation embraced the colour, drama and emotion of religious encounter.

Above: Gian Lorenzo Bernini was the pre-eminent Baroque artist. Allegorical figures representing Charity and Justice adorn his tomb for Urban VIII in St Peter's.

EXTRAVAGANT 'BAROQUE'

These works of art were not called Baroque at the time. The label 'Baroque' was originally a term of abuse in art criticism. It was used to describe painting, sculpture and architecture that was bizarre or extravagant, which did not follow the conventional proportions and rules; right up to the end of the 19th century 'Baroque' meant art that was overdone or strange, with too much decoration. The word may derive from the Italian *barocco* (originally a philosophical term that came to mean a convoluted process of thought).

Baroque art generally belongs to the 17th century. In some places – for example, in Germany and in European colonies in South America – some of the finest flowerings of the style grew up in the 1700s. But in Italy, and particularly in Rome – the birthplace of the

style – Baroque architecture and art began to appear in the second half of the 16th century.

In Rome, the Chiesa dei Gesù (Church of the Gesù), the mother church for the Society of Jesus or Jesuits, was begun in 1568 in the pontificate of Gregory XIII (1572–85) and is widely seen as the first great example of Baroque architecture. The church was begun to plans by architect Giacomo da Vignola; but his designs, largely in the prevailing Mannerist style, were transformed by Giacomo della Porta, with the assistance of Giovanni Tristano.

The Gesù – a single nave without aisles that focuses attention on the high altar, with a great dome above the crossing of the nave with the transepts – was highly influential on the design of churches built throughout the Baroque period. Its interior – completed in the following century – is lavishly decorated, a riot of marble and gilt ornamentation, frescoes, columns and statues.

The nave ceiling vault features one of the great masterpieces of Baroque sacred painting – a fresco entitled *Triumph of the Name of Jesus* by Giovanni Battista Gaulli, painted 1678–9. Another dramatic Baroque sacred painting, *The Burial of St Petronilla*, was made in 1623 by Guercino (Giovanni Francesco Barbieri) for Gregory XV in St Peter's Basilica.

SPECTACLE

Baroque architecture set out to create a dramatic spectacle. The styles – developed by architects including Carlo Maderno (1556–1629), Francesco Borromini (1599–1667) and Gian Lorenzo Bernini (1598–1680) – laid emphasis on monumental size, created drama using space and light and took pleasure in lavish interior decoration using colour, texture and fine materials.

Carlo Maderno was architect to Pope Paul V and worked on St Peter's Basilica. He designed the Church of Santa Maria della Vittoria ('Our Lady of Victory' –

the church that contains one of the greatest and most celebrated pieces of Baroque sculpture, Bernini's *Ecstasy of St Teresa*), and worked with his nephew Francesco Borromini on the Palazzo Barberini for Urban VIII (1623–44). Borromini also worked on the Church of Sant'Agnese in Agone, part of Pope Innocent X (1644–55)'s reworking of the Piazza Navone.

THE GENIUS OF BERNINI

But the greatest Baroque architect and sculptor was Gian Lorenzo Bernini, who worked for popes from Urban VIII to Alexander VII (1655–67), creating a long series of masterpieces. Bernini took over the Palazzo Barberini for Urban VIII while still a prodigy in 1629; he also designed the Triton Fountain in the Piazza Barberini before the palazzo. For this pope he additionally created the magnificent baldachin or bronze canopy

Above: The altar in the Cornaro chapel of Carlo Maderno's church of Santa Maria della Vittoria. Bernini's exuberant Ecstasy of St Teresa – *one of the greatest pieces of Baroque sculpture – is visible behind.*

over the high altar in St Peter's and an extravagant tomb, also in St Peter's. For Innocent X he created the extraordinary 'Fountain of the Four Rivers' in the Piazza Navona.

He designed another series of great works for Pope Alexander VII (1655–67), including the colonnade on St Peter's Piazza together with the *Cathedra Petri* ('Chair of St Peter') and Alexander's tomb in the basilica. Also under this pope's patronage, Bernini worked on the Chigi Chapel in the Church of Santa Maria del Popolo and restored the Scala Regia, the staircase that links the Vatican to St Peter's, as well as reworking a number of Roman squares.

CLEMENT IX TO INNOCENT XII, 1667–1700
POPES ARE INCREASINGLY MARGINALIZED

The majority of popes from Clement IX to Innocent XII clashed with Louis XIV of France over control of the French church. Some also gave valuable support to campaigns against the Ottoman Turks in Europe. Generally these popes struggled with the consequences of the papacy's ever-declining temporal power.

POET AND LIBRETTIST
Clement IX (1667–9) has a most unusual distinction among popes: he wrote the libretti to several operas – and

Above: Cardinal Pietro Ottoboni became Pope Alexander VIII in 1689. One of the acts of his two-year reign was to buy Queen Christina of Sweden's books and manuscripts for the Vatican Library.

indeed is credited with having created the genres of sacred opera and comic opera. Among his works were the comic opera *Chi soffre Speri* ('The One who suffers also hopes'), where his libretto, based on tales by Giovanni Boccaccio, was set to music by Virgilio Mazzocchi and Marco Marazzoli; he also wrote the

sacred opera *Sant' Alessio* (St Alexis), with music by Stefano Landi. Both were written in the 1630s, well before Giulio Rospigliosi (as he was then known) became pope. The future Clement IX was also a notable poet and a patron of French painter Nicolas Poussin, from whom he commissioned the celebrated painting *A Dance to the Music of Time*. He carried on his artistic interests during his pontificate, opening Rome's first public opera house.

As pope he was known for his charity and kindliness, and he brought about a brief respite for the Jansenists in his Peace of Clement IX, signed in January 1669, and also was a mediator in the negotiations between France, Spain, England and the Netherlands that brought about the Peace of Aachen in 1668.

SUCCESS AGAINST OTTOMANS
Clement X (1670–6) was elected in his 80th year and his administration was largely conducted by Cardinal Paluzzi degli Albertoni, to whom he was distantly

Below: This bust of Clement X was one of Gian Lorenzo Bernini's last sculptures. He was 79 when elected pope and initially said 'I am too old to bear such a burden'.

connected by marriage after Clement's niece had married the cardinal's nephew. The cardinal channelled wealth shamelessly to his family and the pope's reputation was damaged as a result.

Clement contributed to a major success against the Ottomans, sending financial support to Polish general John Sobieski who defeated the Ottomans in November 1673 and thereafter became King of Poland. The pope also clashed with King Louis XIV of France over Louis's claim that the French king should take control over appointments to and revenues from bishoprics in France.

GALLICAN CHALLENGE TO PAPAL AUTHORITY

Relations with France worsened further under Innocent XI (1676–89). After Innocent warned Louis XIV that his aggressive claims were nothing less than an insult to God, the majority of the French clergy signed up in March 1682 to four Gallican articles, which denied

the papacy authority in temporal matters and declared that a general council of the Church was superior to the pope. Innocent rejected these articles and the relationship with Louis continued to deteriorate. In January 1688 Innocent excommunicated Louis and his ministers and in September that year Louis once again occupied Avignon and the surrounding area.

Elsewhere papal support of King John Sobieski of Poland reaped benefits: in 1683 Sobieski drove the Ottomans back from the very gates of Vienna; Innocent put together a Holy League combining Holy Roman Emperor Leopold I, Sobieski, Venice and Russia, which succeeded in forcing the Ottomans out of Hungary in 1686 and freeing Belgrade in 1687.

Innocent was a highly devout man of undoubted integrity who lived a simple, frugal life as pope. He is generally viewed as the finest pontiff of the 17th century. In the penultimate year of his reign Catholicism suffered a setback in England in 1688 when the Catholic King James II was ousted from the English throne and replaced by his

Below: Spanish mystic St John of the Cross was a key figure of the Counter-Reformation. He was beatified on 26 January 1675 by Clement X and canonized by Benedict XIII in 1726.

Above: The funeral monument of Innocent XI in St Peter's was made by French sculptor Pierre-Etienne Monnot. The tomb features a bas-relief celebrating John Sobieski's defeat of the Turks at Vienna.

Protestant daughter Mary and her Dutch husband William of Orange. The following year, on 12 August 1689, Innocent died.

IN DEFENCE OF ORTHODOXY

A former head of the Roman Inquisition, Alexander VIII (1689–91) took a hard line in support of doctrinal orthodoxy. He once again condemned Jansenism, and issued a censure to followers of Spanish mystic and priest Miguel de Molinos, who had been sentenced to life imprisonment in Innocent XI's reign for his teaching of Quietism (which promoted mental tranquillity as a truer means of religion than formal worship).

Innocent XII (1691–1700) was elected after a five-month conclave. His first act as pope was to take a stand against nepotism, issuing a papal bull in 1692 that banned popes from giving offices, revenues or estates to their relatives and did away with the office of cardinal nephew. He declared that the poor were his nephews, and began a programme of charitable care for the needy. He made the Lateran Palace into housing for the unemployed and greatly enlarged the orphanage of the Ospizio di San Michele.

CLEMENT XI, 1700–21
PAPACY HUMBLED IN WAR OF THE SPANISH SUCCESSION

The status and authority of the papacy suffered severely in the War of the Spanish Succession (1701–14). Clement XI was unable to mediate in the conflict, and the treaties that ended the war distributed papal territories to new rulers while the pope could only watch.

Born in Urbino to a noble family, Giovanni Francesco Albani was a brilliant scholar, known by the age of 18 for the elegance of his translations from Greek into Latin, educated in Rome and taken up there by Queen Christina of Sweden and her coterie of men of letters. He became a doctor of canon and civil law, and served successively as Governor of Rieti, Sabina and Orvieto. He later became Vicar of St Peter's, Secretary of Papal Briefs and Cardinal-priest of San Silvestro. During this period he drafted Pope Innocent's condemnation of nepotism.

In contrast to several elderly predecessors, he was only 51 years old when he was elected to the papacy on 23 November 1700. But his relative youth and vigour were not enough to enable him to make a mark on the international stage at a time when the papacy and its political interests were sidelined.

THE SPANISH SUCCESSION
During the 46-day conclave that delivered Pope Clement XI, King Charles II of Spain died. At the close of Innocent XI's reign, the pope had recommended

Above: Clement is represented in procession across St Peter's Square in this painting by Pier Leone Ghezzi. He made improvements to the Piazza del Pantheon.

to Charles II, who had no children, that he should choose as his heir Louis XIV's grandson, Philip of Anjou, rather than Holy Roman Emperor Leopold I's son Charles, Archduke of Austria; Charles II changed his will to this effect.

Now on his death Louis XIV despatched Philip to Madrid to claim the throne as King Philip V of Spain. But naturally enough Leopold contested the will – conflict was inevitable; yet no one could have known that this struggle, the War of the Spanish Succession, would last 13 years from 1701 to 1714.

Before becoming pope Clement had been one of the cardinals who had advised Innocent on his decision; as pope, Clement favoured the accession of Philip – and, indeed, he sent a letter to Madrid congratulating the new Spanish king. At the beginning of the war, however, he attempted to maintain a position of neutrality and to position himself as mediator. In this he failed.

French troops captured Milan but in 1706 the imperial general Eugene of Savoy drove them out. In 1707 the troops of Leopold's son, Holy Roman Emperor Joseph I, invaded the papal states and captured Naples, and Clement was forced to abandon Philip V and recognize

Below: Clement XI was pope for around 20 years and died at the age of 71 in March 1721. He was unable to prevent the loss of papal territories.

Leopold's younger son (and Joseph's brother) Charles as the rightful king of Spain. Philip abruptly ended diplomatic relations with Clement.

But then the unexpected death of Joseph I – from smallpox, at the age of just 33 – changed everything. Were Charles to succeed to the Spanish throne and, as was inevitable, also succeed his brother as Holy Roman Emperor, he would become vastly powerful. When a new status quo was thrashed out at the treaties of Utrecht and Rastatt of 1713–14, the papacy was no more than a bystander. Various papal possessions – including Naples, Parma, Sardinia and Sicily – were handed to new rulers in the settlement without regard to papal claims. The pope was not strong enough to intervene and had to accept it.

CONFLICT OVER JANSENISM
Clement issued a stern bull *Unigenitus Dei Filius* ('The Only-begotten Son of God') condemning the Jansenists in France. It provoked an outcry: four bishops challenged it, with the backing of 12 others and some 3,000 clergy. In August 1718 Clement excommunicated the four bishops but the churchmen

Below: St Louis Cathedral, which stands in the French Quarter of New Orleans, is the oldest cathedral in the United States. It was founded in Clement's reign, in 1718.

maintained their opposition and renewed their appeal against the bull in 1720. Gallicanism, which sought to restrict the papacy's power in France, was resurgent and the prestige of the pope was ever-declining. The controversy rumbled on until Clement's death on 19 March 1721.

CHINESE RITES
Clement also provoked major difficulties for Jesuit and Dominican missionaries in China. The Chinese Rites Controversy centred on whether – as a way of easing conversions – it was permissible for missionaries to accept certain local ceremonies in honour of Ancient Chinese philosopher Confucius and ancestors of the Chinese emperors. Clement decreed in 1704 and again in 1715 that this practice was not permissible and after the second ruling many Chinese turned against the missionaries and began to persecute Christians in China. Several missions were closed down.

PATRON OF ARTS
In Rome, Clement founded an academy of painting and sculpture in the Campidoglio and made alterations to the Piazza del Pantheon and the Church of Santa Maria degli Angeli e dei Martiri, where he added a celebrated sundial. A learned and virtuous man, he enriched the collections of the Vatican Library.

Above: The controversy over the Jansenists (followers of Dutch theologian Cornelius Jansen) is represented in this satirical engraving of 1714. Clement made a declaration against the Jansenists.

JANSENISM
The reform movement of Jansenism derived from the writings of Dutch theologian Cornelius Jansen, in particular his four-volume *Augustinus*, published in 1640. In this work Jansen, who served as professor of theology at Louvain in 1630 and Bishop of Ypres in 1636, defended writings of St Augustine of Hippo on free will and divine grace and attacked the teachings of the Jesuits on these issues – and in particular emphasized the necessity of divine redeeming grace for the salvation of a soul damaged by original sin. Jansenism became closely associated with Gallicanism – a movement that sought to restrict the power of the papacy in France. Innocent X (1644–55) and Alexander VII (1655–67) made declarations against the Jansenists, as well as Clement XI. After the promulgation as French law in 1730 of Clement's *Unigenitus* bull, Jansenists mainly took refuge in the Netherlands.

INNOCENT XIII TO CLEMENT XII, 1721–40
POPES BEAUTIFY ROME BUT THEIR PRESTIGE FAILS

From Innocent XIII (1721–4) to Clement XII (1730–40), three elderly popes were unable to prevent the continuing decline in the papacy's prestige and international standing. But in their pontificates the Baroque splendour of Rome was further enhanced, with the addition of the famous 'Spanish Steps' and the magnificent Trevi Fountain.

THE CONTI POPES
Innocent XIII (1721–4) was – like his distant predecessors Innocent III (1198–1216), Gregory IX (1227–41) and Alexander IV (1254–61) – a member of the noble Conti family. He was the last pope to take the name 'Innocent'. Elected pope on 8 May 1721 after a lengthy conclave dominated by disputes between French and imperial cardinals, he was already 66, overweight and in poor health. But he was known also for his kindness and intelligence.

There was no hiding the political weakness of the papacy. Innocent had to invest Holy Roman Emperor Charles VI with sovereignty over Naples and Sicily, recently prized papal possessions, and curried favour with France by making a cardinal of the French councillor of state, the dissolute and highly unsuit-

Above: Clement XII in a painting by Agostino Masucci. He defied old age and poor health, including blindness, to be an energetic and effective pope.

able Abbé Guillaume Dubois. Nevertheless Innocent maintained a hard line on Jansenism, firmly refusing a request that his predecessor's *Unigenitus* bull be recalled, and was strict with the Jesuits – in the light of the Chinese Rites Controversy, banning the Jesuits from carrying on their mission in China and from taking in new members.

Innocent supported the exiled claimant to the English throne, James Edward Stuart (known as the 'Old Pretender'), and allowed Stuart and his court to remain in residence in the Palazzo Muti, which Clement XI had given to the exile.

DEVOUT BUT NAÏVE
The pontificate of Benedict XIII (1724–30) was a political and diplomatic disaster. The Church's new leader had many qualities: scholarly, pious and frugal, he lived as a Dominican friar while pope, visited the sick and cared for the poor. He regularly waited on the poverty-stricken at his table and sought to curb the ostentation of many cardinals, in particular banning the wearing of wigs. But he was also naïve, far too trusting of the man to whom he handed control of other papal business – the corrupt and self-interested Cardinal Niccolò Coscia, who took bribes and sold offices for his own financial gain.

Benedict also caused a diplomatic crisis by refusing when King John V of Portugal sought to nominate candidates

Below: James II of England's Catholic son, James Edward Stuart, lived in Rome as a guest of Clement XI and Innocent XIII.

THE OLD PRETENDER
James Francis Edward Stuart – known as 'the Old Pretender' – was the son of King James II of Great Britain. As a Roman Catholic from 1671, James II had been ousted in the revolution of 1688 in which his Protestant daughter Mary and her Dutch husband William of Orange came to the throne as William III and Mary II. After his father's death in 1701 James Francis Edward Stuart was proclaimed his successor in France and recognized as such by King Louis XIV. However, attempts to restore him to the throne, including the Jacobite Rebellion of 1715, all failed – and after Louis's death he came to Rome, where Clement XI gave him the Palazzo Muti as his residence and Innocent XIII granted him a lifetime annuity. He maintained a 'Jacobite court' in Rome, where his son Charles was born. This young man – the Young Pretender, also known as 'Bonnie Prince Charlie' – failed in his attempt to reclaim his throne in 1745–6 and lived out his life in exile, claiming the title King Charles III of Great Britain after his father's death in 1766.

Above: Another of Rome's Baroque masterpieces, the vast Trevi Fountain was designed by architect Nicola Salvi for Pope Clement XII and constructed in 1732–62.

to the Sacred College, as many other European royal courts did; John broke off relations and attempted to stop the paying of Portuguese alms to Rome.

SPANISH STEPS

Benedict's reign also saw the completion and inauguration in 1725 of the Scalinata della Trinità dei Monti, the famous 'Spanish Steps' that climb from the Piazza di Spanga to the Piazza Trinità dei Monti in Rome.

ELDERLY BUT ENERGETIC

Clement XII (1730–40) was 78 on his election, and during his pontificate was often bedridden and was completely blind from 1732 onwards – his hand had to be positioned in the correct place for him to sign papal documents. Yet for all his declining physical and mental powers, this elderly man somehow remained full of energy. He arrested, tried and imprisoned for ten years the corrupt Cardinal Niccolò Coscia and took various measures to try to reinvigorate papal

finances – including reintroducing the Roman lottery, which Benedict XIII had outlawed.

On the international stage he could do little in the face of the new spirit of indifference to papal territorial and political interests: Holy Roman Emperor Charles VI simply annexed former papal territories and Don Carlos of Spain marched through the papal states and helped himself to Naples and Sicily.

Clement did deliver effective support for missionary work, for example despatching Franciscans to Ethiopia, and issued a papal bull in 1738 condemning Freemasonry and threatening with excommunication any Catholic who joined the masons.

In Rome, Clement was a patron of many fine works – including the new façade for the archbasilica of San Giovanni in Laterano and the superb Corsini Chapel within, both designed by Alessandro Galilei, and the laying out of the Piazza di Trevi and the construction there of the extraordinary Fontana di Trevi (Trevi Fountain): 86 feet (26

Right: St Vincent de Paul helps the plague-ridden in a painting by Antoine Ansiaux. He was canonized by Clement XII in 1737.

metres) high, it is a baroque masterpiece designed by architect Niccola Salvi. Clement also enriched the holdings of the Vatican Library and on the Capitol opened a public museum of antique sculptures, the first of its kind in Europe.

Long a sufferer of gout, he developed a hernia and trouble with his bladder and died on 6 February 1740 at the close of what, given his age, very poor health and the international circumstances, was a remarkably successful pontificate.

BENEDICT XIV, 1740–58
MODERNIZING POPE WHO CORRESPONDED WITH VOLTAIRE

At a time when the Catholic Church was facing severe criticism from philosophers of the European Enlightenment, Benedict XIV was an engaging and learned pope who won widespread admiration for his moderate approach to the difficulties encountered by the papacy and especially for his wit, intelligence and dedicated support for higher learning and the study of science and history. He became popular throughout Europe, liked and praised by Protestants as well as Catholics.

THEOLOGIAN AND LAWYER

A gifted and determined scholar, Prospero Lambertini (the future Benedict XIV) was awarded doctorates in theology, canon law and civil law by the University of Rome at the age of 19. He was made a cardinal in 1728 by Benedict XIII, and served with great distinction as first Bishop of Ancona and then Archbishop of Bologna.

The conclave from which he emerged as pope lasted a full six months following the death of Clement XII on 6 February 1740; finally, Lambertini emerged as a surprise candidate and was elected pope on 17 August, taking the name Benedict in tribute to the pope who had raised him to the cardinalate. He famously said

to the cardinals, referring to the two other leading candidates: 'If you want to elect a saint, choose Gotti; a statesman, Aldobrandini; a good man, elect me.'

Above: Benedict XIV raises his arm to deliver a blessing. He was a great reformer and educational patron. The portrait is by French artist Pierre Subleyras.

Left: Benedict presents an encyclical addressed to the bishops of France to the Comte de Stainville. Painting by Pompeo Girolamo Batoni.

> **FACT BOX**
> **Original name** Prospero Lambertini
> **Born** 31 March 1675
> **Origin** Bologna, papal states
> **Date elected pope** 17 August 1740
> **Died** 3 May 1758
> **Key fact** Highly popular pontiff and a major patron of education

He was a good choice: in addition to being learned and serious-minded, he was kindly and accessible, funny and witty, happy to meet the people of Rome during his regular walks in the city. He engaged with a lively society of intellectuals in Rome and corresponded with many of the leading intellectual figures of the day. These included the French historian-philosopher Voltaire who dedicated his 1741 tragic play *Mahomet* to Benedict.

AUSTRIAN TROUBLES

His papacy was quite effective politically: he improved relations with Spain and Portugal, coming to an agreement in 1740 under which the Portuguese monarch had rights of patronage over all abbeys and bishoprics in his kingdom and another in 1753 under which the Spanish crown gained the right to appoint to some 12,000 church livings. However, he got into some difficulty over the disputed succession to the Holy Roman Empire following the death in 1740 of Emperor Charles VI. His initial refusal to decide and then his support for Charles Albert of Bavaria after he was elected Emperor Charles VII soured relations with Queen Maria Theresa of Austria, daughter of Charles VI and wife of the other candidate, Francis of Lorraine, Grand Duke of Tuscany: in 1742 she announced the seizure of church benefices in Austria. In the event Charles VII died only three years later and Francis succeeded as Holy Roman Emperor Francis I. Relations were restored after Benedict formally recognized him.

PATRON OF LEARNING

Benedict was one of the greatest of papal patrons, but in education rather than architecture and painting. In Rome he created four academies for the study of Christian and Roman antiquities, church history and canon law and liturgy. At the city's university he established professorial chairs of chemistry, physics and mathematics; at the University of Bologna, his native city, he created a chair of surgery. He also initiated the

cataloguing of the Vatican Library. He drew up new rules for the Index of Prohibited Books, so that books could only be banned with the pope's approval. His ecclesiastical writings, notably the *Institutiones Ecclesiasticae,* were honoured. He wrote what is still regarded as the standard official work on canonization.

REFORMS

Benedict was an active reformer, setting to work to improve priestly education, the breviary (the Church's book of liturgical rites) and the calendar of feasts. He issued an encyclical in 1745 condemning usury and effectively stamped it out. A bull of 1748 defined the conditions under which mixed marriages between Protestants and Catholics were permissible; these notably included that the children of the marriage should be brought up in the Catholic faith.

To save money he refrained from creating any cardinals for four years. He improved financial revenue from the papal states by introducing changes to agricultural practices and was able to cut taxes. He delivered himself of forthright decisions on the Jesuits and the 'Rites

Above: Silvio Valenti Gonzaga was Benedict's secretary of state. He was a devoted art collector, and this painting by Giovanni Paolo Pannini shows his gallery.

Controversy' and the driving of South American peoples into slavery. His popularity across Europe with intellectuals and others of religious backgrounds made Catholics and Romans proud. When he died on 3 May 1758 the city of Rome was plunged into grief.

LAWS ON MISSION

Benedict issued two bulls, *Ex quo singulari* in 1742 and *Omnium sollicitudinum* in 1744, prohibiting the native customs such as ancestor worship that the Jesuits had allowed in missions to native peoples. He required missionaries to take an oath that they would not allow such practices in future; many converts abandoned the Christian faith. In 1741 another of his bulls, *Immensa Pastorum Principis*, spoke out against the enslavement of native peoples in South America.

CLEMENT XIII, 1758–69

POPE OVERWHELMED BY SERIES OF ATTACKS ON JESUITS

The pontificate of Clement XIII was dominated by a major scandal involving the Jesuits, in the course of which they were driven out of Portugal, France, Spain, Naples and Parma. When European rulers then demanded the dissolution of the Society of Jesus, Clement was forced to summon a consistory to bring this about, but he died in February 1769 on the night before it was due to meet.

Clement was in fact a staunch supporter of the Jesuits, in contrast to his predecessor who had had distinctly mixed feelings about the Society. Born in Venice, the future Clement XIII was educated by the Jesuits in Bologna before becoming governor of first Rieti and then Fano. Raised to the cardinalate by Clement XII in 1737, he became Bishop of Padua in 1743 and was elected pope on 6 July 1758 as a compromise candidate after the French had vetoed the conclave's earlier choice.

SAINTLY BUT INDECISIVE

He was not the character needed to deal effectively with the coming storm over the Jesuits. He was by no means the impressive wit and philosophical thinker that his predecessor had been. He lacked imagination and verve – he ordered, as Paul V had done, the covering up or even painting out of some of the more risqué elements of the papacy's Renaissance art, including sections of the Sistine Chapel frescoes. Strong in

faith, moderate, a lover of justice, he may have had elements of the saint about him – but he was unable to come up with a decisive response to the onslaught of Enlightenment thinkers against the Jesuits and the Church.

Within two months of his election he faced the crisis. King Joseph I of Portugal, believing that members of the Society of Jesus had been involved in a conspiracy to murder him, confiscated their riches and drove them out of his country, sending them to the Roman seaport of Civitavecchia as a 'gift' to the pope. Diplomatic relations were broken off.

Above: Rezzonico was educated by the Jesuits in Bologna and once installed as Pope Clement was a supporter of the Society of Jesus.

FRENCH ONSLAUGHT

The flames of anti-Jesuit feeling spread through France, which was primed already by the presence there of the writer and philosopher Voltaire and the *philosophes*, free-thinking intellectuals who increasingly saw the Church (which they privately called the *Infâme* or 'infamous one') as ridiculous and dangerous – an enemy of freedom.

FACT BOX

Original name Carlo della Torre Rezzonico

Born 7 March 1693

Origin Venice

Date elected pope 16 July 1758

Died 2 February 1769

Key fact Added French *Encyclopédie* to Index of Prohibited Books

---

Above: Clement's magnificent marble tomb in St Peter's was commissioned by his nephew, Senator Abbondio Rezzonico, and designed by the neoclassical sculptor Antonio Canova.

Voltaire – despite his open admiration for Benedict XIV – was scathing about religion, the Church and the Jesuits. He wrote to Frederick the Great, 'So long as there are rogues and fools in the world, there will always be religion … ours is the most ridiculous, absurd and bloodthirsty that ever infected the earth.' He and the philosophes saw an attack on the Jesuits as the first step in bringing down the Church herself – Voltaire wrote to French philosopher Claude Adrien Helvétius, 'When we have destroyed the Jesuits, we shall have easy work with the *Infâme*.'

The Jesuits came under strong attack and in 1764 Louis XV, influenced by philosophes at court, issued a decree declaring the Society of Jesus abolished in France and expelling all Jesuits from his country.

In Spain, Charles III held the Jesuits responsible for riots and may even have been persuaded that they were plotting against him. He banished them on 27 February 1767, and in the course of that year and 1768 the Jesuits were also expelled from Naples, Sicily, Malta and the Duchy of Parma and Piacenza.

WHAT TO DO WITH THE HOMELESS JESUITS?

Initially Clement, fearing the potential consequences of the influx of so many exiled Jesuits, refused to allow them to come to Rome or the papal states. Many settled in Corsica but had to move on again when the French purchased the island in 1768. Then Clement showed compassion, and allowed the bedraggled and impoverished Jesuits to settle in the papal states.

CLASH WITH PARMA

When the Duke of Parma and Piacenza, a former papal territory, issued a proclamation in 1768 that forbade all appeals to Rome unless with the duke's permission, and banned all papal edicts including bulls, Clement was affronted and pronounced the duke's decree and other earlier anticlerical laws null and void, declaring for good measure that those responsible were to be excommunicated by his bull *In Coena Domini*. This provoked widespread outrage. France took possession of Avignon; Naples seized Benevento. Voltaire even made the statement that it was not fitting for the pope to rule any territory at all.

Above: Charles III of Spain. Clement's bull Quantum ornamentum *of 1760 approved his request to invoke the Immaculate Conception as Patroness of Spain.*

Then in January 1769 came a demand from the ambassadors of France, Spain and Naples that the Society of Jesus be abolished. Clement never recovered his equanimity. He ordered a consistory to consider the matter on 3 February, but the night before its opening he died in Rome following a stroke.

THE ENCYCLOPÉDIE AND THE ENLIGHTENMENT

The French *L'Encyclopédie, ou dictionnaire raisonné des sciences, des arts ets des métiers* ('The Encyclopedia, or systematically arranged dictionary of arts and crafts') was published in 28 volumes in 1751–72. Edited by Denis Diderot and initially also by Jean le Rond d'Alembert, the work included criticism of the Roman Catholic Church – including attacks on the monastic way of life and clerical celibacy – and Clement XIII had it placed on the Index of Prohibited Books.

Right: Pope Clement XIII had Denis Diderot's 'Encyclopedie' placed on the Index of Prohibited Books. 'The Art of Writing' is an engraved plate from the encyclopedia.

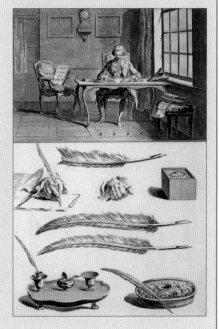

CHAPTER ELEVEN

POPES IN AN AGE OF REVOLUTION

CLEMENT XIV TO LEO XIII, 1769–1903

Pope Pius VII was crowned on 21 March 1800 with a tiara made of papier-mâché and in the Benedictine monastery on the island of San Giorgio Maggiore, Venice, rather than in Rome. When his predecessor Pius VI died in captivity in France, Rome was not safe due to severe unrest following its occupation by the French in 1798, and the conclave from which Pius VII was elected was held on San Giorgio Maggiore under the protection of Holy Roman Emperor Francis I. Pius was crowned with a papier-mâché tiara because the French had taken possession of the original when they occupied Rome.

At the start of his pontificate Pius set about repairing relations with the French Republic. He signed a concordat in 1801 with Napoleon, at this point First Consul of France. But when the pope travelled by invitation to Napoleon's coronation as emperor, he was a mere spectator – Napoleon crowned himself and his empress Josephine. The relationship soured quickly: Napoleon occupied Rome and annexed the papal states, Pius excommunicated Napoleon in 1809 and was then imprisoned by him from 1809–14. As in the previous century, the papacy was unable to hold its own on the international stage.

At the Congress of Vienna in 1814, the papal states and Rome were restored to the pope. The popes were not yet ready to give up their standing as temporal rulers; they felt they needed worldly power in order to exercise spiritual authority. Yet they were unable to hold on to this worldly power. The establishment of the Kingdom of Italy in 1860 during the pontificate of Pius IX saw the papal states annexed and the pope's temporal power wiped out.

Left: French power, papal humiliation. Rather than performing the coronation himself, Pope Pius VII merely looks on as Napoleon crowns his empress, Josephine, in Notre Dame de Paris on 2 December 1804.

CLEMENT XIV AND PIUS VI, 1769–99
POPES WHO FACED A TIME OF REVOLUTION

After Clement XIV (1769–74) carried out the dissolution of the Jesuits that had been pressed so forcefully on his predecessor, Pius VI (1775–99) ruled for 24 years – the longest pontificate up to this date in the history of the papacy. Pius had to face the consequences of the French Revolution of 1789, not least the invasion of the papal states by French general Napoleon Bonaparte.

At the start of his pontificate Clement XIV managed to hold off international pressure to dissolve the Jesuits for four years. Initially he set out to restore peace, renouncing papal claims to Parma and so regaining control of Avignon and Benevento, then reconnecting with Portugal by appointing as a cardinal Paulo de Carvalho, brother of the Portuguese Secretary of State

the Marquis of Pombal, and sending a papal ambassador to the Portuguese royal court.

Clement was intelligent, approachable, frugal and honest. He was well versed in church history and theology and known for his fine speech and educated conversation. But he had no diplomatic experience and was slow to take decisions; he wanted to keep the peace, but lacked the necessary strength of character.

BULL OF DISSOLUTION

Finally, under the threat that unless he wound up the Jesuits Spain and France would break off relations with the papacy, he dissolved the Society of Jesus in his bull *Dominus ac Redemptor noster* ('Our Lord and Saviour') of 16 August

Above: A relatively youthful pope, Clement died aged just 68 in 1774. His neoclassical tomb was designed by Antonio Canova and is in the Church of the Santi Apostoli, Rome.

NAPOLEON

Corsican-born French general Napoleon Bonaparte was First Consul in 1799–1804, then Emperor of the French in 1804–15. He was forced to abdicate and

exiled on the island of Elba in 1814 then returned to power in March 1815 until he was defeated at the Battle of Waterloo and forced again into exile on St Helena.

Despite his intermittent conflict with the papacy, he was a Roman Catholic throughout his life. In 1796, at the head of the French army, he had orders to invade Rome and depose the pope, but signed a treaty that guaranteed Pius VI safety in Rome. In 1800 as First Consul he declared his interest in achieving reconciliation between France and the Holy See, but his relationship with Pope Pius VII was fiery: Napoleon annexed the papal states, occupied Rome and imprisoned the pope, and for his troubles was excommunicated. When the defeated and captive Napoleon was in exile on St Helena at the end of his life Pius exhibited forgiveness by sending him a chaplain.

Left: Napoleon Bonaparte invades. The French army occupied the papal states, proclaimed a Roman Republic and announced the deposition of the pope as the head of state.

Right: Clement dissolves the Jesuits in 1773. He had tried to resist pressure from France and Spain to wind up the Society.

1773. He declared as one of the reasons for his decision that it was impossible to restore 'a true and lasting peace' in the Church while the Society was in existence. Many Jesuits found refuge in Russia and Prussia, where the authorities declined to implement the bull.

Being effectively forced to carry out the dissolution hit Clement hard. He had been educated by the Jesuits in his hometown of Rimini, and in his 30s he had dedicated a theological work to the founder of the Jesuits, Ignatius of Loyola.

After signing the bull of dissolution, Clement was filled with remorse, suffered from depression and lived in fear of his life – convinced that he was going to be assassinated. When he died at the relatively young age of 68 on 22 September 1774, there were whispers that he had been poisoned, but an autopsy established that he had died of natural causes.

RETURN OF NEPOTISM
With Pius VI (1775–99), in an era of crisis when an exceptional pope such as Benedict XIV was needed, the papacy fell back into bad, old ways – nepotism and profligacy. Pius was proud and somewhat vain: tall and good-looking, he lacked seriousness and was not profoundly spiritual. He constructed the Palazzo Braschi in Rome for his nephew Luigi Braschi Onesti: a throwback to the

Renaissance that proved to be the last such palace financed and built by a pope for his relatives. He spent very freely on the arts, particularly on expanding the Museo Pio-Clementino in the Vatican.

TROUBLE WITH THE EMPIRE
Pius faced a major difficulty with Holy Roman Emperor Joseph II who in 1781 introduced church reforms in the empire under which non-Catholic minorities were granted toleration, seminaries were taken under control of the state and would provide trainee priests with a liberal as well as a religious education, some

Below: The French Revolution struck in 1789. Clement is among the powerful brought low in this cartoon depicting 'The Electrical Spark of Liberty that will Topple the Thrones of all Corrupt Monarchs', 1793.

1,300 monasteries were closed and various church festivals and traditions that were deemed superstitious in the era of the Enlightenment were abolished. Pius attempted to intervene and made a personal trip to Vienna in 1782; he was well received but achieved little.

FRENCH REVOLUTION – PAPACY UNDER ATTACK
When the French Revolution struck in 1789, an effigy of the pope was burned in Paris. The inhabitants of Avignon, still a papal territory, declared themselves citizens of France. The French clergy were made state employees. Pius initially took no action but in 1791 after the clergy were required to take an oath of loyalty to the state, he denounced the Revolution and the Declaration of the Rights of Man.

Then in 1796 the French army under Napoleon Bonaparte invaded northern Italy with the intention of taking the papal states and Pius had to sign a humiliating peace treaty at Tolentino on 19 February 1797. When in December that same year a French general was killed in the course of a riot in Rome, the die was cast: the French occupied the city on 15 February 1798 and a republic was declared. The pope was deposed as head of state. Pius died in humiliation and captivity at Valence, in France, on 29 August 1799.

PIUS VII, 1800–23
DIGNIFIED IN DEALINGS WITH NAPOLEON

In the 23-year pontificate of Pius VII, the papacy began to win back lost prestige and international sympathy. After initially making peace with Napoleonic France, Pius acted with courage in challenging and excommunicating Napoleon – and with dignity when he was captured and held in French captivity in 1810–14. He made a triumphant return to Rome following Napoleon's fall from power and regained much of the land lost to French invaders.

Born to a noble family in Cesena in 1742, Barnaba Chiaramonti was related through his mother to the future Pope Pius VI (1775–99). He became a Benedictine aged 16 in 1758 and after working as a professor of theology and philosophy in the order's colleges in Rome and Parma, rose to become cardinal-priest in the basilica of San Callisto and Bishop of Imola in 1785 under his relative Pius VI. He was himself pious and gentle, and proved brave in adversity.

EQUALITY AND DEMOCRACY

While a cardinal, in 1797, Pius had declared in a homily that there was no necessary incompatibility between Roman Catholicism and democracy – stating 'equality is an idea not of the philosophers but of Jesus Christ' – and from the start of his pontificate he set out to establish good relations with the French Republic. His representative Ercole Consalvi, whom Pius appointed

Above: Pius VII initially made peace with France. This portrait by the celebrated French artist Jacques Louis David was made at the Tuileries in 1805.

to the key position of Cardinal Secretary of State, negotiated a concordat in 1801 with Napoleon, at this point First Consul of France, under which dioceses in France were reorganized and Roman Catholicism confirmed as the country's principal religion. However, Pius was forced to protest when additional articles were unilaterally added to the document by Napoleon in 1802; under these, the pope needed the approval of the French government for his rulings in France.

SPECTATOR AT NAPOLEON'S CORONATION

Pius travelled to Paris in 1804 to consecrate Napoleon as Emperor of France. The coronation proved something of a humiliation for the pope: Napoleon not only kept him waiting for a full hour, but also insisted on performing his own coronation, as well as crowning Empress Josephine, while the Pope merely looked on. Pius's role as mere spectator is emphasized in Jacques-Louis David's celebrated painting of the event – with Pius's disgruntlement clear to see.

Relations between pope and emperor were not to recover. Seeking to establish a Kingdom of Italy in his own name,

---

FACT BOX

Original name Luigi Barnaba Gregorio Chiaramonti

Born 14 August 1742

Origin Cesena

Date elected pope 14 March 1800

Died 20 August 1823

Key fact Showed charity to French leader despite ill treatment

---

When the United States won a notable victory over Berber Muslim pirates of northwest Africa in the First Barbary War of 1801–5, Pius declared that in bringing about the defeat of the pirates – who were a scourge of Christian shipping in the Mediterranean – the USA had 'done more for the cause of Christianity than the most powerful nations of Christendom have done for ages'. Pius also approved the establishment of several dioceses in the USA: Boston, New York, Philadelphia and Bardstown in 1808, Charleston (1820) and Cincinnati (1821).

Napoleon occupied Rome in 1808 and declared the papal states annexed to France in 1809. Pius attempted to fight back: he excommunicated Napoleon on 10 June 1809. But he was afterwards seized from the Quirinal Palace and taken first to Grenoble, France, then to Savona, northern Italy, and in 1812 back to France and captivity at Fontainebleau. There Pius – in very poor health and bullied by Napoleon – signed a draft concordat on 25 January 1813 under which the pope would give up all temporal power and the seat of the papacy would be moved from Rome to France.

RETURN TO ROME
Recovering his mind and health, Pius wrote to Napoleon two months later to repudiate the concordat. By this stage Napoleon had his hands full dealing with the collapse of his empire. Pius was released in 1814 and made a triumphant return to Rome: the horses of his carriage were freed and the carriage drawn into the city by 30 young men from Rome's leading families.

At the Congress of Vienna in 1814, with Napoleon defeated and exiled to Elba, the pope regained possession of the papal states and Rome. Napoleon's return, defeat at Waterloo and final exile to St Helena did nothing to change this.

Above: Jacques-Louis David also painted Pius's discomfiture as a mere onlooker at the coronation of Napoleon in Notre Dame, Paris. Napoleon crowned first himself and then his empress.

By 1815 the international standing of the papacy was significantly restored from the low points of the previous century. Napoleon's harsh treatment of the

Below: Antonio Canova, sculptor of tombs for Clement XIII and XIV, was the most celebrated artist of his age in Europe. This portrait is by English portraitist Thomas Lawrence. Canova died in 1822.

pope, Pius's dignified resistance and his behaviour in captivity had won widespread admiration and restored respect for the pope. In the years that remained to him before his death on 20 July 1823 Pius set to work to adapt the Church to the new conditions of the modern world. He signed 20 concordats with different countries, generally having to cede the long-disputed right of the pope to appoint bishops, but achieving the re-establishment of many monasteries and seminaries that had been closed and regaining control of schools.

REVIVAL OF THE JESUITS
In addition, Pope Pius VII revived the Jesuits in 1801 for Russia, in 1813 for Ireland, England and the United States and elsewhere in 1814. He issued condemnations of Protestant Bible Societies and of Freemasons and in 1817 revised the working of the Congregation of Propaganda.

Given the way he was treated in captivity, Pius showed considerable Christian charity towards Napoleon after the French emperor's downfall. He allowed Napoleon's relatives – including his mother Princess Letitia and brothers Lucien and Louis – to settle in Rome and sent Abbé Vignali to St Helena as a chaplain for Napoleon in his exile.

LEO XII, 1823–9
POPE WHO WORKED TO AGENDA OF CONSERVATIVE CARDINALS

The pious, authoritarian Leo XII largely reversed the reforming policies of his predecessor. His rule in the papal states, where a feudal aristocracy and ecclesiastical courts were re-established, won him a reputation as a tyrant and was denounced as 'government by priests'.

Della Genga rose to high ecclesiastical position through being private secretary to Pius VI (1775–99), then served as papal nuncio briefly in Lucerne and for 11 years (1794–1805) in Cologne. He gained significant diplomatic experience – although he was sacked from his position in 1814 by Cardinal Consalvi, who held him responsible for failings in the negotiations to regain control of Avignon. Subsequently cardinal-priest of Santa Maria in Trastevere, he was appointed Vicar General of Rome in 1820 by Pius VII (1800–23).

Below: Rome under Leo's rule, *in 1825, by Silvestr Feodosievich Shchedrin. Life was highly regulated, and all residents had to attend instruction in the Catholic faith. Many Jews left Rome and the papal states.*

PASSION FOR SHOOTING BIRDS

Leo XII was tall, handsome and gifted as a speaker – winning great admiration for the well-judged funeral oration he delivered in the Sistine Chapel in 1790 on the death of Holy Roman Emperor Joseph II. He lived simply, with little furniture, not eating much – and was persistently unwell, troubled in particular by piles; although he had a passion for music and for shooting birds, he was generally puritanical. In outlook he was somewhat narrow-minded, a conservative committed to strict tradition rather than compromise and so naturally opposed to the modernizing reforms of Pius VII.

CONSERVATIVE RULE – CLIMATE OF FEAR

His election as pope on 28 September 1823 after a 26-day conclave at the Quirinal Palace came about through the influence of the *zelanti*, a conservative group of cardinals who wanted firm leadership for the Church. He was 63 years old and in very poor health –

Above: Leo is carried through St Peter's in Rome. A conservative, he introduced regulations and a strict regime that provoked unrest in the papal states.

almost at death's door. However, he recovered – in some accounts, due to the intervention of the Bishop of Marittima, who prayed fervently for his restoration to health – and set to work to deliver on the agenda of the zelanti.

He strengthened the work of the Inquisition and introduced a host of regulations governing daily life in Rome and the papal states. He banned the open sale of alcohol, outlawed the playing of games on feast days or Sundays – with offenders subject to a jail sentence; he declared that dressmakers who made low-cut or transparent dresses would be

FACT BOX

Original name Annibale Sermattei Della Genga

Born 22 August 1760

Origin La Genga, near Spoleto

Date elected pope 28 September 1823

Died 10 February 1829

Key fact Hated for tyrannical rule

Above: The Jesuits, shown here in conclave discussing their accounts, were a resurgent force under Leo and re-established their Collegio Romano.

excommunicated. He banned encores and great ovations in theatres – and even outlawed the ad-libbing of lines by actors – because he felt these encouraged the expression of seditious ideas.

PERSECUTION OF JEWS

He forbade Jews to own property, gave them a very short time to sell what they owned, banned them from doing business with Christians and forced them once again to live in ghettos behind high walls and locked gates. In Rome, he required 300 Jews to attend a weekly Christian sermon. Many Jews left Rome to settle in Tuscany and Lombardy. The economy of the papal states slowed to a crawl.

These rules and strict forms of government were rigidly enforced by a regime that created a climate of fear and made full use of informers. Life was austere under Leo's rule and he was immensely unpopular. His delegate in the south of Italy, Cardinal Palotta, brought in martial law to tame outlaws,

introducing fines for villages found to be harbouring criminals and even abolishing courts of law because he claimed judges might be subject to intimidation. But he was so unpopular that he was

made to stand down after a month and the outlaws financed the singing of Masses of Thanksgiving.

EDUCATION AND ECCLESIASTICAL DISCIPLINE

Under Leo the Jesuits were resurgent. The society's education system was revived and the Collegio Romano re-established. By a papal bull of 1824 Leo put all schools in Rome and the papal states under priestly control.

Leo also reiterated his predecessors' pronouncements against Freemasonry and Protestant Bible Societies and in May 1825 issued a condemnation of indifferentism, the argument that all religions were of equal standing.

In international affairs, he was more successful and maintained good relations with both Protestant and Catholic countries. He supported Roman Catholics in Britain who were under the yoke of discriminatory laws and signed concordats with Hanover in 1824 and the Netherlands in 1827.

CARBONARI AND SANFEDISTI

Two popular groups with enduring influence were in opposition in early 19th-century Italy. The carbonari – 'charcoal burners' – were members of an anti-clerical revolutionary secret society established in Italy in the early 1800s. Pius VII issued a papal constitution, *Ecclesiam a Jesu Christo*, in 1821 under which carbonari were excommunicated and denounced for plotting against the Church and the primacy of the pope. Later Pius IX would issue an encyclical, *Qui Pluribus*, that was seen as an attack on the movement. Their influence fed into the *Risorgimento* movement that led to the unification of Italy in 1861. *Sanfedisti* were members of an anti-Republican movement called *Sanfedismo* ('Holy Faith'). Initially the counter-revolutionary movement was founded by Cardinal Fabrizio Ruffo in 1799 to mobilize peasants from the papal states

against French occupation of the former Kingdom of Naples. The name was applied more generally to religiously inspired peasant armies and to those who rose up against the House of Savoy in the build-up to Italian unification.

Below: The anticlerical carbonari met in secret. This illustration is from an album on the history of the Risorgimento movement that led to the unification of Italy.

PAPAL MISSIONS TO SPREAD THE GOSPEL AROUND THE WORLD

Spreading the Gospel is a responsibility for all Christians, not least the leader of the Roman Catholic Church – from the preaching of St Peter to the globetrotting missions of modern popes such as Paul VI (1963–78) and John Paul II (1978–2005).

THE GREAT COMMISSION

The Church's missionary activity has its origin in the command of the Risen Christ to carry his teachings all over the world. As told in Matthew 28:16–20, Jesus appeared to the disciples after his crucifixion and resurrection and told them, 'All authority in heaven and earth has been given to me. Go therefore and

Left: The Jesuits arrive by ship on the coast of New Granada, bringing the Christian faith to the Spanish territory in the northern part of South America.

make disciples of all nations, baptizing them in the name of the Father and the Son and the Holy Spirit, teaching them to observe all that I have commanded you.' Missionaries call Christ's command to carry the Gospel around the world 'the Great Commission'.

ST PETER THE MISSIONARY

Before becoming leader of the Church in Rome, St Peter himself preached a key sermon to a gathering of Gentiles at Caesarea, as described in the Book of Acts Chapter 10. He declared that God shows no partiality, but accepts those in every nation who fear him and do what is right. He declared himself a witness of all that Jesus did and recalled that Jesus 'commanded us to preach to the people and to testify that he is the one appointed by God to be judge of the living and the dead.' The account continues, 'While Peter was still saying these things, the Holy Spirit fell on all who heard the word. And the believers from among the circumcised who had come with Peter were amazed, because the gift of the Holy Spirit was poured out even on the Gentiles.'

Over the centuries many of Peter's successors supported missionary outreach. The report that Pope Eleutherius (c.175–c.189) sent missionaries to Britain at the request of a British king named Lucius is thought to be apocryphal, but Gregory I (590–604) sent missionaries

Left: The third Mughal emperor, Akbar the Great, welcomed Jesuit missionaries to India and hosted debates between his visitors and local Muslim scholars.

– including St Augustine of Canterbury – to England and they reputedly baptized thousands of locals on Christmas Day 597. In the 8th century Gregory II sent the great missionary St Boniface to what is now Germany.

THE RELIGIOUS ORDERS

In the Middle Ages the great religious orders of the Dominicans and the Franciscans were connected to mission from their foundation. The Dominicans were approved by Honorius III (1216–27) to combat heresy and preach the Gospel; their founder, St Dominic Guzman, was inspired to found the order while taking part in a mission to the heretic Albigensians in the south of France. The Franciscans won the support of Innocent III (1198–1216) in their early years as an order ready to preach orthodoxy and combat heresy. Later the Jesuits – established in the pontificate of Paul III (1534–49) – were also dedicated to education and foreign mission.

Members of these orders carried the Gospel around the world. For example, Nicholas IV (1288–92) sent the Fran-

Below: The Mission San Francisco de Asis is the oldest surviving structure in San Francisco. It was established in June 1776 by the Franciscans.

ciscan John of Montecorvino as the first Roman Catholic missionary to China; Dominican monk Jordanus Catalani (flourished 1321–30) was a key missionary to India. In the 16th century Franciscan and Dominican missionaries travelled to the New World with European explorers and adventurers.

In this work they were encouraged by popes such as Alexander VI (1492–1503) and Paul III (1534–49). In 1493 Alexander VI gave orders that Spain should establish missions through the New World; in 1537 Paul III commanded that the native peoples of the New World be converted to Christianity 'by the preaching of the divine word'.

Jesuits led important missions around the world – in Japan and China, in Brazil and Canada – but were also active throughout Europe as part of the Counter-Reformation, winning back Protestants to Roman Catholicism.

PAPAL MISSIONARY JOURNEYS

In the modern era, while there are specially established Roman Catholic missionary orders – including the Missionaries of the Sacred Heart (founded 1854) and Maryknoll (formerly the Catholic Foreign Missionary Society of America, founded 1911), as well as many members of larger religious orders such as Franciscans and Jesuits working in overseas missions – several popes have personally taken up the missionary mantle, travelling tirelessly to encourage the faithful, strengthen the Church and spread the Gospel.

Paul VI (1963–78) became the first pope to fly by aeroplane and helicopter and landed on six continents. He visited India, Colombia, the USA, Portugal, Turkey and the Holy Land and made a pastoral journey to Africa in 1969.

In his 26-year pontificate, John Paul II (1978–2005) travelled 680,000 miles (1,100,000 km) while visiting 129 countries in the course of 104 official journeys. He attracted vast crowds including four million people for the

Above: Benedict XVI visited Benin on 18–20 November 2011. It was his second visit to Africa, after an earlier mission to Cameroon and Angola in 2009.

Roman Catholic youth festival World Youth Day on January 15, 1995. He was the first pope to visit Mexico and Ireland, the first pontiff in the modern era to visit Egypt and the first reigning pope to visit the UK; in the USA he was the first pope to visit the White House in Washington, D.C., where he was greeted by President Jimmy Carter in 1979.

Benedict XVI (2005–13) also travelled widely on apostolic missions. He made visits to Turkey, Austria and the USA; in Brazil in 2007 he canonized an 18th-century Franciscan friar, Antonio Galvao, the first Brazilian-born saint. He was in Australia for World Youth Day 2008 and in 2009 visited Cameroon, Angola, Israel, Jordan and Palestine.

As the first South American pope, Benedict's successor Francis visited Brazil on his first overseas trip as pontiff, in July 2013. For Roman Catholic World Youth Day he attracted a crowd of three million – many of whom camped out overnight – to hear him celebrate Mass on Copacabana Beach, Rio de Janeiro.

PIUS VIII AND GREGORY XVI, 1829–46
A MODERNIZER FOLLOWED BY AN AUSTERE CONSERVATIVE

Pope Pius VIII (1829–30) and Gregory XVI (1831–46) were starkly contrasting pontiffs. While Pius generally followed in the modernizing footsteps of his mentor Pius VII (1800–23), Gregory reverted to the style of the harsh and authoritarian Leo XII (1823–9). In his 15-year pontificate Gregory fought with little success to turn back the tide of rationalism and the growth of modern developments, even seeking to ban the railroad – which he dubbed *le chemin d'enfer* ('path of hell'), a pun on the French for railroad *le chemin de fer* – from the papal states.

Below: In France Louis Philippe was sworn in as king on 9 August 1830. Pius was quick to back the new regime and grant the title of 'Most Christian King'.

A MAN OF PRINCIPLE
Born in Cingoli in the papal states in 1761, Pius VIII (original name Francesco Saverio Castiglioni) studied canon law and was appointed Bishop of Montalto by Pius VII in 1800. A man of principle and courage, he endured an eight-year imprisonment during the French rule of Italy after refusing to take the required oath of allegiance to Napoleon. He was made a cardinal in 1816 and appointed grand penitentiary, an important position in the Curia, in 1821.

His pontificate as Pius VIII was notable for the 1829 Catholic Emancipation Act in Britain and the agreement of a concordat with France after the coming to the throne of Louis Philippe, Duc d'Orleans, in the July Revolution of 1830. When events in France forced the

Above: Pius VIII. He backed the first convention of bishops in the United States. His 1829 encyclical Traditi humilitati *condemned efforts to put other branches of the faith on a par with Catholicism.*

abdication of the unpopular Charles X, Pius was quick to support Louis Philippe of Orleans as his successor, granting him the title 'Most Christian King' and encouraging French churchmen to back the new regime. Another of Pius's international acts was to issue approval to the statements of the Provincial Council of Baltimore, the first formal convention of bishops in the United States.

Throughout his pontificate he suffered from poor health, in particular from sores on his body and neck. He died on 30 November 1830 in the Quirinal Palace and when an autopsy found no evidence of sickness internally, there were whispers that he had been poisoned. His successor Bartolomeo Alberto Cappellari assumed the papal throne as Gregory XVI, after no fewer than 83 ballots over the course of 64 days, on 2 February 1831.

OPPONENT OF LIBERALISM

Gregory was a Camaldolese monk (an austere version of the Benedictines, who devoted part of their time to living as hermits) from the monastery of San Michele di Murano, on the island of Murano in the lagoon of Venice – the last monk to date to become pope, as well as the last pope to take the name Gregory. Opposed to change, he supported Europe's

Below: Gregory XVI's 1839 apostolic letter In supremo apsotolatus *condemned the Atlantic slave trade.*

1829 CATHOLIC EMANCIPATION ACT IN BRITAIN

Under the 1829 Catholic Emancipation Act Roman Catholics were able to sit in the Houses of Parliament at Westminster and hold most public offices. The background to the passing of the act was the winning in 1828 by Irish Catholic lawyer Daniel O'Connell of the seat for Clare, Ireland; under previous law he was forbidden to take his seat, but he waged a lively campaign for change on the issue.

Below: Pius supported British Catholics, who were suffering under discriminatory laws. The Roman Catholic Relief Act of 1829 opened the higher Civil Service and judiciary to middle-class British Catholics.

conservative monarchies and clamped down very hard on those arguing for democracy, republicanism and liberalism. He condemned the liberal French priest H. F. R. de Lammenais, founder of the newspaper *L'Avenir* ('The Future'), which argued for freedom of conscience and the separation of church and state, and placed his works on the Index of Prohibited Books. In his encyclical *Mirari Vos* ('We think that you wonder…') of August 1832 Gregory denounced the claim of freedom of conscience as an erroneous doctrine, or rather delirium'.

Gregory fiercely put down revolts in the papal states with Austrian help and using execution with sentences of hard labour and exile, and the territory was occupied by foreign troops. When Polish Roman Catholics rose up against the tyrannical rule of Tsar Nicholas I of Russia, to whom they had been subject since the Third Partition of 1795, Gregory did not support them but issued a papal brief in which he condemned

them for having used religion as a cover while setting themselves against 'the legitimate power of princes'. After a brief initial success, the uprising was brutally put down by Nicholas I in 1831.

MISSIONARY ENTHUSIASM

Yet he energetically supported international Roman Catholic missionary work, which he reorganized and placed under papal control, creating near to 200 missionary bishops while establishing 70 new dioceses around the world. In 1839 he condemned slavery in his bull *In Supremo Apostolatus* ('At the summit of Apostolic power'), in which he called the slave trade 'a shame' and 'absolutely unworthy of the Christian name'.

Gregory died on 1 June 1846 in Rome after a very bad attack of erysipelas of the face – the condition, marked by red swellings and lesions accompanied by fever and vomiting, sometimes known as 'holy fire' or 'St Anthony's fire'.

PIUS IX, 1846–78
POPE WHO BEGAN THE FORMATION OF THE MODERN PAPACY

In his 32-year pontificate, the longest papal reign to date, Pius IX oversaw a vast range of changes, including the establishment of the Kingdom of Italy in 1860 and the consequent shrinking of papal territories to what they are today – the Vatican and its immediate surroundings. Pius's period in power also saw the definition of the dogma of the Immaculate Conception and the doctrine of papal infallibility as the papacy attempted to concentrate on matters of faith and spirituality.

Born to a noble family in Senigallia, Giovanni Maria Mastai-Ferretti studied theology in Volterra and Rome. His studies were almost cut short by his epilepsy, but with the support and encouragement of Pope Pius VII (1800–23), he continued and in time entered papal service: on behalf of Pius VII he served on a mission to the newly created South American republics – the first pope to visit the Americas.

Under Pope Leo XII he was appointed Archbishop of Spoleto at the age of 35, then in 1839, after being moved

FACT BOX
Original name Giovanni Maria Mastai-Ferretti
Born 13 May 1792
Origin Senigallia, papal states
Date elected pope 16 June 1846
Died 7 February 1878
Key fact Presided over First Vatican Council

Right: Pius IX was the first pope to be photographed. Particularly at the start of his pontificate, he was generally progressive and open to unfamiliar things – such as the new art of photography.

to Imola, was made cardinal. At this stage of his life, he was committed to charitable work such as helping street children and visiting prisoners in jail. He gained a reputation as a political liberal that carried over into his first years as pope.

He was elected pope after a conclave of just two days on 16 June 1846. He took the name Pius as a tribute to Pius

VII. The election of a liberal pope caused astonishment, for most had expected the triumph of a conservative candidate.

FORWARD-LOOKING
The new pontiff was amicable, warmhearted, approachable, progressive. While cardinal he had been critical of the rule of Gregory XVI (1831–46), and in the first month of his reign he granted amnesties to more than 1,000 exiles and political prisoners. He embraced the modern conveniences his predecessor had rejected – including gas lighting and the railways. Pius IX took important steps towards creating a free press and also did away with the requirement that Jews must listen to a Christian sermon every week.

Everywhere the new pope went Pius found himself celebrated – the crowds in Rome shouted 'A long life for

Left: The First Vatican Council was opened on 8 December 1869. The council underlined the pope's authority to rule on dogma and defined papal infallibility.

Right: Pius aboard the papal train. He embraced modern inventions Gregory XVI resisted. In a pun on the French for railway ('chemin de fer') Gregory had called it the 'chemin d'enfer' ('pathway to hell').

Pius IX!' Even in Protestant England he was praised for his commitment to freedom.

But his popularity melted away and his reputation as a supporter of freedom was lost amid the revolutions of 1848, as he and the papacy were cast as reactionaries blocking the desires of Italian nationalists for a united country. Amid upheaval in Rome, and after the Swiss Guard was disbanded by local ministers, he fled to Gaeta in the kingdom of Naples. A new assembly in Rome declared the establishment of a democratic republic and the end of the papacy's temporal power. Pius made a formal appeal for international help and with the backing of a French army was reinstalled in Rome on 12 April 1850.

THE CAPITAL OF ITALY

This reprieve was only temporary – even though it lasted 20 years. In 1860 the Kingdom of Italy was created and it annexed the papal states. Then in 1870 the French troops on which Pius relied for security left Rome to fight in the Franco-Prussian War of 1870–1. Italian republicans under the command of Giuseppe Garibaldi forced Pius to agree

to a settlement under which the papacy kept the Vatican, which remained independent, but lost Rome.

A plebiscite of 1 October 1870 voted for Rome to become the capital of Italy. Pius was to have full authority within the Vatican and its immediate surroundings and could conduct diplomatic relations with other powers, but elsewhere in Italy, church and state would be separated. Pius did not accept the new situation and regarded himself as a prisoner in the Vatican.

IMMACULATE CONCEPTION

On 8 December 1854 Pius defined the dogma of the Immaculate Conception. According to this, in the moment in which she was conceived by her mother, the Blessed Virgin Mary was made immaculate – was set free from the taint of original sin by which all humankind is touched as descendants of Adam and Eve.

SYLLABUS OF ERRORS

Pius turned away from his early liberalism and became a firm opponent of those pressing for reform in the church.

Left: In this 1860 John Tenniel cartoon from the British magazine Punch, *Garibaldi shows Pius IX the cap of liberty – suggesting that it would be far more comfortable than the heavy papal crown.*

In December 1864 he issued the Syllabus of Errors, which listed 80 of what he identified as the main contemporary errors of thought and notably attacked those who argued that 'the Roman pontiff can and should reconcile and harmonize himself with progress, with liberalism and with recent civilization'. In 1869 he called the First Vatican Council, which asserted the power of the papacy in its definition of papal infallibility.

Pius died in Rome on 7 February 1878. He was beatified by Pope John Paul II on 3 September 2000.

PAPAL INFALLIBILITY

The First Vatican Council of 1869–70 set out the doctrine of papal infallibility: when the pope defines church doctrine concerning faith or morals, speaking ex cathedra and so requiring assent from the whole Church, he cannot be wrong. The pope's authority in this matter derives from the teaching power assigned to the pope as head of the Church by Jesus Christ himself. This was the first formal definition of a position that had been held by many since the medieval period. Papal infallibility lies in the office of pope and is not claimed by the person who happens to be pope.

LEO XIII, 1878–1903
THE 'WORKERS' POPE' IN A CHANGING WORLD

Elected pope close to his 68th birthday and in poor health, Leo XIII might have expected a brief pontificate but he remained on the papal throne for more than a quarter of a century until his death in 1903 aged 93. To the end he kept his energy and keen intellect, and in his reign he succeeded in repositioning the Church in its relationship with science and a swiftly changing world, proving the relevance of the papacy to a new century.

JESUIT EDUCATION
Born the sixth of seven sons to a noble family from Carpineto Romano, near Rome, Vincenzo Gioacchino Pecci studied with the Jesuits in Viterbo and Rome, gaining doctorates in theology, civil law and canon law. Full of energy, with a quick intelligence and a gentle manner, he thrived in the papal service and was legate (governor) of first Benevento and then Perugia before being sent as papal nuncio to Belgium. As Archbishop of Perugia in 1846–77, he was known for his charitable work with the homeless and poverty-stricken; he was made a cardinal in 1853.

He was elected pope on 20 February 1878, shortly before his 68th birthday, on only the third ballot. He chose his papal name in honour of Leo XII, whom he had admired for his commitment to education, his non-confrontational deal-

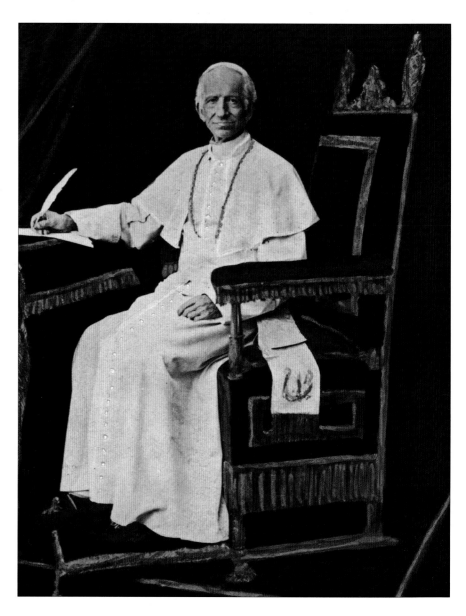

Above: A coloured image of Leo. He was at home in the modern world, the first pope to appear in moving pictures. He was filmed by W. K. Dickson and blessed the movie camera.

ings with secular governments and his interest in building bridges with non-Catholic Christians.

THE KINGDOM OF ITALY
The new pope inherited a difficult position in the Kingdom of Italy, where the government was hostile to the papacy and the Roman Catholic Church. He

was not permitted to bless the faithful from the loggia of St Peter's, as was traditional, and had to hold his coronation in the Sistine Chapel.

His response was measured. His diplomatic experience stood him in good stead and on the international stage he built a good relationship with England, France, Germany, Prussia and Russia, as well as other countries. The expansion of Catholicism begun under his predecessor was continued, with the establishment of dioceses and vicariates around the world.

He attempted to reposition the Church in a swiftly changing world without compromise on major teaching. He issued condemnations of socialism, communism, secular liberalism and Freemasonry, but offered support to the working classes – many of whom were suffering dire conditions in the wake of industrialization – by backing democracy and the right to form unions (see box).

THE CHURCH AND SCIENCE

Leo was determined the Church should not be seen as an enemy of science. He actively encouraged science and astronomy, re-establishing the Vatican Observatory to make clear to people that the Church was 'not opposed to true and solid science', and calling for a return to the study of St Thomas Aquinas's philosophy and theology – both for priests in seminaries and laity in universities. In his encyclical *Aeterni Patris* ('Of the Eternal Father'), he called Aquinas 'the special bulwark and glory of the Catholic faith ... a lover of truth for its own sake' and said that 'richly endowed with human and divine science, like the sun he heated the world with the warmth of his virtues

Below: Leo dictates a phonograph message to American Catholics – he was the first pope whose voice was recorded.

THE WORKERS' POPE

On account of his 1893 encyclical *Rerum Novarum* ('Of new things'), which accepted the creation of trades unions, Leo gained the nickname of 'the workers' pope'. The open letter, sent to all bishops, rejected communism and the unrestricted operation of capitalism and defended an individual's right to own private property, but it recognized the right of workers to form unions and expressed the need for improvements in the miserable and wretched conditions that so many members of the working classes were forced to endure.

and filled it with the splendour of his teaching'. Leo also backed the study of history and of the Bible, and attempted to reach out to Protestants and Orthodox Christians, calling them 'our separated brethren', and inviting them to submit to and unite with Rome.

He did not seem ill at ease in the face of innovation: he was the first pope to make a sound recording and the first to be filmed on a movie camera – film camera pioneer William Kennedy Dickson filmed the pope in the Vatican Gardens in 1898.

Above: Leo XIII. In 1887 the future St Therese of Lisieux met Leo, begging him to authorize her entering the Carmelites aged 15. He said, 'You will enter if God wills it.'

ROSARY POPE

Leo exhibited a particular devotion to the Sacred Heart of Jesus and to the Blessed Virgin Mary. In 1899 he consecrated the whole world to the Sacred Heart of Jesus. He also promoted Marian devotion, issuing eleven encyclicals on the rosary – and became known, as an alternative byname, as the 'Rosary Pope'. He began the custom among Roman Catholics of daily rosary prayer during October and established in 1883 the Feast of the Queen of the Holy Rosary.

In these encyclicals Pius was the first pope fully to engage with and promote the concept of the Virgin Mary as *mediatrix* or mediator, the person through whom the prayers of the faithful are channelled to Christ and God the Father and through whom the grace of God is passed to the world.

He also taught that from the moment of the Annunciation (when she was told by the Angel Gabriel that she would conceive and bear Jesus), Mary was co-redemptrix with Christ: she played a role in the mystery of redemption as the mother of Christ and of all people.

CHAPTER TWELVE

PEACE FOR A TROUBLED WORLD

PIUS X TO FRANCIS, 1903–TODAY

In the first Easter homily of his pontificate, on 31 March 2013, Pope Francis called for peace throughout the world, saying, 'We ask the risen Jesus, who turns death into life, to change hatred into love, vengeance into forgiveness, war into peace.' Through the 20th century his predecessors dedicated themselves to working and praying for peace.

On 1 August 1917 Pope Benedict XV circulated, sadly without success, a peace plan to end the First World War; in 1942, at the height of the Second World War, Pius XII dedicated the entire human race to the Blessed Virgin Mary. In the aftermath of the war John XXIII and Paul VI pressed for peace at the height of the Cold War and John Paul II was on the papal throne when the countries of the communist Eastern bloc saw their hold on power dissolve, and the spectre of Islamic terrorism arose in the 1990s.

In difficult times a succession of popes attempted to return to the original values of the papacy. John XXIII laid far less emphasis on his role as ruler and more on his position as 'servant of the servants of God'. Pope John Paul I passed up the grandeur of a papal coronation for a simple investiture and chose *Humilitas* ('Humility') as the motto of his papacy. The Lateran Treaty of 1929 saw the papacy renounce its claim to expansive papal territories, and the establishment of the pope as ruler of the small independent state of Vatican City.

In years of increasing materialism after the Second World War and in the early 21st century at a time of financial crisis, popes condemned modern consumerism. Throughout his reign, Pope Francis has opposed irresponsible development, and embraced simplicity, action on climate change and concern for the poor.

Left: A pope for the modern age? Armed with smartphones on 'selfie sticks', United Nations peacekeeping troops press around Francis during the Wednesday general audience at Paul VI Audience Hall on 28 January 2015.

PIUS X, 1903–14
TRADITIONALIST POPE WHO LOOKED FOR RENEWAL

Pius X was strongly opposed to liberal and modernist revisions of doctrine, but was not resistant to change in itself and carried through many reforms – recodifying canon law, remodelling the Curia and restructuring seminaries.

Pius performed the duties of a parish priest in his young adulthood and many of his revisions of practice were focused on the daily life of Roman Catholics at the parish level; throughout his pontificate he preached a sermon every Sunday – the only pope of the 20th century to do so. He was canonized by Pius XII on 29 May 1954, the first since his namesake St Pius V (1566–72), to be named a saint.

Below: Pius blesses pilgrims at the Vatican in 1903. His family were far from well off, but he sought no favours for them: his brother carried on working as a postal clerk.

Above: Pius relaxes in the gardens of the Vatican in 1913. He established the Biblical Institute in Rome to be directed by the Jesuits.

Born the son of a postman and a seamstress in Treviso, Venice, Giuseppe Melchiorre Sarto was ordained a priest at the age of 23 and served for eight years as chaplain at Tombolo, performing many of the duties of a parish priest, then was arch-priest of Salzano in the Diocese of Treviso. He filled various other positions before being named Bishop of Mantua in 1884, then cardinal and Patriarch of Venice in 1893.

A decade later he was elected pope with 55 out of a possible 60 votes on 4 August 1903 and was crowned Pius X on 9 August. He was friendly, warm-hearted and practical – as well as being pious and, in the words of his tomb inscription, 'meek and humble of heart'.

'RENEW ALL THINGS IN CHRIST'

His commitment to change was shown when he identified in his first encyclical that the motto of his papacy would be from *Ephesians* 1:10 – 'renew all things in Christ'. He produced the first code of canon law, which was promulgated by his successor Benedict XV on 27 May 1917. He revised the operation of the Curia, cutting the number of its departments from 37 to 19.

He rewrote the catechism and urged that it should be used with adults as well as children, and that a class should be held in every parish around the world. He himself held catechism classes every week in the courtyard of San Damaso in the Vatican.

Pius reformed the breviary. He placed a new emphasis on the ritual of Holy Communion, which he described as 'the shortest and safest way to Heaven', and encouraged the faithful to take communion more frequently – every day or once weekly at the least. He reduced the age of discretion, at which children should take their first communion, from 12 years to 7 years. He decreed that Church music would turn back

Below: Pius watches Andre Beaumont, winner of the Paris-Rome section, fly over the Vatican during the Paris-Rome-Turin air race, in an illustration for Le Petit Journal, *18 June 1911.*

from the recently popular Baroque and classical styles to plainsong and Gregorian chant.

STERN TRADITIONALIST

Yet Pius was no intellectual and certainly no supporter of 'modernists' who wanted to adapt the Church to the new philosophical and psychological ideas of the 19th century.

In 1907 he issued a decree *Lamentabile Sane Exitu* ('On a Deplorable Result') and an encyclical *Pascendi Dominici Gregis* ('On Feeding the Flocks of the Lord') that condemned this modernism in the Church as a 'compendium of all the heresies'. In 1910 he issued a decree ordering all seminary teachers and all clerics on ordination to take an oath supporting these two papal documents and denouncing modernism.

As part of a programme to enforce discipline on these matters he endorsed the creation of the 'Society of Pius V', which functioned almost like a secret police force using underhand methods – including agents who attempted to trap liberal Catholics into incriminating themselves. His use of this body was brought up as a reason against his canonization in the 1950s and was the cause of some controversy.

RELATIONS WITH ITALY AND FRANCE

Pius X maintained papal opposition to the annexation of the papal states by Italy and criticized French president Emile Loubet for making a visit to the Italian King Victor Emmanuel III. When the French issued in 1905 the Law of Separation under which church and state were separated in France, Pius denounced this development and in the end diplomatic relations with France were broken off. In 1907 the French government confiscated all church property in France. Throughout his pontificate Pius refused to recognize the government of Italy, but he did give Roman Catholics permission to vote in general elections.

Above: This initial 'A' in a 13th-century antiphonal depicts St Gregory. Pius brought about a return to plainsong and Gregorian chant in church music.

FIRST WORLD WAR

The outbreak of the First World War crushed Pius. He called on Catholics to turn 'to Him from whom alone help can come, to Christ, the prince of peace' and to pray for peace. He was 79 years old, suffered from gout and had had a heart attack in 1913; the news of the war further set him back and he died in the early hours of 20 August 1914. In his will this saintly pope wrote, 'I was born poor; I have lived poor; and I wish to die poor.'

REFUGEES IN THE APOSTOLIC PALACE

Pius was known for his charity and Christian concern. After a terrible earthquake struck Messina and Reggio Calabria in south Italy on 28 December 1908 he did not wait for the Italian government to act but opened the Vatican to refugees. In his will he left a legacy for 400 children who were made orphans of the earthquake.

BENEDICT XV, 1914–22
PEACEMAKER IN THE TIME OF WORLD WAR

Benedict XV remained impartial during the First World War and attempted with all his might to bring about an end to hostilities. Afterwards he was very disappointed to be excluded from the peace negotiations in 1919 and in 1920 dedicated the papacy to efforts for reconciliation between nations whilst consolidating the position of the Church in Europe.

Born in Pegli, Genoa, to an aristocratic family, Giacomo della Chiesa was initially refused permission to train for the priesthood by his father, who wanted his son to become a lawyer. However, in 1875 – after acquiring a doctorate in law and at the age of 21 – he did gain his father's permission to enter the Church and began training in Rome, where he was ordained on 21 December 1878.

Below: Il piccoletto *('the little fellow'): after being born prematurely, Benedict XV was very short throughout his life. When he became pope there were no robes small enough for him. He had poor eyesight.*

> **FACT BOX**
> **Original name** Giacomo della Chiesa
> **Born** 21 November 1854
> **Origin** Pegli, Genoa
> **Date elected pope** 3 September 1914
> **Died** 22 January 1922
> **Key fact** Spent 82 million lira on war relief

After working in the papal diplomatic service he became Archbishop of Bologna in 1908 and in 1914 was made cardinal, just three months before his election as pope. Benedict had been born extremely prematurely and was very small in stature – in Bologna he had been nicknamed *il piccoletto* ('the little fellow'), and on his election as pope there were no robes small enough for him to wear. He had poor eyesight, one shoulder raised above the other and was not personable or charismatic, but was kind-hearted and very generous – and well loved by those who knew him well.

Above: This statue in Orleans honours St Joan of Arc. After Pius X had beatified her in 1909, Benedict canonized her in 1920. Her feast day is 30 May.

Below: Pope Benedict XV in the garden of the Vatican during the Catholic Congress in Rome, 1921.

Above: A satirical view: Jesus reads the peace plan issued by Benedict, and says (with a nod to Luke 23:34) 'Father, forgive him, for he knows not what he does.'

'PROPHET OF PEACE'

In the war, with Catholics fighting on both sides, he had no choice but to maintain impartiality. He did what he could to bring about an end to the fighting. His first encyclical, on 1 November 1914, was a call for peace and he tried to persuade the combatants to revive the medieval tradition of the 'Truce of God' on Christmas Day, 1914. In August 1917 he circulated a detailed seven-point plan for peace but his proposals were rejected by the warring countries. When in 2005 Benedict XVI chose his papal name it was to honour this pontiff, whom he called 'that courageous prophet of peace'.

RELIEF EFFORTS

In 1914 he established an agency for the repatriation of prisoners of war and wounded that brought about the homecoming of 65,000 people. In 1915 he negotiated the exchange of civilians from occupied areas – this led to 20,000 people being sent to unoccupied southern France. In 1916 he achieved an agreement under which 29,000 prisoners with tuberculosis were sent to neutral Switzerland. Through his intervention many prisoners were spared execution. He organized several humanitarian

missions, particularly to aid children – in Belgium, Lithuania, Russia and elsewhere. He reputedly spent 82 million lira on humanitarian and relief programmes and left the Vatican reserves empty – it is said that after his death Cardinal Gasparri was forced to raise a bank loan in order to pay for the conclave that selected Pope Pius XI.

The success of these initiatives won the respect and admiration of many countries. When the Turks raised a statue in Benedict's honour in Istanbul they described him as 'the benefactor of all peoples, irrespective of nationality or religion'. His humanitarian outlook in the war was one reason why an increasing number of states sent diplomatic representative to the Vatican: these included Britain, who sent a chargé d'affaires in 1915 (the first British diplomat at the Vatican since the 1600s), and France. Relations with France improved after Benedict canonized Joan of Arc in 1920.

ITALY AND RUSSIA

Relations with the Italian government, however, remained very tricky. But Benedict made progress towards a solution by giving official backing to the

---

MARIOLOGY

Benedict – like 'the Rosary Pope', Leo XIII before him – enthusiastically promoted devotion to the Blessed Virgin Mary, particularly emphasizing her role as Co-Redemptrix with Christ. Benedict raised 20 Marian shrines to the status of minor basilicas. In May 1917 he placed the whole world under Mary's protection, a few days before the first of the Virgin's reputed appearances at Fatima, Portugal. To the well-known Litany of the Blessed Virgin Mary (often called 'the Litany of Loreto' because of its early usage at the Shrine to the Virgin at Loreto in Italy) he added the invocation 'Queen of Peace, pray for us'.

Above: Benedict was a devoted Marian. He placed the world under the protection of the Blessed Virgin in the First World War. He authorized the Feast of Mary, Mediator of All Graces.

establishment of the *Partito Populaire* (Italian People's Party) by Sicilian priest Don Luigi Sturzo in 1919. The war raised the prospect of the expansion of Russia and the Orthodox Church but the Russian Revolution of 1917 and the virulently anti-religious policies of the new regime spelled profound trouble for Christianity there. In Rome, Benedict established the Congregation for the Eastern Church and the Pontifical Eastern Institute.

AN EYE FOR TALENT

Benedict promoted two future popes to important positions. He appointed Eugenio Pacelli (the future Pius XII) to lead the work on prisoners of war at the Vatican and afterwards sent him as papal nuncio to Munich. He took the distinguished paleographer Achilles Ratti (the future Pius XI) from his position working as prefect at the Vatican Library and sent him in 1918 as papal representative to Poland; afterwards he was made Archbishop of Milan.

Pope Benedict died unexpectedly young, at the age of just 67 and following an attack of pneumonia, on 22 January 1922.

PIUS XI, 1922–39
FIRST SOVEREIGN OF THE INDEPENDENT VATICAN CITY

The pontificate of Pius XI saw the establishment of the pope as sovereign ruler of the independent state of Vatican City. The Lateran Treaty that delivered this outcome stated that the papacy would be permanently neutral in diplomatic and military conflicts and recognized the creation of the Kingdom of Italy.

LASTING HATRED OF COMMUNISM

Achille Ratti came to the papacy at the age of 65 after a distinguished career as a palaeographer and a librarian. He was plucked from his position as prefect of the Vatican Library by Benedict XV (1914–22), who in 1919 sent him as papal nuncio to newly independent Poland. There he showed great bravery and won respect by refusing to flee to Rome when the invading Bolsheviks marched on Warsaw in 1920; he remained in place in the Polish capital while Marshal Jozef Pilsudski, Chief of

Below: Pius XI was a distinguished palaeographer and librarian who became the first sovereign ruler of the independent state of Vatican City.

FACT BOX

Original name Ambrogio Damiano Achille Ratti
Born 31 May 1857
Origin Desio, Lombardy
Date elected pope 6 February 1922
Died 10 February 1939
Key fact Initially tolerant of fascist regimes, he later attacked them

---

State, masterminded 'the miracle on the Vistula' and drove the Russians back. These events convinced Ratti that communism was the greatest threat of all those faced by the countries of Christian Europe in these highly troubled times.

Back in Italy in 1921, he was made cardinal and then Archbishop of Milan, and in February 1922 – after what must have seemed a whirlwind three years since he left the Vatican Library – he was pope. Ruling in the era of the Spanish Civil War and the build-up to the Second World War, Pius used as his papal motto the phrase *Pax Christi in Regno Christi* ('The Peace of Christ in the Kingdom of Christ') and attempted to work for international cooperation.

RELATIONS WITH FASCISM

Pius's administration made pacts with the fascists both in Italy and in Germany, but the pope also issued attacks on both in encyclicals of the 1930s. By the Lateran Treaty that established the Holy See as an independent neutral state – signed on 11 February 1929 by Prime Minister Benito Mussolini and Pius's Secretary of State, Cardinal Pietro Gaspari – the pope received financial compensation equivalent to around £21 million for renouncing his claim to papal territories, Roman Catholicism was recognized as the only state religion in Italy, all anticlerical laws were scrapped and canon law was recognized in addition

---

Above: Pius offers a blessing. He was an admirer of Thérèse of Lisieux and fast-tracked her path to sainthood. She was beatified in 1923 and canonized in 1925.

to state law. The terms were by no means bad, but there was no getting away from the fact that the papacy had implicitly backed fascism.

Then on 20 July 1933 Pius's new secretary of state, Cardinal Eugenio Pacelli (the future Pope Pius XII), signed a concordat with Franz von Papen, Hitler's

---

CHRIST THE KING

In 1925 Pius initiated the Feast of Christ the King in his encyclical *Quas Primas* ('In the first'). At first celebrated on the last Sunday in October, in 1969 Paul VI moved it to the last Sunday of the liturgical year. Pius described the Church as 'the kingdom of Christ on earth' and said she should 'with every token of veneration salute her Author and Founder in her annual liturgy as King and Lord, and as King of Kings'. He added that when people recognize that Christ is King they will receive the 'great blessings of real liberty, well-ordered discipline, peace and harmony'.

Above: Pius was the first pope to make a radio broadcast. Here he is with radio pioneer Guglielmo Marconi in the Vatican in January 1933.

Vice-Chancellor, in Rome. Under this treaty the Church and its schools gained privileges in Germany but agreed to give up social and political activity in the country, and as a result the Centre Party, the second most powerful in the German Reichstag under the leadership of Monsignor Ludwig Kaas, was terminated – opening the way for the progression of the Nazis.

FORTHRIGHT ENCYCLICALS

Pius issued encyclicals attacking Italian fascism in *Non abbiamo bisogno* ('We need not acquaint you', June 1931) and the rule of the Nazis in *Mit brennender Sorge* ('With Profound Anxiety', 1937). But it is undeniable that the pope issued no condemnation of the Nazis' anti-Semitic Nuremberg race laws of 1935 nor of the terrible events of the *Kristallnacht* pogrom against the Jews of 9–10 November 1938 in which 91 Jews were slain and 30,000 arrested and taken to concentration camps.

A third encyclical, *Divini redemptoris* ('Our Divine Redeemer', 1937), issued a forthright condemnation of communism. Pius prepared a fourth that was to explicitly condemn anti-Semitism and persecution of the Jews but died before he could deliver it in 1939.

MISSION AND LEARNING

Pius was also active in other areas. He oversaw a great expansion in the number of native priests and bishops overseas, notably in China and India. He attempted, with little success, to bring about reconciliation with the Eastern Orthodox Churches. Devoted as he was to learning, he founded several higher education bodies, including the Pontifical Institute of Christian Archaeology in 1925 and the Pontifical Academy of Science in 1936.

He built the Pinacoteca as a home for the Vatican's ever-expanding picture collection and moved the Vatican Observatory to Castel Gandolfo. In 1931 he installed a radio in the Vatican. He became the first pope to make a radio broadcast.

By 1938 Pius's health was very poor. Already suffering badly from diabetes,

he had two heart attacks in a single day on 25 November. He struggled on, desperately trying to stay alive to deliver his final encyclical, intended as a denunciation of fascist dictators, but died on 10 February 1939.

Below: Pope Pius XI instituting celebration of the social reign of Jesus Christ, in a drawing by Damblans from the French paper Le Pelerin, *3 January 1926.*

PIUS XII, 1939–58
CONTROVERSIAL SILENCE OVER WORLD WAR II ATROCITIES

Pius XII maintained a position of impartiality through the Second World War. For some, the fact that he did not issue a forthright condemnation of the outrages perpetuated by the Nazis against the Jews was a terrible failure. Others emphasize the work he did to help the victims of war and point out that he was celebrated after the war by leading Jewish figures.

DESTINED FOR THE CHURCH

Eugenio Pacelli was born in 1876 to a family with a long and distinguished history of papal service. His great-grandfather was Pope Gregory XVI's minister of finance, his grandfather Pius IX's undersecretary of the interior, his father dean to the lawyers at the Vatican. According to his sister, as a boy he used to dress as a priest and enact his own celebration of the Mass in his bedroom.

Below: Pius soon after his coronation in 1939. Only one day long, the conclave that elected him was the shortest for 300 years.

Above: As a cardinal, the future Pius XII (at head of table) signs a concordat with Franz von Papen (second from left), Hitler's vice-chancellor, in Rome on 20 July 1933.

He took degrees in law and theology, was ordained in 1899 at the age of 23 and under Pius X worked on the recodification of canon law. He served as papal nuncio to Germany, and became a lover of that country, before returning to Rome and becoming secretary of state in 1930. He negotiated concordats with Austria and Nazi Germany.

He was elected pope on his 63rd birthday, 2 March 1939, on the very first day of the conclave – the shortest for three centuries.

Pacelli was a cautious figure, highly intelligent and a fine diplomat. He did not issue the encyclical condemning anti-Semitism on which his predecessor had been working, but he set about trying to dissuade the governments of Europe from entering the looming war. He did not condemn the German invasion of Poland on 1 September 1939. He sought to maintain a position not of neutrality (since this might imply indifference to suffering) but of impartiality.

THE SILENCE OF PIUS XII?

Many historians criticize Pius for not denouncing the atrocities committed by the Nazis during the war. When he did make public references to the suffering he spoke in curiously veiled terms. For example, in his Christmas broadcast in 1942 – at the end of a year in which he had repeatedly rebuffed requests to condemn German massacres of Jews (including one from US President Roosevelt) – he spoke of 'persons who, without any fault on their part, sometimes only because of their nationality or race, have been consigned to death or to a slow decline' – not mentioning the Jews or Nazis by name.

> **FACT BOX**
> **Original name** Eugenio Mafria Giuseppi Giovanni Pacelli
> **Born** 2 March 1876
> **Origin** Rome
> **Date elected pope** 2 March 1939
> **Died** 9 October 1958
> **Key fact** Invoked papal infallibility in defining dogma of the Assumption of Blessed Virgin Mary

BOTCHED EMBALMING

Pius died of heart failure on 9 October 1958 at Castel Gandolfo. In his last years his medical treatment had been almost exclusively in the hands of his personal physician Riccardo Galeazzi-Lisi, who now took responsibility for the embalming of the pope's body – claiming that he would rely on the same method used for Jesus Christ himself. Unfortunately this did not work as predicted and the pope's body suffered many indignities, including the loss of fingers and his nose, while his skin turned black.

When the Nazis occupied Rome and began to drag off 1,259 of the Jews of Rome to a terrible end in the Auschwitz death camp, still Pius did not issue an open condemnation of their actions, although according to some accounts the Vatican managed to rescue and give refuge to 252 Jews at this time.

Below: The first pope to become familiar to the world through TV and radio, Pius gives a radio broadcast in 1941. His failure to issue outright condemnations of the Nazis in these broadcasts remains controversial.

Those who defend Pius's action argue that he not only wanted to maintain an impartial position, but had a responsibility to avert reprisals against the Church and perhaps feared that denunciation would provoke further and even more savage atrocities against the powerless. They point out, moreover, that he established the Vatican Information Service that discreetly saved the lives of many hundreds of thousands of Jews in the course of the war and he was praised for his actions by prominent Jews after the war – for example, on Pius's death in 1958 Israeli Prime Minister Golda Meir declared, 'When fearful martyrdom came to our people in the decade of Nazi terror, the voice of the pope was raised for the victims. The life of our times was enriched by a voice speaking out on the great moral truths, above the tumult of daily conflict. We mourn a great servant of peace.'

AFTER THE WAR

A lifelong opponent of communism, Pius issued condemnations of communist expansion in Eastern Europe. In a decree of 1949 he attacked the Soviet Union and threatened excommunication for any Catholics joining the Communist Party or collaborating with communists.

Above: Czeslawa Kwoka, a Polish Catholic girl, was sent to the Nazi-run death camp at Auschwitz in December 1942 and photographed there, aged 14. She and her mother were dead within three months.

Now in his 70s, the pope became increasingly entrenched in traditional doctrinal positions, for example on birth control and marriage relations. He issued a condemnation of the questioning attitudes of a new wave of theology in France in his 1950 encyclical *Humani generis* ('Concerning the Human Race') and in 1953 terminated what had been proving a successful pastoral experiment in which worker priests laboured alongside workers in factories.

ASSUMPTION OF THE VIRGIN MARY

In 1950 he invoked papal infallibility in defining the dogma of the Assumption of the Virgin Mary – the teaching that Mary was taken body and soul into heaven on her death. This was the first use of papal infallibility since the doctrine of infallibility had been proclaimed at the First Vatican Council in 1869–70. One of his final appointments, on 4 July 1958, was of Karol Wojtyla (the future Pope John Paul II) as Auxiliary Bishop of Krakow.

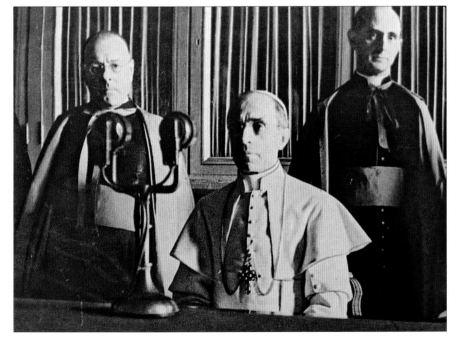

JOHN XXIII AND PAUL VI, 1958–78
TWO POPES WHO CARRIED THROUGH CHANGE

Remembered with affection as 'The Good Pope', John XXIII (1958–63) believed strongly in equality and was committed to change. He called the Second Vatican Council (1962–5). Paul VI (1963–78) carried on the work his predecessor called *aggorniamento* ('bringing up to date'), seeing the Council through its latter stages and travelling widely – he was the first pope to travel by aeroplane and helicopter and the first to visit the Holy Land.

John XXIII was born Angelo Giuseppe Roncalli, one of 13 children of a modest tenant farmer in Sotto il Monte, a tiny Lombardy village. He studied in nearby Bergamo and in Rome, eventually taking a doctorate in canon law and becoming secretary to the Bishop of Bergamo. He served as papal diplomat in Bulgaria, Greece and Turkey and then from 1944 in France; he was made a cardinal and Patriarch of Venice by Pius XII in 1953. He was a compromise candidate when he was elected pope on the twelfth ballot on 28 October 1958.

'JOHNNY WALKER'
John reigned at a time of high political tension in the Cold War between West and East and urged nations to live together in peace – in particular, winning the respect of US President Kennedy and Soviet Premier Khrushchev for his input during the Cuban Missile Crisis of 1962.

Above: Front page news. The front cover of Paris Match, *a weekly news magazine, reported the election of Cardinal Roncalli as Pope John XXIII. He was elected on 28 October 1958.*

He followed Leo XII in stressing the need for the rich to help the poor. He was unaffected, humble and approachable – once he stopped to hold the hand of a peasant woman who had reached up to him as he was being carried through St Peter's, saying to her there was no reason why she should not be allowed as close to him as the King of Jordan had been on a recent encounter.

Left: Paul VI's meeting with United States President John F. Kennedy at the Vatican on 3 July 1963, was deliberately low key. Paul had good English and the meeting was conducted in that language.

John liked to go out incognito at night and walk the streets of Rome – and was reputedly nicknamed 'Johnny Walker' after the celebrated brand of whisky. He published a diary of spiritual reflections in book form under the title *Journal of a Soul*.

He was also committed to furthering reconciliation among Christians and between faiths. In 1960 he set up a Secretariat for Christian Unity and received a visit in Rome from the Archbishop of Canterbury, the first since the 1300s, and in 1961 he sent brotherly greetings to the Patriarch of Constantinople.

RELATIONS WITH THE JEWS

As papal nuncio in the war years, he saved the lives of thousands of Jews during the Holocaust, for example by facilitating the passage of refugee Jews who had reached Istanbul to Palestine. As pope he removed the word 'perfidious' as relating to Jews from the Good Friday liturgy and made a confession for

Below: John XXIII was approachable, humble and committed to equality. He famously said, 'We were all made in God's image and thus we are all Godly alike.'

the church of the sin of anti-Semitism over the centuries. He prayed in 1965: 'We are conscious today that many, many centuries of blindness have cloaked our eyes so that we can no longer see the beauty of Thy chosen people… Forgive us for the curse we falsely attached to their name as Jews. Forgive us for crucifying Thee a second time in their flesh.'

SECOND VATICAN COUNCIL

John announced that he would be calling an ecumenical council soon after his election as pope. He was 77 and seen by some as a caretaker pope, and conservative elements in the Curia did what they could to delay the calling of the council in the hope that the pope might pass on and the project be dropped. However, John survived long enough to see the opening session of the Second Vatican Council.

Paul VI (1963–78), original name Giovanni Battista Montini, carried through the reforms of the Second Vatican Council. He introduced changes that provoked fierce opposition among traditionalists – such as the use of vernacular languages rather than universal Latin for most of the liturgy. But he also upset modernizers when he took a firm stand on some issues – for example he insisted that priests must be celibate and in his 1968 encyclical *Humanae vitae* condemned artificial birth control.

Above: President Lyndon Johnson visited the Vatican on 23 December 1967. Paul had previously met him in the US in 1965.

'PILGRIM POPE'

Paul VI, who visited six continents on his travels, was nicknamed the 'pilgrim Pope'. He travelled to the USA in October 1965, where he met President Johnson, visited the United Nations and celebrated Mass in the Yankee Stadium. He was the first modern pope to visit the Holy Land and to travel to India. He even reached out to the Moon: he sent one of the 73 Goodwill messages carried to the Moon by *Apollo 11* in 1969. After a quote from Psalm 8, it stated, 'To the glory of the name of God who gives such power to men, we ardently pray for this wonderful beginning.'

IN THE HOLY LAND

Paul VI was the first modern pope to visit the Holy Land. On his two-day trip in January 1964 he met Ecumenical Patriarch Athenagoras I on the Mount of Olives in Jerusalem. He also met President Shazar of Israel in Megiddo and King Hussein of Jordan, celebrated Mass at the Church of the Holy Sepulchre in Jerusalem and in Bethlehem, and toured the shores of the Sea of Galilee.

THE SECOND VATICAN COUNCIL TO REVITALIZE THE CHURCH

The Second Vatican Council of 1962–5 was a major landmark in the history of the modern Roman Catholic Church, bringing about changes in tone and attitude, in liturgy and the life of the Church. Pope John XXIII (1958–63) called the Council. He was concerned above all to promote Christian unity, and saw the need for a spiritual renewal in the Church, a reform of institutions and structures – a process he characterized in the Italian word *aggiornamento* ('updating' or 'revitalization').

'A NEW ENTHUSIASM'

The pope opened the first session on 11 October 1962. He said, 'What is needed … is a new enthusiasm, a new joy and serenity of mind in the unreserved acceptance by all of the entire Christian faith, without forfeiting that accuracy and precision in its presentation which characterized the proceedings of the Council of Trent and the First Vatican Council.' He

Below: The council in session. Its Decree on Ecumenism called for the reuniting of Christendom and declared ecumenism should be a matter of concern for all the faithful.

said doctrine was 'certain and immutable' and the faithful owed it obedience, but it should be 'studied afresh and reformulated in contemporary terms'.

The first session ended on 8 December 1962. Pope John XXIII died on 3 June 1963 and the council might have ended with him, for an ecumenical council is automatically suspended on

Below: John XXIII is carried through St Peter's. He called the council having discerned the need for spiritual renewal – 'a new enthusiasm, a new joy' – in the Church.

Above: Bishops exit St Peter's during the Second Council session, November 1963.

the death of the pope who called it; but John's successor Paul VI, elected on 21 June 1963, announced that the council would continue. There were three more sessions: 29 September–4 December 1963; 14 September–21 November 1964; and 14 September–8 December 1965.

The Second Vatican Council was the 21st ecumenical council of the Church. The First Vatican Council was held in 1869–70, under Pius IX (1846–78), and is remembered above all for its definition of papal infallibility. Before that the previous ecumenical council of the Church was the Council of Trent (1545–63).

EFFECTIVE COMMUNICATION

The overall impetus of the Second Vatican Council's work was to try to make the Church more effective at delivering the Gospel in the 20th century. The Church would be more open, there would be a greater role for lay Catholics in the Mass, as well as more use of English and other vernacular languages rather than traditional Latin.

The Council approved 16 documents (see panel). The Constitution on the

Sacred Liturgy ordered a revision of the liturgy to increase the involvement of lay people in the Mass and other rites, while the Decree on the Ministry and Life of Priests reaffirmed the requirement of celibacy for priests. It presented committing to a life of celibacy as an act of charity on behalf of a priest – which provided 'in a special way a source of spiritual fruitfulness in the world'.

The Declaration on the Relationship of the Church to Non-Christian Religions spoke out against denunciations of the Jews. It declared: 'True, the Jewish authorities and those who followed their lead pressed for the death of Christ; still, what happened in His passion cannot be charged against all the Jews, without distinction, then alive, nor against the Jews of today ... the Jews should not be presented as rejected or accursed by God, as if this followed from the Holy Scriptures.'

COLLEGE OF BISHOPS

The Decree on the Bishops' Pastoral Office in the Church identified the bishops as a college that succeeded the Apostles in governing and teaching the Church. A note clarified the college did not challenge the authority of the pope.

The Dogmatic Constitution on the Church was a statement on the character and identity of the Roman Catholic Church. It talked of the 'common priesthood of the faithful' as interrelated with the ministerial priesthood; the faithful exercise their priesthood by 'joining in

Above: Chinese cardinal Thomas Tien Kensin takes a meal in the Vatican during the first session of the council in October 1952. This photograph appeared in Life *magazine.*

the offering of the Eucharist' and 'in receiving the sacraments, in prayer and thanksgiving, in the witness of a holy life, and by self-denial and active charity'.

PAUL VI MASS

In the wake of the Council, Paul VI (1963–78) introduced a revised form of the Mass in 1969. The Mass would be in the vernacular rather than the traditional Latin and the priest would face the congregation while saying it rather than facing the altar as was usual practice. A number of Roman Catholics rebelled against this reform. In particular French Archbishop Marcel Lefebvre led a movement to use the Tridentine Mass, the Latin liturgy approved by the Council of Trent in the 16th century, as contained in the 1962 Missal. Pope John Paul II excommunicated Lefebvre in 1988.

In 2007 Benedict XVI (2005–13) declared celebrating Mass according to the 1962 Missal would be made easier. Previously groups wishing to use the Tridentine Mass had had to ask the permission of their bishop but they could now ask their local priests to allow it. He issued a letter to allay concerns that this move might be seen as undermining the decrees of the Second Vatican Council: he stated that the Mass of Paul VI would remain the norm and that no priest could refuse to use the Paul VI Mass.

FOUR POPES

Four churchmen present at the opening session of the Second Vatican Council went on to become pope: Cardinal Giovanni Battista Montini, later Pope Paul VI; Bishop Albino Luciani, later Pope John Paul I; Bishop Karol Wojtyla, later Pope John Paul II; and Father Joseph Ratzinger, later Pope Benedict XVI. Father Ratzinger was theological consultant to the Archbishop of Cologne at the Council.

Panel Documents approved by the Second Vatican Council
Promulgated 4 December 1963
• Constitution on the Sacred Liturgy (*Sacrosanctum Concilium*).
• Decree on the Instruments of Social Communication (*Inter Mirifica*).

Promulgated 21 November 1964
• Dogmatic Constitution on the Church (*Lumen Gentium*).
• Decree on Ecumenism (*Unitatis Redintegratio*).
• Decree on Eastern Catholic Churches (*Orientalium Ecclesiarum*).

Promulgated 28 October 1965
• Decree on the Bishops' Pastoral Office in the Church (*Christus Dominus*).
• Decree on Priestly Formation (*Optatam Totius*).
• Decree on the Appropriate Renewal of the Religious Life (*Perfectae Caritatis*).
• Declaration on the Relationship of the Church to Non-Christian Religions (*Nostra Aetate*).
• Declaration on Christian Education (*Gravissimum Educationis*).

Promulgated 18 November 1965
• Dogmatic Constitution on Divine Revelation (*Dei Verbum*).
• Decree on the Apostolate of the Laity (*Apostolicam Actuositatem*).

Promulgated 7 December 1965
• Declaration on Religious Freedom (*Dignitatis Humanae*).
• Decree on the Ministry and Life of Priests (*Presbyterorum Ordinis*).
• Decree on the Church's Missionary Activity (*Ad Gentes*).
• Pastoral Constitution on the Church in the Modern World (*Gaudium et Spes*).

JOHN PAUL I, 1978
'SMILING POPE' WHOSE REIGN WAS CUT SHORT

Remembered as *il papa del sorisso* ('the smiling Pope'), John Paul I was an unexpected choice as pontiff. He was a cardinal without diplomatic or curial experience but with warmth and great good humour who seemed determined to sweep away formality and to humanize the office of pope, but who died of a heart attack after just 33 days so that the character of his pontificate was never developed or fully revealed.

Born in Forno di Canale in the Veneto region, northern Italy, Albino Luciani was the son of a bricklayer. He was ordained in 1935 and taught theology, canon law and sacred art at a seminary before gaining a doctorate in theology. He was appointed Bishop of Vittorio Veneto by John XXIII and then made Patriarch of Venice in 1970 and a cardinal in 1973 by Paul VI.

A cardinal Luciani wrote a series of letters to historical and fictional characters, which were later collected in the book *Illustrissimi*, published in 1976. These included letters to Jesus Christ,

Below: Pope Paul VI, his predecessor, with Albino Luciano, the future John Paul I, visiting Venice in 1972.

FACT BOX
Original name Albino Luciani
Born 17 October 1912
Origin Forno di Canale
Date elected pope 26 August 1978
Died 28 September 1978
Key fact Died of heart attack after just 33 days

Right: The smiling pope. John Paul I's inner joy and great good humour are plain in this photograph of his first official ceremony after his election. Cardinal Basil Hume said of him, 'he was God's candidate'.

Pinocchio, Figaro (the barber in French playwright Pierre Beaumarchais' plays *The Barber of Seville* and *The Marriage of Figaro*) and Mark Twain. He was elected on the fourth ballot of the conclave following the death of Paul VI, on 26 August 1978.

FIRST DUAL NAME
He chose the first dual name in papal history to honour his two immediate predecessors, John XXIII and Paul VI. He announced that he would continue the

implementations of the decrees of the Second Vatican Council while upholding traditional discipline. He refused to be crowned – choosing an investiture with the pallium of an archbishop rather than a coronation. He chose as his papal motto *Humilitas* ('Humility').

His decision to forgo the splendour of a papal coronation was popular in some quarters, but may have fuelled doubts about him among more conservative elements in the Church. Moreover, he was known to have had significant concerns about the ban on contraception in his predecessor's encyclical *Humanae vitae* and in 1968 while Bishop of Vittorio Veneto had recommended to Paul VI that use of the contraceptive pill be permitted – a recommendation the then pope rejected.

Some sources suggest that John Paul was not respected as an intellectual within the highest echelons of the Church and was seen as naive and idealistic – one unnamed cardinal is said to have dismissively said 'They have elected Peter Sellers', a reference to the British comic actor particularly famous at that time for his portrayal of the bumbling yet inexplicably successful Inspector Clouseau in the *Pink Panther* movies.

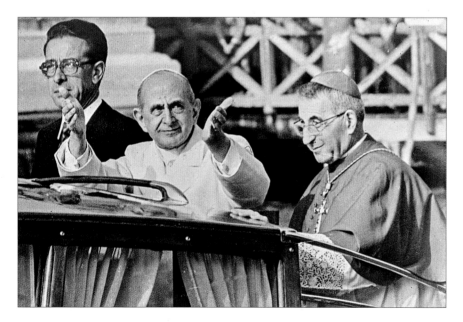

'GOD'S CANDIDATE'

Yet other voices hailed his election as divinely inspired. English cardinal Basil Hume declared of the conclave in which John Paul I was elected, 'Seldom have I had such an experience of the presence of God … for me he was God's candidate.'

John Paul was immediately popular. His friendly manner, humility and warm smile were allied with skill as an orator. He came across extremely well. Mother Teresa of Calcutta said of him, 'He has been the greatest gift of God, a sun ray of God's love shining in the darkness of the world.'

Below: After John Paul I's sudden death, 111 Cardinals were sealed inside the Sistine Chapel to elect his successor. After eight ballots, they chose Polish cardinal Karol Wojtyla. He chose the name Pope John Paul II.

SUDDEN DEATH

On the morning of 29 September 1978 John Paul was found dead. The previous night the pope had dined quietly in his Vatican apartment with his two secretaries, Father Diego Lorenzi and Father John Magee, then gone to bed just after 9pm. When discovered, he was sitting up in bed still clasping the papers he had been reading.

There were later inconsistencies in the reported facts, which fuelled some conspiracy theories that he had been murdered. The usual details given are that he was discovered by Sister Vincenza Taffarel – who had brought him his morning coffee for decades – just after 4.30am, his normal rising time. She then raised the alarm; Cardinal Jean Villot, Secretary of State, called the papal embalmers; and Dr Renato Buzzonetti, deputy head of the Vatican's health service, determined that Pope John Paul had had a heart attack at 11pm the previous night.

No post-mortem was held and the Vatican, when questioned, declared that post-mortems were not held for popes – despite the fact that they had been performed in previous reigns, such as that of Clement XIV (1769–74). It later

Above: Pope John Paul I with Cardinal Karol Wojtyla, who was to succeed him as pope in October 1978.

emerged that the pope's personal doctor, Giuseppe da Ros, had given John Paul a medical examination less than a week before and concluded that John Paul was not only well, but in robust health.

CONSPIRACY THEORIES

Some conspiracy theorists argue that the pope was about to expose a Mafia-connected financial scheme involving the Vatican Bank, and that those involved, desperate to prevent this, had him murdered; others propose that the pope was planning to demote prominent churchmen who could have been tempted to stop his reforms before they started. However, while there do seem to have been puzzling inconsistencies and departures from normal procedure within the Vatican after John Paul's death, the conspiracy theories have little force and there seems no doubt in truth that he died from natural causes.

After lying in state, John Paul's body was buried on 4 October 1978 in a tomb designed by Francesco Vacchini in the crypt of St Peter's Basilica.

JOHN PAUL II, 1978–2005
POLISH POPE WHO CONNECTED POWERFULLY WITH THE YOUNG

Pontiff for 26 years and five months, John Paul II was the third longest-reigning pope in history after St Peter (roughly 35 years) and Pius IX (21 June 1846– 7 February 1878, 31 years seven months). Seeking to develop an understanding between nations and faiths, he travelled very widely – visiting more than 129 countries in the course of 104 journeys.

He was the first Polish pope and the first non-Italian pope since the Dutch Hadrian Florenszoon Boeyens who ruled as Hadrian VI in 1522–3; Wojtyla's early years in Poland under first Nazi and then Soviet domination profoundly influenced his attitudes – he helped to inspire the collapse of communist rule in his native country and Eastern Europe.

FACT BOX

Original name Karol Józef Wojtyla
Born 18 May 1920
Origin Wadowice, Poland
Date elected pope 16 October 1978
Died 2 April 2005
Key fact Inspired peaceful resistance to communist rule

Right: Shortly after his death, John Paul II joined Leo I, Gregory I and Nicholas I in being referred to as 'the Great'. Pope Francis recognized him as a saint in 2014.

Karol Wojtyla lost his mother, his beloved older brother 'Mundek' and his father by his early 20s. By this stage the Nazis had invaded Poland and he was forced to take various jobs, including working in a quarry and a chemical factory. He began to train for the priesthood in secret and illegal classes during the war and was ordained in November 1946, by which time the Soviets had taken over from the Nazis as occupiers of Poland.

In his youth Wojtyla played soccer (as a goalkeeper), studied languages and was a playwright. After the war he wrote and anonymously published poetry, taught philosophy and served as professor at the Catholic University of Lublin. Pius XII made him Auxiliary Bishop of Krakow

Below: John Paul II is welcomed by President Lech Walesa to Poland in 1991. This was the pope's fourth pilgrimage to his native land.

in 1958 and Paul VI appointed him Archbishop of Krakow in 1963. Wojtyla was made a cardinal in 1967.

He was elected pope on the third day of the second conclave of 1978. He followed his predecessor in dispensing with the traditional coronation and having a simple investiture instead.

As pope, John Paul II supported the reforms of the Second Vatican Council and otherwise maintained a traditional line in many of his teachings, rejecting calls for the use of artificial contraception, the end of priestly celibacy, and the ordination of women priests, speaking out against abortion, against sex before marriage and against practising as a homosexual – although he made no condemnation of homosexual orientation.

'BE NOT AFRAID' – NON-VIOLENT PROTEST

In his installation Mass on 22 October 1978 John Paul II invoked the biblical phrase 'Be not afraid!', a command given in these or similar words by God to Abraham (Genesis 46:3), by Gabriel in the Annunciation (Luke 1:30) and Jesus himself to his disciples (for example, in Matthew 14:27). These words became a byword for his papacy, and notably they looked forward to the peaceful campaigns for political and religious freedom and for human rights that the pope promoted during his pontificate.

JOHN PAUL II AND COMMUNISM

John Paul II visited his native Poland on his second official trip, in June 1979, and declared to vast audiences that they had the right to be free. He repeated the message of his homily at his installation Mass: 'Be not afraid!' He was an inspiration for those seeking freedom from communist rule, those who formed the Polish trade union federation Solidarity that forced the first multi-party elections in the Soviet bloc of countries. These brought about the ousting of the communist regime in Poland and the collapse of communist rule across Eastern Europe. Some hold that the Vatican Bank secretly funded Solidarity. Mikhail Gorbachev, the former Soviet leader, said, 'The collapse of the Iron Curtain would have been impossible without John Paul II' – a reference to the 'curtain' said to divide the capitalist West from the communist East during the Cold War.

Below: John Paul II walks with Mother Teresa in 1988. He said she found strength and perseverance 'in prayer and in the silent contemplation of Jesus Christ'.

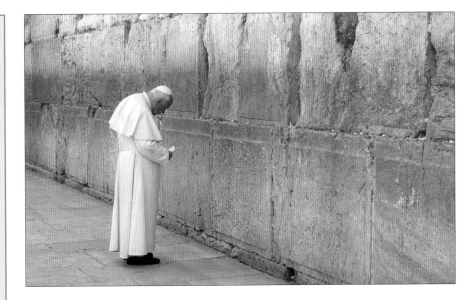

Above: In 2000 John Paul II prayed at the Wailing Wall in Jerusalem. On this visit Israeli prime minister Ehud Barak met him with the words, 'Blessed are you in Israel'.

He was a strong critic of the apartheid system and called for economic sanctions against South Africa. He opposed the US-led invasion of Iraq in 2003. He taught that 'Wars do not in general solve the problems for which they are fought, and therefore prove ultimately futile.'

INTERFAITH INITIATIVES

Through his travels and other engagements John Paul worked hard to bring about reconciliation among Christian denominations and between Christianity and other world faiths. In 1982, he prayed in Canterbury Cathedral alongside Archbishop of Canterbury Robert Runcie; in 1983 he was the first pope to visit a Lutheran church; in 1990 he pronounced anti-Semitism a sin against God and humanity and in 1993 he established diplomatic relations between the Holy See and the state of Israel; in 1995, during a visit to Buddhist-majority Sri Lanka, he expressed admiration for Buddhism and its 'four great values of … loving kindness, compassion, sympathetic joy and equanimity'; in 2001, during a visit to Damascus in Syria, he became the first pope to set foot in and pray in an Islamic mosque.

ASSASSINATION ATTEMPT – SAVED BY THE VIRGIN?

On 13 May 1981 John Paul survived an assassination attempt: while John Paul was being driven through St Peter's Square, a 23-year-old Turkish man named Mehmet Ali Agca shot and wounded him. He was struck four times and suffered severe blood loss.

John Paul later said that he was saved by the Virgin Mary, who diverted the bullet away from his heart; on the first anniversary of the attack he visited the shrine of the Virgin in Fatima, Portugal, and performed a consecration of the modern world to the Immaculate Heart of Mary.

DECLINING HEALTH

Fit and athletic when he became pope, John Paul enjoyed swimming and even jogging in the Vatican Gardens – in an Irish newspaper article, he was dubbed the 'keep-fit pope'. But for the last decade or more of his life, he was in declining health.

As early as 1991 there were the first signs that he might be developing Parkinson's disease, although this was not officially confirmed until 2003. Towards the end of his life, he suffered from osteoarthritis and hearing difficulties. He died on 2 April 2005. His final words were 'Allow me to depart to the House of the Father'.

BENEDICT XVI, 2005–13
FIRST POPE TO ABDICATE SINCE 1415

Benedict XVI is remembered above all for his decision, announced on 11 February 2013, to abdicate as pope. His eight-year pontificate was generally conservative and overshadowed somewhat by a series of sexual abuse scandals involving Roman Catholic clerics.

Born the youngest of three children to a hotel cook and a policeman in Bavaria, Ratzinger was six years old when the Nazis came to power in Germany. His parents were fervent Catholics and were anti-Nazi but after beginning training as a priest the young Joseph Ratzinger was made to join the Hitler Youth in 1941 and then drafted into the German army in 1943. He deserted in April 1945 and was a prisoner of war for a short period after being captured by the Americans.

After the war he was ordained a priest in 1951 and embarked on a distinguished academic career, taking a doctorate in theology and teaching at the universities of Bonn, Munster, Tubingen and Regensburg. He served as the Archbishop

Below: Pope Benedict XVI with US President George W. Bush at the White House, Washington, on 16 April 2008, the day the pope celebrated his 81st birthday.

of Cologne's expert assistant at the Second Vatican Council before in 1977 Paul VI appointed him Archbishop of Munich and elevated him to the cardinalate.

'GOD'S ROTTWEILER'

From 1978 onwards he was a close friend of John Paul II and in 1981 the pope appointed him prefect of the Congregation for the Doctrine of the Faith, the body responsible for enforcing doctrinal orthodoxy and the modern equivalent of the Inquisition. In more than 20 years in this role he won a reputation for being a stern authoritarian and was nicknamed 'God's rottweiler', in a reference to the originally German breed of dogs.

A highly intelligent and humble man, Ratzinger certainly has a gentle side – while a cardinal, he was known as a lover of cats, prone to adopting strays from the streets in Rome. In his younger years he was an accomplished pianist, particularly devoted to the works of Bach and Mozart. As his friend John Paul II did, Ratzinger speaks several languages very well.

When he was elected pope on 19 April 2005 he was already 78 and was the oldest new pope since Clement XII who was the same age on his election in 1730. Benedict indicated that he would follow John Paul II's traditionalist

Above: Benedict blesses the faithful in 2005. In his encyclical 'God is Love', he declared, 'Prayer, as a means of drawing ever-new strength from Christ, is concretely and urgently needed'.

line on matters concerning sexuality and priestly celibacy and intended to continue his predecessor's work to bring Christian denominations and world faiths together.

However, early in his pontificate he faced controversy when a speech in Germany in September 2006 offended many Muslims. In his speech he quoted some words, originally spoken by the Byzantine emperor Manuel II Palaeologus: 'Show me just what Muhammad brought that was new and there you will find things only evil and

> **FACT BOX**
> **Original name** Joseph Alois Ratzinger
> **Born** 16 April 1927
> **Origin** Marktl am Inn, Germany
> **Date elected pope** 19 April 2005
> **Abdicated** 28 February 2013
> **Key fact** Issued apologies for sexual abuse by priests

inhuman, such as his command to spread by the sword the faith he preached.' He apologized for causing offence and later that year visited Turkey, where he prayed inside the celebrated Blue Mosque. He also met the Ecumenical Patriarch of Constantinople, Bartholomew I.

Benedict taught frequently on the need for people to open themselves to friendship with Jesus Christ. In his first homily he declared, 'Only in this friendship do we experience beauty and liberation ... open wide the doors to Christ – and you will find true life.'

'POPE OF AESTHETICS'

Benedict was noted for wearing very fine ecclesiastical vestments; he revived the use of traditional papal garments including red papal shoes, the *camauro* (red velvet cap bordered with white fur) and the wide-brimmed *cappello romano*, also red. He was nicknamed 'the pope of aesthetics'; he also revitalized the link between the Church and the world of the arts, holding a meeting with artists in the Sistine Chapel in 2009 'to express and renew the Church's friendship with the world of art' and declaring that 'art is like an open doorway to the infinite, towards a beauty and truth that go beyond everyday reality.'

APOLOGY FOR PRIESTLY SEXUAL ABUSE

During a visit to the United States in 2008 Benedict met victims of priestly sexual abuse and spoke out condemning perpetrators. In the same year in Australia he apologized for abuse by priests, saying 'I would like to ... acknowledge the shame which we have all felt as a result of the sexual abuse of minors by some clergy and religious in this country.'

ABDICATION

Pope Benedict XVI announced on 11 February 2013 his decision to abdicate as pope with effect from 28 February. He was 85 years old. Benedict said, 'My strengths, due to an advanced age, are no longer suited to an adequate exercise of the petrine ministry.' Press reports suggested he was suffering from

Below: Pope Benedict and Ecumenical Orthodox Patriarch Bartholomew I in Istanbul, 2006. They discussed how to bring an end to the Catholic/Orthodox divide.

Above: The faithful made a pictorial puzzle to welcome Benedict to the Dos Coqueiros stadium in Luanda, Angola, 2009. He called for further evangelization of Africa.

deafness and had lost the sight in one eye; there was also speculation that he was upset after his butler Paolo Gabriele was found to have been leaking the pope's private correspondence.

However, Benedict later revealed that the decision came as a result of a 'mystical experience' in which he experienced an 'absolute desire' to step down from public life and give himself to a secluded life of prayer.

Then in an interview on 28 June 2016 his successor Pope Francis emphasized that the resignation was an act of church government. He said of Pope Benedict 'his brain and memory are functioning perfectly', adding 'He was a revolutionary. His resignation brought to life all the Church's problems. His resignation ... was an act of government. His last act of government.'

FRANCIS, 2013–
FIRST LATIN AMERICAN AND FIRST JESUIT POPE

Argentinian cardinal Jorge Mario Bergoglio, the former Archbishop of Buenos Aires, was 76 when he was elected pope on 13 March 2013. His pontificate began with a call for peace and for the Church to embrace the needs of the poor. He chose the name Francis to honour St Francis of Assisi, and at his first media audience, praised his saintly namesake as 'the man who gives us this spirit of peace, the poor man.'

Pope Francis is known for his humility. On the night of his election he rode back in a bus to his hotel rather than take the papal car. He tends to adopt a 'no frills' style, dressing plainly and living simply. He chose to live in the Domus Sante Marthae (St Martha's House), a guesthouse adjacent to St Peter's Basilica rather than in the papal apartments of the Apostolic Palace.

The new leader of the Church – the first pope from Latin America as well as the first Jesuit pope – was known from his time as Archbishop of Buenos Aires as being committed to social justice. In the first months of his pontificate he called on world leaders to avoid the 'cult of money', which he said was making

Below: Pope Francis is the first pope from the Americas and the first Jesuit pope. He met members of sports associations for the 70th anniversary of Centro Sportivo Italiano, Vatican City in June 2014.

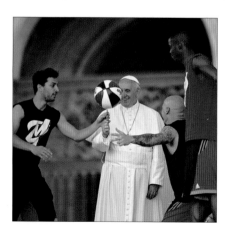

Above: Francis greets pilgrims during the 2016 Jubilee of Mercy. He is said to be approachable, informal and reportedly introduces himself on the phone as 'Hi, it's Pope Francis here!'

people unhappy, and attacked a 'throw away culture' in which 'human beings themselves are … considered as consumer goods which can be used and thrown away'. He said 'in circumstances like these, solidarity, which is the treasure of the poor, is often considered counterproductive, opposed to the logic of finance and the economy.'

In his 2013 exhortation *Evangelii gaudium* ('The Joy of the Gospel') he denounced market autonomy and declared, 'Just as the commandment "Thou shalt not kill" sets a clear limit in order to safeguard the value of human life, today we also have to say "thou shalt not" to an economy of exclusion and inequality. Such an economy kills.' In 2015 he declared 'Poverty is at the centre of the Gospel.'

At the same time he was, like his two predecessors, generally conservative on matters of morality and sexuality, unresponsive to modern calls for the ordination of women or for priests to be allowed to marry. He declared that there would be no going back on the possibility of women priests: 'John Paul II made the Church's stance definitive. The door is closed.' However, he argued that women had a special role in the Church: 'Our Lady was more important

than the Apostles, bishops, deacons and priests. Women play a role that's more important than that of bishops or priests. How? This is what we have to explain better publicly.'

ENVIRONMENT AND THE 'CULTURE OF ENCOUNTER'

On his election Francis said one reason he chose his papal name was because Francis of Assisi 'teaches us profound respect for the whole of creation and the protection of our environment'. The pope later argued in favour of using renewable energy sources rather than

> **FACT BOX**
>
> **Original name** Jorge Mario Bergoglio
> **Born** 17 December 1936
> **Origin** Buenos Aires, Argentina
> **Date elected pope** 13 March 2013
> **Key fact** Shares Vatican with pope emeritus

traditional fuels, but also emphasized that consumerism must be brought under control – we should distinguish between human needs and human appetites; the first can be met, but the second are potentially beyond limit. On 18 June 2015, Francis published the encyclical, *Laudato si* ('Praise be to You') calling for 'swift and unified global action' to counter global warming.

Shortly after becoming pope, Francis called for interreligious dialogue in order to 'help to build bridges connecting all people'. On 20 March 2013 he reached out to non-believers, saying that people of no religious tradition who were 'searching for truth, goodness and beauty' were the Church's 'valued allies in the commitment to defending human dignity, in building a peaceful coexistence between peoples and in safeguarding and caring for creation,' adding in a homily on 22 May that God 'redeemed all of us, with the Blood of Christ: all of us, not just Catholics, Everyone! … even the atheists!' He called for a 'culture of encounter': 'we must meet one another doing good'.

'ALWAYS CONSIDER THE PERSON…'

In an interview with Jesuit journal *La Civilta Cattolica* on 19 September 2013 Francis called for a less condemnatory attitude in the Church towards divorced people, women who have had an abortion and gays. He said, 'We must always consider the person … In life, God accompanies persons, and we must accompany them, starting from their situation.' Earlier that year, on 28 July, he had said, 'If someone is gay and is searching for the Lord and has good will, then who am I to judge him?'

He remained strongly opposed to gay marriage, which he said in January 2015 would 'disfigure God's plan for creation'. But on 26 June 2016 he said the Church owed gay people an apology for how it had treated them and added: 'they should not be discriminated against, they should be respected, accompanied pastorally.'

In his comments on 26 June 2016 Francis suggested that the Church owed an apology to other groups as well: 'I think that the Church not only should apologize … to a gay person whom it offended but it must also apologize to the poor as well, to the women who have been exploited, to children who have been exploited by [being forced to] work. It must apologize for having blessed so many weapons.'

Below: The modern face of the Vatican. Francis is the first pope to create an Instagram account. He gained more than 1 million followers in the first 12 hours.

REFUGEE CRISIS, TERROR ATTACKS

In 2016 Francis engaged with the refugee crisis that engulfed Europe, as thousands of migrants fled Syria, Iraq, Afghanistan and African countries. He visited the Moria migrant camp on the Greek island of Lesbos on 16 April.

In 2017 he responded to the wave of terrorist attacks on leading cities, invoking 'God's blessings of peace, healing and strength' upon England after the attack in Manchester on 22 May, and on 4 June praying for victims of the previous night's attack on London Bridge: 'May the Holy Spirit grant peace to the whole world … May He heal the wounds of war and of terrorism.'

Francis emphasized mercy as the most powerful part of Jesus's message. He urged people never to give up seeking God's forgiveness. On 31 May 2017 he urged Christians to 'sow hope', adding: 'The Holy Spirit makes us not only able to hope, but also to be sowers of hope, that we too are, like Him and thanks to Him – the "paraclete" – consolers and defenders of our brothers.' Then on 24 June 2017, in his weekly Angelus Address, he taught that while God does not shield us from failure and suffering, He never abandons His followers – 'Jesus does not leave us alone, because we are precious to Him.'

INDEX

Entries in bold refer to illustrations.

Above: Callistus II.

Below: Clement I.

Below: Gregory XV.

Above: Julius II.

Above: Sixtus IV.

Below: Urban II.

ACKNOWLEDGEMENTS

This edition is published by Lorenz Books,
an imprint of Anness Publishing Ltd,
108 Great Russell Street, London WC1B 3NA;
info@anness.com

www.lorenzbooks.com; www.annesspublishing.com;
twitter: @Anness_Books

Anness Publishing has a picture agency outlet for
images for publishing, promotions or advertising.
Please visit our website www.practicalpictures.com
for more information.

© Anness Publishing Ltd 2017

A CIP catalogue record for this book
is available from the British Library.

Publisher: Joanna Lorenz
Editors: Joy Wotton and Felicity Forster
Designer: Nigel Partridge

PUBLISHER'S NOTE
Although the information in this book is believed
to be accurate and true at the time of going to press,
neither the authors nor the publisher can accept
any legal responsibility or liability for any errors
or omissions that may have been made.

PAGE 1: *St Peter's Basilica and Ponte Sant Angelo, Rome, Italy.*
PAGE 2: *Portrait of Pope Julius II by Raphael, 1511.*
PAGE 3: *Christ passing to Peter the key that represents
papal authority over the church; mosaic from St Peter's in Rome.*
Endpapers: *Clement XI in procession across St Peter's Square;
painting by Pier Leone Ghezzi.*

PICTURE CREDITS
Alamy: Heritage Image Partnership Ltd 4iii, 56–7, 69t;
John Kellerman 90b; Peter Horree 134–5; REUTERS
246b, 247t, 247b.
Bridgeman Images: 60b, 79t, 190t, 201, 240br; Aachen
Cathedral Treasury, Aachen, Germany / De Agostini Picture
Library / A. Dagli Orti 105; Alinari 242b, 243t, 243b;
Archivio di Stato, Siena, Italy 156t; Archivo General de
Simancas, Valladolid, Spain / Index 161r; Art Gallery of
New South Wales, Sydney, Australia 59t; Basilique Saint-
Denis, France 68b; Bayerische Staatsbibliothek, Munich,
Germany / De Agostini Picture Library 86b; Biblioteca
Marucelliana, Florence, Italy 191b; Biblioteca Monasterio
del Escorial, Madrid, Spain / Mithra-Index 124b; Bibliotheca
Nazionale, Turin, Italy / Index 72; Bibliothèque de la
Sorbonne, Paris, France / Archives Charmet 133bl;
Bibliothèque Historique de la Ville de Paris, Paris, France /
Archives Charmet 233tl; Bibliothèque Municipale, Amiens,
France 136r; Bibliothèque Municipale, Castres, France 77t,
78, 104t; Bibliothèque Municipale, Laon, France 58b, 231t;
Bibliothèque Nationale, Paris, France 98b, 100t, 103t, 122,
140t, 205t, 255; Bibliothèque Nationale, Paris, France /

Archives Charmet 83t, 224b; Bibliothèque Nationale, Paris,
France / De Agostini Picture Library / J. E. Bulloz 130b;
Bischöfliches Dom- und Diözesanmuseum, Mainz,
Germany / Bildarchiv Steffens / Bischöfliches Dom- und
Diözesanmuseum Mainz 59b; The Bowes Museum,
Barnard Castle, County Durham, UK 202t; Brancacci
Chapel, Santa Maria del Carmine, Florence, Italy 79b;
British Library, London, UK 137r; British Library, London,
UK / © British Library Board, All Rights Reserved 88b,
112b, 123b; British Museum, London, UK 181br;
Buyenlarge Archive / UIG 237t; California Historical
Society / Gift of M. Calder 221b; Casa Buonarroti,
Florence, Italy 165l; Castello Sforzesco Civiche Raccolte
Archeologiche E Numismatiche Museo Della Preistoria
E Protostoria, Milan, Italy / De Agostini Picture Library
82b; Catacombs of San Callisto, Rome, Italy 33; Chartres
Cathedral, Chartres, France / Photo © Paul Maeyaert 89t;
Château de Versailles, France 110b, 199b, 222b; Church of
St. Gall, Prague, Czech Republic 143b; Church of St. Luke,
Bath, Somerset, UK 68t; Church of St.Marien, Wittenberg,
Germany 168t; Church of the Gesù, Rome, Italy 183b;
Collection of the Duke of Devonshire, Chatsworth House,
UK / © Devonshire Collection, Chatsworth / Reproduced
by permission of Chatsworth Settlement Trustees 166l;
CSU Archives / Everett Collection 238b; De Agostini
Picture Library 9t, 40t, 85b, 119t, 126, 131t, 133t, 147t,
157b, 162b, 193t; De Agostini Picture Library / A. Dagli
Orti 12r, 18–19, 24b, 61tl, 61tr, 71, 86t, 102t, 138b, 146b,
178b, 183t, 193b, 210, 217b; De Agostini Picture Library /
A. De Gregorio 61b, 132, 177b, 179b; De Agostini Picture
Library / F. Ferruzzi 152t; De Agostini Picture Library /
G. Cigolini 81b; De Agostini Picture Library / G. Dagli
Orti 5i, 55t, 83b, 84b, 101b, 104b, 108b, 130t, 141b, 154l,
154r, 155t, 160b, 176b, 192l, 214b, 218t, 222t, 223b, 250;
De Agostini Picture Library / G. Nimatallah 121t, 178t; De
Agostini Picture Library / L. Pedicini 163b, 187tr; De Agostini
Picture Library / L. Romano 96b; De Agostini Picture
Library / M. Seemuller 41b, 97b, 139r, 220t; De Agostini
Picture Library / R. Carnovalini 99t; De Agostini Picture
Library / S. Vannini 119b, 136l; Detroit Institute of Arts,
USA / Gift of Mrs. Edgar R. Thom 200b; Deutsches
Historisches Museum, Berlin, Germany / © DHM 166r,
169b, 170t; © Devonshire Collection, Chatsworth /
Reproduced by permission of Chatsworth Settlement
Trustees 219t; Duomo, Florence, Italy 144b; Église Saint-
Louis-en-L'Île, Paris, France 189t; Elvehjem Museum of
Art, Madison, WI, USA 49; Forum 11b, 17r, 244t, 244b;
Galleria Borghese, Rome, Italy 188t; Galleria degli Uffizi,
Florence, Italy 164t, 167t, 188b, 253; Galleria Doria Pamphilj,
Rome, Italy 194; Galleria Nazionale d'Arte Antica,
Italy / Photo © Stefano Baldini 202b; Galleria Nazionale
delle Marche, Urbino, Italy 204t, endpapers; Gallerie
dell'Accademia, Venice, Italy / Cameraphoto Arte Venezia
43; Germanisches Nationalmuseum, Nuremberg, Germany
128t; Godong/UIG 31b, 76, 221t; Gonville and Caius
College, University of Cambridge, UK / © Leemage 139l;
J.T.Vintage 230b; Koninklijk Museum voor Schone
Kunsten, Antwerp, Belgium / © Lukas - Art in Flanders
VZW 106; Kunsthistorisches Museum, Vienna, Austria 24t,
58t; Louvre, Paris, France 5iii, 5v, 92–3, 120l, 131b, 158t,
174–5, 212–13, 216, 217t, 254; Maison Jeanne d'Arc,
Orléans, France 153t; Minneapolis Institute of Arts, MN,
USA / The William Hood Dunwoody Fund 208b;
Monastero di San Benedetto, Subiaco, Italy 127t;
Mondadori Portfolio / Archivio Grzegorz Galazka /
Grzegorz Galazka 5vi, 10, 172–3, 228–9, 245t, 245b, 246t,
248t, 248b, 249; Mondadori Portfolio / Electa / Bruno
Balestrini 179t; Mondadori Portfolio / Electa / Sergio
Anelli 214t; Monte Cassino Abbey Museum, Cassino,
Italy 97t; Musée Bonnat, Bayonne, France 29b; Musée
Calvet, Avignon, France 143tl; Musée Cantonal des Beaux-
Arts de Lausanne, Switzerland / De Agostini Picture
Library / G. Dagli Orti 184b; Musée Conde, Chantilly,
France 115b; Musée Crozatier, Le Puy-en-Velay, France
45t; Musée de l'Assistance Publique, Hôpitaux de Paris,
France 207b; Musée de la Ville de Paris, Musée Carnavalet,
Paris, France 181t, 215b; Musée des Beaux-Arts, Béziers,
France 189b, 252; Musée des Beaux-Arts, Marseille, France
209; Musée des Beaux-Arts, Nantes, France 81t; Musée des
Beaux-Arts, Orléans, France / Roger-Viollet, Paris 152b;
Musei Capitolini, Rome, Italy / Photo © Stefano Baldini
195tl; Museo Civico, Bologna, Italy / Mondadori Portfolio
/ Electa / Antonio Guerra 142; Museo Correr, Venice,

Italy 115t; Museo de Bellas Artes, Seville, Spain / Index
182t; Museo del Risorgimento, Bologna, Italy / De
Agostini Picture Library / A. Dagli Orti 215t; Museo e
Gallerie Nazionale di Capodimonte, Naples, Italy 176t,
182b; Museo Lazaro Galdiano, Madrid, Spain 211tr;
Museum Europaischer Kulturen, Berlin, Germany / De
Agostini Picture Library 171t; National Gallery, London,
UK 2; Ognissanti, Florence, Italy 42b; Ospedale di Santa
Maria della Scala, Siena, Italy / Alinari 118t; Palazzo
Barberini, Rome, Italy 167b, 190b; Palazzo Chigi, Ariccia,
Italy 198b; Palazzo dei Conservatori, Musei Capitolini,
Rome 158b; Palazzo Pubblico, Siena, Italy 4v, 94–5,
113t; Photo © CCI 241; Photo © Everett Collection 239t;
Photo © Patrick Morin 240t; Photo © PVDE 26t, 28t, 32t,
42t, 51l, 51m, 51r, 143tr, 235b; Photo © Stefano Baldini 4i,
20, 35, 123t, 165r; Photo © Tallandier 148t, 236t; Photo
© Tarker 5ii; Photo © Zev Radovan 47t; Piazza del
Campidoglio, Rome, Italy 195b; Pictures from History 99b,
129, 137l; Pierluigi Praturlon / Reporters Associati &
Archivi / Mondadori Portfolio 11t; Pinacoteca Ambrosiana,
Milan, Italy / De Agostini Picture Library 138t;
Pinacoteca di Brera, Milan, Italy 149b; Pinacoteca
Nazionale, Siena, Italy 153b; Prado, Madrid, Spain 159b;
Private Collection 7b, 65b, 77b, 80b, 110t, 145t, 145b, 146t,
180, 184t, 186, 191t, 206t, 219b, 224t, 225t, 232bl, 235t,
236b, 238t; Private Collection / Archives Charmet
88t; Private Collection / © Bianchetti / Leemage 84t,
96t; Private Collection / © Coll. Farabola / Leemage 242t;
Private Collection / © Costa / Leemage 38l, 38r, 64t, 66t,
70t, 87b, 133br, 160t; Private Collection / De Agostini
Picture Library 220b; Private Collection / Index 203b;
Private Collection / © Look and Learn 25t, 44t, 62t, 66b,
82t, 87t, 90t, 107t, 108t, 109t, 112t, 114t, 144t, 157t, 230t,
231b, 234b; Private Collection / © Look and Learn /
Rosenberg Collection 227t; Private Collection / Photo
© Agnew's, London 207t; Private Collection / Photo ©
Christie's Images 5iv, 159t, 196–7, 204b, 208t; Private
Collection / Photo © Ken Welsh 28b, 70b, 149t;
Private Collection / Photo © Philip Mould Ltd, London
206b; Private Collection / Photo © Rafael Valls Gallery,
London, UK 181bl; Private Collection / Photo © Tarker
7t, 54t, 63b, 67t, 98t, 227b; Private Collection / The
Stapleton Collection 69b, 73t, 113b, 127b, 161l, 169t, 187tl,
211b; S. Agostino, San Gimignano, Italy 53t; Saint Louis Art
Museum, Missouri, USA / Museum purchase, by exchange
67b; San Clemente, Rome, Italy 25b, 251; San Francesco,
Upper Church, Assisi, Italy 4vi, 116–17, 124l; San Martino,
Monte San Martino, Italy 53b; San Vitale, Ravenna, Italy
55b; Santa Maria della Concezione, Rome, Italy 195tr;
Santa Maria della Vittoria, Rome, Italy / De Agostini
Picture Library / G. Nimatallah 185b; Santi Giovanni e
Paolo, Venice, Italy / Cameraphoto Arte Venezia 125;
Scala Regia, Vatican Museums, Vatican City 199t;
SeM/Universal Images Group 239b; Sizergh Castle,
Cumbria, UK / National Trust Photographic Library 128b;
St. Peter's, Vatican City 148b, 198t, 200t, 240bl; St. Peter's
Basilica, Vatican City 211tl, 256; Statens Museum for Kunst,
Copenhagen, Denmark 192r; SZ Photo / Scherl 91t,
232br; Tino Soriano / National Geographic Creative 203t;
Topkapi Palace Museum, Istanbul, Turkey 155b; Tretyakov
Gallery, Moscow, Russia 218b; United Archives / Carl
Simon 234t; Universal History Archive / UIG 41t, 168b,
225b, 237b; Vatican City 162t; Vatican Library, Vatican City
80t; Vatican Museums and Galleries, Vatican City 4ii, 36,
48t, 150–1, 156b; Vatican Museums and Galleries, Vatican
City / Artothek 171b; Vatican Museums and Galleries,
Vatican City / Photo © Stefano Baldini 4iv, 74–5, 89b;
Victoria & Albert Museum, London, UK 65t; Yale Center
for British Art, Paul Mellon Collection, USA 223t.
Fotolia: 30t; Pisa Cathedral, Italy 102b.
iStock: 1, 16r, 100b, 187b; _laurent 232t; © HultonArchive
226; AndreaAstes 52t; annavee 140b; bbstanicic 85t;
Borisb17 27l, 62b; Brzozowska 111b; Claudiad 12l; clodio
64b; DeniseSerra 27r; duncan1890 14m, 101t, 105t, 114b,
118b; Faabi 107bl; FabrizioBernardi 46b; FilippoBrandini
14l; frankix 39t; Gerardo_Borbolia 8t, 164b; gkuna 103b;
Jorisvo 52b; parys 30b; pavlemarjanovic 6, 34b; Peter
Zelei 32b; peterspiro 45b; photovideostock 9b, 141t;
Pilin_Petunyia 60t; redstallion 63t; savcoco 23b; sedmak 3,
22b, 23t, 29t, 47b, 109b, 233tr; seraficus 50; Terryfic3D
121b; Tramont_ana 31t; traveler1116 177t; treeffe 163t;
uschools 12m, 22t; Vladyslav Danilin 39b; whitemay 13m,
107br; ZU_09 34t, 40b, 44b, 48b, 73b, 91b, 111t, 124r, 147b.

Below: Tomb of Clement XIII.